THE PROCESS OF
INTERNATIONAL
ARBITRATION

THE PROCESS OF
INTERNATIONAL
ARBITRATION

KENNETH S. CARLSTON
PROFESSOR OF LAW, UNIVERSITY OF ILLINOIS

33703

COLUMBIA UNIVERSITY PRESS

NEW YORK   1946

FOREWORD

Recourse to arbitration by States at variance reflects their common and lofty aspiration to adjust by judicial process controversies that have baffled diplomacy and also their common expectation that justice is obtainable and a reasonable adjustment to be had by reference to accepted principles of international law. In very many instances the hopes of arbitrating States have been shattered, partly because of the failure of arbitrators to perceive and heed the scope of the functions entrusted to them, and partly also because of the failure of the States at variance to take the trouble to make comprehensive and exact terms indicative of their own design, and not opening the way to divergent interpretations of their contractual arrangements.

Mr. Carlston has in the present work done yeoman service to show States how they may wisely contract and make arbitration feasible and helpful as a means of adjusting international problems. He has done this by showing the pitfalls into which arbitrating States have fallen. His story is both a warning and a guide. He has shown the propensity of disgruntled losers on good and bad grounds to deny the validity of their arrangements. He has shown how judges have departed from terms of submission and have exceeded the jurisdiction conferred upon them. He has portrayed some notorious instances where arbitrators have handed down decisions upon matters outside the scope of a *compromis;* he has noted cases where the arbitrators failed to apply the law prescribed by a *compromis;* and he has constantly been watchful of situations where for various reasons it could fairly be maintained that an excess of jurisdiction was asserted and exercised. He has also discussed the failure of litigating States to raise in a timely manner their jurisdictional objections. He has dwelt upon the doctrine of "essential error." He has not lost sight of the problems pertaining to the finality of an award. The jurisdiction of a court to grant a rehearing, in all that it implies, has been faithfully dealt with. The whole matter of revision has been discussed. The problem of appeal has not been overlooked. Timely suggestions have been offered as to the growth of a system of international arbitral jurisprudence.

The outstanding feature of Mr. Carlston's contribution is the fact that in the light of his offering, States at variance have right before their eyes concrete suggestions, the use of which should enable them to make recourse to arbitration both safe and wise. He shows them how to banish difficulties that heretofore have so often been ruinous to arbitral effort. In a word, the careful reader of his text, especially if he be a governmental draftsman or counsellor, is shown how to make a *compromis* responsive to the exact design of the contracting parties. He is also warned as to matters concerning which those parties should, in such an instrument, focus attention and express their thought. With the prospect of greatly increased recourse to arbitration by States at variance, of which their freedom under Article 33 of Chapter VI of the Charter of the United Nations would seem to be prophetic, Mr. Carlston's study is bound to be widely utilized. Before it is, the writer cheerfully points to the expectant fact.

CHARLES CHENEY HYDE

New York
February 15, 1946

PREFACE

International arbitration is a judicial process, involving the settlement of disputes between States by tribunals acting as courts of law. While a large literature exists upon the Continent concerning various aspects of international arbitration considered as a judicial process, our writers have tended to ignore this field and have concerned themselves more with the substantive law applied by the international tribunal than the functioning of the tribunal as a judicial institution. Yet study of the international court itself is as important as that of the law laid down by the court. States must have confidence not only in international law itself but also in the judicial quality of the tribunal which administers it.

Certain questions are fundamental in the consideration of international arbitration as a judicial process. What procedural difficulties have arisen in the conduct of international arbitrations and how can these be remedied by improvement of procedural rules? What guaranties of justice do States have in entering upon a settlement of a dispute by arbitral means? What limitations exist upon international tribunals, both in the conduct of their hearings and in the rendering of their awards? What may be done to correct excess of jurisdiction or error by a tribunal before its final dissolution? What should be done towards the creation of a means for appeal or review of arbitral decisions? If these questions can be answered in some degree, if the channels of future growth can be marked at least in part, a sound groundwork for the wider acceptance by States of the system of arbitration as a means for the settlement of international controversies will have been laid.

A word about the organization of the book is in order. An unusual degree of attention has been given to a study of cases. Aside from the fact that they are a primary source of the law, detailed analyses and reporting of the precedents have been included for the reason that much of their source material is not readily available, being largely found in libraries and archives in Washington, D.C., and in libraries possessing large international law collections. A number of Central and South American precedents have been included, in addition to the study of the more customary French, German, and English sources. The study of problems of international law requires the broadest possible examination of all relevant material, and we have somewhat tended to overlook the precedents and writers of our sister nations to the south. Detailed case analysis has also been necessary in order to develop adequately the intricate jurisdictional and legal issues involved.

Much of the material in Sections 1 to 7 and 53 to 56 of the text previously appeared in articles in the *American Journal of International Law,* the *International Arbitration Journal,* and the *Journal du Droit International.* The author gratefully acknowledges permission to include it in this volume.

The translations are by the writer unless otherwise indicated. In certain instances this fact is specifically noted, when departures were made from an available printed translation.

KENNETH S. CARLSTON

Bronxville, New York
February 18, 1946

CONTENTS

3. Jurisdiction

4. DOCTRINE OF ESSENTIAL ERROR

5. FINALITY OF THE AWARD

6. REHEARING

7. Appeal

8. Future Progress

BIBLIOGRAPHICAL ABBREVIATIONS

A.B.A. JOUR., American Bar Association Journal.

AM. J. INT. LAW, American Journal of International Law.

AM. SOC. INT. LAW, American Society of International Law.

ANALES, Anales de la Corte de Justicia Centroamericana.

ANNUAIRE, Annuaire de l'Institut de Droit International.

BRITISH YEARBOOK, The British Yearbook of International Law.

CT. CLS., Cases Decided in the Court of Claims of the United States.

COL. L. REV., Columbia Law Review.

CONG. REC., Congressional Record.

DE MARTENS, Martens, G. Fr. de, Nouveau recueil général de traités.

FORD. L. REV., Fordham Law Review.

FOR. REL. U.S., Papers Relating to the Foreign Relations of the United States.

GEORGETOWN L.J., Georgetown Law Journal.

HARV. L. REV., Harvard Law Review.

ILL., Reports of Cases at Law and in Chancery Argued and Determined in the Supreme Court of Illinois.

ILL. L.Q., Illinois Law Quarterly.

IND., Reports of Cases Decided in the Supreme Court of the State of Indiana.

JOUR. DU DROIT INT. (Clunet), Journal du Droit International (Clunet).

JOUR. D.C. BAR ASS'N, Journal of the District of Columbia Bar Association.

KY. L.J., Kentucky Law Journal.

L.J., Law Journal.

L.Q. REV., Law Quarterly Review.

MALLOY, TREATIES, Malloy, W. M., Treaties, Conventions, International Acts, Protocols, and Agreements between the United States of America and Other Powers (1910).

TREATIES (Malloy Supp., 1923), Treaties, Conventions, International Acts, Protocols, and Agreements between the United States and Other Powers, 1910–1923.

MICH. L. REV., Michigan Law Review.

MOORE, INT. ADJ., Moore, J. B., International Adjudications.

MOORE, INT. ARB., Moore, J. B., History and Digest of the International Arbitrations to Which the United States Has Been a Party.

MOORE, DIG., Moore, J. B., A Digest of International Law.

N.W., The Northwestern Reporter.

Op. Att'y Gen., Official Opinions of the Attorneys General of the United States.

Proceedings Am. Soc. Int. Law, Proceedings of the American Society of International Law.

Ralston's Report, Venezuelan Arbitrations of 1903, Ralston's Report.

Recueil des Cours, Academie de Droit International, Recueil des cours.

Recueil des Décisions, Recueil des Décisions des tribunaux arbitraux mixtes.

Rev. de Droit Int., Revue de Droit International.

Rev. de Droit Int. L.C., Revue de Droit International et de Législation Comparée.

Rev. de Droit Pub. S.P., Revue de Droit Public et de la Science Politique.

Rev. Gen. de Droit Int. Pub., Revue Générale de Droit International Public.

Stat., United States Statutes at Large.

Tex. L. Rev., Texas Law Review.

U.S., United States Reports.

Va. L. Rev., Virginia Law Review.

Vt., Reports of Cases Argued and Determined in the Supreme Court of the State of Vermont.

Wis., Reports of Cases Determined in the Supreme Court of Wisconsin.

THE PROCESS OF
INTERNATIONAL
ARBITRATION

CHAPTER 1

PROCEDURE

1. FUNCTION OF PROCEDURAL RULES.—The drafting of procedural rules for the conduct of an international arbitration is not merely the writing of a timetable for the introduction of pleadings and evidence. Many different factors must be taken into account in the formulation of procedural rules if they are to serve their function of facilitating a prompt and just disposition of the cases to be arbitrated. The requirements of dispatch, of protecting litigants from needlessly protracted procedural steps, must be harmonized with the necessity of ensuring an adequate hearing in the interests of justice. Rules must be adjusted to fit the problems and the difficulties peculiar to the particular arbitration. Differences in types of cases must be recognized. It is obvious, for example, that a case involving intricate questions of fact and law will require, for a proper hearing, a more detailed course of pleadings and argument than one whose facts are simple and involve no other legal issue than whether there has been a failure to meet a recognized international obligation. Differences in the legal systems of the parties must likewise be foreseen and guarded against. If one party is accustomed to the system of the English common law while the other is familiar with that of the Continental civil law, clashes will occur as to the proper contents of the pleadings and the rules applicable to the introduction of evidence. These and all other foreseeable sources of misunderstanding must be minimized by explicit and detailed directions. Provision should be made for enforcement of established rules, but not at the expense of a just decision.

Upon the careful and skilled drafting of the procedural rules, therefore, the successful conduct of an international arbitration will often depend. On the one hand, rules may serve to reconcile the many conflicting demands involved in the conduct of the arbi-

tration, or, on the other hand, they may be merely an arbitrary
mechanism thrusting upon the parties burdens and delays which a
more realistic and careful approach would have avoided. Procedure
is no unalterable and immutable course of conduct to which all
tribunals must adhere. On the contrary, procedural rules should be
carefully adapted to the requirements of each arbitration as it arises
so that it may be consummated speedily, economically and justly.

2. IMPORTANCE OF ADEQUATE PROCEDURAL RULES.—International tribunals are occasionally only too prone to borrow their rules of
procedure from one another without considering their suitability
for the particular arbitration at hand.[1] It must be recognized that
the hurry and pressure attendant upon the opening of an arbitration often makes this unavoidable. Agents and counsel are anxious
to proceed with the preparation of their cases. During the course
of the arbitration the ever-nearing date fixed for its completion, the
mounting expense of maintaining the staffs, and the burden of
other official duties awaiting the arbitrators and advocates after the
completion of their tasks, all tend to discourage the deliberate consideration of matters of procedure. Though the need for procedural
reform was long ago recognized,[2] the problem has received relatively little attention from writers.[3] Their attention has for the

---

[1] Thus, the General Claims Commission, United States and Mexico, under the
convention of September 8, 1923, 43 STAT. 1730, adopted the method of presentation by memorial followed in the prior Mexican claims arbitration of 1868 (Rules
and Regulations, Art. 3, 3 MOORE, INT. ARB., 2153), despite the fact that four extensions of time were required by the earlier commission to settle the considerably
fewer claims docketed with it (2 *ibid.* 1297–1298). The rules of the General Claims
Commission in turn spread, with some modification, to the rules of the other
claims commissions charged with settling claims against Mexico, see p. 22, n. 1.
This is not to say that uniformity by commissions in recognizing certain basic
principles of procedure is not desirable as tending to the establishment of customary rules of procedural law, see SANDIFER, EVIDENCE BEFORE INTERNATIONAL
TRIBUNALS (1939) 31.

[2] Dennis, *The Necessity for an International Code of Arbitral Procedure* (1913)
7 AM. J. INT. LAW 285; Lansing, *The Need of Revision of Procedure before International Courts of Arbitration* (1912) 6 PROCEEDINGS AM. SOC. INT. LAW 158.

[3] RALSTON, THE LAW AND PROCEDURE OF INTERNATIONAL TRIBUNALS (1926) 191–
213, and SUPPLEMENT TO 1926 REVISED EDITION OF THE LAW AND PROCEDURE OF IN-
TERNATIONAL TRIBUNALS (1936) 96–108, devotes in each case only one chapter to
procedure. BISHOP, INTERNATIONAL ARBITRAL PROCEDURE (1930) is primarily descriptive in its approach. CALDWELL, A STUDY OF THE CODE OF ARBITRAL PROCEDURE
ADOPTED BY THE HAGUE PEACE CONFERENCES OF 1899 AND 1907 (1921) is necessarily

most part been directed to a description of existing procedural practices. Critical analysis and investigation of the relation of procedural rules to the successful conduct of international arbitrations is almost entirely lacking in the literature on the subject. This neglect of the procedural aspects of international arbitrations has been not only the source of unnecessary disputes between litigants but also a cause of the expensive, leisurely, protracted course for which international arbitrations have at times been condemned.[4] In at least one international arbitration of note the fail-

restricted in scope. A condensed but most interesting description of procedural processes appears in HUDSON, INTERNATIONAL TRIBUNALS (1944) 84–98. ACREMENT, LA PROCÉDURE DANS LES ARBITRAGES INTERNATIONAUX (1905) is a thoughtful early study. An illuminating analysis of procedural problems and suggestions for reform with respect to functioning of the American and Panamanian General Claims Arbitration established under the Conventions of July 28, 1926, and December 17, 1932, appears in REPORT OF THE AGENT FOR THE UNITED STATES, DEPARTMENT OF STATE, ARBITRATION SERIES No. 6 (1934) 7–29. Some excellent procedural suggestions out of his ripe experience as an international judge are found in a few pages of NIELSEN, INTERNATIONAL LAW AS APPLIED TO RECLAMATIONS (1933) 67–69, 72–74. WITENBERG, L'ORGANISATION JUDICIAIRE, LA PROCÉDURE ET LA SENTENCE INTERNATIONALES (1937) 110–261, while comprehensive and well documented, is also primarily descriptive of procedural steps rather than a critical study. HOIJER, LA SOLUTION PACIFIQUE DES LITIGES INTERNATIONAUX (1925) 250–270, is broadly descriptive in content. Of the early studies on arbitration see MÉRIGNHAC, TRAITÉ THÉORIQUE ET PRATIQUE DE L'ARBITRAGE INTERNATIONAL (1895) 244–282, 435–439; KAMAROWSKY, LE TRIBUNAL INTERNATIONAL (1887) 175–180, 510–512; DREYFUS, L'ARBITRAGE INTERNATIONAL (1892) 271–296. An extensive literature on the Mixed Arbitral Tribunals created under the Treaty of Versailles and the other treaties of peace exists, however; see bibliography collected in TEYSSAIRE AND SOLERE, LES TRIBUNAUX ARBITRAUX MIXTES (1931) 231–243. See also Nielsen, *Progress in Settlement of International Disputes by Judicial Methods* (1930) 16 A.B.A. JOUR. 229; Garnier-Coignet, *Procédure judiciaire et procédure arbitrale* (1930) 6 REV. DE DROIT INT. 123; the author's article *Procedural Problems in International Arbitration* (1945) 39 AM. J. INT. LAW 426.

4 See remarks in 75 CONG. REC. 14424. As to the costs of international arbitrations, consider the following examples.

Appropriations for arbitrations embodying a single issue or claim:
        Landreau claim (U.S.) v. Peru $45,000, 42 STAT. 336
        Norwegian Claims Case   60,000, 42 STAT. 336
For arbitrations embodying many claims:
        United States–Germany Mixed Claims Commissions ⎱ 1922–1932
        Tripartite Claims Commission   ⎰ $1,339,863 *
        United States–Mexican Mixed Claims Commissions   1924–1932
                                  $2,574,730 **

* 42 STAT. 1051; 43 STAT. 215, 1023; 44 STAT. 359, 1189; 45 STAT. 74, 913, 1105; 46 STAT. 183, 886, 1581; 47 STAT. 25.
** 43 STAT. 691, 1024; 44 STAT. 340, 865, 1190; 45 STAT. 74, 1105; 46 STAT. 184, 1318; 47 STAT. 25.

ure to adapt the procedural rules to the necessities of the arbitration led to its abandonment and the transfer of its task to a domestic body. During the first eight years of its existence, the Special Claims Commission, United States and Mexico, created under the convention of September 10, 1923, decided 18 claims. In a corresponding period of time the General Claims Commission, United States and Mexico, decided 148 claims, making an aggregate of 166 claims decided out of some 5,736 claims filed with both commissions.[5] Yet the Special Mexican Claims Commission, functioning as a statutory national commission under the Act of April 10, 1935,[6] and not under the Convention of September 10, 1923, and untrammeled by elaborate procedural rules, decided 2,833 claims in a little more than two and one-half years, and this on a budget of less than $90,000 a year, as against an aggregate expenditure by the commissions during their existence of more than $2,000,000 when they functioned in the traditional manner of international tribunals.[7]

As the web of international commerce is again woven into its intensely intricate pattern in the postwar years, every means must be taken to lessen the strains to which differences in language, laws and culture will subject it. Disputes and misunderstandings will inevitably arise because of clashes caused by varying national back-

---

The foregoing computations, of course, fail to take into consideration any unexpended appropriations turned back to the Treasury. Deduction of a specified percentage from awards to cover the expenses of the arbitration is sometimes made, 56 STAT. 1058, 1063, but this only adds to the burden of claimants without affecting the amount of expenses incurred.

5 See FELLER, THE MEXICAN CLAIMS COMMISSIONS, 1923–1934 (1935) 60, 68; Turlington, *Comments on the Rules of the Special Mexican Claims Commission* (1936) 3 JOUR. D.C. BAR ASS'N 22, 23; McDonald and Barnett, *The American-Mexican Claims Arbitration* (1932) 18 A.B.A. JOUR. 183, 184.

6 49 STAT. 149.

7 See McKernan, Special Mexican Claims (1938) 32 AM. J. INT. LAW 457, 461. It was recognized that the commission had at its disposal "a veritable mine of information" collected by the former agency and that its task was confined to a review of the records and did not include the preparation and prosecution of cases undertaken by the former agency, *ibid.* 463; *Rules and Regulations of the Special Mexican Claims Commission,* Rules II and VII. Moreover, approximately 500 claims were submitted to the former commission by the American agency in memorial form, of which 150 were briefed as to facts and law, and evidence probably sufficient for memorialization was obtained by the agency on some 200 additional claims. Turlington, *supra* note 5, fn. 11.

grounds. If arbitration is to carry out successfully its task of solving amicably such disputes, the utmost consideration must be given to its procedural aspects. Unless the details of the presentation of the case and the pertinent evidence are thoroughly explored and settled in advance, the final disposition of the dispute to be arbitrated may very well be wrecked upon the shoals of a procedural argument. At best, a haphazard course of procedure does not conduce either to a sound award or to satisfaction with arbitration as a means for the settlement of disputes.

To be successful, therefore, an arbitration in the international sphere will have to be undertaken by the parties with full recognition of the fundamental differences existing between their respective national backgrounds and legal systems, and every effort will have to be made to carry the arbitration forward in carefully marked channels.

3. PROCEDURAL PROBLEMS IN ARBITRATIONS LIMITED TO A SINGLE CASE. —Procedural difficulties are necessarily much less likely to arise when the arbitration is confined to the decision of a single dispute instead of many. Generally these difficulties concern the scope of the pleadings and the time and manner of introducing the evidence.

Pleadings, in general, fall into one of two systems of nomenclature. In certain recent multi-claims arbitrations the opening pleading (i.e., the complaint) is termed the "memorial," and it is followed successively by the answer, the reply, and the rejoinder, or the answer to the reply. In the arbitration of single disputes, the opening pleading is often designated the "case" and is followed by the counter-case, or answer, and the reply.

Argument as to the scope of pleadings is not likely to be provoked when the arbitration goes forward under the direction of counsel whose legal experience has been under similar systems of law.[1] But when one of the countries adheres to the civil law, while

[1] American counsel were engaged by both litigants in the Tacna-Arica arbitration, where it happened that the cases and the counter-cases of each were generally similar in scope, though the exposition of facts tended to be presented within the structure of a legal analysis, ARBITRATION BETWEEN PERU AND CHILE UNDER PROTO-

the other upholds the common law, dissension between the respective agents may well be expected to arise. Those trained under the latter system tend to regard the function of the first pleading as the narration of the facts upon which the position of their government is grounded, to which is joined the evidence in support of their contentions.[2] On the other hand, those possessing the civil law background appear to view the function of the first pleading as a discussion of law as well as of fact.[3] Material disadvantage will be less likely to result to either party because of this variance of views if their true positions as plaintiff and defendant are frankly recognized. When the rules provide that the plaintiff government is to file its case first, to be followed in turn by the answer of the respondent and subsequent pleadings, each party is afforded an opportunity to meet the pleadings of the other no matter to what lengths they may go.[4] A disparity of position, however, can readily be created if the parties are limited by the *compromis* to the simultaneous exchange of cases and counter-cases, with no opportunity to come to a full understanding concerning the scope of each.

The facts of a case can rarely be grasped by the lawyer or the

COL AND SUPPLEMENTARY ACT OF JULY 20, 1922, CASE, COUNTER-CASE OF THE REPUBLIC OF CHILE, CASE, COUNTER-CASE OF PERU. Likewise, in an arbitration taking place under civil law conceptions, an identity in function of pleadings followed, AFFAIRE DE LIMITES ENTRE LA COLOMBIE ET LE VÉNÉZUÉLA (Sentence Arbitrale du Conseil Fédéral Suisse sur Diverses Questions de Limites pendantes entre la Colombie et le Vénézuéla, Berne, 24 mars 1922) *Première Mémoire, Réponse, Réplique des États-Unis du Vénézuéla, Première Mémoire, Mémoire Responsif, Réplique de la République de Colombie.*

[2] See memorial of the United States, PIOUS FUND OF THE CALIFORNIAS, REPORT OF JACKSON H. RALSTON, FOR. REL. U.S. 1902, 2 APP. 21; Chamizal arbitration, CASE OF THE UNITED STATES, 6, COUNTERCASE OF THE UNITED STATES, 3-4; Orinoco Steamship Company Case, CASE OF THE UNITED STATES, 6, COUNTER CASE OF THE UNITED STATES, 4-6. Exceptions to this practice may occur as the result of restrictions imposed by the protocol, see the pleadings in the Alsop claim (U.S.) v. Chile, or for other reasons; *cf.* I NORTH ATLANTIC COAST FISHERIES ARBITRATION, FINAL REPORT OF THE AGENT OF THE UNITED STATES, 11.

[3] See the *Demanda* and *Réplica* of Mexico in the Chamizal arbitration, *supra* note 2, and the *Premier Mémoire* and *Réplique* of Colombia and Venezuela, respectively, in their boundary arbitration of 1922, *supra* note 1. This approach is followed in the Rules of Court, Permanent Court of International Justice, Article 42, STATUTE AND RULES OF COURT (1936) 28 at 43.

[4] *Cf.* Lansing, *The Need of Revision of Procedure before International Courts of Justice* (1912) 6 PROCEEDINGS AM. SOC. INT. LAW; see the Landreau arbitration (U.S.) v. Peru, Protocol of May 21, 1921, Art. 10, CASE OF THE UNITED STATES, 5-6.

judge without at least partially fitting them into a legal frame-work.[5] Accordingly, that party which first makes clear to the arbitrator its legal position is most likely to influence the decision in its favor. On the other hand, in one respect the restriction of the case to a narration of fact places the more venturesome opponent, who has discussed both the facts and the law in its case, at a disadvantage. Although he has thus disclosed his position, he labors in the dark when making an answer to his opponent's pleading in that he must endeavor to anticipate undisclosed legal grounds. Thus, we find the agent of Sweden, in the arbitration with the United States under the special agreement of December 17, 1930, complaining:

> The function of the answers in the present arbitration . . . was to enable each party to answer and rebut, with additional evidence and argument, the statement of the case and supporting evidence previously filed by the opposing party, and thus to bring the parties to an issue upon the facts and the law applicable thereto. The answer of the United States can be so directed because of the full statement of the case contained in the printed documents previously filed by Sweden.

> But the Agent for Sweden finds the greatest difficulty in making such an answer. . . . The Statement filed by the United States sets forth much of the legislation of the United States, and the contemporaneous correspondence, both diplomatic and otherwise, relating to the detention of the two vessels, which is printed in the Appendix to the Case of Sweden. It also sets forth the subsequent diplomatic correspondence in which the Government of Sweden presented its claim for indemnity and the Government of the United States disputed it. But whether or not the positions taken by the Government of the United States in this correspondence are now adhered to is not disclosed. . . . But it is fair to say that the Statement of the Case of the United States does not—and for wholly understandable and proper reasons—present the conclusions of fact and law upon which the United States will rest its defense to the claim of Sweden for indemnity. This answer must, therefore, be written without, for the most part, a knowledge of what defense the Government of Sweden will be called upon to rebut.[6]

[5] The concept of *operative* facts is illustrative, HOHFELD, FUNDAMENTAL LEGAL CONCEPTIONS (1923) 32; CLARK, CODE PLEADING (1928) 84.

[6] ANSWER OF THE KINGDOM OF SWEDEN, DEPARTMENT OF STATE, ARBITRATION SERIES No. 5, 1–2. See also the Norwegian Claims Case, COUNTER CASE OF THE

The point was succinctly put by The Netherlands in the *Palmas Island* arbitration.

Whereas the first memoranda were statements of the case independent of one another, the counter-memoranda for the first time could take into account the point of view of the other party, and it was only by the counter-memoranda that each party knew the attitude of the other towards his own statements.[7]

In the *Orinoco Steamship Company* arbitration, although the Venezuelan case consisted in an argument of various questions of law and fact, the United States, in its counter-case, announced that it would adhere to its views respecting the functions of the case and the counter-case.[8] The issue in this arbitration was primarily one of law, namely, the validity of a prior arbitral award as falling within its terms of submission. In such a case there can be little purpose in refraining from entering upon a discussion of the law until the argument. When slight dispute as to the facts exists, the case and counter-case should have the function of clarifying both the factual and the legal issues involved.

In the *Venezuelan Preferential Claims Case*, at The Hague, the tribunal was requested to require Great Britain, Germany, and Italy to submit first their statement of their case, on the ground that they were in fact the plaintiffs. The resulting argument between the Powers was settled by ordering the simultaneous presentation of pleadings.[9] In the *Norwegian Claims Case* the United States recognized itself as the defendant.[10] Again, in the *Chamizal* arbitration the United States contended that in fact Mexico was the claimant government and that the circumstance that both parties filed the pleadings simultaneously was not inconsistent with

KINGDOM OF NORWAY, 1–2, and the Alaska boundary proceedings (Great Britain v. U.S., 1903) IV PROCEEDINGS OF THE ALASKAN BOUNDARY TRIBUNAL, COUNTER CASE OF THE UNITED STATES, 1–2; ACREMENT, LA PROCÉDURE DANS LES ARBITRAGES INTERNATIONAUX (1905) 110.

[7] EXPLANATIONS OF THE NETHERLANDS GOVERNMENT, 11. But *cf.* REJOINDER OF THE UNITED STATES, 3–4.

[8] *Supra* note 2, COUNTER CASE OF THE UNITED STATES, 6.

[9] REPORT OF WILLIAM L. PENFIELD (1905) 55, 62.

[10] United States–Norway arbitration under the special agreement of June 30, 1921, CASE OF THE UNITED STATES, 7.

this contention, because such practice was common.[11] Possibly disputes of this nature are in part induced by a desire to fix upon the opposing party the burden of proof.

The practice of concurrently filing the cases and subsequent pleadings has at times led to unnecessary duplication in the submission of evidence. In the support of their respective positions, the parties will unavoidably to some degree adduce the same documentary evidence. And when evidence becomes as voluminous as it did in the *North Atlantic Coast Fisheries* arbitration, such duplication of effort, with its resulting heightening of the cost of the arbitration, is regrettable.[12] This could be avoided by the use of stipulations of fact entered into between the agents or by their reaching some definite understanding as to what evidence shall be produced with their respective cases. For example, the documents in the *Pious Fund Case* were by the consent of both governments printed in one volume.[13]

In view of the difficulties attendant upon the simultaneous filing of the successive pleadings, it was long ago recommended that this device be discarded.[14] It seems unlikely that it will be entirely abandoned, in view of its value to foreign offices as a means of avoiding the decision of the often ticklish question as to who is properly the plaintiff and who the defendant. While the responsibility for this decision might be escaped by leaving it to the tribunal to decide who shall be the plaintiff and who the defendant and then directing the filing of alternate pleadings, in such cases an adjournment to permit of the preparations of such pleadings would probably be necessary, with consequent protraction of the arbitration.

Other sources of difficulty lie in the production of evidence. When must it be introduced? In what form and to what extent must it be produced? Often tribunals are loath to regulate ques-

[11] *Supra* note 2, ARGUMENT OF THE UNITED STATES, 4.

[12] I *op. cit. supra* note 2, at 11.

[13] See TRANSCRIPT OF RECORD OF PROCEEDINGS BEFORE THE MEXICAN AND AMERICAN MIXED CLAIMS COMMISSION WITH RELATION TO THE PIOUS FUND OF THE CALIFORNIAS.

[14] Lansing, *supra* note 4, at 161–163; BISHOP, INTERNATIONAL ARBITRAL PROCEDURE (1930) 238.

tions such as these in their rules, with the result that parties proceed haphazardly and often end in disputes which greater foresight would have avoided. A notable example is the failure of the government of The Netherlands in the *Palmas Island* arbitration to include with its first pleading the greater portion of the documents referred to therein, informing the arbitrator that authentic copies thereof were available and would be produced if desired.[15] Its action was apparently taken in entire good faith [16] and was the result of its belief in the applicability of the principle of civil law which denied a defendant the power to require, without good reason, the plaintiff to accumulate evidence in support of every fact mentioned.[17] A like course was followed in its second pleading.[18] On the part of the United States, it was insisted that such a procedure was without precedent and that assertions made without supporting proof must fall to the ground. It was contended that under the assumption of The Netherlands the tribunal would be denied the exercise of the judicial function of deciding a controversy in the light of the evidence before it.[19] In the *impasse* The Netherlands sought to rely on Article III of the treaty, which empowered the arbitrator to call upon either party for further explanations as a means whereby the required evidence could be introduced.[20] Unfortunately, such a solution placed the United States at a disadvantage. Its evidence had been disclosed with its first pleading; The Netherlands was given six months to answer it and to introduce

[15] MEMORANDUM OF NETHERLANDS GOVERNMENT, [Preliminary] Note.

[16] See EXPLANATIONS OF THE NETHERLANDS GOVERNMENT, 12: "The note was inserted by the Netherlands Government as a natural and simple matter, and it seems hardly necessary to add that there was not behind it some sinister design to prejudice the other party's position; any such intention (supposing that a party to this dispute was capable of having it) would be futile in view of article III of the special agreement."

[17] *Ibid.* at 5, citing German Code of Civil Procedure, par. 130, Nos. 3, 4, 5, par. 272, 282, 350; French Code of Civil Procedure, Art. 34; Code of Civil Procedure of Swiss Canton of Basel-Stadt, secs. 98, 289.

[18] COUNTER-MEMORANDUM OF THE NETHERLANDS GOVERNMENT, [Preliminary] Note.

[19] COUNTER-MEMORANDUM OF THE UNITED STATES, 2–3; REJOINDER OF THE UNITED STATES, 3–8.

[20] EXPLANATIONS OF THE NETHERLANDS GOVERNMENT, 15.

evidence in rebuttal, whereas, in making its rejoinder to the further explanations of The Netherlands, the United States was limited to three months and apparently was denied the opportunity of submitting further rebuttal evidence.[21] Though the tribunal could hardly have done otherwise than to permit this irregular use of further explanations as a vehicle for late evidence, in view of the fact that The Netherlands had acted in good faith, the cause of arbitration would have been better served had there been rules to regulate this question in advance. This was, in fact, done in the subsequent arbitration convention of March 18, 1938, with The Netherlands.[22]

On the other hand, in the *Norwegian Claims Case,* before the Permanent Court of Arbitration, the American agent admirably formulated the general rules applicable to a request for the late introduction of evidence after the written pleadings had been filed.

The United States does not, however, desire to offer any captious opposition to the introduction of further documentary evidence on the part of Norway and should not oppose the introduction of such evidence if desired by Norway, always provided: (1) that some reasonable explanations be forthcoming as to why this evidence was not seasonably presented, (2) that the evidence be really relevant and of a character to assist the Tribunal in coming to a just decision, (3) that reciprocal consent, similarly conditioned, be accorded by Norway to the United States for the introduction of new evidence, (4) that suitable opportunity be given the United States for the consideration of this evidence and the presentation of rebutting evidence if necessary, and (5) *especially* that new evidence should not be admitted if such rebutting evidence is necessary and cannot be procured without delay.[23]

[21] Art. 3, agreement of January 23, 1925, United States and The Netherlands (1928) 22 AM. J. INT. LAW 869. *Cf.* REPORT OF FRED K. NIELSEN 39–40; Jessup, *The Palmas Island Arbitration* (1928) 22 AM. J. INT. LAW 735, 751, 752. For an instance in which a correct use of further explanations was made see the boundary arbitration between Colombia and Venezuela of 1922, RENSEIGNEMENTS COMPLÉMENTAIRES PRÉSENTÉS PAR LES ÉTATS-UNIS DU VÉNÉZUÉLA AU HAUT CONSEIL FEDERAL SUISSE (1921).

[22] 53 STAT. 1564, 1565, Art. I.

[23] PROCEEDINGS OF THE TRIBUNAL (1922) Protocol II, Meeting of July 25, 1922, p. 16.

In each instance the tribunal refrained from actively intervening in the matter, and the agents came to an agreement which was satisfactory to each.[24]

Other disputes which have arisen after sittings of the tribunal have begun concern the order of debates [25] or the submission of pleadings not provided for in the *compromis*. In the *Pious Fund Case* the tribunal permitted the filing by the United States of what was termed a replication, though no provision for it was made in the *compromis*. However, the consent of Mexico was first obtained, and that consent was given only upon the condition that Mexico be allowed a rejoinder.[26]

4. PROCEDURAL PROBLEMS IN MULTI-CLAIMS ARBITRATIONS.—Far more complicated are the procedural problems faced by arbitrations having for their purpose the settlement of numerous claims pending between States. The conflicting conceptions of procedure and evidence, on which comment has heretofore been made, clash with increased frequency. Interests of claimants must be reconciled with the insistent demands of economy and dispatch. Opportunities for dilatoriness must be minimized, but provision for the adequate preparation of cases varying widely in their complexity and importance must be made, and the commands of the *compromis* must ever be heeded. The essential problem is well stated by Judge Nielsen.

International tribunals created to adjust international claims are often required to determine a considerable, and sometimes a very large, number of cases. No efforts looking to a just disposition of each one should be spared in view of its importance from the standpoint of both private and public interest. But without any sacrifice in thoroughness of presentations and judicial determination, it would be feasible to simplify voluminous rules that are conducive to delays, prolonging the final presentation of cases;

---

24 Palmas Island arbitration: see Award of Tribunal (1928) 22 AM. J. INT. LAW 870–871; Norwegian Claims Case, *op. cit. supra* note 23, Protocol V, Meeting of July 28, 1922, Protocol VIII, Meeting of August 2, 1922.

25 Dennis, *The Necessity for an International Code of Arbitral Procedure* (1913) 7 AM. J. INT. LAW 285, 295–296, sets forth several instances in which differences of opinion arose concerning the order of oral argument.

26 *Op. cit. supra* note 2, at pp. 513, 514, 523. *Cf.* the incident in the Alabama claims arbitration reported by ACREMENT, *op. cit. supra* note 6, at 116–117.

that teem with obscurities, frequently multiplying questions requiring judicial determination; that permit undesirable repetitions in the presentation of cases; and that, because of uncertainties, are in a measure responsible for friction between counsel.[1]

When cases are few in number, when no time limit exists for the completion of hearings, when counsel possess similar views with respect to pleadings and presentation of evidence, and when the respective governments desire that full consideration be given to the merits of each case, simple procedural rules are possible. These circumstances in large measure led to the successful conduct of the American and the British claims arbitration under the agreement of August 18, 1910.[2] The pleadings to be filed were given a very brief description.[3] No specific date was required for their filing, only that they should be prepared "with all dispatch" and filed "as soon as may be reasonably possible." [4] With a full hearing accorded to each case, it is not surprising that some five years were consumed in deciding the fifty-two groups of claims submitted.[5] But remove any one of these favorable factors, and such leisurely processes will no longer be possible.

The various tribunals set up between the Allied and the Central Powers under the treaties of peace closing World War I had facing them the duty of settling an unprecedented number of claims.[6]

1 Nielsen, International Law as Applied to Reclamations (1933) 67.

2 Cf. Le Roy, American and British Claims Arbitration Tribunal (1926) 12 A.B.A. Jour. 156; for the text of the special agreement of August 18, 1910, and the rules of procedure see American and British Claims Arbitration, Report of Fred K. Nielsen (1926) 3, 11.

3 Rules 11–18, ibid. 12, 13.   4 Rule 10, ibid. 12.

5 Ibid. 24–36; Le Roy, supra note 2, at 157.

6 The British-German Clearing Office dealt with 382,464 claims of which about 10,000 had to be considered by the Anglo-German, Mixed Arbitral Tribunal, Hart, Experiment in Legal Procedure (1931) 72 L.J. 392. The United States–German Mixed Claims Commission had 20,430 claims filed before it, of which more than 12,000 were under the first treaty, that of August 10, 1922. 6,187 awards were rendered totaling $186,813,901.56, the remainder of the claims being dismissed or withdrawn, Hearing before the Sub-committee of House Committee on Appropriations, First Deficiency Appropriation Bill for 1933, 72d Cong., 2d Sess. 113. The foregoing sum does not include the award of approximately $31,400,000 made in Lehigh Valley R. Co. et al. (U.S.) v. Germany, Opinions and Decisions in the Sabotage Claims Handed down June 15, 1939, and October 30, 1939, at 324. The Tripartite Claims Commission between the United States, Austria, and Hungary had 1,631 claims filed before it, Report of Robert W. Bonynge (1930) 3.

Expedition accordingly became the one primary requisite of procedure. Yet the procedural rules adopted by the European Mixed Arbitral Tribunals show little evidence of conscious effort to meet this requirement. The institution of the Clearing Offices, which inestimably lightened their task by the direct settlement of private debt claims, was not their creation, but rather that of the authors of the peace treaties. The payment of debts which were admittedly due or as to which an agreement could be reached, by means of debiting and crediting of accounts between Clearing Offices representing each of the States, provided a simple and expeditious way of disposing of claims outside the tribunals.[7] The casting of the burden of preparation and defense of their claims upon individual creditors and debtors [8] and the provisions made for the presentation of joint claims and the joinder of parties [9] were impelled by the fact that most of the litigation which came before the Mixed Arbitral Tribunals was of a private nature. The requirement that the pleadings were to be filed within fixed periods one after another was not novel.[10] One interesting suggestion is afforded by the rules of the Anglo-German Tribunal, which directed that no reply or rejoinder need be filed if it were only desired to deny the facts alleged in the preceding pleading.[11] A further saving of time could well have been attained by dispensing entirely with these secondary pleadings,[12] instead of permitting their optional filing; while

[7] Treaty of Versailles, Art. 296, Annex, particularly clauses 6–10, 112 BRITISH AND FOREIGN STATE PAPERS (1919) 1, 140; Treaty of Saint-Germain, Art. 248, ibid. 317, 428; Treaty of Trianon, Art. 231, 113 ibid. 486, at 579; cf. Hart, supra note 6.

[8] Cf. Treaty of Versailles, Art. 296, Annex, clauses 16, 18, 112 op. cit. supra note 7, at 144; Rules of Procedure, Anglo-German M.A.T., par. 3, I RECUEIL DES DÉCISIONS (1922) 110; Rules of Procedure, Franco-German M.A.T., Art. 6, ibid. 46.

[9] Joint claims: Anglo-German M.A.T., par. 16, ibid. 112; German-Belgian M.A.T., Art. 44, ibid. 39; cf. Franco-German M.A.T., Art. 16, ibid. 47. Joinder of parties: Anglo-German M.A.T., par. 17–21, ibid. 112–113; German-Belgian M.A.T., Art. 37–43, ibid. 38–39; Franco-German M.A.T., Art. 19–22, ibid. 48.

[10] Anglo-German M.A.T., par. 8, ibid. 110; Franco-German M.A.T., Art. 13, 26, 28, ibid. 47, 49.

[11] Art. 15, ibid. 111. Cf. Rule 19, rules of procedure of the Nicaraguan Mixed Claims Commission, providing that absence of answer would be equivalent to a general denial, REPORT OF THE NICARAGUAN MIXED CLAIMS COMMISSION (1915) 26.

[12] Cf. Williams, The Tribunal for the Interpretation of the Dawes Plan (1928) 22 AM. J. INT. LAW 797, 799. The rules of the United States–Panama Mixed Claims Commission (convention of July 28, 1926) make provision only for a memorial, answer, brief, and reply brief and expressly prohibit amendments thereto, Art.

the clarification of the issues of the case would still have been reasonably preserved through the filing of the answer.[13]

More noteworthy are the contributions of the German-American Mixed Claims Commission and the Tripartite Claims Commission between the United States, Austria, and Hungary. They found very early that the laborious process of presentation by memorial and answer was too unwieldy an instrument for the rapid disposition of the many claims filed. If their task were not to be dragged out for years, some form of direct settlement was essential. The innovations of the administrative decision and the use of agreed statements of facts furnished the solution. Owing to the fact that the claims were to be judged upon the basis of interpretation of treaty clauses,[14] it was possible to segregate them into certain classifications with regard to the disposition of which general rules could be laid down by the commission in what were termed "administrative decisions." The task of the application of these rules to specific cases was assumed by the respective agencies. Through direct negotiation they arrived at agreed statements of facts of individual cases. These were referred to the commission for final action. Usually the review of the commission was *pro forma* in nature and award was made in accordance with the recommendation of the agents. When no agreement as to the facts of a case was possible submission by the customary means of memorial and answer was utilized or statement was made to the commission of the views of the respective agencies.[15]

Had the basis for decision been responsibility under the general

---

13–17. The regulations of the Central American Court of Justice look primarily to the filing of a declaration, answer and dilatory pleas. Written or oral arguments may, however, be made, Art. 50, 57, 73, 74 and 79, (1914) 8 AM. J. INT. LAW, SUPP. 205, 206, 210, 211.

[13] Art. 26, 28, Franco-German M.A.T., *op. cit. supra* note 8, at 49; Art. 31, German-Belgian M.A.T., *ibid.* 37.

[14] Art. 1, Agreement of August 10, 1922, United States and Germany, 42 STAT. 2200; Art. 1, agreement between the United States and Austria and Hungary of December 12, 1925, 44 STAT. 2213. See Administrative Decision No. II (1923), DECISIONS, MIXED CLAIMS COMMISSION, UNITED STATES AND GERMANY (1925) 5, 7; Opinion construing the phrase "naval and military works or materials" (1924), *ibid.* 75, 76; (Note) (1927) 40 HARV. L. REV. 752, 753.

[15] Morgan, *The Work of the Mixed Claims Commission, United States and Germany* (1926) 4 TEX. L. REV. 399, 401–402.

principles of international law instead of responsibility as admitted in treaty clauses, it is not probable that effective classification of cases could so readily have been made. The application of those rules to each case would raise factual and legal questions too intricate to be disposed of by broad generalizations. Not that administrative decisions would have been altogether precluded,[16] but these novel procedural methods could be effectively used only because the cases, arising as they did principally out of the provisions of the Treaty of Versailles or its analogues and relating to acts of war and war legislation of the Central Powers, naturally fell into distinct groups.[17] And to this tendency further impetus was given by the simple legal basis decreed for their decision.

The conciliatory and business-like spirit in which the respective agents approach their duties indicates a second factor on which will depend the success of any attempt to shift the power of settlement from the tribunal to the agents.[18] That is, the existence on the part of agents, and in turn upon their respective governments, of a genuine desire not to insist upon their every legal privilege. Hence it is not believed that the same degree of success would necessarily follow the unqualified adoption of similar methods by the typical international mixed claims arbitration. Much of its task is addressed to the final resolution of claims pending between nations which all the resources of diplomatic negotiations have failed to settle. Granted the existence of the utmost spirit of conciliation on the part of the agents, it is not likely that they could arrive at an agreement for the settlement of cases which have for so long been the cause of such sharp differences of opinion on the part of their respective governments. Moreover, it is no criticism of agents to point out that theirs is the approach of an advocate,

---

[16] Cf. Opinion in the Lusitania Cases (1923), op. cit. supra note 14, at 17; Administrative Decision No. III (1923), ibid. 61.

[17] Cf. Morgan, supra note 15, at 401, 402.

[18] Cf. Addresses of Mr. Morris, agent of the United States, and Dr. von Lewinski, agent of Germany, at the opening meeting of the German-American Mixed Claims Commission, FIRST REPORT OF ROBERT C. MORRIS, MIXED CLAIMS COMMISSION, UNITED STATES AND GERMANY (1922) 9–11; Morgan, supra note 15, at 403.

rather than that of a conciliator. It is their duty to present their government's case to the tribunal in the strongest possible light; hence only rarely will settlement between agents supplant the traditional role of the tribunal. The experience of the General Claims Commission, United States and Mexico, as constituted under the Protocol of April 24, 1934,[19] is illuminating in this connection. It was contemplated that the cases would be decided by agreement between two commissioners, one for each government, with no third commissioner to act as umpire; in other words a system of direct settlement between representatives of each State. It is understood, however, that the commissioners were able to agree upon favorable awards in only 121 cases, 1,050 remaining undecided, and the remainder being dismissed.

The experience of the American war claims arbitrations does, however, suggest a highly desirable procedural reform, which, it is believed, should be introduced in arbitrations of this type. Agents should be expressly granted the discretionary power to differentiate among claimants in the presentation of their cases and to negotiate settlements under the guidance of administrative decisions of the commission. Hitherto the principle that each claimant must have his day in court has been deemed to include the consequence that each *prima facie* case is to be presented through the same course of procedure. But cases vary in complexity, importance, and quality of supporting evidence. An adequate presentation of a claim involving a simple legal issue, such as a claim based on a charge of harsh and unusual treatment during imprisonment, can be procured without resorting to all the procedural steps necessary to clarify as complex a case as one involving the validity of a Calvo clause. Similarly, a case whose evidence is insufficient and doubtful does not justify recourse to the lengthy and expensive process of presentation by way of memorial, answer, reply, brief, counter-brief, and oral argument. If procedure is to facilitate in the most effective way the functioning of the tribunal—which is its only role in any

[19] 48 STAT. 1844.

judicial system—it must recognize that these differences in cases exist and enable counsel and tribunal to use for them special methods of treatment.

In his able handling of the interests of the United States before the American and Panamanian General Claims Arbitration, the American agent took the step of rejecting, without submitting to the commission, 40 out of a total of 133 claims, in which it was clear that awards for damages would be unprocurable. Claims were also presented in groups rather than individually, when possible, 93 claims being encompassed by 15 sets of pleadings.[20] With regard to the great mass of cases in which evidence is entirely lacking on one or more vital points such as nationality, and the time for the submission of evidence has passed, authority exists in any agent to submit them directly to the commission for dismissal.[21] Settlement through agreed statements could be utilized in cases where the evidence is somewhat weak but sufficient to justify an award *ex aequo et bono*.[22] However, as has been observed before, the successful performance of these and similar functions by the agents can only be expected if they, and in turn their respective governments, possess a sincere desire that claims shall be decided on their merits and not on technicalities.

Whatever cases cannot be disposed of by direct negotiation between agents or by dismissal—and in the usual mixed claims commission there will be many—must be handled by some form of procedure. For the presentation of claims involving intricate issues of fact and law the customary procedural processes of memorial, answer, and subsequent pleadings, including brief and argument, suffice. But for less complex claims, in which the issue is usually whether as a matter of fact there has been a failure to meet a recognized international obligation, some simpler form of procedure seems sufficient. Provision that all pleadings after the me-

[20] REPORT OF THE AGENT FOR THE UNITED STATES, DEPARTMENT OF STATE, ARBITRATION SERIES NO. 6 (1934) 10–12.
[21] *Ibid.*
[22] Lasry (U.S.) v. Venezuela (1903), RALSTON'S REPORT (1904) 37.

morial and the answer are to be optional [23] does not always result in the elimination of superfluous pleadings.[24] Once let a defined course of procedure be begun, and it is unlikely that the agent who is zealous to protect the interests of his government will overlook any one of its steps. It is thought that only by providing special forms of procedure for the presentation of simple claims of this nature to the commission will dispatch be achieved without an undue sacrifice of the interests of claimants. This approach was taken in the Nicaraguan Mixed Claims Commission, in which the rules of procedure provided for the filing of memorial and answer, but exception was made for several thousands of claims, small in amount, which had been filed with local boards. Such claims were considered upon their proofs, without memorial or answer.[25] Another possible approach would be to utilize the *mémoire*, or case, as conceived of in the civil law, containing a discussion of the legal basis as well as the facts of a claim, for the presentation of such claims. The pleadings could then close with an answer prepared along similar lines. It would even be possible in some cases to go to the commission upon the first pleading by providing that the absence of an answer should be deemed equivalent to a general denial.[26]

5. PROBLEMS IN THE ENFORCEMENT OF PROCEDURAL RULES.—Once procedural rules are established by a commission, the difficulties then most likely to arise concern the matter of procuring adherence to the established rules and ensuring adequate protection for the interests of the party aggrieved by departure from them. Divergence of viewpoint as to the form and content of pleadings seems largely

---

[23] Rule IV, par. 4 (a), Rule X, par. 2, General and Special Claims Commissions, United States and Mexico; Art. 15 (a), 16, 37, German-Mexican Claims Commission; Art. 15 (a), 16, 40, 41, Spanish-Mexican Claims Commission; Rule IV, par. 13 (a), 14, Rule XI, par. 41, Anglo-Mexican Claims Commission.

[24] Compare replies of the United States in joint claims of B. E. Chattin, et al. (Gen. Docket Nos. 40, 41, 42, 43), and in Charles E. Tolerton (Gen. Docket No. 921).

[25] *Op. cit. supra* note 11, at 24–26.

[26] See the interesting suggestions of Judge Nielsen in INTERNATIONAL LAW AS APPLIED TO RECLAMATIONS (1933) 68. Compare Rule 19, Nicaraguan Mixed Claims Commission, *op. cit. supra* note 11, at 26.

to have been overcome by the precise and complete description of the various pleadings contained in the rules adopted by recent arbitral bodies.[1] The practice of filing the pleadings in succession followed before commissions of this type also eliminates most of the handicaps to which the simultaneous exchange of pleadings gives rise.

Occasion may be taken, however, to advert to the tendency toward the introduction of dilatory motions which has manifested itself.[2] In general, they are to be indulged in only when time does not press,[3] and then only upon the condition that full freedom for amendment be permitted.[4] When, however, a defective or tardy pleading is filed, a motion to reject or similar dilatory plea serves

[1] The rules adopted by the General Claims Commission, United States and Mexico, have had a considerable influence in this direction. Their careful description of the memorial and of the answer and reply, Rule IV, par. 2, 3 (b), 4 (b), was adopted in identic or similar language by the Special Claims Commission, United States and Mexico, ibid.; the Anglo-Mexican Claims Commission, Rule IV, par. 10, 12 (b), 13 (b); the German-Mexican Claims Commission, Art. 11, 14 (b), 15 (b); Spanish-Mexican Claims Commission, Art. 13, 14 (b), 15 (b); the Franco-Mexican Claims Commission, Art. 11, 14, 15. As the result of this explicit description, it was the experience of the General Claims Commission, United States and Mexico, that the memorials and replies of Mexico in claims on behalf of her citizens were similar in form to the corresponding pleadings in American claims. E.g., Memorial and Reply of Mexico in Francisco Quintanilla (Mexico) v. United States (Gen. Docket No. 532); Garcia and Garza (Mexico) v. United States (Gen. Docket No. 292).

[2] Motions to dismiss or reject: The rules of the General Claims Commission, United States and Mexico, as at first adopted permitted the filing of motions to dismiss or reject. Rule VII, par. 1–4. By a later provision their filing was denied on and after October 25, 1926. Rule VII, par. (6). Motions to dismiss or reject were, however, permitted by the rules of the Special Claims Commission, United States and Mexico, Rule VII, par. 1–4, of the Anglo-Mexican Claims Commission, Rule VII, of the German-Mexican Claims Commission, Art. 21–24, and motions to dismiss were permitted by the Spanish-Mexican Claims Commission, Art. 25–27, and the Franco-Mexican Claims Commission, Art. 21–24. Demurrers (excepciones dilatorias), as provided for in the rules of the Anglo-Mexican Claims Commission, Rule V, the German-Mexican Claims Commission, Art. 18, 19, and the Franco-Mexican Claims Commission, Art. 18, 19, were intended to raise matters of defense not going to the merits of the claim such as nationality.

[3] Cf. Lynch (Great Britain) v. Mexico (1929), DECISIONS AND OPINIONS OF COMMISSIONERS, CLAIMS COMMISSION, GREAT BRITAIN AND MEXICO, 1929–1930, 20. The German-Mexican Claims Commission considered dilatory pleas in connection with the decision on the merits. Feller, The German-Mexican Claims Commission (1933) 27 AM. J. INT. LAW 74–76.

[4] "No objection to procedural methods should be entertained unless it includes an adequate provision for curing the fault complained of." Sunderland, Joinder of Actions (1920) 18 MICH. L. REV. 571, 588.

the salutary purpose of sharply presenting to the tribunal the problem of the terms and conditions upon which departure from its
rules shall be permitted. Fundamental in the consideration of the
problem of a departure from the rules is not only the protection
of the interests of the opposing litigant [5] but also the fact that numerous other claims are clamoring for decision by the tribunal.
Exaction of a reasonable compliance with its rules thus becomes
essential. The implications attendant upon delay in the filing of
pleadings were graphically shown in the United States–Panama
Mixed Claims Commission under the convention of July 28, 1926.
Its rules were drafted in specific contemplation of Article VI of
the treaty which required the commission to decide all claims within
one year from the date of its first meeting.[6] The rules stipulated
a fixed date after which memorials should not be filed and declared
that not more than two months should elapse between the filing,
respectively, of the answer, the brief, and the reply brief. Dilatory
proceedings of any kind were expressly prohibited.[7] Consequently,
delays on the part of the agent of Panama in filing his pleadings
aggregating 62 months and 11 days created a great burden upon
the agent for the United States in preparing his responsive pleadings within the time fixed for the completion of the arbitration.[8]

In principle, the parties are expected in the course of the written
pleadings to state all the facts and disclose all the evidence upon
which they intend to rely.[9] In the *Rio Grande* case [10] before the
American and British claims arbitration under the agreement of
August 18, 1910, the British agent attempted the late filing of a
voluminous reply. The American agent objected. The tribunal held

[5] *Cf.* Stroobant v. Wanner-Brandt (1921) I Recueil des décisions 296 (German-
Belgian M.A.T.).
[6] 47 Stat. 1915, 1921.
[7] Rules, Articles 11, 14–17.
[8] Report of the Agent for the United States, Department of State, Arbitration Series No. 6 (1934) 18.
[9] See Lister (Great Britain) v. Germany, VI *op. cit. supra* note 5, at 34, 37 (British-
German M.A.T., 1925); Sandifer, Evidence before International Tribunals
(1939) 35.
[10] Rio Grande Irrigation and Land Company, Ltd. (Great Britain) v. United
States (1923), American and British Claims Arbitration, Report of Fred K.
Nielsen (1926) 336.

that it had no power to permit the introduction of the document. The American agent, however, consented to its introduction upon condition that full opportunity for the production of evidence by both sides be allowed. In these circumstances the filing of the document was permitted. The case itself was decided upon the jurisdictional questions raised by the American agent in filing a motion to dismiss. No provision was made in its rules for such a plea, but the privilege of the agent to present it was sustained upon the ground of the inherent power of the tribunal to raise for itself preliminary points going to its jurisdiction. The motion was in part based upon defects existing in the British memorial. It was asserted that his pleading was not drawn by the British agent, that the exhibits relied upon were not included therewith, and that its citations and quotations were so inaccurate as to render it unfit for presentation to any judicial tribunal. Though it was held by the tribunal that these defects were not an adequate ground for dismissal, a different view might have been entertained had the motion related merely to the admissibility of the pleading.

The ruling of the General Claims Commission, United States and Mexico, in the *Deutz* claim [11] is significant in this connection. The Mexican agent filed an answer in which he made a general denial of the allegations of the United States and reserved the right to clarify his position. Upon a request by the American agent for a ruling on the pleadings, the commission stated that it recognized "no right on the part of either Agent to make reservations implying a right to present pleadings or amendments thereto or evidence in any manner at variance with the Rules." It further remarked that defenses which were properly for the answer could not be formulated after the answer was filed, that evidence not accompanying the pleadings could not be received, except through a stipulation entered into between the agents, and that compliance with its reasonable rules was indispensable to the just determina-

[11] Adolph and Charles Deutz (United States) v. Mexico (Gen. Docket No. 2042). See MINUTES OF FORTY-SECOND SITTING, FIFTH SESSION, GENERAL CLAIMS COMMISSION, UNITED STATES AND MEXICO, June 29, 1927.

tion of claims.[12] Criticism has been voiced against the action of the German-Mexican Claims Commission in deferring the consideration of dilatory pleas until the final decision on the merits. It was contended that the German agency was by this practice left uninformed as to what course it should follow in the preparation of pleadings, as, for instance, in the matter of who are proper parties.[13] It would seem preferable to have these and similar questions of law common to many cases settled as far as possible by means of administrative decisions rendered before the preparation of pleadings and the obtaining of evidence has begun. Administrative decisions need not be restricted merely to the enunciation of rules of conduct to be followed by agents in settling cases by agreement, but may well be extended to the function of guiding them in the development of claims for the litigious procedure.[14] Such a solution would minimize the delay and the expense of deciding every dilatory plea as it was presented. These pleas tend to be concerned with objections of no consequence beyond the particular case and do not justify prolonging the sessions of the commission in order that they may be immediately settled when they arise.

Analogous questions of procedure are created when late submissions of pleadings or evidence are attempted. Here, the enforcement of the established procedural rules conflicts with a strong conviction on the part of tribunals that in the interest of a sound decision no pertinent document should be excluded. As stated in the Judgment of June 7, 1932, of the Permanent Court of International Justice respecting late submissions by the French government: ". . . because the decision of an international dispute of the present order should not mainly depend on a point of procedure, the

---

12 *Cf.* in this connection Gonzalez (Mexico) v. United States (1926) OPINIONS OF COMMISSIONERS, GENERAL CLAIMS COMMISSION, UNITED STATES AND MEXICO, 1926–1927, at 10 (final decision on motion to dismiss postponed for thirty days in order to give opportunity to amend inadequate allegations). Accord, when jurisdiction is at issue: Kunkel (Germany) v. Poland, VI *op. cit. supra* note 5, at 334, 974 (German-Polish M.A.T., 1925); Vaterlaendischer Frauenverein à Czarnkow (Germany) v. Poland, *ibid.* 346 (German-Polish M.A.T., 1925).

13 Feller, *supra* note 3, at 75, 76.

14 *Cf.* Administrative Decision No. V (1924) DECISIONS, MIXED CLAIMS COMMISSION, UNITED STATES AND GERMANY (1926) 175.

Court thinks it preferable not to entertain the plea of inadmissibility and to deal on their merits with such of the new French arguments as may fall within its jurisdiction." [15] In the incident occurring in the *Rio Grande* case, cited above, the American and British Claims Tribunal said: "It would be most undesirable from every point of view if the Tribunal should attempt to decide a case without having all the documents before it which might turn out to be material in the course of the trial." [16] But if late evidence be admitted in accordance with this view, the premise equally justifies granting to the opposing party an opportunity to obtain and submit rebuttal evidence. In the cases of the *Sidra* and the *Coquitlam* before the same tribunal, Great Britain filed with its reply evidence which the United States considered should have been filed with the affirmative case. The United States accordingly deemed it proper to present, presumably in accordance with Rule 19,[17] additional evidence as a supplemental answer.[18]

The question of the admissibility of evidence should be entirely removed from controversy by providing in the *compromis* that the commission shall be bound to receive and to consider all documents submitted,[19] or by ensuring that the rules of procedure enunciate

[15] SER. A./B., No. 46 (1932) 96, at 155–156.

[16] *Op. cit. supra* note 10, at 334.

[17] *Ibid.* 13. But *cf.* the action of the tribunal in the Fishing Claims, Group I (U.S.) v. Great Britain, *ibid.* 555–564.

[18] *The Sidra*, SUPPLEMENTAL ANSWER OF THE UNITED STATES; *The Coquitlam* (U.S.) v. Great Britain, SUPPLEMENT TO THE ANSWER. In Le Bas (Great Britain) v. Mexico (1929) *op. cit. supra* note 3, at 65, final decision on a motion to dismiss was suspended in order to give the Agents opportunity to submit supplementary evidence. In the Alaskan boundary proceedings, the British Agent requested an extension of two months for the filing of his counter-case. After some correspondence, the Secretary of State informed the British Ambassador that the United States was not in a position to accede to the request, since it was not shown that special difficulties had arisen, as required by the treaty, Secretary of State Hay to Sir Herbert, June 16, 1903, (1903) FOR. REL. U.S. 512; I PROCEEDINGS OF THE ALASKAN BOUNDARY TRIBUNAL, REPORT OF JOHN W. FOSTER, AGENT OF THE UNITED STATES, 10; *cf.* Cobham (Great Britain) v. Venezuela (1903), RALSTON'S REPORT (1904) 409. See ACREMENT, LA PROCÉDURE DANS LES ARBITRAGES INTERNATIONAUX (1905) 109: "An arbitral tribunal cannot refuse to take cognizance of a fundamental document under the stupid pretext that the period for its production has expired. The tribunal may not have recourse to exclusion except in the presence of evident bad faith." See also SANDIFER, *op. cit. supra* note 9, sec. 2.

[19] Clauses to this effect have been included in the following arbitration agreements: United States–Mexico, July 4, 1868, Art. II, 1 MALLOY, TREATIES 1129;

in the most categorical terms what course of conduct it will follow.[20] When the *compromis* and rules are vague,[21] and even when they indicate rather clearly the intention that all forms of evidence shall be admissible,[22] disputes on this point arise. The adoption of such a rule should not be difficult, since it seems to be well established that commissions are not bound by municipal rules of evidence and are free to consider all documentary evidence submitted to them and to give to it such weight as it may merit.[23]

There are certain facts concerning international claims commissions charged with the disposition of an accumulation of claims which should be more appreciated. One is the complexity of the litigation with which they have to deal. Theirs is the work of an arbitration of a single dispute many times multiplied. As instance

United States–Peru, December 4, 1868, Art. II, II *ibid.* 1412; United States–Great Britain, May 8, 1871 (Treaty of Washington), Art. XIII, XXIV, I *ibid.* 706, 710; United States–France, January 15, 1880, Art. V, *ibid.* 537; United States–Haiti, May 28, 1884, Art. III, *ibid.* 933; United States–Chile, August 7, 1892, Art. V, *ibid.* 186–187; United States–Venezuela, February 17, 1903, Art. II, II *ibid.* 1871; Mexico-Venezuela, February 26, 1903, Art. II, RALSTON'S REPORT (1904) 876–877; Netherlands-Venezuela, February 28, 1903, Art. II, *ibid.* 891; Belgium-Venezuela, March 7, 1903, Art. II, *ibid.* 262–263; Sweden and Norway-Venezuela, March 10, 1903, Art. II, *ibid.* 946–947; Spain-Venezuela, April 2, 1903, Art. II, *ibid.* 918–919; Great Britain–Venezuela, May 7, 1903, par. 8, *ibid.* 295; Germany-Venezuela, May 7, 1903, Art. III, *ibid.* 516–517; Italy-Venezuela, May 7, 1903, Art. III, *ibid.* 646; United States–Germany, August 10, 1922, Art. VI, 42 STAT. 2200.

20 *Cf.* Rule V (b), Mixed Claims Commission, United States and Germany. By Order No. 3, November 15, 1922, this Commission expressly ruled that it would receive ex parte affidavits or depositions.

21 Shufeldt claim (U.S.) v. Guatemala (1929), DEPARTMENT OF STATE, ARBITRATION SERIES NO. 3 (1932) 9–14.

22 Convention between the United States and Mexico, September 8, 1923, creating the General Claims Commission, Art. II, 43 STAT. 1730; convention between Great Britain and Mexico, November 19, 1926, creating the British-Mexican Claims Commission, Art. 4, 23 DE MARTENS (3d ser., 1931) 8: Rules, German-Mexican Claims Commission, Art. 25. The convention of March 16, 1925, providing for the latter commission, was silent upon the admissibility of evidence, FELLER, THE MEXICAN CLAIMS COMMISSIONS, 1923–1934 (1935) 442.

23 The Montijo (U.S.) v. Colombia, 2 MOORE, INT. ARB. 1427, 1434, 1435; Parker (U.S.) v. Mexico (1926) *op. cit. supra* note 12, at 35, Cameron (Great Britain) v. Mexico, British-Mexican Claims Commission (1929) *op. cit. supra* note 3, at 33; Ernesto H. Goeldner (Germany) v. Mexico (No. 48) German-Mexican Claims Commission under Convention of March 16, 1925 (MS copy); Shufeldt (U.S.) v. Guatemala (1929) *op. cit. supra* note 21, at 851; see SANDIFER, *op. cit. supra* note 9, sec. 2–4. *Cf.* Murphy (U.S.) v. Chile (Case No. 36) United States and Chilean Claims Commission under convention of August 7, 1892, discussed in SHIELDS, REPORT OF THE AGENT OF THE UNITED STATES (1894) 150–157. See Act of July 3, 1930, 46 STAT. 1005.

of this, it is sufficient to point out that one memorial alone filed
before the General Claims Commission, United States and Mexico,
contained 1,148 printed pages.[24] Many of the claims filed before
commissions have been the subject of lengthy negotiations between
States.[25] Obviously they cannot be settled with the rapidity achieved
by domestic administrative bodies when handling far simpler matters of municipal law. Rules must be drafted with a view to the
nature of the disputes to be arbitrated, their complexity, the extent
to which questions of fact or of law predominate, and the character
of the evidence to be presented. It should also be remembered that
the creation of an international claims commission does not relieve
either foreign offices or agents of the responsibility to determine
what claims merit being brought before it.[26] A government should
not lend its support to the vigorous prosecution of a claim before
an international commission unless the evidence and the law applicable to it would justify similar action in the diplomatic channel. Either through its foreign office or its agent, a government
should determine what claims merit active prosecution before the
commission. The temptation to evade this responsibility under the
pressure and importunities of claimants and to cast upon the commission the task of reviewing and rejecting worthless, deficient, or
fraudulent claims may at times be difficult to resist. Yet a more
energetic performance of this duty, such as, for example, occurred

---

[24] Sheldon L. Butler et al. (U.S.) v. Mexico (Gen. Docket No. 2404). The Memorial in another was 484 printed pages in length, John W. De Kay (U.S.) v.
Mexico (Gen. Docket No. 2718).

[25] The American and British claims arbitration under the agreement of August
18, 1910, was the first general arbitration between the two States since that established under the convention of February 8, 1853. The Civil War claims were settled by the commission sitting under the Treaty of Washington of May 8, 1871.
1 MOORE, INT. ARB. 683–702. The General Claims Commission, United States and
Mexico, had jurisdiction over all unsettled claims presented to either government
for its interposition with the other since the signing of the claims convention of
July 4, 1868, see Art. I, convention of September 8, 1923, 43 STAT. 1730.

[26] Cf. Frelinghuysen v. Key, 110 U.S. 63, 72–73 (1884) in connection with the
Weil and La Abra cases, 2 MOORE, INT. ARB. 1324; Report of Secretary of State
Bayard, January 20, 1887, in connection with the Pelletier and Lazare cases, ibid.
1749, 1793; BISHOP, INTERNATIONAL ARBITRAL PROCEDURE (1930) 169, 170; see also
Z. & F. Assets Realization Corp. v. Hull, 311 U.S. 470, 486, 487 (1941).

in the Panama claims arbitration discussed above, would considerably simplify the task of expediting proceedings of tribunals.

6. PROCEDURAL REFORM AND THE RULE-MAKING POWER.—To what extent will a codification of established international arbitral procedure eliminate procedural difficulties? It must be recognized that the statement of rules upon which there can be a general agreement among States, in a field as broad as this, will inevitably tend to be confined to those very points where problems are least likely to arise. The progress to be made in this direction by general agreement therefore tends to be slight, though the work preparatory to the formulation of a code of international arbitral procedure may very well be expected to be of great value.[1] The experience of the Institute of International Law is illuminating. At its first meetings in 1874 and 1875 the Institute adopted a project of rules for international arbitral procedure, which laid down the general principle that the conduct of any one arbitration is to be formulated by the particular *compromis* or by the arbitrators.[2] For the rest, the *projet* of the Institute chiefly addressed itself to the statement of such self-evident facts as "the *compromis* is concluded by a valid international treaty," [3] or "the *compromis* gives to each of the contracting parties the right to address itself to the arbitral tribunal," [4] or "each of the parties may constitute one or several representatives before the arbitral tribunal," [5] and to the consideration of such uncontroversial matters as the naming of the arbitrators, the determination of the place of sitting, and the manner of rendering the award.[6]

---

[1] See Report of the First Committee on the Progressive Codification of International Law to the Assembly of the League of Nations, September 27, 1927, LEAGUE OF NATIONS, OFFICIAL JOURNAL (Spec. Supp. No. 54) Annex 35 (Document A. 105. 1927. V); ACTS OF THE CONFERENCE FOR THE CODIFICATIONS OF INTERNATIONAL LAW (1930), BASES OF DISCUSSION (1929), (Nos. C. 351. M. 145. 1930. V., C. 75. M. 69. 1929. V).

[2] *Projet de règlement pour la procédure arbitrale internationale*, Art. 12 and 15, (1877) ANNUAIRE 126, 129, 130.

[3] *Ibid.*, Art. 1.

[4] *Ibid.*, Art. 2.

[5] *Ibid.*, Art. 13.

[6] *Ibid.*, Art. 2–9, 21–24. *Cf.* the criticism made of the project by the Fourteenth Commission of the Institute in its report of 1927 (1927) *ibid.* 571–593.

In relatively few cases were provocative procedural problems attacked.[7] The Hague Conferences of 1899 and 1907, though a step forward, did not greatly advance the solution of procedural problems.[8] The Convention for the Pacific Settlement of International Disputes, as finally adopted, again left to the discretion of the tribunal the issuance of rules of procedure for the conduct of the case, in the absence of specific directions in the *compromis*.[9] It is true that reference was made to the filing of cases, counter-cases, and replies, but the form, order, and time in which these must be made were to be defined by the *compromis*.[10] This is not to say that the convention did not exhibit a realistic approach to some extent. Given its task of creating an all-embracing code of rules for international tribunals, whatever their form and whatever their task, it recognized that the formulation of procedural rules should proceed on an *ad hoc* basis, with the tribunal being empowered to determine its own procedural rules to fit its own problems.

The variability in the factors affecting the successful conduct of any international arbitration is too great to enable the creation of any one comprehensive code which would furnish an unfailing guide for the conduct of all arbitrations. Inevitably, such a code would suffer from lack of flexibility and technical refinement.[11] Rules that may function well enough in one arbitration may lead to a complete breakdown when introduced in another arbitration possessing totally different characteristics. Each arbitration presents

[7] (1877) *ibid.* Art. 27, relating to the nullity of awards, has had much influence upon the arbitral law governing nullity. See also Art. 14, 16 and 17. At its session of 1927 the Institute decided to begin the elaboration of a code of arbitral procedure, in view of the progress made in arbitration, (1927) *ibid.* 319, 320, 324.

[8] See Dennis, *The Necessity for an International Code of Arbitral Procedure* (1913) 7 Am. J. Int. Law 285, 290, 291.

[9] Art. 52, 74. I Proceedings of the Hague Peace Conferences, Conference of 1907 (Carnegie trans., 1920) 599, 608, 611.

[10] Art. 52, 63, *ibid.,* at 608, 610.

[11] *Cf.* Moses, *International Legal Practice* (1935) 4 Ford. L. Rev. 244. With regard to the difficulties in legislative reform of municipal procedure, Sunderland, *The Machinery of Procedural Reform* (1924) 22 Mich. L. Rev. 293, 297–300. Thus a commentary on the new Federal Rules of Civil Procedure, which were established only so recently as 1938, runs into four volumes, Moore's Federal Practice (1938), and the Federal Rules Service started in 1939 has extended into eight volumes. But see p. 261 *infra.*

its own peculiar problems. In one the respective governments may be primarily interested in the precedents to be established by the decision; an elaborate procedure, with ample opportunity to develop through a series of pleadings and oral argument the issues involved, best serves such an end. Thus, the careful and detailed rules of the Permanent Court of International Justice have worked very well in their orbit, when an exhaustive presentation of its case is the paramount desire of each litigant. But in other instances (for example, an arbitration of many small claims) dispatch may be the primary requisite, so that pleadings and hearings must be reduced to a minimum. If the litigants live under different systems of law (for example, the Continental civil law as against the English common law), great care must be taken in defining in the rules the scope and nature of the pleadings and the time and manner of the introduction of evidence. The nature of the disputes to be decided and the extent to which they involve complex questions of law and fact must also be borne in mind. When the issues are simple, protracted, and refined, procedural steps are superfluous. In claims and similar arbitration proceedings the body charged with the power and duty of providing rules of procedure has generally been the tribunal itself. But the members of the tribunal are not chosen because of their previous familiarity with the arbitration entrusted to them. Rather, the contrary is the case. Though possessing distinguished attainments in international law, rarely do they have a long background of experience as arbitrators. Hence the tribunal, capable as it may be of deciding the disputes to be submitted to it, is not necessarily best qualified to exercise the rule-making power. The task of determining the rules for the tribunal should rather be delegated to that body most likely to possess an accumulation of experience in international arbitrations. It is believed, therefore, that foreign offices should be more active in assuming this task, for with the growing use of arbitration as a means for the settlement of international disputes they have come to possess a reservoir of experience in this field. In some cases it might be left to the respective agents to arrive at an agreement in advance as to rules of procedure, with the tribunal empowered to settle any undecided questions by prescribing applicable rules or by way of interlocutory decision or otherwise. Such rules, whether prepared by the respective foreign offices or by the agents, could serve as a basis for procedure before the tribunal until later amended by it. In any event, rules drafted with a view to the specific problems of the arbitration technique would go far towards smoothing the paths of arbitral bodies and in advancing the cause of international arbitration.

The most hopeful avenue for improvement, therefore, lies in a greater exercise of the rule-making power by the parties themselves through the incorporation of detailed rules of procedure in the *compromis*. The rules of procedure in such case are binding on both tribunal and litigants and only the form and manner of presentation prescribed by the rules can be permitted by the tribunal when a threat to depart from the rule occurs. Thus, a precise definition in the *compromis* of the times for the introduction of pleadings and evidence eliminates disputes on the disposition of late filings by rendering the tribunal powerless to receive them. While this would be desirable in order to bind a tribunal charged with the prompt disposition of numerous claims, in order that it might not be tempted to sanction delays and departures from the rules, the case of tribunals charged with the decision, on a fair and lasting basis, of important disputes long pending between States is not so clear. Some area of judicial discretion may in such case be desirable in order to insure that full justice shall be done. To establish by the *compromis* inexorable rules of conduct governing all action of the tribunal and of the advocates involves the sacrifice of flexibility.[12] In general, some opportunity must exist for modifying and supplementing procedural rules when the occasion demands.[13]

---

[12] ACREMENT, LA PROCÉDURE DANS LES ARBITRAGES INTERNATIONAUX (1905) 107.

[13] At least one attempt to define in the arbitration agreement the contents of the pleadings to be filed failed to achieve an entirely satisfactory solution. Notwithstanding a rather precise description of the pleadings contained in the exchange of notes between the United States and Guatemala providing for the arbitration of the Shufeldt claim (U.S.) v. Guatemala (1929) DEPARTMENT OF STATE, ARBITRATION SERIES NO. 3 (1932) 9–14, see particularly p. 10, par. 4, 6 and 7, the

Accordingly, as suggested in one claims arbitration, the *compromis* should include a preliminary statement of procedural rules, and power should be vested in the tribunal to amend them as required after its sessions have begun.[14] Such an approach would not only conduce to a more satisfactory conduct of the arbitration but also avoid the delay incident to having the tribunal meet solely for the purpose of adopting rules, only to adjourn thereafter pending the preparation of the case or cases in accordance with such rules.

7. PREPARATION OF THE COMPROMIS.—The following agenda of certain of the principal factors involved in the formulation of a *compromis* will serve to summarize some of the principles discussed above, as well as to furnish the introduction into the discussion of other problems in the following chapters.

Definition of Question for Decision.—Here is, of course, the heart of the arbitration; how can the difficulties be overcome of focusing into a precise statement all the rancors, the charges and counter-charges, the conflicting interests involved in the case? It is only too easy to by-pass the arduous task of defining the exact question on which decision is necessary and instead to turn everything en masse over to the arbitrator for settlement. Unless he be gifted beyond the attainments of most men, this is a temptation to be sternly resisted. For to the extent to which his area of action is not strictly defined and limited, he will tend to assume more the role of the mediator, the conciliator and the seeker for compromise than the judicial role of arbitrator.

The arbitrator has such powers of decision as the parties confer upon him. Unless his powers are clearly stated and the exact ques-

---

reply of Guatemala was much more elaborate than its case. *Ibid.* 407. The United States was placed somewhat at a disadvantage as a result in that it could not then file additional evidence, which would have been open to it in replying to Guatemala's first pleading, and it was limited to thirty days in which to prepare the written argument to meet Guatemala's reply while sixty days would have been available to it had the matter been included in Guatemala's case. *Ibid.* 10, par. 6, 7. See also the remarks of the Mexican Agent before the Hague Court in the Pious Fund Case. PIOUS FUND OF THE CALIFORNIAS, REPORT OF JACKSON H. RALSTON, FOR. REL. U.S. 1902, 2 APP. 515–516.

14 See REPORT OF THE AGENT FOR THE UNITED STATES, DEPARTMENT OF STATE, ARBITRATION SERIES No. 6 (1934) 21.

tion at issue is precisely stated, dissatisfaction with his award may easily provoke the charge that he has exceeded his jurisdiction. A clear definition of the question to be arbitrated tends to expedite the proceedings—through demarking the irrelevant and the admitted, elevating the arbitration to a more judicial sphere, conducing to a more acceptable award, and diminishing the possibility of attack by a dissatisfied litigant.

Agreed Statement of Facts.—To the extent that the parties can determine in advance what facts are agreed upon, so will the arbitration be speeded and its expense reduced.

Pleadings.—Is the case of such a nature as to require, say, preliminary written statements by each side, followed by replies, or can it be presented directly upon written evidence and, when necessary, oral testimony? A case whose facts are complicated and in dispute will benefit from a rather formal and defined course of procedure. On the other hand, one whose emphasis is upon the determination of the applicable law will demand a careful definition of the time, manner, and scope of arguments of counsel. Moreover, it should ever be borne in mind that if divergence in legal systems exists between the parties meticulous description should be given of the scope of the pleadings and the extent to which they shall include discussion of law.

The customary clause in arbitration provisions that the arbitral tribunal shall fix its own rules of procedure is only too often regarded as an inevitable concomitant of recourse to arbitration. The clause should rather provide that the tribunal shall have the power to establish rules of procedure not otherwise determined in the terms of submission and to amend its rules of procedure governing the arbitration.

Time and Manner of Introduction of Evidence.—Shall the written evidence accompany such pleadings as are contemplated? To what extent can the parties agree upon in advance, and jointly file, the documentary evidence and thereby avoid the duplication and expense incurred when each presents the same evidence with their respective cases? If times are fixed for the presentation of evidence, what shall be done with late evidence?

Rectification, Rehearing and Revision of the Award.—What exceptions shall apply to the customary provision that the award shall be final? For example, shall means for revision be provided if new evidence is found which is of a character calculated to produce a change in the tribunal's views had it known of such evidence?

Appeal.—Shall means of review be provided to regulate questions of validity or of error which may arise after the tribunal has dissolved? Strong reason exists to support the view that an assertion that an award is void should be judicially determined rather than be left to the regulation of the parties. If so, is it desired that a right of appeal on grounds of nullity alone be established, or should it extend to include error of law as well? Shall the appellate tribunal be confined merely to declaring the existence of nullity or mistake, permitting the original tribunal to reform its decision, or shall it be directed itself to render judgment on the merits, if it shall declare the decision under review to be wholly or partly null? [1]

---

[1] In connection with this section see the author's article *Importance of Procedural Rules in International Arbitration* (1945) 1 INT. ARB. JOUR. 58.

CHAPTER 2

MINIMUM PROCEDURAL STANDARDS

8. FUNDAMENTAL PROCEDURAL RIGHTS.—Up to this point we have been concerned with the technique of conducting an international arbitration; our task has been confined to the examination of the disputes and the difficulties concerning procedure which have arisen in the past and to the determination of the steps to be taken towards lessening their occurrence in the future. This is but a part of the larger task, to which this study is addressed, of ascertaining the legal rights of States with respect to an international arbitration. A State, in submitting its dispute with another to the decision of an international tribunal, has certain fundamental rights which it may expect in full confidence will be respected. The power of the tribunal is not arbitrary. As stated by Judge Moore: "The international judicial tribunals so far created have been tribunals of limited powers." [1] The tribunal must respect the law governing its creation and defining its powers as laid down in the *compromis,* and it must likewise observe certain other established rules of a fundamental character which inherently, under the generally accepted rules of law and justice, regulate the conduct of any judicial body. By creating the tribunal and presenting their controversy to it for decision States do not renounce these rights as a consequence of the rule that the award shall be final. [2]

The assurance that certain fundamental procedural rights will be respected in the course of the arbitration is essential to the growth of confidence of States in the system of arbitration as a means for the settlement of international disputes. In the words of Borel:

[1] Mavromattis Palestine Concessions case, Permanent Court of International Justice, SER. A., Judgment No. 2, August 30, 1924, p. 60; see *infra* sec. 21.
[2] See *infra* sec. 64.

Recourse to international justice and, in particular, to arbitration is a matter of confidence by States, free to adopt it or to abstain. The system of international justice will gain more if States may be assured as to the manner in which it accomplishes its task, and, in particular, guaranteed against risks which it may be reasonably supposed they could not be asked to accept in advance.[3]

Secretary of State Root said:

There can be no doubt that the principal objection to arbitration rests not upon the unwillingness of nations to submit their controversies to impartial arbitration, but upon an apprehension that the arbitrations to which they submit may not be impartial. It has been a very general practice for arbitrators to act, not as judges deciding questions of fact and law upon the record before them under a sense of judicial responsibility, but as negotiators effecting settlements of the questions brought before them in accordance with the traditions and usages and subject to all the considerations and influences which affect diplomatic agents. The two methods are radically different, proceed upon different standards of honorable obligation, and frequently lead to widely differing results. It very frequently happens that a nation which would be very willing to submit its differences to an impartial judicial determination is unwilling to subject them to this kind of diplomatic process.[4]

A certain fear exists that the arbitration will not proceed as a judicial process and in a judicial manner and that the arbitrators will substitute a political for a legal decision and succumb to the human tendency to compromise.[5] Legal guarantees exist, however, against arbitrary conduct by a tribunal.

There is, in the view of Morelli, a certain "fundamental procedural norm . . . from which the decision draws its legal effect."[6] This norm or standard comprises certain fundamental rules of pro-

3 Borel, *Les Voies de recours contre les sentences arbitrales* (1935) 52 RECUEIL DES COURS 89.

4 Instructions to the American Delegates to the Hague Conference, May 31, 1907 (1907) FOR. REL. U.S., Part 2, 1128, 1135. See also Root, *The Importance of Judicial Settlement* (1910) PROCEEDINGS OF AMERICAN SOCIETY FOR THE JUDICIAL SETTLEMENT OF INTERNATIONAL DISPUTES 9, 11.

5 Dennis, *Compromise—The Great Defect of Arbitration* (1911) 11 COL. L. REV. 493.

6 Morelli, *La Théorie générale du procès international* (1937) 61 RECUEIL DES COURS 286.

cedure inherent in the judicial process [7] or generally recognized in all procedures.[8] It does not lie in a simple error of form.[9] It must be a material *("essentiel")* departure from established procedural rules.[10] Thus, the error *in procedendo* consists in the failure to apply a rule considered necessary for establishing the reasoned approach of the judge.[11]

Clearly, a breach of the formalities prescribed by the *compromis* under penalty of nullity will lead to an invalid award.[12] It may likewise be said with logical exactitude that the inobservance of any procedural rule stipulated by the *compromis* will result in an excess of jurisdiction [13] or nullity of the award,[14] even if the *compromis* should be silent as to the consequences to follow from such failure to observe its procedural rules. It is felt more consonant with theory and practice to say that there are certain fundamental procedural rights upon which a State may rely in any international arbitration and of which no State would consent to be deprived. When they are denied to a party by a tribunal, and when that party has sought in vain to obtain a fair hearing, it is privileged not to comply with the decision so reached.

Not all failures to observe procedural stipulations contained in the *compromis* will lead to nullity of the award. The legal effect of such a failure is not to be judged upon the purely abstract basis of whether it constitutes a departure from terms of submission. The question is rather: Does the departure constitute a deprivation of a fundamental right so as to cause the arbitration and the resulting

[7] BALASKO, CAUSES DE NULLITÉ DE LA SENTENCE ARBITRALE EN DROIT INTERNATIONAL PUBLIC (1938) 133, 194.

[8] Hertz, *Essai sur le problème de la nullité* (1939, 3d ser.) 20 REV. DE DROIT INT. L.C. 462.

[9] 3 CALVO, LE DROIT INTERNATIONAL (5th ed., 1896) 486.

[10] Borel, *supra* note 3, at 98–99; WITENBERG, L'ORGANISATION JUDICIAIRE, LA PROCÉDURE ET LA SENTENCE INTERNATIONALES (1937) 368.

[11] Rundstein, *La Cour Permanente de Justice Internationale comme instance de recours* (1933) 43 RECUEIL DES COURS 91.

[12] 2 CARNAZZA-AMARI, TRAITÉ DE DROIT INTERNATIONAL PUBLIC (1882) 564.

[13] Castberg, *L'Excès de pouvoir dans la justice internationale* (1931) 35 RECUEIL DES COURS 389.

[14] Goldschmidt, *Projet de règlement pour tribunaux arbitraux internationaux* (1874) 6 REV. DE DROIT INT. L.C. 447 (Section 32 (8)); *cf.* ACREMENT, LA PROCÉDURE DANS LES ARBITRAGES INTERNATIONAUX (1905) 163.

award to lose its judicial character? Unless its effect is to prejudice materially the interests of a party, the charge of nullity should not be open to a party.[15] Thus, the denial of a fair hearing, of an adequate opportunity to present its case, will justify a party in taking the position that the ensuing award is void. As an additional fundamental procedural right Schätzel suggests the rule that the collection of evidence should take place in full freedom and independence.[16] The Tacna-Arica arbitration is interesting in this connection.[17]

A further limitation upon the privilege to invoke faults of procedure as producing nullity lies in the requirement that such complaints be made as soon as is reasonably possible, in order to avoid a charge of waiver of the right to contest through acquiescence and tacit ratification.[18] However, the proof required to establish waiver of the right to contest validity will be much stricter than that necessary to establish the loss, through silence, of the privilege to object to procedural departures involving only momentary and incidental advantages or handicaps occurring during the course of the litigation.[19]

9. PRIVATE LAW ANALOGIES.—The conception that there are certain fundamental procedural guarantees for litigating parties finds recognition in various domestic legal systems. The French Code of Civil Procedure affords the remedy of the *requête civile* when a judgment has been procured through fraud or false evidence.[1] The German Code of Civil Procedure allows judgments to be reopened by proceedings in nullity and proceedings in restitution. The former may be availed of when the judge was not duly qualified, possessed bias or a personal interest in the litigation, or was otherwise disqualified to act as a judge. Proceedings in restitution may be

---

[15] SCHÄTZEL, RECHTSKRAFT UND ANFECHTUNG VON ENTSCHEIDUNGEN INTERNATIONALER GERICHTE, 6 FRANKFURTER ABHANDLUNGEN ZUM KRIEGSVERHÜTUNGSRECHT (1928) 68, citing examples of inconsequential departures in the practice of the Mixed Arbitral Tribunals.

[16] *Ibid.*, 71.

[17] *Infra* sec. 60.

[18] *Infra* sec. 51; SCHÄTZEL, *op. cit. supra* note 15, at 61–71.

[19] See comments at close of sec. 13 *infra*.

[1] French Code of Civil Procedure (1936) Art. 480.

resorted to for the correction of violations of fundamental rules of procedure, such as obtaining a judgment through deceit, fraud, or false documents or in violation of oath.[2] Under our system of law a judgment may be set aside in equity by a party to the action "if in the action he had no reasonable opportunity to have determined impartially a meritorious claim or defense which he had." [3] Among the circumstances justifying such relief is fraud in the procurement of such judgment.[4]

10. RIGHT TO BE HEARD: THE "UMPIRE CASES."—One of the most elemental procedural rights is the right of a party to be heard, to present its arguments and proofs. A number of writers are in agreement that if that be denied the award may be considered null.[1] Bluntschli, in a particularly illuminating passage, aptly expresses their views.

Arbitral procedure is a judicial procedure and, therefore, although not subject to any particular code of procedure, it is nevertheless subject to the natural fundamental principles of all codes of procedure. The award cannot, therefore, be attacked and declared void on account of mere errors of form, but if the above-mentioned fundamental principles have been violated in a glaring and indubitable manner, as if, for instance, the parties have been afforded no opportunity to present their arguments and refute those of the adversary, then they do not need to acquiesce in so arbitrary an award.[2]

This principle found judicial recognition in the "Umpire Cases" before the United States–Colombian Mixed Commission of 1864, in which it was held that claims decided by the umpire of a prior commission between the same governments, wherein an opportunity

---

[2] German Code of Civil Procedure (1930) Art. 578–580.
[3] AMERICAN LAW INSTITUTE, RESTATEMENT OF THE LAW OF JUDGMENTS (1942) sec. 118.
[4] Hazel-Atlas Glass Co. v. Hartford Empire Co., 322 U.S. 238 (1944).
[1] BONFILS, MANUEL DE DROIT INTERNATIONAL PUBLIC (1898) 488; BLUNTSCHLI, LE DROIT INTERNATIONAL CODIFIÉ (1886) 289; 2 CARNAZZA-AMARI, TRAITÉ DE DROIT INTERNATIONAL PUBLIC (1882) 564; 1 FAUCHILLE, TRAITÉ DE DROIT INTERNATIONAL PUBLIC (1926) Part IV, at 552; GENET, TRAITÉ DE DIPLOMATIE ET DE DROIT DIPLOMATIQUE (1932) 587; HEFFTER, DAS EUROPÄISCHER VÖLKERRECHT DER GEGENWART (8th ed., Geffcken, 1888) 233; 6 PRADIER-FODÉRÉ, TRAITÉ DE DROIT INTERNATIONAL PUBLIC 434; 3 OLIVART, TRATADO DE DERECHO INTERNACIONAL PÚBLICO (1903) 14.
[2] BLUNTSCHLI, op. cit. supra note 1, at 289.

for a hearing had not been given to one of the parties, were un-settled cases within the meaning of the *compromis* of the 1864 com-mission.

The convention of September 10, 1857, between New Granada (now Colombia) and the United States provided for the hearing of a certain class of claims by a board of two commissioners, one to be chosen by each government, who were to examine and decide upon all claims. They were to name an umpire, to whom would be submitted for decision claims upon which the two commission-ers could not agree. The following provision was made with respect to the finality of awards.

The proceedings of this Commission shall be final and conclusive with re-spect to all the claims before it, and its awards shall be a full discharge to New Granada of all claims of citizens of the United States against that Republic which may have accrued prior to the signature of this convention.[3]

The commission was unable to complete its work within the time allotted and a convention was signed on February 10, 1864, creat-ing a new commission for the hearing of the undecided cases. Be-fore this commission were brought four of the so-called "Umpire Cases," namely, five cases under the titles *Constancia, Good Return, Medea,* John D. Danels, and R. W. Gibbes. The Colombian com-missioner had protested the regularity of the awards by the um-pire in these cases and had refused to sign the certificates of award. His protest was based upon the contention that the awards were "null and void according to the stipulations of the treaty and to the universal principle of justice that no party can be condemned before having been heard in defense."[4] He asserted that in none of these cases had he been given an opportunity to enter his views as to the merits, the reference to the umpire having been merely upon a jurisdictional question. The American commissioner en-tered a counterprotest contesting the declarations of the Colombian commissioner,[5] whereupon the umpire filed a statement that "as the commission had expired, it did not seem to me the cases could

---

[3] Art. 5, 1 MALLOY, TREATIES 321.   [4] 2 MOORE, INT. ARB. 1401, 1402.
[5] *Ibid.*, 1402.

be opened again, except on an extension of the commission, when, perhaps for cause shown, it might be done." [6] The Colombian government refused to make provision of payment for the cases, "because the umpire presumed to decide them, without authority, upon points which had not been submitted to him." [7] The United States steadily maintained the validity of the awards. However, upon advice by the Attorney-General that it was intended that the new commission should be a continuation of the old, that it had power only to decide such claims as were undetermined by the old commission and consequently must declare what cases were undetermined,[8] Secretary of State Seward expressed to the commission the view that if it should decide that a case had not been lawfully allowed by the commission of 1857 a rehearing could be had.[9]

All the "Umpire Cases," except that of Gibbes, were referred to the umpire, who held that there were grounds for belief that the Colombian commissioner's statements were well founded and that the claims must be submitted *de novo* to the new commission. After argument on the merits, all four claims were disallowed.[10]

The claimant Gibbes refused to prosecute his case before the new commission and obtained payment in full of his claim from the United States. The United States then insisted that Colombia should in turn pay to it the amount of the award with compound interest. The demand for compound interest was dropped, and Colombia paid the principal of the award with simple interest, "not . . . because the Government of Colombia thinks itself under obligations to pay it," but "as a compromise . . . for the settlement of the matter." [11]

As will be observed in the following section, the "Umpire Cases" are also illustrative of the principle that a party is entitled to due and proper consideration of his case by the entire tribunal.

11. RIGHT TO DUE DELIBERATION BY A TRIBUNAL DULY CONSTITUTED.— The parties are entitled to a decision emanating from the tribunal

---

[6] *Ibid.*, 1405.

[7] *Ibid.*, 1406.

[8] 11 OP. ATT'Y. GEN. 402 (1865).

[9] 2 MOORE, INT. ARB. 1407.

[10] *Ibid.*, 1407–1409.

[11] *Ibid.*, 1410–1411.

designated by them in the *compromis*,[1] in its capacity as a tribunal, not as the personal opinions of its members,[2] joined in by a majority of the arbitrators,[3] rendered after due and joint deliberation,[4] and supported by reason.[5] All these conditions are essential to the validity of the tribunal's decision.

The parties have a right to expect that the tribunal shall function as a judicial body. Its members must scrupulously observe the forms of judicial decorum and ethics. Manifest partiality in the conduct of the hearings must be avoided. They must confer and act jointly. They are selected, not as individual arbitrators, but as members of a judicial body. Accordingly, their judgment must be exercised, not in separate solitude, but in joint discussion, debate, and deliberation with one another as a single judicial body.

The views of writers upon this point are somewhat divided, but a careful analysis of them will help to clarify the exact issues here involved. Calvo [6] and Balasko [7] lay down the requirement that absence of one of the members of the tribunal will prevent all subsequent proceedings. Hudson [8] guardedly remarks that the presence of all members has been thought necessary to constitute the tribunal. Mérignhac [9] denies that absence of an arbitrator caused by bad faith can paralyze the action of the tribunal, which Witenberg [10] extends to a case of refusal to take part in the voting on the judgment. Hyde [11] states that after extended participation in the

[1] *Infra* sec. 14; see Hertz, *Essai sur le problème de la nullité* (1939, 3d ser.) 20 Rev. de Droit Int. L.C. 458.

[2] Balasko, Causes de nullité de la sentence arbitrale en droit international public (1938) 124.

[3] 7 Moore, Dig. sec. 1074.

[4] *Infra* this section and secs. 12 and 13.

[5] *Infra* sec. 15.

[6] 3 Calvo, Le Droit international (5th ed., 1896) 481–482.

[7] Balasko, *op. cit. supra* note 2, at 117, 124.

[8] Hudson, International Tribunals (1945) 115, but *cf.* 71, 74 (default judgments).

[9] Mérignhac, Traité théorique et pratique de l'arbitrage international (1895) 276–277.

[10] Witenberg, L'Organisation judiciaire, la procédure et la sentence internationales (1937) 281.

[11] 2 Hyde, International Law, Chiefly as Interpreted and Applied by the United States (2d ed., 1945) 1629.

work of the tribunal a member cannot by withdrawal render it powerless. Phillimore [12] suggests a possible line of reconciliation of these views in his statement that malicious abstention of an arbitrator from the deliberations need not prevent the others from proceeding, but that death of an arbitrator would dissolve the arbitration.

It does seem necessary to distinguish between a willful and personal refusal of an arbitrator to join in the deliberations of the tribunal and the absence of an arbitrator caused by the direction of his government. The former is a defect which may be waived by the parties, and if no objection be raised by either of them the remaining members of the tribunal are justified in proceeding. The latter, however, deprives the tribunal of its judicial quality and power to decide. Thus, the withdrawal of the Mexican commissioner and the other Mexican representatives from the French-Mexican Commission of 1924 under instructions of their government was recognized by the two governments as one of the circumstances requiring examination *de novo* of decisions thereafter rendered by the remaining members who constituted a majority.[13] It is true that repudiations by a State of the authority of a tribunal to proceed farther should not be arbitrarily exercised. It is not clear from the records so far made public whether the action of the German government to this end in the *Sabotage Cases* was justified in the circumstances.[14] But power must exist in a party to protect itself from manifest excesses of jurisdiction by a tribunal, and it need not await the rendering of the award to make its protest effective.

12. SAME: DISRUPTION OF THE MIXED CLAIMS COMMISSION, UNITED STATES AND MEXICO.—It is significant that the break-up in 1926 of the Special Claims Commission, United States and Mexico, established under the convention of September 10, 1923, and the disruption in 1931 of the work of the General Claims Commission between the same governments created under the Convention of Sep-

---

[12] 3 PHILLIMORE, COMMENTARIES UPON INTERNATIONAL LAW (1857) 4.
[13] *Infra* sec. 13. [14] *Infra* sec. 14.

tember 10, 1923, were both attended by the circumstance that the commissioners rendered their opinions without joint deliberation. In the opinion of American Commissioner Perry of the Special Claims Commission in the *Santa Isabel* cases appears the following statement:

Because of ill health, or otherwise, the Presiding Commissioner did not meet in conference with his associates to discuss the case. Because of continued ill health he went to Cuba where he wrote his final decision, one of the Commissioners being at his home in Mexico and the other in the United States. If there could have been just one conference; if there could have been just one opportunity to present and have answered one question perhaps it would have been unnecessary to write this dissenting opinion.[1]

The break-up of the General Claims Commission in July of 1931, in the undiplomatic language of the public press, was stated to have occurred when the Mexican commissioner and the presiding commissioner "held secret conferences to formulate their conclusions."[2] In the two published opinions of that month[3] American Commissioner Nielsen entered dissenting opinions in which he adverted to Rule XI (1), of the Rules of Procedure, providing that awards shall be rendered at a public sitting of the commission, and stated:

The other two Commissioners have signed the "Decision" in this case. However, no meeting of the Commission was ever called by the Presiding Commissioner to render a decision in the case, and there has never been any compliance with the proper rule above quoted.[4]

No further information appears to have been made public by the Department of State in relation to these incidents, but it is believed that if these untoward procedural practices had been accompanied by other evidence indicating bad faith and partiality

---

[1] (1932) 26 AM. J. INT. LAW 172, 184, 188. Lack of joint deliberation was admitted by the Presiding Commissioner, Letter to Editor, N.Y. TIMES, May 8, 1926, p. 17.

[2] WASHINGTON POST, July 26, 1931, at 1.

[3] Dickson Car Wheel Company (U.S.) v. Mexico, OPINIONS OF COMMISSIONERS, GENERAL CLAIMS COMMISSION, UNITED STATES AND MEXICO (1931) 175; International Fisheries Company (U.S.) v. Mexico, *ibid.*, 207.

[4] *Ibid.*, 206, 286.

on the part of the arbitrators the United States would clearly have been justified in refusing to recognize the validity of these decisions.

13. SAME: DISRUPTION OF FRENCH-MEXICAN COMMISSION OF 1924.— In the episode occurring in connection with the French-Mexican Commission of 1924, the question of lack of joint deliberation was presented in a different and much more serious form. There the absence of the national commissioner of Mexico from the deliberations of the tribunal took place apparently under the instructions of his government and as an incident of the abstention of all of its representatives from their respective roles under the view that the powers of the tribunal had lapsed by virtue of the expiration of its *compromis*. Decisions rendered by the tribunal in these circumstances were, by agreement of the governments concerned, later considered *de novo* by a new commission.

The French-Mexican Commission established under the convention of September 25, 1924, reached the expiration of its treaty period, without completing its work, on December 26, 1928. Nearly four months later the arbitrating parties exchanged notes extending the life of the commission for nine months from December 26, 1928. The presiding commissioner then called a session of the commission in Mexico City, to which he received a reply from the Mexican government, addressed to him in his capacity as presiding commissioner, requesting that this session be postponed because of the inability of the Mexican commissioner to attend. The presiding commissioner denied this request in view of the fact that only five months of the commission's life remained. He requested the Mexican government to appoint a substitute commissioner as provided in the convention, but the Mexican government then took the position that his role as presiding commissioner ceased on December 26, 1928.[1] The presiding commissioner convoked the commission to meet on May 29, 1929, and the commission met on June 3, the Mexican com-

[1] See generally, concerning this section, FELLER, THE MEXICAN CLAIMS COMMISSIONS, 1923–1934 (1935) 69–76; BALASKO, CAUSES DE NULLITÉ DE LA SENTENCE ARBITRALE EN DROIT INTERNATIONAL PUBLIC (1938) 277–280.

missioner, agent, and secretary being absent. Its first decision sustained the act of the presiding commissioner in convoking the commission on the ground that he was still possessed of his powers.[2] Its second decision (No. 22 of June 3, 1929) held that the lack of representation of Mexico was not a bar to the rendering of decisions by a majority of the commission in cases previously pleaded in the presence of the three commissioners.[3] Thereafter the two commissioners handed down awards in 23 claims, the Mexican commissioner absenting himself throughout. On June 24, in its Decision No. 23, the commission decided to adjourn until it could be fully constituted.[4] The presiding commissioner nevertheless continued to affirm that the two commissioners had the power to continue the sessions and that Mexico could not escape its obligations under the treaty.

By a convention of August 2, 1930, a new commission was provided for, which was to decide, among others, the claims which the "rump commission" had purported to decide.

The fact relied upon as evidencing consent by Mexico to extension of the life of the commission, the letter addressed by Mexico to Mr. Verzijl in his capacity of presiding commissioner after the life of the commission would otherwise have terminated according to the *compromis,* lacked that clear showing of intent to waive jurisdictional objections necessary to support a conferment of jurisdictional powers otherwise lacking.

14. SAME: SABOTAGE CASES.—The history of the so-called *Sabotage Cases,* or the *Black Tom and Kingsland Cases,* before the Mixed Claims Commissions, United States and Germany, under the agreement of August 10, 1922, is replete with procedural moves ending finally in the retirement of the German commissioner and agent from the tribunal in 1939. While many of the petitions of the parties related to questions of rehearing and may, therefore, be more properly dealt with in the discussion on rehearings later

---

[2] FELLER, *op. cit. supra* note 1, at 72–73.
[3] *Ibid.,* 73–74.   [4] *Ibid.,* 75.

herein, they will briefly be summarized to bring out all the circumstances attending the rendering of the award of the umpire of October 30, 1939.

On October 16, 1930, the commission rendered a decision disallowing, for lack of evidence as to the responsibility of Germany, the claims for damage from sabotage in *Lehigh Valley R. Co. et al. (U.S.)* v. *Germany.*[1] A petition for rehearing by the American agent, based on no new evidence or arguments, was dismissed.[2] A supplemental petition for rehearing, based on newly submitted evidence, was then filed by the American agent. This was denied by the umpire on December 3, 1932, for lack of sufficient evidence, no ruling being made on the jurisdictional question of the power of the commission to entertain the petition.[3]

The American agent next filed on May 4, 1933, a petition for rehearing the 1930 decision on the ground of fraud and collusion among some of the witnesses. The two national commissioners disagreed on the power of the commission to reopen its former decision on the merits and entered a certificate of disagreement.[4] The umpire sustained the jurisdiction of the commission to reopen the cases on the ground of fraud in a decision of December 15, 1933.[5]

On July 29, 1935, the umpire held that the cases would not be reopened until the moving party had proved its charges that fraud had been practiced upon the commission.[6]

On June 3, 1936, the commission set aside the decision of December 3, 1932, expressly leaving unimpaired by such action the 1930 decision on the merits. The parties were held to be authorized to submit evidence and arguments as to whether that decision should be reopened.[7]

The parties thereafter proceeded accordingly, the cases being closed in January, 1939. Conferences of the commission were begun the following month, but on March 1, 1939, the German commis-

---

[1] Mixed Claims Commissions, United States and Germany, Administrative Decisions and Opinions of a General Nature (1926–1932) 967.

[2] *Ibid.*, 995.   [3] *Ibid.*, 1004.   [4] *Ibid.* (1933–1939), 1084, 1086, 1097.
[5] *Ibid.*, 1115.   [6] *Ibid.*, 1173.   [7] *Ibid.*, 1175.

sioner announced his retirement from his post.[8] The German agent thereafter withdrew from the meetings of the commission in accordance with his letter to the commission of June 10, 1939.[9] On the same day the German chargé d'affaires *ad interim* notified Secretary of State Hull that it was considered that the commission was without jurisdiction and that no legal basis existed for any further meetings by it.[10] Under date of October 3, 1939, the chargé outlined his reasons for his assertions, concluding that any awards which might be entered would be "null and void."[11]

The German commissioner based his action on the alleged action of the umpire in bringing up new and previously unconsidered points in the deliberations of the tribunal and upon acts in the course of the deliberations said to evidence bias. He stated that he could "no longer cooperate in a procedure which no longer offers to both parties equally the usual guarantees of a decision arrived at in a really judicial way." The chargé d'affaires referred to "serious irregularities" in the proceedings and presented the legal reasons leading to the view of his government that proceedings of the tribunal subsequent to the withdrawal of the German commission were without legal effect. Principal among these was the contention that the commission could not function as a validly constituted tribunal under the treaty in the face of the withdrawal of the German commissioner.

In these circumstances the American commissioner filed on June 15, 1939, a certificate of disagreement and opinion, holding that the 1930 decision should be set aside and that the liability of Germany had been clearly established by the evidence.[12] These conclusions were sustained in the "Decision of the Commission Rendered by the Umpire," of the same date.[13] On October 30, 1939, awards were made in the sum of $21,157,227.01, which, with inter-

---

[8] MIXED CLAIMS COMMISSION, UNITED STATES AND GERMANY, OPINIONS AND DECISIONS IN THE SABOTAGE CASES HANDED DOWN JUNE 15, 1939, AND OCTOBER 30, 1939, 4, Appendix i.
[9] *Ibid.*, Appendix viii.   [10] *Ibid.*, Appendix ix.
[11] *Ibid.*, Appendix xi.   [12] *Ibid.*, 5.   [13] *Ibid.*, 310.

est, amounted to approximately $31,400,000 as of January 1, 1928.[14]

The full facts concerning the circumstances leading to the German commissioner's retirement are not known. The umpire replied to his charges of partiality in a letter dated March 2, 1939, in part as follows:

I do not propose to enter into any controversy with respect to the statements contained in your letter other than to say that they are unjustified and, in my opinion, present a wholly false picture of our deliberations with respect to the motion pending before the Commission.[15]

15. RIGHT TO A REASONED JUDGMENT.—The right to a reasoned judgment is a guarantee to States that the decision shall be in accordance with law and pursuant to the *compromis*. Not only is it a source of the authority of the decision as a precedent, it is also a condition of the legal effect of the decision. International tribunals may not avail themselves of the *per curiam* decision if they expect their decisions to be respected by litigants. The practice of tribunals to support their decisions by reasons has been so crystallized in thousands of cases, the views of writers are in such harmony upon this point, and its importance to the parties is so grave that the inclusion of reasons in support of the judgment has in international arbitral practice assumed the status of a fundamental rule of procedure the violation of which will lead to nullity.

Fiore[1] makes the categorical statement that if an award is not reasoned it may be proved to be void. Hoijer[2] affirms that its absence is equivalent to an excess of jurisdiction. In his view the sanction for its absence is nullity. Castberg[3] is of the opinion that the rule that arbitral decisions must be reasoned was definitely fixed in positive international law by Article 52 of the Hague Convention of 1899. Audry[4] notes that one may find many awards not supported by reasons, but holds that a failure to support a judg-

---

[14] *Ibid.*, 324; see also Z. & F. Assets Realization Corp. v. Hull, 311 U.S. 470 (1941).
[15] *Op. cit. supra* note 8, at Appendix iv.
[1] 2 FIORE, NOUVEAU DROIT INTERNATIONAL PUBLIC (Antoine trans., 1885) 643, 644.
[2] HOIJER, LA SOLUTION PACIFIQUE DES LITIGES INTERNATIONAUX (1925) 277.
[3] Castberg, *L'Excès de pouvoir dans la justice internationale* (1931) 35 RECUEIL DES COURS 389.
[4] AUDRY, LA REVISION DE LA SENTENCE ARBITRALE (1914) 60, 63.

ment by reasoning involves a failure to recognize a universally admitted principle. Lammasch [5] considers that the failure to support the decision by reasoning gives cause to doubt it and remarks that it will possess a higher value because of its reasoning. Schätzel [6] concludes that according to modern international practice failure to give reasons results in an excess of jurisdiction and nullity. Balasko [7] considers a statement of reasons to be indispensable and its absence to be a cause of nullity.

The lack of reasons in an award has been invoked as a cause for its nullity in the *Chamizal* arbitration [8] and in the *Norwegian Claims Case*.[9] In the *Cayuga Indians* case a departure from the terms of submission was asserted thereby to have resulted.[10] Writers have also criticized the awards of President Cleveland in the *Cerruti case*,[11] of President Loubet in the *Panama—Costa Rica Boundary* arbitration,[12] of the President of the Argentine Republic in the *Bolivia-Peru* boundary arbitration of 1909,[13] and of King Edward VII in the *Argentine-Chile* boundary arbitration [14] for the absence of reasons to support them.

In the project of Goldschmidt [15] it was considered discretionary

---

[5] LAMMASCH, DIE RECHTSKRAFT INTERNATIONALER SCHIEDSSPRÜCHE (1913) 82–88.

[6] SCHÄTZEL, RECHTSKRAFT UND ANFECHTUNG VON ENTSCHEIDUNGEN INTERNATIONALER GERICHTE, 6 FRANKFURTER ABHANDLUNGEN ZUM KRIEGSVERHÜTUNGSRECHT (1928) 73.

[7] BALASKO, CAUSES DE NULLITÉ DE LA SENTENCE ARBITRALE EN DROIT INTERNATIONAL PUBLIC (1938) 127.

[8] (1911) FOR. REL. U.S. 598.

[9] (1923) 17 AM. J. INT. LAW 287, 289.

[10] AMERICAN AND BRITISH CLAIMS ARBITRATION UNDER THE SPECIAL AGREEMENT OF AUGUST 18, 1910, REPORT OF FRED K. NIELSEN (1926) 304.

[11] BRY, PRÉCIS ÉLÉMENTAIRE DE DROIT INTERNATIONAL PUBLIC (1910) 491; BUREAU, LE CONFLIT ITALO-COLOMBIEN (AFFAIRE CERUTTI) (1899) 87; Pierantoni, *La Nullité d'un arbitrage internationale* (1898) 30 REV. DE DROIT INT. L.C. 461; Darras, *De certains dangers de l'arbitrage international; affaire Cerruti entre la Colombie et l'Italie* (1899) 6 REV. GEN. DE DROIT INT. PUB. 547.

[12] ANDERSON, EL LAUDO LOUBET. CONTRIBUCION AL ESTUDIO DE LÍMITES ENTRE COSTA RICA Y PANAMÁ (1911) 48.

[13] Weiss, *Le Arbitrage de 1909 entre la Bolivie et le Pérou* (1910) 17 REV. GEN. DE DROIT INT. PUB. 134.

[14] Alvarez, *Des occupations des territoires contestés à propos de la question de limites entre le Chili et la République Argentine* (1903) 10 REV. GEN. DE DROIT INT. PUB. 681.

[15] Goldschmidt, *Projet de règlement pour tribunaux arbitraux internationaux* (1874) 6 REV. DE DROIT INT. L.C. 445 (Section 28).

with the tribunal whether it would add any statement of reasons to its award. Article 13 of the project of the Institute states that "the arbitral award should be drawn up in writing, and contain a statement of reasons, unless dispensed with by the stipulations of the *compromis*." [16] At the Hague Conference of 1899, in the examination in committee of the Russian draft of an arbitral code, Dr. Zorn moved that Article 22 should require that the award "must state the reasons upon which it is based." [17] The article in question then read: "The award given by a majority of votes should be drawn up in writing and signed by each member of the arbitral tribunal." [18] Mr. Martens opposed the motion upon what now seems the rather remarkable ground that it would impose upon arbitrators "one of the most delicate of obligations," and would perhaps embarrass them in their task.[19] Chevalier Descamps favored the motion, remarking that to abandon a statement of the reasons for the award would be injurious from the judicial point of view.[20] Mr. Asser felt that it was a strong guaranty for impartiality and against arbitrariness of action.[21] The motion was adopted by the Committee of Examination [22] and was eventually adopted by the conference as a part of Article 52 of the final draft.[23] The material part of the article as adopted reads: "The award, given by a majority of votes, must state the reasons upon which it is based." [24] Its counterpart in the Convention of 1907 is Article 79, which, as here material, reads: "The award must state the reasons on which it is based." [25] The same rule is adopted in Article 56 of the Statute of the Permanent Court of International Justice, reading: "The judgment shall state the reasons on which it is based." [26]

[16] (1877) Annuaire 132.
[17] Proceedings of the Hague Peace Conferences, Conference of 1899 (Carnegie trans., 1920) 740.
[18] *Ibid.*, 801, 803.   [19] *Ibid.*, 740.
[20] *Ibid.*, 741.   [21] *Ibid.*, 748.
[22] *Ibid.*   [23] *Ibid.*, 91.   [24] *Ibid.*, 98.
[25] 1 Proceedings of the Hague Peace Conferences, Conference of 1907 (Carnegie trans., 1920) 612.
[26] Statute and Rules of Court (1936) 25.

Admittedly, arbitration is a judicial process. The requirement that a decision be reached by a formally stated process of reasoning would, therefore, seem to be essential.[27] It need not be in meticulous detail; a statement indicating in a general way the legal reasons upon which the award is based will be valid and binding.[28] The circumstance, however, that upon certain aspects of the opinion reasons were lacking cannot reasonably be considered to result in the nullity of the entire decision.[29]

16. RIGHT TO A TRIBUNAL FREE FROM CORRUPTION.—The parties have a right to a decision of a tribunal free from corruption and manifest and willful partiality. The tribunal should conduct itself in a judicial manner and should not in bad faith violate the principle of impartiality. When fraud and corruption of the arbitrators exist, their decision will lose its authority. Frivolous and trivial charges of partiality, however, are not sufficient to justify a disregard of the tribunal's decision. Partiality of an arbitrator to be a cause of nullity must be fully demonstrable, exercised in bad faith, and the source of substantial prejudice to the party. The practical difficulties of admitting mere partisanship as a cause of nullity are evident from the following remarks of Lord Salisbury:

If the matter in controversy is important, so that defeat is a serious blow to the credit or the power of the litigant who is worsted, that interest becomes a more or less keen partisanship. According to their sympathies, men wish for the victory of one side or the other.

Such conflicting sympathies interfere most formidably with the choice of an impartial arbitrator. It would be too invidious to specify the various forms of bias by which, in any important controversy between two great powers, the other members of the commonwealth of nations are visibly affected. In the existing condition of international sentiment each great power could point to nations whose admission to any jury by whom its interests were to be tried it would be bound to challenge; and in a litiga-

[27] Cf. STOYKOVITCH, DE L'AUTORITÉ DE LA SENTENCE ARBITRALE EN DROIT INTERNATIONAL PUBLIC (1924) 92.
[28] But cf. the complaints of the United States in the Chamizal arbitration, Norwegian Claims Case and Cayuga Indians case infra secs. 49, 50.
[29] Castberg, supra note 3, at 390.

tion between two great powers the rival challenges would pretty well exhaust the catalogue of the nations from which competent and suitable arbiters could be drawn.[1]

Schätzel [2] has an unusually thoughtful discussion of this phase of the topic of the nullity of arbitral awards. Reference is made by him to those impalpable elements, which, it may be supposed, will always influence in some measure the judicial temper. Of these he mentions the influence of war psychology in allowing claims against the loser.[3] It would appear that account can hardly be taken of such influences. Yet he submits that if the prejudice or partiality of a judge be manifest and timely objection thereto be raised, the parties are privileged to revise the judgment.[4] He notes that the practice of placing national judges on a tribunal to protect the interests of the State is a recognized institution. Such a member of a tribunal preserves his judicial character and the fact of his appointment can give rise to no complaint.[5] A corrupt judge is defined by him to be one who violates in bad faith the principle of impartiality or even in good faith shows a markedly favorable attitude towards one party. The apt comment is made that the means of corrupting judges which States can use are now so finely cultivated that a criminal corruption could not be absolutely established. The conferral of honorary decrees, favors and other subtle methods may be among them.[6] In general, it may be said that gross breaches of good faith and honesty, the use of force against witnesses, and attempts to influence the neutral or opposing judge are justifications for a refusal to proceed further before a tribunal.[7] He

---

[1] Lord Salisbury to Sir Julian Pauncefote, March 5, 1896 (1896) For. Rel. U.S. 222–223; see also Clarke, *A Permanent Tribunal of International Arbitration: Its Necessity and Value* (1907) 1 Am. J. Int. Law 343, 402.

[2] Schätzel, Rechtskraft und Anfechtung von Entscheidungen Internationaler Gerichte, 6 Frankfurter Abhandlungen zum Kriegsverhütungsrecht (1928) 18–55.

[3] *Ibid.*, 18–19.

[4] *Ibid.*, 54.

[5] *Ibid.*, 32–41. *Cf.* Art. 31 of the Statute of the Permanent Court of International Justice permitting the retention of judges of the nationality of a contesting party. Statute and Rules of Court (1936) 19.

[6] Schätzel, *op. cit. supra* note 2, at 20.

[7] *Ibid.*, 19–20.

concludes that the trust in international arbitral processes can only be improved if success is attained in instituting the necessary procedural remedies against partiality of arbitrators.[8]

Writers are unanimously agreed that the corruption or bad faith of the arbitrators will lead to the nullity of an arbitral award.[9] Pufendorf [10] was the earliest to remark on this cause of nullity, stating that a party to an arbitration was not obliged to submit to the decision of the arbitrator when he had been bribed or when there was collusion between him and the other party. Calvo [11] affirms that an arbitrator is in a state of incapacity when he has a concealed interest in the outcome of the dispute. Presumably as evidence of bad faith, Phillimore [12] speaks of "a sentence bearing upon its face glaring partiality." Lammasch [13] states that corruption must be proved and requires a conviction of the corrupt

---

8 *Ibid.,* 55.

9 In addition to references *infra* this section notes 10–21, see: *Monographs:* ACREMENT, LA PROCÉDURE DANS LES ARBITRAGES INTERNATIONAUX (1905) 163; AUDRY, LA REVISION DE LA SENTENCE ARBITRALE (1914) 44; BISHOP, INTERNATIONAL ARBITRAL PROCEDURE (1930) 242; GUERMANOFF, L'EXCÈS DE POUVOIR DE L'ARBITRE (1929) 41; HOIJER, LA SOLUTION PACIFIQUE DES LITIGES INTERNATIONAUX (1925) 278; MÉRIGNHAC, TRAITÉ THÉORIQUE ET PRATIQUE L'ARBITRAGE INTERNATIONAL (1895) 314; STOYKOVITCH, DE L'AUTORITÉ DE LA SENTENCE ARBITRALE EN DROIT INTERNATIONAL PUBLIC (1924) 208; *Treatises:* BONFILS, MANUEL DE DROIT INTERNATIONAL PUBLIC (1898) 488; BLUNTSCHLI, LE DROIT INTERNATIONAL CODIFIÉ (Lardy trans., 1895) 281; BRY, PRÉCIS ÉLÉMENTAIRE DE DROIT INTERNATIONAL PUBLIC (1910) 491; 2 CARNAZZA-AMARI, TRAITÉ DE DROIT INTERNATIONAL PUBLIC (1882) 564; DE LOUTER, LE DROIT INTERNATIONAL PUBLIC POSITIF (1920) 154; 1 FAUCHILLE, TRAITÉ DE DROIT INTERNATIONAL PUBLIC (1926) Part IV, at 552; 2 FIORE, NOUVEAU DROIT INTERNATIONAL PUBLIC (Antoine trans., 1885) 643; GENET, TRAITÉ DE DIPLOMATIE ET DE DROIT DIPLOMATIQUE (1932) 587; HALL, INTERNATIONAL LAW (8th ed., 1924) 420; HEFFTER, DAS EUROPÄISCHE VÖLKERRECHT DER GEGENWART (8th ed., Geffcken, 1888) 233; 6 PRADIER-FODÉRÉ, TRAITÉ DE DROIT INTERNATIONAL PUBLIC (1894) 434–435; 2 RIVIER, PRINCIPES DU DROIT DES GENS (1896) 185; 1 PLANAS SUÁREZ, TRATADO DE DERECHO INTERNACIONAL PÚBLICO (1916) 440; TAYLOR, A TREATISE ON INTERNATIONAL LAW (1901) 379–380; 2 TWISS, THE LAW OF NATIONS (2d ed., 1875) 8; 2 VATTEL, LE DROIT DE GENS (ed., 1758, Fenwick trans., 1916) 224; *Articles, etc.:* Nys, *La Revision de la sentence arbitrale* (1910, 2d ser.) 12 REV. DE DROIT INT. L.C. 600, at 621; Scelle, *Une Instance en revision devant la Cour de la Haye, l'affaire de la Orinoco Steamship Company* (1911) 18 REV. GEN. DE DROIT INT. PUB. 190; Goldschmidt, *Projet de règlement pour tribunaux arbitraux internationaux* (1874) 6 REV. DE DROIT INT. L.C. 447 (Section 32); Art. 27, *projet* of the Institute of International Law (1877) ANNUAIRE 133.

10 2 PUFENDORF, LE DROIT DE LA NATURE ET DE GENS (1734) 176.

11 3 CALVO, LE DROIT INTERNATIONAL (5th ed., 1896) 485.

12 3 PHILLIMORE, COMMENTARIES UPON INTERNATIONAL LAW (1857) 5.

13 LAMMASCH, DIE RECHTSKRAFT INTERNATIONALER SCHIEDSSPRÜCHE (1913) 168.

arbitrator as a condition for further proceedings to nullify the award. The suggestion has been advanced that if one of several arbitrators constituting a tribunal were proved corrupt, the remaining arbitrators would be privileged to declare the award null, exclude the corrupted arbitrator, and render a new decision after appointment of a substitute arbitrator.[14] Castberg [15] requires the integrity of the entire membership of the tribunal as a condition of validity of its award. He points out, with sound reasoning, that one or more of the members of the unaffected majority might have decided otherwise had they retained their freedom of judgment intact. Balasko [16] concurs in this, affirming that any corruption will vitiate the ensuing award of the tribunal. Morelli [17] holds that a decision which is the product of corruption of the judge is null. Hertz [18] states that corruption of the arbitrator should include not only venality but also every personal defect that deprives him of the quality of a judge.

Oppenheim [19] summarizes the general doctrine on the point of fraud in a lucid statement.

Should they [the arbitrators] have been bribed, or not followed their instructions, should their award have been given under the influence of coercion of any kind, or should one of the parties have intentionally and maliciously led the arbitrators into an essential and material error, the award would have no binding force whatever.

An award rendered by a corrupt judge is not only void but also entirely lacking in legal meaning or authority as a precedent. It does not flow from a judge and has no judicial quality. It may not be resorted to as an expression or source of international law.

---

[14] Lisboa, *Revision des sentences arbitrales* (1902, 3d ser.) 4 REV. DE DROIT INT. L.C. 62, at 64, 65; *cf.* ACREMENT, *op. cit. supra* note 9, at 120.

[15] Castberg, *L'Excès de pouvoir dans la justice internationale* (1931) 35 RECUEIL DES COURS 441, 442.

[16] BALASKO, CAUSES DE NULLITÉ DE LA SENTENCE ARBITRALE EN DROIT INTERNATIONAL PUBLIC (1938) 119.

[17] Morelli, *La Théorie générale du procès international* (1937) 61 RECUEIL DES COURS 327.

[18] Hertz, *Essai sur le problème de la nullité* (1939, 3d ser.) 20 REV. DE DROIT INT. L.C. 492.

[19] 2 OPPENHEIM, INTERNATIONAL LAW (4th ed., 1928) 28.

It is, with a certainty not approached by any other type of arbitral award which the parties are privileged to disregard, an absolute nullity.[20]

17. SAME: UNITED STATES–VENEZUELA CLAIMS COMMISSION OF 1866.— Following the completion of the work of the commission for the settlement of claims created under the convention between the United States and Venezuela of April 25, 1866,[1] the Venezuelan government protested against the awards rendered, alleging irregularity in the appointment of the umpire and fraud in the proceedings and findings. The Committee on Foreign Affairs of the United States House of Representatives found that the commission was a conspiracy and that its proceedings were tainted with fraud. The United States commissioner, together with the American minister to Venezuela and another individual, was charged with having irregularly procured the appointment of an umpire, with influencing the making of awards, and with defrauding claimants by exacting attorney's fees. A joint resolution was approved that the proceedings should be set aside and a rehearing be had by a new commission.[2]

A convention creating a new commission was eventually concluded on March 15, 1888. This commission held its purpose to be the rehearing of the original claims. It declared that it could concede no " 'force and legal effect' " to the former adjudications and that the claims stood before the commission substantially as they stood before the former commission.[3] Thus, the fraud or partiality of an arbitrator was held to render void the awards made by him.

18. RIGHT TO PROCEEDINGS FREE FROM FRAUD.—The parties are entitled to the assurance that the proceedings before the tribunal will not be influenced by fraud, false documents, malicious deceit, or any other act, such as bribery, which would lead the tribunal into

---

20 See *infra* p. 58.

1 Art. 5 of this convention provided that: "The decisions of this commission and those (in case there may be any) of the Umpire, shall be final and conclusive as to all pending claims at the date of their installation. Claims which shall not be presented within the twelve months herein prescribed will be disregarded by both Governments, and considered invalid." 2 MALLOY, TREATIES 1856, 1857.

2 2 MOORE, INT. ARB., 1660–1664.   3 *Ibid.*, 1675, 1687.

a decision not based on truth and an impartial, honest judgment. To be distinguished, however, are complaints such as were made by Chile in the *Tacna-Arica* arbitration that the case of Peru contained numerous partial quotations and misquotations which gave a false impression.[1] Such a complaint of counsel is often to be expected in the course of an arbitration. We are here concerned rather with the protection of one party from the effects produced by the fraudulent acts of the other.

It will be recalled that Oppenheim includes as a cause of nullity not only the instance of a corrupt arbitrator but also the case where one of the parties has "intentionally and maliciously" led him into error.[2] The principle that an award procured through false evidence or other fraud is void has been sustained by a number of writers. Since their discussion of this point has principally occurred in connection with the topics of essential error and revision, reference is made to the discussion of those questions later in this text.[3] It is clear that authority and practice sustain the conclusion that an award fraudulently procured is without obligatory force.[4]

19. SAME: WEIL AND LA ABRA CASES.—The well-known *Weil* and *La Abra* cases between the United States and Mexico afford occasion for indicating a distinction between the legal effects of a decision rendered by a corrupt arbitrator and one procured by the fraud of a party from competent tribunal of unquestioned integrity. The first is, of course, entirely without legal significance. The second will likewise entrain no responsibility upon the respondent government to execute it. But the latter decision can, to a certain extent, be regarded as an expression and a source of international law, notwithstanding that the facts upon which the tribunal rendered its judgment are proved to be false.[1] An explanation is believed thereby to

---

1 COUNTER-CASE OF THE REPUBLIC OF CHILE 2–7.
2 2 OPPENHEIM, INTERNATIONAL LAW (4th ed., 1928) 28.
3 *Infra* Ch. iv and secs. 75–79.
4 Cases *infra* secs. 19, 20.
1 *Cf.* Castberg, *L'Excès de pouvoir dans la justice internationale* (1931) 35 RECUEIL DES COURS 451–452.

be afforded for the position taken by Secretary of State Evarts [2] and Umpire Thornton [3] that decisions allowing fraudulent claims, as were here involved, should not be reviewed by another or the same international tribunal. If it were ascertained by the claimant government that the claims were unfounded, no necessity existed for their resubmission to a new tribunal. The claimant government would no longer be in a position to press their collection.

Awards were rendered by Umpire Thornton, of the United States–Mexico Claims Commission of 1868, in behalf of Benjamin Weil and the La Abra Silver Mining Company, respectively, in the sums of $285,000 and $385,791.06, Mexican gold.[4] Mexico attempted to enter a reservation against these awards,[5] but later contented itself with announcing that while it might take measures to establish that the claims were based on perjury, it would "conscientiously fulfill the obligations imposed on it" by the treaty.[6] The question of the status of the award thus raised was made the subject of a report to the President by Secretary of State Evarts, under date of August 13, 1879, in which he concluded that since regular hearings had been held before a tribunal of unquestioned integrity, the awards should not be opened or the cases retried before a new international tribunal, but that in view of the grave doubt cast upon the claims by Mexico, the honor of the United States required that the claims be investigated.[7] Nevertheless, no immediate action was taken by the United States, and $240,683.06 was distributed on the *La Abra* claim and $171,889.64 on the *Weil* claim.[8] In 1882 a convention was signed with Mexico providing for a resubmission of the claims to arbitration, but in 1886 it was rejected by the Senate.[9] Further distribution of the awards, however, ceased, and efforts by assignees of the claimants to compel the Secretary of State,

---

[2] *Infra* this section, note 7.   [3] 2 MOORE, INT. ARB. 1329.
[4] *Ibid.*, 1327, 1329.   [5] *Ibid.*, 1330.
[6] *Ibid.*, 1331–1332. Under Article II of the convention of July 4, 1868, the parties considered the decisions of the commission "as absolutely final and conclusive." 1 MALLOY, TREATIES 1128, 1130.
[7] 2 MOORE, INT. ARB. 1334.   [8] *Ibid.*, 1337.
[9] *Ibid.*, 1337–1339.

through court action, to distribute the funds in his hands failed.[10] Finally, in 1892, Congress authorized the United States Court of Claims to investigate both cases and to determine whether the charges of fraud were well founded.[11] The Court held that the awards were obtained by fraud.[12]

Subsequently, in 1900, the sums of $403,030.08 in the *La Abra* case and $287,833.77 in the *Weil* case, the unpaid balances received and retained by the United States, were returned to Mexico.[13] On March 6, 1902, the sum of $412,572.70, received on account of both claimants and paid over to them by the United States, was returned to Mexico,[14] following the appropriation therefor in the urgent deficiencies act of February 14, 1902.[15]

The judgment of the United States Court of Claims in this affair would, of course, not be conclusive upon Mexico; [16] though attempt has been made to rest its authority upon a tacit mandate of Mexico and an express mandate of the United States.[17] Question of its authority was not raised, inasmuch as its judgment was favorable to Mexico and the United States thereafter returned to Mexico the sums received towards payment of the awards. But it would seem that the judgment would have no greater authority than that of any other judgment of a national court and that Mexico would have been privileged to attack it if it had been unfavorable to her allegations. It would then have been seen that

[10] Frelinghuysen v. Key, 110 U.S. 63 (1884); United States ex rel. Boynton v. Blaine, 139 U.S. 306 (1891).

[11] 27 STAT. 409, 410.

[12] United States v. La Abra Silver Mining Company, 32 Ct. Cls. 462 (1897), aff'd La Abra Silver Mining Company v. United States, 175 U.S. 423 (1899); United States v. Alice Weil, 35 Ct. Cls. 42 (1900).

[13] Secretary of State Hay to Señor Azpiroz, March 28, 1900 (La Abra) (1900) FOR. REL. U.S. 781; same to same, November 10, 1900 (Weil), *ibid.*, 783.

[14] Secretary of State Hay to the Mexican Ambassador, in COUNTER CASE OF THE UNITED STATES, APPENDIX, UNITED STATES AND VENEZUELAN ARBITRATION AT THE HAGUE (Orinoco Steamship Company Case) 92.

[15] 32 STAT. 5.

[16] Cf. Lapradelle, *L'Arbitrage international en 1897* (Chronique Internationale) (1898) 10 REV. DE DROIT PUB. S.P. (Part 2) 525; Castberg, *supra* note 1, at 451.

[17] Mérignhac, *De l'autorité de la chose jugée en matière de sentence arbitrale* (1898) 5 REV. GEN. DE DROIT INT. PUB. 606, 625.

the judgment was purely advisory to the executive officers of the United States.

20. SAME: MANNESMANN CASE.—Before World War I certain German manufacturers, the Mannesmann brothers, had submitted claims against Morocco, principally concerning the expropriation of mines. In 1914 an arbitral commission was instituted to examine these claims. After the war France reinstituted the commission. Another German company now claimed the mines, the Hamburg Marokko Gesellschaft. This company produced before the commission several important dossiers in order to establish mining activities before 1914. The commission demanded proofs of works completed. The company did not produce, in answer to this order, the original reports of 1912 and 1913, but instead certified translations were submitted. It explained that the originals were in Morocco and had been sequestered by France. The Moroccan government caused the original documents to be sent to France, where they were compared with the translation. It was found that all matter injurious to the claimant's case had been suppressed and that detailed accounts of explorations and works had been inserted which were not to be found in the original documents. The representatives of the Moroccan government notified the tribunal of their discovery, and in 1921 it rendered a decision that the proofs submitted established that the errors were not simple errors in translation, but were intentional. These facts were communicated by the French government to the German government, with the request that action be taken against the forgers.[1]

1 1 FAUCHILLE, TRAITÉ DE DROIT INTERNATIONAL PUBLIC (1926) Part IV, at 567.

CHAPTER 3

JURISDICTION

21. ARBITRATION BASED UPON CONSENT OF THE PARTIES.—Arbitration between States, as well as between persons, is contractual in source and arises solely out of consent. Usually consent to confer power to an arbitral tribunal to settle disputes existing between States is evidenced by an arbitration treaty, agreement, or *compromis*. The scope of the powers of the tribunal, the sphere of the activity permitted to it by the arbitral agreement and by international law, may be said to constitute the jurisdiction of the tribunal. The tribunal must ever endeavor in good faith to keep within the limits of its treaty,[1] and its decisions will have validity only insofar as it keeps within its jurisdiction, express or implied.[2]

These principles are well stated by the Permanent Court of International Justice in the *Mavromattis Palestine Concessions* case,[3]

---

[1] *Cases:* See Van Bokkelen (U.S.) v. Hayti (1888) 2 MOORE, INT. ARB. 1813, 1822; Rudloff (U.S.) v. Venezuela (1903) RALSTON'S REPORT 38, 41; Stevenson (Great Britain) v. Venezuela (1903) *ibid.* 438, 451; Administrative Decision No. V (1922) DECISIONS AND OPINIONS, MIXED CLAIMS COMMISSION, UNITED STATES AND GERMANY (1925) 145, 175, 183; Illinois Central Railroad Company (U.S.) v. Mexico (1923) OPINIONS OF COMMISSIONERS, GENERAL CLAIMS COMMISSION, UNITED STATES AND MEXICO (1927) 15, 16; Norddeutsche Bank, Hamburg v. Board of Trade and Public Trustee (Anglo-German Mixed Arbitral Tribunal, 1922) 2 RECUEIL DES DÉCISIONS (1923) 520, 522. *Writers:* Basdevant, Jèze and Politis, *Le Principes juridiques sur la compétence des juridictions internationales* (1927) 44 REV. DU DROIT PUB. S.P. 45; Borel, *Les Voies de recours contre les sentences arbitrales* (1935) 52 RECUEIL DES COURS 72; Ćastberg, *L'Excès de pouvoir dans la justice internationale* (1931) 35 RECUEIL DES COURS 394; Dumas, *Sanctions of International Arbitration* (1911) 5 AM. J. INT. LAW, 935; HOIJER, LA SOLUTION PACIFIQUE DES LITIGES INTERNATIONAUX (1925) 270; Morelli, *La Théorie générale du procès international* (1937) 61 RECUEIL DES COURS 266; Rundstein, *Le Caractère juridique des différends internationaux* (1934, 3d ser.) 15 REV. DE DROIT INT. L.C. 388; 2 FIORE, NOUVEAU DROIT INTERNATIONAL PUBLIC (Antoine trans., 1885) 630, 642.

[2] Lauterpacht, *The Legal Remedy in Case of Excess of Jurisdiction* (1928) 9 BRITISH YEARBOOK 117, 118; GUERMANOFF, L'EXCÈS DE POUVOIR DE L'ARBITRE (1929) 8–10; Morelli, *supra* note 1, at 314.

[3] Judgment No. 2 (August 30, 1924) SER. A., No. 2; see Borchard, *The Mavromattis Concessions Cases* (1925) 19 AM. J. INT. LAW 729, 738.

which arose out of an attempt by the Greek government to bring the government of Great Britain before the Court by means of a compulsory jurisdiction clause contained in Article 26 of the Mandate of Palestine. A preliminary objection to the jurisdiction was made by the respondent government, in part upon the ground that the conditions stipulated as necessary for compulsory jurisdiction had not been shown to exist. The Court, by a majority vote, overruled the objection. In so doing, however, it recognized that "its jurisdiction is limited, that it is invariably based on the consent of the respondent and only exists insofar as this consent has been given" and "that it must satisfy itself that the suit before it, in the form in which it has been submitted and on the basis of the facts hitherto established, falls to be decided by application of the clauses of the Mandate." [4] This point of view was fully concurred in by the dissenting judges. Thus, Judge Moore stated:

Ever mindful of the fact that their judgments, if rendered in excess of power, may be treated as null, international tribunals have universally regarded the question of jurisdiction as fundamental. . . . The international judicial tribunals so far created have been tribunals of limited powers. Therefore no presumption in favor of their jurisdiction may be indulged. Their jurisdiction must always affirmatively appear on the face of the record.[5]

To similar effect was the dissenting opinion of Lord Finlay.

The jurisdiction of the Permanent Court rests upon consent, and without consent there is no jurisdiction over any State.[6]

In the *Eastern Carelia* case the Permanent Court of International Justice said:

It is well established in international law that no State can, without its consent, be compelled to submit its disputes with other States either to mediation or to arbitration or to any other kind of pacific settlement. Such consent can be given over and for all in the form of an obligation freely undertaken, but it can on the contrary also be given in a special case apart from any existing obligation. The first alternative applies to the Members

[4] *Op. cit. supra* note 3, at 16.
[5] *Ibid.*, 60.
[6] *Ibid.*, 42. See also in this connection Judgment No. 4 (March 26, 1925), SER. A.

of the League, who, having accepted the Covenant, are under the obligation resulting from the provisions of this pact dealing with the pacific settlement of international disputes. As concerns States not Members of the League, the situation is quite different; they are not bound by the Covenant. The submission, therefore, of a dispute between them and a Member of the League for solution according to the methods provided for in the Covenant, could take place only by virtue of their consent. Such consent, however, has never been given by Russia. . . . The Court therefore finds it impossible to give its opinion on a dispute of this kind.[7]

The danger of any other course of action by tribunals was strikingly set forth by Chief Justice White in his award in the Panama–Costa Rica boundary controversy.

Discretion or compromise or adjustment, however cogent might be the reasons which would lead the mind beyond the domain of rightful power, and however much they might control if excess of authority could be indulged in, can find no place in the discharge of the duty to arbitrate a matter in dispute according to the submission and to go no further. No more fatal blow could be struck at the possibility of arbitration for adjusting international disputes than to take from the submission of such disputes the element of security arising from the restrictions just indicated.[8]

The tribunal accordingly derives its life and vitality from the *compromis*. Respect for its constitutive treaty is its cardinal rule of action. Yet, when it is charged with the decision of a dispute in accordance with the rules of international law, it is more than the mere servant of the parties. It is an international court, drawing from the accumulated precedents of past tribunals and in its turn contributing to the growth of international jurisprudence. If, in carrying out the task entrusted to it by the parties, it will refrain from being influenced by considerations of momentary advantage of the litigating parties in the particular controversy and instead give paramount regard to their interest in establishing a reign of law between States, then, indeed, will its decrees be respected and enforced.

[7] Request for advisory opinion concerning the Status of Eastern Carelia (July 23, 1923), Advisory opinion No. 5, SER. B., No. 5, 27–28; see Judgment No. 12, "Rights of Minorities in Upper Silesia," (Apr. 26, 1928) SER. A., No. 15, at 22: "The Court's jurisdiction depends on the will of the Parties."
[8] (1914) FOR. REL. U.S. 1000, 1014.

22. ARBITRATION UNDER AN INVALID COMPROMIS.—The unqualified statement has often been made that an arbitral decision may be considered null and subject to attack when the *compromis* under which it was rendered is invalid.[1] Efforts have been made to formulate the conditions under which a *compromis* may be regarded as validly executed.[2] All that need be said in this connection is that the *compromis*, like any international treaty, must be concluded by regularly authorized representatives of the State and be duly approved and ratified.[3] However, the fact that a State was forced to accept a *compromis* of arbitration has never been invoked as a cause of nullity. Nor would the fact that a new régime had succeeded to the government between the signing of the protocol and the rendering of the award raise a question of capacity.[4]

The statement that an award may be void by reason of an invalid *compromis* will be seen to be incomplete if its practical application be considered, since a treaty is not the only means by which a State may evidence its consent that a tribunal shall be empowered to adjudicate a dispute pending with another State. It may tacitly confer jurisdiction by participating in the arbitration, while fully cognizant of the defect, without raising the objection of the invalidity of the *compromis*. Judge Moore soundly regards it to be "inconceivable that a state should be permitted silently to

[1] 2 BULMERINCQ, VÖLKERRECHT (1887) 352; HEFFTER, DAS EUROPÄISCHE VÖLKERRECHT DER GEGENWART (8th ed., Geffcken, 1888) 233; Art. 27, *projet* of the Institute of International Law adopted at its session at The Hague, 1875 (1877) ANNUAIRE 126, 133; STOYKOVITCH, DE L'AUTORITÉ DE LA SENTENCE ARBITRALE EN DROIT INTERNATIONAL PUBLIC (1924) 189; Hertz, *Essai sur le problème de la nullité* (1939, 3d ser.) 20 REV. DE DROIT INT. L.C. 453, 457.

[2] Thus, Guermanoff states that consent, capacity and a justiciable controversy (*cause licite*) are required for a valid treaty, L'EXCÈS DE POUVOIR DE L'ARBITRE (1929) 38. An elaborate list of requirements is made by Audry, who contends that the *compromis* should (1) be freely entered into, (2) comply with the legislation of each State as to signature and ratification, (3) fulfill the requirements of *droit commun* as to the capacity of the parties and their object, (4) name the arbitrators, set forth the powers conferred upon them and the matters to be decided, and (5) contain the elements susceptible of informing the judge upon the decision, AUDRY, LA REVISION DE LA SENTENCE ARBITRALE (1914).

[3] STOYKOVITCH, *op. cit. supra* note 1, at 45; see also BALASKO, CAUSES DE NULLITÉ DE LA SENTENCE ARBITRALE EN DROIT INTERNATIONAL PUBLIC (1938) 103–104.

[4] MÉRIGNHAC, TRAITÉ THÉORIQUE ET PRATIQUE DE L'ARBITRAGE INTERNATIONAL (1895) 175, 176; but see *supra* note 2.

hold in reserve the question of the validity or continuing force of
its own agreement, until it should have learned, by the results of
the agreement's complete execution, whether it would be advan-
tageous or disadvantageous to raise the question." [5] Goldschmidt,
who was possibly the first to state that a *compromis* not validly concluded was a source of nullity, expressly limited it by the statement that "this reason may not be invoked if the complaining party
has taken part in the procedure before the arbitral tribunal, without objecting to the nullity of the *compromis*." [6]

23. SAME: NICARAGUA-HONDURAS BOUNDARY DISPUTE.—The effect of
the expiration of an arbitration treaty prior to the institution of
the proceedings under it was raised by Nicaragua in the course
of its boundary dispute with Honduras.[1] In order fully to appreciate the position of Nicaragua in this controversy, it is necessary to
detail somewhat at length the procedure established by the Gámez-
Bonilla treaty for the settlement of the dispute.

It created a Mixed Boundary Commission to fix the boundary
between the two States. Such points as the commission could not
agree upon were to be submitted to an "unappealable arbitration"
composed of a representative of each State and a member of the
foreign diplomatic corps accredited to Guatemala to be nominated
by the national arbitrators.[2] Article 5 minutely outlined the pro-

[5] Opinion of John Bassett Moore, Counsellor for Honduras, Honduras-
Nicaragua Boundary Meditation before the Secretary of State of the United States,
1920–1921. 5 COLLECTED PAPERS OF JOHN BASSETT MOORE (1944) 129.

[6] Goldschmidt, *Projet de règlement pour tribunaux arbitraux internationaux,
présenté à l'Institut de Droit International* (Session de Genève, 1874) (1874) 6 REV.
DE DROIT INT. L.C. 421, 447 (Section 32 (1)). Accord: ACREMENT, LA PROCÉDURE
DANS LES ARBITRAGES INTERNATIONAUX (1905) 157; GUERMANOFF, *op. cit. supra* note 2,
at 39; LAMMASCH, DIE RECHTSKRAFT INTERNATIONALER SCHIEDSSPRÜCHE (1913) 166,
167; Lisboa, *Revision des sentences arbitrales* (1902, 2d ser.) 4 REV. DE DROIT INT.
L.C. 62, 63; MÉRIGNHAC, *op. cit. supra* note 4, at 304, 305; REVON, L'ARBITRAGE
INTERNATIONAL, SON PASSÉ-SON PRÉSENT-SON AVENIR (1892) 518; *cf.* HALL, INTERNA-
TIONAL LAW (8th ed., 1924) 385: "Tacit ratification takes place when an agreement,
invalid because made in excess of special powers, or incomplete from want of
express ratification, is wholly or partly carried out with the knowledge and permission of the state which it purports to bind."

[1] For an analogous case see *supra* sec. 13.

[2] Art. 1, 3, Gámez-Bonilla treaty of October 7, 1894, 2 MEDIACIÓN DEL SECRETARIO
DE ESTADO DE LOS ESTADOS UNIDOS EN LA CONTROVERSIA DE LÍMITES ENTRE LA RE-
PÚBLICA DE NICARAGUA Y LA REPÚBLICA DE HONDURAS (1920) 202, at 204.

cedure to be followed by them in the nomination of the third arbitrator and read as follows:

In the event that the foreign Diplomatic Representative declines, the election of another shall be effectuated within the ten days following, and thus successively. When the members of the foreign Diplomatic Corps are exhausted, the election shall, by agreement of the *Comisiones* of Honduras and Nicaragua, fall upon any public personage, foreign or Central American; and if this agreement should not be possible, the controverted point or points shall be submitted to the decision of the Government of Spain, and in default thereof to whatever other [Government] of South America in which the chancelleries of both countries may agree.[3]

Article 10 reserved to the secretaries of foreign relations of the respective States the acceptance of the third arbitrator so named and to this end required the national arbitrators to communicate the fact of his selection to the secretaries.[4]

The boundary commission found itself unable to fix the boundary line from the "Portillo de Teotecacinte" to the Atlantic Ocean and, on August 29, 1904, dissolved itself in order that arbitration might take place.[5] The national arbitrators met in their first session on October 2, 1904, when they proceeded to the election of the third arbitrator. Stating that their action was in accordance with the Gámez-Bonilla treaty, an invitation to accept the office of third arbitrator was extended to the king of Spain. It was understood that if he should accept, there would belong to him exclusively the powers granted by the treaty necessary to reach a decision. The presidents of Honduras and Nicaragua were duly notified of the invitation to the king of Spain to act as arbitrator, and they in turn declared their acceptance of his nomination. On October 17, 1904, the Spanish minister notified the arbitrators and the two presidents by telegram of the acceptance of the post of arbitrator by the king of Spain.[6] Without raising any question of ir-

3 *Ibid.*
4 *Ibid.*, at 205.
5 Acts 5 and 8, *Actas de la Comisión Mixta de Limites,* printed in FONTECHA, EL ARBITRAJE ENTRE HONDURAS Y NICARAGUA, RECTIFICACIÓN DOCUMENTADA (1908) 162, 167.
6 *Op. cit. supra* note 2, at 228–231.

regularity in his appointment, the two governments presented to the arbitrator in Madrid their printed *Alegatos* and *Réplicas,* with supporting proofs.[7] On December 23, 1906, the award was pronounced.[8] Honduras accepted the award unconditionally.[9] The president of Nicaragua stated that the award was accepted, but that explanations of certain obscure points had been requested.[10] On March 23, 1911, after the fall of President Zelaya, the new Nicaraguan government sent a telegram to the president of Honduras that its first fraternal demonstration would be "the complete recognition of the arbitral award of the King of Spain." [11]

Yet on March 19, 1912, the Nicaraguan Minister of Foreign Relations addressed a note to Honduras stating that his government was unable to accept the validity of the award.[12] Towards arriving at a friendly settlement of the dispute which thereby arose, the United States offered its good offices,[13] which were accepted by the two countries.[14] In the mediation which took place before the Secretary of State, Nicaragua contended that the ten-year period fixed for the duration of the treaty of October 7, 1894, was to be determined from the date of its signature and that it had accordingly lapsed before the arbitration before the king of Spain had begun. Necessarily, it was asserted, his award was without the sanction of the treaty.[15] Nor should the participation by the executive in the proceedings before the king of Spain be deemed to bind Nicaragua. That participation was irregular, and just as the signature of the President of the United States did not impose on the United States

---

[7] MEMORANDUM DE HONDURAS, in LÍMITES ENTRE HONDURAS Y NICARAGUA, MEDIACIÓN DEL GOBIERNO DE ESTADOS UNIDOS (1921) 7–8.

[8] FONTECHA, *op. cit. supra* note 5, at 113.

[9] Message of President of Honduras to Congress, Jan. 1, 1907, *op. cit. supra* note 7, at 9.

[10] Message of President of Nicaragua to the National Assembly, Dec. 1, 1907, *ibid.;* see telegram of President Zelaya to President Bonilla, Dec. 25, 1906, LÍMITES ENTRE HONDURAS Y NICARAGUA, INCIDENTE SUSCITADA POR NICARAGUA (1912) 80.

[11] *Op. cit. supra* note 7, at 11.

[12] *Op. cit. supra* note 10, at 19, 25.

[13] Telegram from the Secretary of State to the American Minister at Tegucigalpa, Honduras, received Aug. 21, 1918, *op. cit. supra* note 7, at 4.

[14] *Ibid.,* 4–6.

[15] Memorandum of Counsel for Nicaragua, Mar. 1, 1920, EXPOSICIÓN DE NICARAGUA, 1 *op. cit. supra* note 2, at 199 *et sqq.*

the obligations of the Treaty of Versailles, so, it was contended, the executive's irregular action created no obligations upon Nicaragua.[16] At most, the proceedings reached the character of a mediation, not of a positive arbitration.[17]

The Nicaraguan position with regard to the expiration of the treaty was met on its merits by Judge Moore, counsellor for Honduras.[18] Yet even if Nicaragua were correct on this point, its subsequent participation in the arbitration is believed to have precluded it from thereafter raising any question as to the competency of the arbitrator to settle the dispute. It might raise objection to the terms of his judgment, but it could hardly question his authority to render *a* judgment, as occasion will later be taken to demonstrate.[19] In meeting Nicaragua's argument, Judge Moore pointed out that the exchange of ratifications took place on December 24, 1896, while the award was rendered on December 23, 1906, the last day of the ten-year term as computed from the exchange of ratifications. The supposed rule that by international law a provision fixing the duration of a treaty is to be determined from the date of its signature, in the absence of any contrary stipulation, was one which, with all deference, he was obliged to deny. An examination of the treaties of the United States showed that of those treaties which fixed a definite period for their duration, 125 counted the period from the exchange of ratifications as against about 10 that took the date of signature. The constant reiteration of this particular conventional stipulation was, he submitted, proof of the existence of a rule of international law to similar effect, rather than of its nonexistence, as urged by Nicaragua. The rule that a treaty is obligatory for the parties from the date of its signature meant that nothing should be done in opposition to its terms. It did not mean that its performance should be commenced on the

---

16 RÉPLICA DE NICARAGUA AL MEMORANDUM DE HONDURAS, 3 *op. cit. supra* note 2, at 48, 49.

17 *Ibid.*, 16, 50.

18 Opinion of John Bassett Moore, Counsellor for Honduras, Honduras-Nicaraguan Boundary Mediation before the Secretary of State of the United States, 1920–1921. 5 COLLECTED PAPERS OF JOHN BASSETT MOORE (1944) 118.

19 *Infra* sec. 52.

same date. The natural and logical thing to do was to count from the day on which the treaty came into force. A reading of the provisions of the Gámez-Bonilla treaty made it perfectly clear that it was intended to come into force from the date of the exchange of ratifications. Finally, he stated, the interpretation thus advanced was supported by the arbitration itself and by the contemporaneous construction of the treaty by the parties, which was the highest kind of evidence.[20]

24. SAME: EFFECT OF CONSTITUTIONAL LIMITATIONS.—An exception to the principle of tacit ratification noted in the preceding section has been advanced on the ground that if the agents of the State whose participation in the arbitral proceeding is relied upon do not have the constitutional power to renounce the invalidity of the *compromis,* no implied ratification can result from their acts.[1] The suggestion clearly has a bearing upon the question of the *time* when a State will be deemed to have renounced its right to contest an award under an invalid treaty; if its representatives are lacking in the constitutional power to enter into conventional arrangements on its behalf, it may well be that their participation in the proceedings alone would not be sufficient to constitute an implied ratification of a treaty otherwise invalid. But they are under the control of the State[2] and their continued participation after the circumstances of invalidity are known would seem to evidence a waiver by the State of the issue of invalidity.

On the more fundamental question of the right of a State under international law to raise objections of the constitutional incapacity of its representatives signing an arbitration agreement on its behalf as a basis for the invalidity of the treaty, it would seem that such a right is strictly circumscribed. It is true that under munici-

---

[20] *Op. cit. supra* note 18, at 169–181.

[1] Castberg, *L'Excès de pouvoir dans la justice internationale* (1931) 35 RECUEIL DES COURS 357, 363; Basdevant, Jèze, Politis, *Le Principes juridiques sur la compétence des juridictions internationales et, en particulier, des tribunaux arbitraux mixtes organisés par les traités de paix de Versailles, de Saint-Germain, de Trianon* (1927) 44 REV. DU DROIT PUB. S.P. 45, 50.

[2] BALASKO, CAUSES DE NULLITÉ DE LA SENTENCE ARBITRALE EN DROIT INTERNATIONAL PUBLIC (1938) 108; *cf.* Permanent Court of International Justice, Judgment of June 7, 1932, SER. A./B., No. 46, at 170, 209–210.

pal law limitations may exist upon the power of the executive to conclude treaties.[3] This circumstance is well recognized in international practice, and States may be expected to take reasonable care to inform themselves as to the powers of negotiators of a treaty.[4] Indeed, it is the rule to exhibit the full powers of the plenipotentiaries for verification before the signature of a treaty.[5] The step of ratification further affords a means for satisfying constitutional requirements and is a recognized procedural step in the creation of a valid convention.[6] The constitutional requirement of the consent and approval of the United States Senate to treaties may by now be said to have become so well-known to other States as to place them on notice with respect to the necessity of satisfying that step so far as treaties with the United States are concerned. But when a State has done everything in its power to bind itself internationally, it should not be able to plead its failure to satisfy its constitutional requirements as a reason for not being bound by the resulting treaty.[7] McNair points out that it is necessary "to distinguish in relation to a treaty between the perfection of the international obligation and the perfection of the municipal means to carry it out, because the former may exist without the latter." [8] It is his conclusion that:

. . . in concluding a treaty if one party produces an instrument "complete and regular on the face of it" (to borrow an expression from another department of law) though in fact constitutionally defective, the other party, if it is ignorant and reasonably ignorant of the defect, is entitled to assume

[3] 5 MOORE, DIG. 166–171; but cf. Missouri v. Holland, 252 U.S. 416, 433 (1920); 2 BUTLER, TREATY MAKING POWER OF THE UNITED STATES (1902) 350; KENT, COMMENTARIES (13th ed., 1884) 165, 166.

[4] HALL, INTERNATIONAL LAW (8th ed., 1924) 387–388; cf. McNair, Constitutional Limitations upon the Treaty-Making Power, Introduction to ARNOLD, TREATY-MAKING PROCEDURE (1933) 1, 16. See generally on the problem discussed in this section 2 HYDE, INTERNATIONAL LAW CHIEFLY AS INTERPRETED AND APPLIED BY THE UNITED STATES (2d ed., 1945) 1383 et sqq., particularly at 1409.

[5] SATOW, A GUIDE TO DIPLOMATIC PRACTICE (3d ed., 1932) 79. For cases where such powers were not possessed by the representatives, see infra this section, case of the Levantine Valley Tolls and the Panama–Costa Rica boundary dispute.

[6] HALL, op. cit. supra note 4, at 388.

[7] Fitzmaurice, Do Treaties Need Ratification? (1934) BRITISH YEARBOOK 113, 130.

[8] Supra note 4, at 6.

that the instrument is in order and to hold the former to the obligations of the treaty. If that view is correct then the repudiation of such a treaty constitutes an international wrong.[9]

Accordingly it would not be open for a State to refuse to execute an arbitral award in a boundary dispute ordering the relinquishment of territory held by it upon the ground that it was constitutionally incapable of doing so. Arbitration is considered a peculiarly appropriate method for the determination of questions of disputed territories. The losing State in such an arbitration could not avoid the force of the decision by urging its incapacity to consent.[10]

East Griqualand Arbitration.—In this connection, the position taken by the South African Republic in the case involving the ownership of the diamond deposits of East Griqualand seems clearly erroneous. A dispute of some standing had existed between the Boer South African Republic and the South African tribes of Bechuanaland and East Griqualand as to the title to certain territory, which became more pronounced upon the discovery of diamond deposits upon a portion of it. An agreement was finally signed on March 1, 1871, between Pretorius, as president of the Republic, and the chiefs of the tribes in question providing for the submission of the dispute to a joint commission with final review, in case of disagreement, by an arbitrator whose award they agreed "to execute faithfully." The ensuing award gave over almost the entire disputed territory to the tribes.[11] The South African Republic thereafter officially protested against the decision upon the ground that President Pretorius did not have the constitutional authority to sign merely by himself the agreement of March 1, 1871, and, consequently, that the proceedings which followed were null and void. Sir Henry Barkly, governor of Cape Colony, correctly replied that

[9] *Ibid.*

[10] Opinion of John Bassett Moore, Counsellor for Honduras, Honduras-Nicaragua Boundary Mediation before the Secretary of State of the United States, 1920–1921. 5 COLLECTED PAPERS OF JOHN BASSETT MOORE (1944) 128; see 2 HYDE, *op. cit. supra* note 4, at 1400.

[11] 2 LAPRADELLE ET POLITIS, RECUEIL DES ARBITRAGES INTERNATIONAUX (1905) 676, 685, 687, 691.

no consideration need be taken of an internal conflict in the Republic between the executive and the legislative powers and that the authority of the award should be respected. There the matter seems to have rested. Apart from the question of the power of the executive to enter into treaty arrangements without legislative participation, it may well be presumed that he has the power to settle disputes with foreign States or bodies by arbitration or by any other appropriate pacific method.[12]

Case of the Levantine Valley Tolls.[13]—On the other hand, it is exceedingly questionable whether it can fairly be presumed that the deputies of the Canton of Tessin at the federal Diet of Switzerland possessed an authority which would have rendered valid their agreement with the representatives of the Canton of Uri to submit to arbitration a dispute existing between the two cantons concerning their respective shares of the tolls collected in the Levantine Valley. The making of the agreement was in contravention of the express instructions communicated to them by the Council of State of Tessin. When the award of August 15, 1815, was rendered, wholly sustaining the claims of the Canton of Uri, the Council of State was taken by surprise by the unforeseen decision. The council accordingly took the position that the award had no validity, since it was rendered under a *compromis* which the representatives of one of the parties did not have the authority to conclude. New negotiations were thereafter entered into, resulting finally, in 1846, in the settlement of the dispute by the payment of a lump sum to the Canton of Uri.

Panama–Costa Rica Boundary Dispute.—It is, of course, entirely proper for a government to refuse to enter into certain conventional stipulations upon the ground that it is constitutionally incapacitated from doing so. In the negotiations preceding the convention of March 17, 1910, whereby Panama and Costa Rica submitted to

12 In his doctrinal note on the case, Westlake states his opinion to be that President Pretorius had exceeded his powers in signing the agreement, that his act was void and, therefore, that the decision did not have obligatory force for his country, *ibid.*, 700, 705.
13 1 *ibid.*, 269.

arbitration the question of what boundary between them was "under and most in accordance with the correct interpretation and true intention" of the award of President Loubet of France of September 11, 1900,[14] Panama restricted the powers of its representative to the strict acceptance by the contracting parties of the Loubet award as a preliminary basis of discussion and further imposed upon him certain special instructions.[15] When Secretary of State Knox expressed surprise at this action, the Minister for Foreign Affairs of Panama replied that the powers delegated were the most ample that the executive could give in view of the constitution, national laws, and permanent interests of Panama.[16] Its position was later reaffirmed in the words: "My Government is constitutionally unable, even were it disposed, to consent to the annulment of the Loubet award and the resubmission of the whole question to a new arbitrator." [17] Though such a position could properly be taken with reference to the future creation of conventional obligations, its validity is questionable as a defense to the action of Costa Rica in seeking redress in regard to certain disposals of territory made by President Loubet which it conceived to lack legal authority.[18]

25. POWER OF A TRIBUNAL TO DECIDE QUESTIONS OF ITS OWN JURISDICTION.—The competence of an arbitral tribunal to decide questions of its own jurisdiction is unquestionably firmly established as a principle of international arbitral law. Precedent [1] and the views of writers [2] are uniformly to this effect. The power to decide

[14] (1910) FOR. REL. U.S. 820.

[15] Secretary of State Knox to Dr. Porras, Feb. 2, 1910, *ibid.*, 804, 805.

[16] Minister for Foreign Affairs Lewis to Chargé Weitzel, Feb. 5, 1910, *ibid.*, 806.

[17] Dr. Porras to Secretary of State Knox, Feb. 20, 1910, *ibid.*, 808.

[18] *Infra* sec. 34. For other pertinent cases see McNair, *supra* note 4.

[1] Advisory Opinion No. 16 (August 28, 1928), Permanent Court of International Justice, SER. B., 20; see Hargous (U.S.) v. Mexico (1839), 2 MOORE, INT. ARB. (1898) 1267; Flutie Cases (U.S.) v. Venezuela (1903), RALSTON'S REPORT (1904) 38, 41; Rudloff (U.S.) v. Venezuela (1903) *ibid.* 182, 183, 192; statement of Secretary of State Webster, Jan. 21, 1842, regarding the claim of the *Topaz*, 2 MOORE, INT. ARB. 1242; Secretary of State Evarts to the Spanish Minister, Mar. 4, 1880, 3 MOORE, INT. ARB. 2599; 7 MOORE, DIG. 33–35; the *Betsey infra* this section. Holdings to this effect are also implied in the innumerable cases in which jurisdictional objections have been raised by one of the parties and considered by the tribunal.

[2] *Monographs:* BALASKO, CAUSES DE NULLITÉ DE LA SENTENCE ARBITRALE EN DROIT INTERNATIONAL PUBLIC (1938) 185; Castberg, *L'Excès de pouvoir dans la justice*

whether contemplated action lies within the scope of the authority granted to it, is a reasonable and necessary one to the effective functioning of any tribunal. Thus, we find the Hague Convention of 1907 providing in part that: "The tribunal is authorized to declare its competence in interpreting the *compromis*." [3] The Statute of the Permanent Court of International Justice provides that: "In the event of a dispute as to whether the Court has jurisdiction, the matter shall be settled by the decision of the Court." [4]

The case of the *Betsey* [5] before the Mixed Commission under Article 7 of the Jay Treaty is one of the earliest and most notable instances in which the power of an international commission to decide questions of its own jurisdiction was upheld. A difference of opinion arose between the commissioners upon the question whether the decisions of the Lords Commissioners of Appeal in Prize Cases affirming the condemnatory sentences of the lower English prize courts must be regarded in all respects as final and conclusive. The two British commissioners withdrew, contending that the commission was not competent to decide on its own jurisdiction. The two American commissioners, Gore and Pinkney, an-

---

internationale (1931) 35 RECUEIL DES COURS 426, 432; LAMMASCH, DIE RECHTSKRAFT INTERNATIONALER SCHIEDSSPRÜCHE (1913) 70; MÉRIGNHAC, TRAITÉ THEORIQUE ET PRATIQUE DE L'ARBITRAGE INTERNATIONAL (1895) 254; GUERMANOFF, L'EXCÈS DE POUVOIR DE L'ARBITRE (1929) 16; POLITIS, LA JUSTICE INTERNATIONALE (1924) 78; STOYKOVITCH, DE L'AUTORITÉ DE LA SENTENCE ARBITRALE EN DROIT INTERNATIONAL PUBLIC (1924) 55; *Treatises:* BLUNTSCHLI, LE DROIT INTERNATIONAL CODIFIÉ (Lardy trans., 1895) 280; 3 CALVO, LE DROIT INTERNATIONAL (5th ed., 1896) 481; 2 FIORE, NOUVEAU DROIT INTERNATIONAL PUBLIC (Antoine trans., 1885) 641; 6 PRADIER-FODÉRÉ, TRAITÉ DE DROIT INTERNATIONAL PUBLIC (1894) 421; but see BONFILS, MANUEL DE DROIT INTERNATIONAL PUBLIC (2d ed., 1898) 485. *Rules adopted by the Hague Conferences and other sources:* Article 73, Convention for the Pacific Settlement of International Disputes of 1907, 1 PROCEEDINGS OF THE HAGUE PEACE CONFERENCES, CONFERENCE OF 1907 (Carnegie trans., 1920) 611; Article 14, *projet* of the Institute of 1875 (1877) ANNUAIRE 129, 130; Goldschmidt, *Projet de règlement pour tribunaux arbitraux internationaux, présenté à l'Institut de Droit International* (Session de Genève, 1874) (1874) 6 REV. DE DROIT INT. L.C. 440 (Section 18); Auer, *The Competency of Mixed Tribunals* (1928) 13 TRANSACTIONS OF THE GROTIUS SOCIETY xxvii.

[3] Art. 73, SCOTT, REPORTS TO THE HAGUE CONFERENCES OF 1899 AND 1907 (1917) 305. This was Art. 48 in the 1899 Convention, *ibid.*, 40.

[4] Art. 36, STATUTE AND RULES OF COURT (1936) 21.

[5] Mixed Commission under Article 7 of the treaty of November 19, 1794, between the United States and Great Britain, 4 MOORE, INT. ADJ. (1931) 81, 179; 1 LA-PRADELLE ET POLITIS, RECUEIL DES ARBITRAGES INTERNATIONAUX (1905) 51.

swered this contention in written opinions. The fifth commissioner concurred in their views. Yet it was not until the British government failed to sustain the views of their commissioners, Lord Chancellor Loughborough remarking "that the doubt respecting the authority of the commissioners to settle their own jurisdiction, was absurd; and that they must necessarily decide upon cases being within, or without, their competency," [6] that proceedings were resumed. Said Commissioner Gore in his opinion:

> A power to decide whether a claim preferred to this board is within its jurisdiction, appears to me inherent in its very constitution, and indispensably necessary to the discharge of its duties. . . .
> To decide on the justice of the claim it is absolutely necessary to decide whether it is a case described in the article. It is the first quality to be sought for in the examination.[7]

The impossibility of any other rule is aptly put in the statement: "To say that the international judge cannot decide upon the exception of lack of jurisdiction is to maintain, in effect, the thesis that each time this contention is presented, he must admit it." [8]

In the *Rio Grande* case, the British and American Claims Tribunal noted that "there is in this and every legal Tribunal a power, and indeed a duty, to entertain, and, in proper cases, to raise for themselves, preliminary points going to their jurisdiction to entertain the claim." [9]

The legal process involved is set forth by the Mixed Claims Commission, United States and Germany, with some detail.

[6] 4 MOORE, INT. ADJ. 85.
[7] *Ibid.*, 183, 186.
[8] Doctrinal note, 1 LAPRADELLE ET POLITIS, *op. cit. supra* note 5, at 86, 104–105. See also Report to the Conference on Draft Convention for the Pacific Settlement of International Disputes, PROCEEDINGS OF THE HAGUE PEACE CONFERENCES, CONFERENCE OF 1899 (Carnegie trans., 1920) 106, 147: "Not to accept this view would be to place the tribunal in the condition of a court incapable of acting, and obliged to divest itself of jurisdiction of the controversy every time that it might please one of the parties to maintain, even against the evidence, that the tribunal could not take cognizance of such a question."
[9] Rio Grande Irrigation and Land Co., Ltd. (Great Britain) v. United States (1910), AMERICAN AND BRITISH CLAIMS ARBITRATION UNDER THE SPECIAL AGREEMENT OF AUGUST 18, 1910, REPORT OF FRED K. NIELSEN (1926) 336, 342.

. . . at the threshold of the consideration of each claim is presented the question of jurisdiction, which obviously the Commission must determine preliminarily to fixing the amount of Germany's financial obligations, if any, in each case.

When the allegations in a petition or memorial presented by the United States bring a claim within the terms of the Treaty, the jurisdiction of the Commission attaches. If these allegations are controverted in whole or in part by Germany, the issue thus made must be decided by the Commission. Should the Commission so decide such issue that the claim does not fall within the terms of the Treaty, it will be dismissed for lack of jurisdiction. But if such issue be so decided that the claim does fall within the terms of the Treaty, then the Commission will prescribe the measure of damages, apply such measure to the facts in the particular case as the Commission may find them, and fix the financial obligation of Germany therein. The Commission's task is to apply the terms of the Treaty of Berlin to each case presented, decide those which it holds are within its jurisdiction, and dismiss all others.[10]

In Advisory Opinion No. 16 the Permanent Court of International Justice affirmed "the principle that, as a general rule, any body possessing jurisdictional powers had the right in the first place itself to determine the extent of its jurisdiction." [11] The Convention for the Exchange of Greek and Turkish Populations of January 30, 1923, established a Mixed Commission the duties of which were to supervise the emigration provided for in the convention and to carry out the liquidation of certain property. Further powers were entrusted to it by a Declaration of July 24, 1923, and by the Agreement of December 1, 1926, between Greece and Turkey. A Final Protocol was annexed to the last-mentioned agreement, Article 4 of which provided that:

Any questions of principle of importance which may arise in the Mixed Commission in connection with the new duties entrusted to it by the Agreement signed this day and which, when that Agreement was concluded, it was not already discharging in virtue of previous instruments defining its

[10] Administrative Decision No. II (1922), DECISIONS AND OPINIONS, MIXED CLAIMS COMMISSION, UNITED STATES AND GERMANY (1925) 6, 7.
[11] Permanent Court of International Justice. Advisory Opinion No. 16 (August 28, 1928) SER. B., 20.

powers, shall be submitted to the President of the Greco-Turkish Arbitral Tribunal sitting at Constantinople for arbitration. The arbitrator's awards shall be binding.

A dispute arose in the commission as to the wording of certain communications. The Greek members suggested that it be referred to arbitration. The president thereupon asked the commission to decide whether the dispute constituted a principle of some importance concerning its new duties so as to be within the Final Protocol. To this proposal the Greek members objected that only the two States were entitled to appeal to the arbitrator and that the Greek government had already referred the matter to him. The Turkish members contended that a decision of the Mixed Commission was a prerequisite to a reference to the arbitrator.

The matter was brought to the Permanent Court of International Justice by means of a request for an advisory opinion made by the Council of the League. The Court sustained the Turkish contention and held that it was for the Mixed Commission alone to determine whether the conditions required by Article 4 for a submission to the arbitrator were fulfilled. The Court remarked that although the article contained no express provision governing by whom or when the questions with which the instrument dealt were to be referred to the arbitrator, the power should be deemed to rest with the Mixed Commission itself. Article 4 contemplated only questions arising in the course of the commission's deliberations and, "that being so, it is clear—having regard amongst other things to the principle that, as a general rule, any body possessing jurisdictional powers has the right in the first place itself to determine the extent of its jurisdiction—that questions affecting the jurisdiction of the Mixed Commission must be settled by the Commission itself without action by any other body being necessary." [12]

26. SIGNIFICANCE OF THE TERM "JURISDICTION."—The *compromis* being the source of the tribunal's powers, it is the *compromis* which must be primarily examined in determining whether the tribunal is competent to decide both in respect of the parties (*ratione personae*)

[12] *Ibid.*

and of the subject matter (ratione materiae).[1] Moreover, the com-promis often lays down the rules to govern the tribunal in conduct-ing its hearings and in reaching its decisions. Infractions of these rules may also raise jurisdictional questions in the broad sense of the term.

The term "competence" has been said to signify the capacity of a tribunal to take cognizance of a particular case.[2] The solution of a question of competence in this sense presents almost no prob-lems when the tribunal is expressly charged with the designation of one or more specific disputes. In contrast, the term "jurisdiction" has been said to relate to the capacity of the tribunal generally to decide cases brought before it by the States by which it was consti-tuted.[3] Thus Morelli[4] states that with the creation of the Perma-nent Court of International Justice one could for the first time speak of jurisdiction.

It is true that jurisdictional questions, using that term in its broadest meaning as relating to the scope of the powers of the tri-bunal under its compromis, will be more likely to arise when the tribunal is charged with the decision of numerous cases or claims which are described as a class in general terms. The compromis will in such a case include certain criteria which the tribunal is required to consider in determining whether or not a particular case happens to fall within its jurisdiction. Thus, it is said that: "It is the nature and not the justice of the claim that determines jurisdiction."[5] The distinction between the preliminary judgment on the issue of jurisdiction to consider the case and the decision

---

[1] RALSTON, LAW AND PROCEDURE OF INTERNATIONAL TRIBUNALS (1926) 37, 39; HUDSON, INTERNATIONAL TRIBUNALS (1944) 67.

[2] Cf. BALASKO, CAUSES DE NULLITÉ DE LA SENTENCE ARBITRALE EN DROIT INTERNA-TIONAL PUBLIC (1938) 139.

[3] Ibid.; cf. Bruns, Opinion in Hungarian Optants Case, 2 SOME OPINIONS, ARTICLES AND REPORTS BEARING UPON THE TREATY OF TRIANON AND THE CLAIMS OF THE HUNGARIAN NATIONALS WITH REGARD TO THEIR LANDS IN TRANSYLVANIA 147, 152.

[4] Morelli, La Théorie générale du procès international (1937) 61 RECUEIL DES COURS 312.

[5] Opinion of M. Joseph Barthélémy (Hungarian Optants case), 1 op. cit. supra note 3, at 105, 106. See also Joint Opinion of Sir Henry Slesser and Mr. Ralph Sutton, Hungarian Interests in Roumania, 2 ibid., 3, 4; Opinion of Professor Edwin M. Borchard, ibid., 23, 33–36.

of the case on the merits, and the necessity of not prejudging the latter when considering the former, was recognized by the Permanent Court of International Justice in Judgment No. 6.[6]

Unlike municipal courts, however, jurisdictional questions may present themselves in what would seem to be the decision on the merits.[7] For in international law jurisdiction is fundamentally "the power of a tribunal to determine a case conformably to the law creating the tribunal."[8] The *compromis* constitutes the primary source of that law, and it may circumscribe the powers of the tribunal with respect to the ascertainment of the law applicable to the case as well as with respect to the preliminary issue of whether the case itself is within the tribunal's power to decide. Thus, the treaty of February 2, 1897, providing for the arbitration of the boundary between British Guiana and Venezuela, fixed for the arbitrators a fifty-year period of prescription in the ascertainment of title.[9] The rules of decision thus laid down occupy somewhat the relation of legislation to common law in Anglo-American jurisprudence. An international arbitral tribunal would, as a matter of custom and practice, be compelled to adopt international law as the basis for its decision of a case, even in the absence of its designation as such in the *compromis*.[10] If, however, the *compromis* decreed rules for decision which varied from customary international law, the tribunal would be constrained to follow them just as a munici-

[6] PUBLICATIONS, SER. A., No. 6, pp. 15–16.

[7] *Cf.* Castberg, *La Compétence des tribunaux internationaux* (1925, 3d ser.) 6 REV. DE DROIT INT. L.C. 310, 342, 343.

[8] See Blair (U.S.) v. Mexico (1923), OPINIONS OF COMMISSIONERS, GENERAL CLAIMS COMMISSION, UNITED STATES AND MEXICO (1929) 107, 108 (Dissenting opinion of Commissioner Nielsen).

[9] 1 MOORE, DIG. 297.

[10] *Cf.* Judge Moore's statement that "as one to whose lot it has fallen actually to examine the work of international arbitrators, from the earliest times to the latest, I am prepared to pronounce unjustified the invidious imputation to them of a disposition to substitute diplomatic compromises for conclusions based on law and justice," *Specific Agencies for the Proper Conduct of International Relations;* 5 COLLECTED PAPERS OF JOHN BASSETT MOORE (1944) 308; Professor Borchard is of a similar view: "A somewhat exhaustive analysis of the hundreds of arbitrations to be found in Mr. Moore's monumental work and in repositories like Ralston and La Fontaine and other works, has convinced me that principles of law are constantly and almost uniformly applied by international tribunals of arbitration." *Strength and Weakness of the New International Court* (1922) 4 ILL. L.Q. 67, 68.

pal court would be required to apply legislation as superior to the common law. The international tribunal, however, would lack power or jurisdiction to do otherwise.[11] Consequently, even after it has disposed favorably of the preliminary question of jurisdiction, it may be confronted with further jurisdictional questions in disposing of a case.

27. DEPARTURE FROM TERMS OF SUBMISSION: LACK OF JURISDICTION (INCOMPÉTENCE) AND EXCESS OF JURISDICTION (EXCÈS DE POUVOIR).— If the international tribunal is a body of limited jurisdiction, its powers being derived from and limited by the *compromis,* the problem arises concerning the consequences of its failure to observe the rules of its charter. Will such acts be null and void?

Most writers have agreed that an arbitral award is null in the measure that the tribunal has manifestly and in a substantial manner passed beyond the terms of submission, express or implied. The Institute of International Law, in its *projet* of 1875, states that an award may be null in case of an "excès de pouvoir" (excess of jurisdiction).[1] The meaning which it intended to attribute to this term may be fairly held to be expressed in the rule of the *projet* of Goldschmidt, upon which the *projet* of the Institute was founded, that an arbitral award could be attacked "if the tribunal has exceeded the bounds of jurisdiction which the *compromis* gave it."[2] Bidau states: "The arbitrators may not, without executing a void act, exceed the limits indicated by the parties."[3] Bluntschli holds that an award may be considered null to the extent to which the arbitral tribunal has exceeded its powers.[4] Bonfils,[5] Fauchille,[6] and Genet[7]

---

[11] *Cf.* Commissioner Nielsen's dissent in International Fisheries Company (U.S.) v. Mexico (1923), *op. cit. supra* note 8 (1931) 207, 225 discussing distinction between jurisdictional issue and decision on the merits in Calvo clause cases.

[1] (1877) ANNUAIRE 133. For similar use of term see BISHOP, INTERNATIONAL ARBITRAL PROCEDURE (1930) 242.

[2] Goldschmidt, *Projet de règlement pour tribunaux arbitraux internationaux* (1874) 6 REV. DE DROIT INT. L.C. 447 (Section 32 (6)).

[3] 2 BIDAU, DERECHO INTERNACIONAL PÚBLICO (4th ed., 1924) 21.

[4] BLUNTSCHLI, LE DROIT INTERNATIONAL CODIFIÉ (Lardy trans., 1895) 281.

[5] BONFILS, MANUEL DE DROIT INTERNATIONAL PUBLIC (1898) 488.

[6] 1 FAUCHILLE, TRAITÉ DE DROIT INTERNATIONAL PUBLIC (1926) Part IV, Book I, at 552.

[7] GENET, TRAITÉ DE DIPLOMATIE ET DE DROIT DIPLOMATIQUE (1932) 587.

state that the award is not obligatory if the arbitrators have decided *ultra petita*. This defect is defined by Planas Suárez [8] and Ulloa [9] to be the exceeding of the powers fixed by the *compromis* or the decision of matters not submitted to the arbitrators. Bry,[10] Bulmerincq,[11] and Rouard de Card [12] speak of the violation of the arbitral agreement as producing nullity. Calvo [13] states that a party may refuse to accept and to execute an award when the arbitrators have decided without the terms of the *compromis*. Carnazza-Amari [14] states that a decision is null when the arbitral tribunal has exceeded the powers granted by the act by which it was constituted and has determined questions that are not within its competence. In the view of Fiore, the *compromis* establishes the limits of the powers attributed to the arbitrators,[15] and their award may, therefore, he proved to be null when they have decided upon points not indicated in the *compromis*.[16] Audry,[17] Heffter,[18] Le Fur,[19] Pradier-Fodéré,[20] and Rivier [21] likewise look to the disregard by the arbitrators of the prescriptions of the *compromis* as effecting nullity. Oppenheim [22] uses the phrase "not followed their instructions" to indicate one of the conditions under which an award by arbitrators would have no binding force. Hall [23] states that "an arbitral decision may be disregarded . . . when the tribunal has clearly exceeded the powers given to it by the instrument of submission." To similar effect are

[8] 1 PLANAS SUÁREZ, TRATADO DE DERECHO INTERNACIONAL PÚBLICO (1916) 440.

[9] 2 ULLOA, DERECHO INTERNACIONAL PÚBLICO (1929) 202.

[10] BRY, PRÉCIS ÉLÉMENTAIRE DE DROIT INTERNATIONAL PUBLIC (6th ed., 1910) 491.

[11] BULMERINCQ, VÖLKERRECHT (1887) 352.

[12] ROUARD DE CARD, DROIT INTERNATIONAL; L'ARBITRAGE INTERNATIONAL DANS LE PASSÉ, LE PRÉSENT ET L'AVENIR (1877) 53.

[13] 3 CALVO, LE DROIT INTERNATIONAL (5th ed., 1896) 485.

[14] 2 CARNAZZA-AMARI, TRAITÉ DE DROIT INTERNATIONAL PUBLIC (1862) 564.

[15] 2 FIORE, NOUVEAU DROIT INTERNATIONAL PUBLIC (Antoine trans., 1885) 630.

[16] *Ibid.*, 642.

[17] AUDRY, LA REVISION DE LA SENTENCE ARBITRALE (1914) 44.

[18] HEFFTER, DAS EUROPÄISCHE VÖLKERRECHT DER GEGENWART (8th ed., GEFFCKEN, 1888) 233.

[19] LE FUR, PRÉCIS DE DROIT INTERNATIONAL PUBLIC (1937) 481.

[20] 6 PRADIER-FODÉRÉ, TRAITÉ DE DROIT INTERNATIONAL PUBLIC (1894) 433.

[21] 2 RIVIER, PRINCIPES DU DROIT DES GENS (1896) 185.

[22] 2 OPPENHEIM, INTERNATIONAL LAW (4th ed., 1928) 28.

[23] HALL, A TREATISE ON INTERNATIONAL LAW (8th ed., 1924) 420.

Taylor[24] and Twiss.[25] Hyde[26] declares that "excessive action on the part of an arbitral tribunal may be due to a misconstruction of its powers, manifest in the reasons given in the award." Vattel was probably the first to formulate the concept now under discussion. He states that "in the case of a vague and indefinite agreement" it may happen "that the arbitrators will exceed their powers and decide points which have not really been submitted to them. Having been appointed to decide what satisfaction a State owes for an offense, they condemn it to become subject to the offended State. Clearly the offending State never gave them such extensive power, and their absurd sentence is in no way binding upon it."[27]

Nys[28] states that an excess of jurisdiction occurs when the arbitrators exceed the mission given them. Lammasch has a broader definition. He considers that within the concept of excess of jurisdiction is a decision by the arbitrator on matters not entrusted to him, a failure to apply the rules of law prescribed, an inobservance of procedural rules such as rendering a decision before the submission of the required briefs or failure to hear the parties, or failure to give reasons as required by the *compromis*.[29] Balasko[30] considers excess of jurisdiction (*excès de pouvoir*) occurs in a failure to observe the jurisdictional limits of the tribunal as defined by the parties. Castberg apparently distinguishes between excess of competence and excess of jurisdiction. Action falling within the former

---

[24] TAYLOR, INTERNATIONAL LAW (1901) 379: "the arbitral decision or award may be honorably disregarded when the tribunal has exceeded the powers conferred upon it by the articles of submission."

[25] 2 TWISS, THE LAW OF NATIONS (2d ed., 1875) 8: "a clear departure from the terms of reference."

[26] 2 HYDE, INTERNATIONAL LAW CHIEFLY AS INTERPRETED AND APPLIED BY THE UNITED STATES (2d ed., 1945) 1637.

[27] 2 VATTEL, LE DROIT DES GENS (ed. 1758, Fenwick trans., 1916) Sec. 329, p. 224. The entire passage is discussed *infra* sec. 57.

[28] Nys, *La Revision de la sentence arbitrale* (1910, 2d ser.) 12 REV. DE DROIT INT. L.C. 621.

[29] LAMMASCH, DIE RECHTSKRAFT INTERNATIONALER SCHIEDSSPRÜCHE (1913) 167, 168.

[30] BALASKO, CAUSES DE NULLITÉ DE LA SENTENCE ARBITRALE EN DROIT INTERNATIONAL PUBLIC (1938) 153.

category is considered to create no obligation upon the parties,[31] while excess of jurisdiction is used by him in the sense of a violation of law on the part of a tribunal, without regard to whether in the particular case it is at the same time such a departure as not to bind the parties.[32] Schätzel classifies excess of jurisdiction as being either material or formal. The first involves a real exceeding of its jurisdiction by a court by mistakenly defining its competence and expressing its opinion upon facts not submitted to its judgment,[33] while the second involves errors resulting from the court's failure to heed the rules of procedure laid down for it.[34] Stoykovitch [35] points out that an excess of power may occur as to the object, that is, in deciding what was not submitted, and as to the extent of the powers, that is, in misapplying the rules of the *compromis.*

On the whole, however, little juridical purpose is believed to be served by the introduction of subcategories, such as lack of jurisdiction (*incompétence*) and excess of jurisdiction (*excès de pouvoir*), in the determination of jurisdictional questions in the case of the international tribunal. Terms such as these may have significance and usefulness in domestic legal systems, when we are concerned with an established, organized judicial system and legal process. But they lose their usefulness when transplanted to the international judicial process, and they tend to become distinctions without mean-

---

[31] Castberg, *La Compétence des tribunaux internationaux* (1925, 3d ser.) 6 REV. DE DROIT INT. L.C. 310, 342, 343: "Primarily, the competence of the tribunal may signify its power or its capacity to bind the parties by its decision. If the tribunal exceeds its competence in this sense, its decision does not bind the parties. That maxim is in fact tautological. That the tribunal has exceeded its competence signifies only that it has proceeded outside of the sphere where it possesses the power to compel the parties.

". . . It may also signify the *law* of the tribunal, comprising the totality of the measures which it is justified to take. Any action on the part of the tribunal which imports a violation of its obligations could be criticized as an excess of its 'competence' in this latter sense."

[32] Castberg, *L'Excès de pouvoir dans la justice internationale* (1931) 35 RECUEIL DES COURS 361.

[33] SCHÄTZEL, RECHTSKRAFT UND ANFECHTUNG VON ENTSCHEIDUNGEN INTERNATIONALER GERICHTE, 6 FRANKFURTER ABHANDLUNGEN ZUM KRIEGSVERHÜTUNGSRECHT (1928) 57, 74.

[34] *Ibid.,* 57.

[35] STOYKOVITCH, DE L'AUTORITÉ DE LA SENTENCE ARBITRALE EN DROIT INTERNATIONAL PUBLIC (1924) 193.

ing.[36] Whether a tribunal lacks jurisdiction or exceeds its jurisdiction involves an analysis of the scope of its powers in the light of the provisions of its *compromis* and the principles of international law. That analysis is directed to the investigation of the single question of whether the tribunal in fact and in law possessed jurisdiction or authority to perform the questioned act. Solution of that question is in no wise aided by first classifying it as one involving "lack" or "excess" of jurisdiction. This is not to place all questions involving absence of jurisdiction in a rigid, logical formula; rather, the nature of each must be examined in the light of its particular circumstances and of the principles made the subject of the present work. Not all departures from the terms of the *compromis* will lead to nullity. It is a matter of the substantial character of the departure, the prejudice involved, the importance of the departure from the standpoint of the practice of tribunals, and whether the injured party has by failure to object and subsequent participation in the conduct of the arbitration waived its right to contest validity.

Nevertheless, since the arbitral agreement or *compromis* constitutes the primary source of the tribunal's powers, it is of decisive importance in determining whether in any respect the tribunal has exceeded those powers. In each case, to ascertain whether the tribunal's decision constitutes an obligation which the parties must fulfill, it is necessary to analyze its opinion in the light of the terms of the agreement and the action of the parties before it. In general, the award should confine itself to the question presented, should conform to the rules of decision expressly or impliedly established by the parties, and should be reached in a fair and impartial manner. In decisions involving jurisdictional questions the *compromis* will constitute the primary test of validity. Says Weiss,

It is in the *compromis*, in the *compromis* alone that the arbitrator possesses the right to adjudicate the dispute submitted to him. It is the *compromis*, chart of his temporary magistracy, which fixes the character and the

[36] Rundstein, *La Cour Permanente de Justice Internationale comme instance de recours* (1933) 43 RECUEIL DES COURS 90, at note 1, 95–96; Borel, *Les Voies de recours contre les sentences arbitrales* (1935) 52 *ibid.,* 37.

limits of the jurisdiction with which he is invested. Thus, if he exceeds the mandate which he has received, that jurisdiction vanishes, the decision which he pronounces under such conditions, having no legal basis, has neither validity nor obligatory force for the parties whose intentions he has ignored.[37]

The departure from the terms of submission should be clear to justify the disregarding of the decision. Claims of nullity should not captiously be raised. Writers who have given special study to the problem of nullity are agreed that the violation of the *compromis* should be so manifest as to be readily established.[38] In order that a tribunal's decision or a jurisdictional issue shall be considered null, it must, in general, be arbitrary, not merely doubtful or arguable.[39]

It may be noted that the term *excès de pouvoir* has a definite meaning in French internal law, and occasionally reflections of that meaning, as well as of the accompanying term *incompétence,* are in the background of their discussions of the international law phases of the problem of jurisdiction of tribunals. A large literature exists concerning *excès de pouvoir.*[40] From this standpoint the term may be defined as embodying those cases in which a court has exceeded the normal regular functions of any court *qua* court. Thus, if it attempts to enter upon the legislative or administrative domain, it commits an *excès de pouvoir.* A case of *incompétence,* however, oc-

---

[37] Weiss, *L'Arbitrage de 1909 entre la Bolivie et le Pérou* (1910) 17 REV. GEN. DE DROIT INT. PUB. 105, 118–119; see also in this relation ACREMENT, LA PROCÉDURE DANS LES ARBITRAGES INTERNATIONAUX (1905) 163; Fiore, *La Sentence arbitrale du président de la République Argentine dans le conflit de limites entre la Bolivie et le Pérou* (1910) 17 REV. GEN. DE DROIT INT. PUB. 225, 240, 241; GUERMANOFF, L'EXCÈS DE POUVOIR DE L'ARBITRE (1929) 10, 60; Hertz, *Essai sur le problème de la nullité* (1939, 3d ser.) 20 REV. DE DROIT INT. L.C. 458; MÉRIGNHAC, TRAITÉ THE-ORIQUE ET PRATIQUE DE L'ARBITRAGE INTERNATIONAL (1895) 313; POLITIS, LA JUSTICE INTERNATIONALE (1924) 91; HOIJER, LA SOLUTION PACIFIQUE DES LITIGES INTERNA-TIONAUX (1925) 270, 273; Pierantoni, *La Nullité d'un arbitrage international* (1898) 30 REV. DE DROIT INT. L.C. 445, 455; Scelle, *Une instance en revision devant la Cour de la Haye, l'affaire de la Orinoco Steamship Company* (1911) 18 REV. GEN. DE DROIT INT. PUB. 164, 187 *et sqq.*

[38] Castberg, *L'Excès de pouvoir dans la justice internationale* (1931) 35 RECUEIL DES COURS 443; Lapradelle, *L'Excès de pouvoir de l'arbitre* (1928) 2 REV. DE DROIT INT. 14; STOYKOVITCH, *op. cit. supra* note 35, at 194; Verdross, *L'Excès de pouvoir du juge arbitrale dans le droit international public* (1928, 3d ser.) 9 REV. DE DROIT INT. L.C. 225, 231.

[39] GUERMANOFF, *op. cit. supra* note 37, at 64.

[40] See KELLERSHOHN, DES EFFETS DE L'ANNULATION POUR EXCÈS DE POUVOIR (1915).

curs when a court takes cognizance of a matter properly belonging within the jurisdiction of another court.[41] Politis makes the following distinctions:

The notion of *excès de pouvoir* implies an activity of the authorities which, while vitiated by illegality, is produced wholly within their proper sphere. It is distinguished in this respect from usurpation of power which implies an activity exercised beyond the administrative sphere, for example an arrest or confiscation which only the judicial authorities may decide.

Taken in its largest sense, the term *excès de pouvoir* implies every violation of law and is confused with the term, sometimes employed, of abuse of power (*abus de pouvoir*). There is between them only one difference. An *excès de pouvoir* is applied to acts of a judicial nature, while abuse of power is applied to a material situation.[42]

Erich [43] states:

Incompétence means, notably, that one of the primary conditions of procedure is lacking, for example, if one of the parties was not duly cited, if the tribunal sat without the required number of members present, if the *compromis* had not been duly established, etc. On the other hand, *excès de pouvoir* signifies that the tribunal has gone beyond the limits of the task conferred upon it by the *compromis*. *Incompétence* always indicates a flagrant and conscious departure from the fundamental rules which determine the activity of the tribunal. A precise and practical distinction between the two terms is not easy to establish.

28. DECISIONS ON MATTERS OUTSIDE THE SCOPE OF THE COMPROMIS.— The simplest aspect of excess of jurisdiction is represented by a decision of a tribunal upon issues not within the scope of the *compromis*, though the solution of a question of this nature may be exceedingly complex in a particular case.[1] In each such case, the question of excess of jurisdiction will be determined by an analysis and comparison of the award in the light of the definition of the

---

[41] 2 BOITARD, LEÇONS DE PROCÉDURE CIVILE (13th ed., 1879) Section 768, pp. 136–137.

[42] Politis, *Le Problème des limitations de la souveraineté et la théorie de l'abus des droits dans les rapports internationaux* (1925) 6 RECUEIL DES COURS 5, 84.

[43] Erich, *Le Projet de conferer à la Cour Permanente de Justice Internationale des fonctions d'une instance de recours* (1931, 3d ser.) 12 REV. DE DROIT INT. L.C. 268, 276.

[1] *Infra* sec. 37.

dispute submitted for decision as laid down in the *compromis*. Thus, an arbitrator to whom has been submitted the task of determining which of two boundary lines is the true boundary between the litigating States cannot fix upon a third.[2] A tribunal created to adjudicate all disputes arising between the parties would seem to require a specific conferral of authority to enable it to order the parties to cease measures of mobilization when one of those disputes was leading to war.[3] An arbitrator cannot confer rights upon parties strangers to the arbitration,[4] nor can he prejudice the rights of such third parties.[5] Decisions upon matters collateral to the question submitted will have no binding force, though otherwise the judgment would be unaffected by such a departure.[6]

29. SAME: NORTHEASTERN BOUNDARY DISPUTE.—After attempts by negotiation had failed to fix the Northeastern boundary between the United States and Canada in accordance with the Treaty of Peace of 1783, it was agreed by the convention of September 29, 1827, to submit the dispute to the arbitration of some friendly sovereign. The king of The Netherlands was accordingly appointed arbitrator. To the end that "a just and sound decision" should be reached, he was empowered by Article VI of the convention to call for further evidence and information upon such points as he should desire. If he should find the topographical evidence insufficient, he was authorized to order the making of additional surveys.[1] By Article VII it was provided that "the decision of the Arbiter, when given, shall be taken as final and conclusive; and it shall be carried, without reserve, into immediate effect, by Commissioners appointed for that purpose by the contracting parties."[2]

Notwithstanding his broad powers, in his award of January 10, 1831, the arbitrator not only refrained from making a final judgment of a decisive character, but did so in part upon the ground that the arguments and proofs advanced could not "be considered as sufficiently preponderating to determine a preference in favor of

---

[2] *Infra* secs. 29, 32, 34, and 45.   [3] *Infra* sec. 35.
[4] *Infra* secs. 31 and 33.   [5] *Infra* sec. 38.
[6] *Infra* secs. 30 and 36.   [1] 1 MALLOY, TREATIES 646, 649.
[2] *Ibid.*

either one of the two lines" claimed by the two governments. He further declared that since "the nature of the difference and the vague and not sufficiently determinate stipulations of the Treaty of 1783, do not permit us to award either of those lines to one of the said Parties, without violating the principles of law and equity with regard to the other . . . it will be suitable to adopt" ³ a certain boundary duly described by him.

Two days after the award was announced the American minister at The Hague entered "a Protest against the Proceeding, as constituting a departure from the power delegated by the High Parties interested, in order that the rights and interests of The United States may not be supposed to be committed, by any presumed acquiescence on the part of their Representative near His Majesty the King of the Netherlands." ⁴

Since the award was stated to be of a purely mediatory character and accordingly possessed no binding force, the question of excess of jurisdiction may well be viewed as academic.⁵ The case has, however, so often been referred to upon this question that it merits further analysis. Clearly, by entering an opinion recommendatory in character when a definitive decision was demanded by the treaty, the arbitrator exceeded his powers.⁶ Though mediation may at the present time be undertaken by a government without the prior consent of the parties between whom a dispute exists,⁷ no private person has such a power, even though he be given the office of arbitrator. A judicial, not a political, solution is desired of him, and he may not arrogate to himself authority to propose any other. Nor does the circumstance that in the case under discussion the arbitra-

---

³ 1 MOORE, INT. ARB. 119, 133, 134.
⁴ Minister Preble to Baron Verstolk de Soelen, Jan. 12, 1831, 22 BRITISH AND FOREIGN STATE PAPERS (1833–1834) 772, 775.
⁵ Cf. Mr. Livingston to Mr. Bankhead, July 22, 1832, ibid., 788, 789; Renault, Une Nouvelle mission donée aux arbitres dans les litiges internationaux (1894) 1 REV. GEN. DE DROIT INT. PUB. 44, 45.
⁶ Cf. Doctrinal note by M. Asser, 1 LAPRADELLE ET POLITIS, RECUEIL DES ARBITRAGES INTERNATIONAUX (1905) 391, 397.
⁷ Art. 3, Hague Convention of 1899 for the Pacific Settlement of International Disputes, PROCEEDINGS OF THE HAGUE PEACE CONFERENCES, CONFERENCE OF 1899 (Carnegie trans., 1920) 236.

tor was a sovereign vary this conclusion. If he found it impossible, upon the basis of the proofs submitted, to fix the boundary, the obligation first rested upon him by Article 6 of the treaty to call for further evidence. If a legal decision should then prove impossible, the obligation rested upon him under customary law to pronounce a *non liquet*.[8]

It may be noted that the dispute was finally settled by the negotiation of the Webster-Ashburton treaty of August 9, 1842.[9]

30. SAME: AVES ISLAND CASE.—Though no charge of excess of jurisdiction was made by the parties, who apparently found in the award a satisfactory solution of the dispute between them, it is believed that the award of the queen of Spain as arbitrator in the *Aves Island* case was in part invalid for excess of jurisdiction.

Aves Island, situated about 600 miles from the coast of Venezuela, was occupied in 1854 by a colonel of the Venezuelan army in the name of Venezuela. Holland protested upon the ground that her sovereignty over the island had been established. For the settlement of the dispute thereby arising a convention was signed on August 5, 1857, in which it was agreed that "the question of the right of dominion and of sovereignty over the Island of Aves shall be submitted to the arbitration of a friendly power, previously chosen by common agreement."[1]

The queen of Spain was chosen arbitrator, and on June 30, 1865, she rendered her decision. It recited that the property (*la propriété*) of the island belonged to Venezuela, charged with the duty of indemnifying the Dutch subjects, who had there been accustomed to fish, if they were deprived of fishing privileges. The question submitted to the arbitrator concerned only the ownership of the island. Accordingly, in determining the wholly distinct question of whether a servitude existed, it would seem that the arbitrator committed an excess of jurisdiction.[2]

---

[8] Balasko, Causes de Nullité de la Sentence Arbitrale en Droit International Public (1938) 300; see *infra* sec. 46.

[9] 1 Malloy, Treaties 650.

[1] 2 Lapradelle et Politis, Recueil des Arbitrages Internationaux (1905) 408.

[2] *Ibid.*, 420; Balasko, Causes de Nullité de la Sentence Arbitrale en Droit International Public (1938) 290.

31. SAME: CERRUTI CASE.—The question whether an arbitrator, while nominally paying respect to the jurisdictional limitations of the *compromis,* can in the decretal part of his judgment require of the respondent government measures which would enure to the benefit of strangers to the arbitration and go beyond the dispute submitted to him was raised in the *Cerruti* case between Italy and Colombia.[1]

Cerruti, a native-born Italian, emigrated to Colombia in 1869, where he established his residence, married, and engaged in business. A copartnership *(societa en comandita)* under the name of E. Cerruti et Cie. was there formed by him with certain Colombian subjects.[2] In 1885 the local administrative authorities imprisoned him and confiscated his personal property and the entire property of his firm by reason of his alleged participation in rebellion. The Italian government interposed on his behalf. Attempt was made to settle the dispute by the processes of both mediation and arbitration in an agreement signed on May 24, 1886, but the arbitral commission lapsed without having reached a decision, principally because of the difficulty of determining whether an award should compensate Cerruti for his interest in the partnership.[3] Subsequent diplomatic negotiations likewise failed until a formula of agreement was reached in the protocol of Castellamare of August 18, 1894.[4] It was thereby agreed to invite the President of the United States to arbitrate the claims of Cerruti and upon his acceptance of the post of arbitrator to invest him with: "full power, authority, and jurisdiction to do and perform, and to cause to be done and performed, all things, without any limitation whatsoever, which in his judgment may be necessary or conducive to the attainment in a fair and equitable manner of the ends and purposes which this agreement is intended to secure." [5] It was this clause, paragraph 4, which later became the principal source of controversy as to the

---

[1] Lapradelle, *L'Arbitrage international en 1897* (Chronique Internationale) (1898) 10 REV. DU DROIT PUB. S.P. (Part 2) 523, 526.

[2] BUREAU, LE CONFLIT ITALO-COLOMBIEN (AFFAIRE CERRUTI) (1899) 5, 6.

[3] *Ibid.,* at 30 *et sqq.* For the report of the Mediator, dated Jan. 26, 1888, see (1912) 6 AM. J. INT. LAW 1003.

[4] (1895) FOR. REL. U.S., Part 2, 959.

[5] Par. 4, *ibid.*

validity of the arbitrator's decision. His duties were, first, to determine what claims among those advanced by Cerruti were proper for international adjudication and, secondly, what claims should be pursued before the territorial courts of Colombia. If any claims were held to be within the first category, he was "to declare the amount of indemnity, if any, which the claimant, Sig. E. Cerruti, be entitled to receive from the Government of Colombia through diplomatic action." In respect to the claims falling within the second class, he was enjoined to "take no further action" than to declare them to be of such a character.[6] A most detailed statement as to the finality of the award was made, as follows:

The two Governments solemnly bind themselves to abide by the decisions and awards of the arbitrator, which shall be final and conclusive and not subject either to discussion or appeal. And they further agree not to re-open negotiations or diplomatic discussions on any point or points which the arbitrator may decide or dispose of or which he may declare to have already been disposed of in conformity with public law; nor upon any claim or claims of Sig. E. Cerruti which the arbitrator may declare to have an internal and territorial character.[7]

The position of arbitrator was duly accepted by President Cleveland,[8] who, on March 2, 1897, rendered his award.[9] The award briefly stated that after the proofs had been examined, it was decided that the claims of Cerruti as an individual and for his interest in the firm of E. Cerruti et Cie. were proper claims for international adjudication, that the claim for personal damages was disallowed, as was also the claim for moneys expended in the prosecution of his case, but that the claims for losses and damages to his individual property and his interest in E. Cerruti et Cie. were allowed in the sum of 60,000 pounds sterling.

No protest against this portion of the award was entered by Colombia, and it appears clearly to have been in conformity with the *compromis*. Article 5 of the award proved to be the cause of

---

[6] Par. 5, *ibid.*
[7] Par. 8, *ibid.*
[8] Mr. Gresham to Mr. MacVeagh, Mar. 1, 1895, *ibid.*, 960.
[9] (1898) FOR. REL. U.S. 245.

ensuing controversy. By that article the property, real and personal, of Cerruti in Colombia which had been made the subject of the instant litigation, was decreed to belong to the government of Colombia, while in turn Colombia was required to "guarantee and protect Signor Ernesto Cerruti on account of the debts" of E. Cerruti et Cie. and save him from loss in any sums which he might have to expend to defend such claims. This further decree was declared to rest on the authority granted the arbitrator under paragraph 4 of the protocol.

Immediately thereafter, under notes of March 3 and May 1, 1897, the Colombian chargé d'affaires entered a protest against Article 5 of the award, while recognizing its validity in other respects.[10] That article was asserted to be invalid and outside the scope of submission of the protocol because it failed to conform thereto in the following specific respects: (1) It did not determine the amount which the claimant was entitled to receive through diplomatic action. (2) It not only failed to put an end to a subject of disagreement between the two governments, but provided a prolific source of disagreement between them. (3) It was no final disposition of any claim of Cerruti. (4) It imposed upon the government of Colombia an uncertain liability, the amount of which was not determined by the President as arbitrator. (5) It was a delegation to others of the authority of the President to determine the indemnity due. These others were, moreover, "to be ascertained by some other persons and tribunals, not named in the protocol nor specifically provided for in the award." [11] In response to the request, made in the second of these notes, that the award be reconsidered, the United States replied:

The President of the United States, whether he be the individual who acted as arbitrator or his successor in office, became, under any circumstances, *functus officio*, so far as the arbitration was concerned, upon the rendition of his award, and could not undertake to reopen the arbitration and reconsider the award under any just view of the powers conferred upon him as arbitrator by the protocol under which he acted. Should the

10 *Ibid.*, 246, 247.   11 *Ibid.*, 249.

parties to the arbitration invite the reconsideration of the award in question, in whole or part, or request its interpretation in any respect, that could only be accomplished by a new submission and arbitration.[12]

The award was finally complied with by Colombia when Italy sent a naval mission to enforce it. The claims of the creditors of E. Cerruti et Cie. were settled at 20 percent, with the concurrence of the Italian government and a large number of the creditors.[13] Nevertheless, it is generally agreed by commentators, including the Italian publicist Pierantoni,[14] that the award was null for excess of jurisdiction. Bureau, in his monograph on this case, indicates the reasons for which Article 5 of the award sought to protect Cerruti from liability for the debts of the partnership.[15] The firm was insolvent by reason of the confiscations of which it was a victim. So far as Cerruti was concerned, unless protected from the firm's creditors, an award would be illusory. So far as the creditors were concerned, they would gain the benefit of "an intervention strictly limited . . . to the defense of the rights of an Italian subject," whatever their nationality might be. Despite the suggestion so advanced by him, he insists that the arbitrator exceeded his powers in condemning Colombia to pay, even though indirectly, creditors of the firm who were necessarily strangers to the arbitration.

The award of President Cleveland does not seem to find support in the terms of the protocol. Paragraph 4 of the protocol seems primarily intended to confer on him the necessary authority to establish rules of procedure. In any event, it must be read in the light of the other paragraphs. Under them he was restricted to awarding an indemnity for the international claims, and, as to the remainder of the claims, was expressly prohibited from taking any other action than to segregate them from the international claims. In the proto-

[12] Secretary of State Sherman to the Colombian Minister, May 5, 1897, *ibid.*, 250, 251.

[13] Bureau, *op. cit. supra* note 2, at 123–127.

[14] Pierantoni, *La Nullité d'un arbitrage internationale* (1898) 30 Rev. de Droit Int. L.C. 459, 460; Bureau, *op. cit. supra* note 2, at 100, 101; but *cf.* Darras, *De certains dangers de l'arbitrage international; affaire Cerruti entre la Colombie et l'Italie* (1899) 6 Rev. Gen. de Droit Int. Pub. 533 (holding award void only for absence of reasoning).

[15] Bureau, *op. cit. supra* note 2, at 93, 96, 100–101.

col there appeared no express authorization for the arbitrator to order the respondent to take measures directly redounding to the benefit of third parties which were strangers to the arbitration. Only the claim of Cerruti was submitted. Such an express authorization would seem to be necessary, particularly in view of the rule of arbitral law that creditors have no standing before mixed claims commissions.[16]

The final incident in the history of the case may briefly be noted. One creditor, Mazza, refused to accede to this settlement and brought suit in the Italian courts for the debt owed him by the firm, where he recovered judgment. Whether the payment of this judgment by Cerruti together with legal expenses incurred in defending this and other suits should be repaid him by Colombia and other questions incident to the settlement of the award were submitted to another arbitration by a *compromis* of October 28, 1909. The tribunal held that the Mazza claim was one validly against the firm and that Colombia should accordingly reimburse Cerruti for the payment of the judgment. Since a number of the suits defended by Cerruti were not valid claims against the firm, the tribunal fixed a lump sum approximation of the proper legal expenses to be paid by Colombia.[17]

32. SAME: ARGENTINE-CHILEAN BOUNDARY DISPUTE.—An arbitrator charged with the duty of fixing one of two lines as the boundary between two States could hardly, without exceeding his jurisdiction, fix upon a third line as the definitive boundary. Yet, in effect, this was what was done by King Edward VII as arbitrator in the dispute between Argentina and Chile concerning the proper boundary between them under the terms of Article I of the treaty of July 23, 1881.[1] By that article the line of separation was for a certain distance fixed at the highest points of the Andean Range marking

[16] See Benner (U.S.) v. Spain (1871) 3 MOORE, INT. ARB. 2335; Mora & Arango (U.S.) v. Spain (1871) *ibid.*, 2336.

[17] (1912) 6 AM. J. INT. LAW 1018 (Award rendered July 6, 1911); *cf.* Hagerup, *Affaire Cerruti—sentence arbitrale du 6 juillet 1911* (1912) REV. GEN. DE DROIT INT. PUB. 268.

[1] (1901) 1 TRATADOS, CONVENCIONES, PROTOCOLES Y DEMÁS ACTOS INTERNACIONALES VIGENTES CELEBRADROS POR LA REPÚBLICA ARGENTINA 232.

the water-divide. In fixing the boundary it was found that in one district the summits of the Andes tended towards the Pacific Ocean, while the line of the water-divide went inland. Argentina consequently contended that the line of the summit conformed to the treaty, while Chile supported the opposite construction. It seems probable, however, that in making the treaty both governments had assumed that the two lines would coincide.[2] To resolve the dispute an agreement was entered into on April 17, 1896,[3] to submit it to the decision of the English sovereign. The arbitrator was charged by Article 2 of the agreement with applying strictly the provisions of the treaty of 1881. No provision was made as to the finality of the award.

The award of King Edward VII of November 20, 1902,[4] merely set forth a description of the boundary thereby established. A report of a commission appointed to aid him in reaching his award,[5] however, stated the basis upon which the award was determined. It was there concluded that the two lines were irreconcilable, that neither conformed to the spirit of the treaties made the basis of decision, that the terms of the treaties were inapplicable, and that in consequence the question for decision was not only which of the two lines was correct, but also, between the extreme contentions of either party, what exact line would best conform to the intention of the documents submitted.

It may be admitted that the lines were irreconcilable, but this does not sustain the violent interpretation of the treaties which was made. In fact, the arbitrator was presented with a controversy impossible of arbitration. The criticism has been advanced, and, it is believed, correctly, that the arbitrator was limited to determining one of the two lines as the correct one. If he thought neither to be within the language of the treaty, he should have so informed the

[2] Alvarez, *Des occupations des territoires contestés à propos de la question de limites entre le Chili et la République Argentine* (1903) 10 REV. GEN. DE DROIT INT. PUB. 651, 665.

[3] *Op. cit. supra* note 1, at 432.

[4] (1902) DESCAMPS ET RENAULT, RECUEIL INTERNATIONAL DES TRAITÉS DU XXe SIÈCLE 372.

[5] *Ibid.*, 375.

parties and asked for new powers.[6] Thus, the emperor of Russia, when asked in 1889 to act as arbitrator in a dispute between France and The Netherlands concerning the boundaries of the Guianas, refused to accept unless he were authorized to designate an intermediary line between the two boundaries contested. By a supplementary treaty he was so authorized.[7] It has also been criticized upon the ground that it fixed the line so as to give to Argentina the territory occupied by her during the dispute, contrary to international law and the express intention of the parties.[8] But any question of nullity was ended by the tacit ratification by the parties, who received the decision with satisfaction and thereafter adhered to it.[9]

33. SAME: CASE OF THE CARACAS GENERAL WATERWORKS COMPANY.— The award of the umpire of the Belgian-Venezuelan Mixed Claims Commission of 1903 in the case of the *Caracas General Waterworks Company* [1] recognized one claimant and rendered an award ostensibly in its favor, but nevertheless ordered that the sum allowed be paid to a different person.

The Caracas General Waterworks Company was a Belgian corporation holding a concession for the distribution of water in Caracas. By contract of October 31, 1895, it transferred to the government of Venezuela its concession and all of its property in Venezuela in return for 10,792,440 bolivars in bonds of the special debt of the waterworks of Caracas (Deuda Especial Interna de las Aguas de Caracas) created by executive decree of the same date. These bonds were payable to bearer, bore interest at 5 percent, and were taken by the company at 40 percent of their nominal value. Venezuela later suspended the payment of the interest and sinking-fund payments on the bonds for reasons not here material. Claim for the unpaid balance of the bonds, with interest, was brought by the liquidators of the company before the Belgian-Venezuelan Mixed

---

[6] Alvarez, *supra* note 2, at 678, 681.
[7] 1 LAPRADELLE ET POLITIS, RECUEIL DES ARBITRAGES INTERNATIONAUX (1905) 399.
[8] Alvarez, *supra* note 2, at 681.
[9] *Ibid.*, 688.
[1] Compagnie Générale des Eaux de Caracas (Belgium) v. Venezuela (1903) RALSTON'S REPORT (1904) 271.

Claims Commission established under the protocol of March 7, 1903. The protocol provided for the examination and decision by the commission of "all Belgian claims which have not been settled by diplomatic agreement or by arbitration between the two Governments." It was to decide such claims "upon a basis of absolute equity without regard to objections of a technical nature or of the provisions of local legislation." It was agreed that the decisions "shall be final and conclusive." [2]

Upon a preliminary objection to the jurisdiction the Venezuelan commissioner held that since the bonds of the special debt were payable to bearer, the company should show that it was the legitimate holder of the bonds outstanding for which it claimed payment or to limit its claim to the number of bonds which it had in its possession. He pointed out that the bonds had been distributed and were in general circulation. They were doubtless owned by citizens of various nationalities besides Belgian, and a number belonged to Venezuelan citizens. The company was considered to be vested with no legal right to represent the bearers of the bonds, and no legal relation existed between it and the bearers. The commissioner's position was that the company, even though of Belgian nationality, was not the owner of the claim it advanced. Yet upon the ground that the company was Belgian and the claim presented by it was one which remained unsettled between the two governments, the umpire overruled the objection to the jurisdiction.

In the decision upon the merits, the Venezuelan commissioner reaffirmed his previous position and adduced specific proof that some of the bonds were owned by persons not of Belgian nationality. He submitted that the only right which the company had was to exact the fulfillment of the executive decree which created the debt, namely, the re-establishment of the interest and amortization payments. Nevertheless, an award was rendered by the umpire in the sum of 10,565,199 bolivars and 55 centimes in gold, payable as

[2] Art. 1, protocol of March 7, 1903, *ibid.*, 261, 262.

stipulated in Article 5 of the protocol.³ He grounded his award primarily upon the nonperformance of the contract of October 31, 1895. The differences relative to the requisite proof of ownership were disposed of by the argument that the claim of the company was based upon such nonperformance and the following statement:

That this contract, insofar as it goes, is the law between the parties, contains in itself the proof that the company is the owner of its claim, and that the Belgian character of the claimant has not been disputed. It is not to be considered whether foreign bondholders can indirectly take advantage of its action.⁴

He decreed that the sum awarded was to be paid, not to the representatives of the company which had submitted the claim and whose Belgian nationality and contractual relations with Venezuela were held to justify the award, but to the Société Générale pour Favoriser l'Industrie Nationale at Brussels, to be distributed by it to the holders of the bonds upon their presentation. The agent for Venezuela duly entered a protest against the award before the commission and reserved all rights of his government to invoke its nullity.⁵

The efforts of Venezuela to escape the payment of the award proved unsuccessful, but in the contentions advanced in support of its position the case was analyzed with admirable lucidity and force. Its representative before the Hague Tribunal in the *Venezuelan Preferential Claims Case,* Mr. Paúl, entered a request that it exclude from the distribution of the revenues set aside for the payment of claims, the amount awarded by the umpire in the claim of the Caracas General Waterworks Company, "because this claim consisted of bonds of the public debt, a class of claims excluded by the protocols." ⁶ The tribunal first replied that it considered Mr. Paúl's statement as a simple declaration, not having the char-

³ For comment on the equity aspect of this award, see *infra* sec. 47.
⁴ *Op. cit. supra* note 1, at 289.
⁵ Protest of Aug. 26, 1903 (1907) VENEZUELA. LIBRO AMARILLO. MINISTRO DE RELACIONES EXTERIORES 79, 81.
⁶ Meeting of Nov. 10, 1903, VENEZUELAN ARBITRATION BEFORE THE HAGUE TRIBUNAL, 1903, REPORT OF WILLIAM L. PENFIELD, AMERICAN AGENT (1905) 83.

acter of a reservation,[7] and then later requested him to desist from protesting any findings of the mixed commissions as these were outside the competence of the tribunal.[8]

The same contention that the special debt was a part of the public debt of Venezuela and not subject to the jurisdiction of any of the arbitral tribunals of 1903 was advanced by Venezuela in its protest of the decision to Belgium.[9] It was alleged that the owners of the bonds of the special debt, realizing the impossibility of bringing any claim for the suspension of payments before the commission, resorted to bringing claim through the liquidators of the extinct Waterworks Company purely as a device. The company was not the owner of the bonds. By the contract of October 31, 1895, the company transferred all its property to Venezuela in return for bonds of the Venezuelan debt. The company then turned over these bonds to its creditors and own bondholders, thereby completing the liquidation of its assets and liabilities. When this transfer was made to its bondholders, the company ceased to be their debtor. Their mortgage security was thereby extinguished. The bonds were now in the hands of unknown persons, and no proof was made that even a part of them were held by Belgian subjects. The bonds were payable to bearer, and their production was the only proof of ownership. Since the umpire found himself confronted with the fact that the Venezuelan government was bound to pay the holders, and since the bonds were held, not by the company, but by persons foreign to it, the solution occurred to him— which, however, was outside the powers conferred on him—of ordering that the sum which Venezuela was required to pay be deposited with the Society for the Protection of National Industries at Brussels for distribution to the holders, although the award stated that the company was the owner of the action and legally qualified to bring it. The point was later added that this society was unknown to Venezuela and had no claim against it.[10] Revert-

[7] Meeting of Nov. 11, 1903, *ibid.*, 86.
[8] Meeting of Nov. 13, 1903, *ibid.*, 90.
[9] Minister Paúl to Baron de Favereau, Mar. 7, 1904 (1905) VENEZUELA. EXPOSICIÓN DE MINISTRO DE RELACIONES EXTERIORES 256, 259.
[10] Minister Paul to Baron de Favereau, Apr. 12, 1904, *ibid.*, 273.

ing to and elaborating its first contention, Venezuela pointed out that 30 percent of the customs receipts of La Guaira and Puerto Cabello were set aside by Venezuela in the Washington protocols for the payment of claims which did not arise from a failure to make payments on the domestic or foreign debts of Venezuela. Therefore, when the umpire applied some of the funds otherwise than in direct payments to the claimants, when he ordered that this 30 percent should serve up to the amount of 10,565,199.44 bolivars as a sinking fund for the redemption of the bonds of a debt whose status was identical with that of the discount loan, the English foreign debt, the diplomatic 3 percent debt, and the consolidated 6 percent debt, held by persons of different nationalities, he usurped powers not conferred upon him by the protocol, thereby rendering the award void.

A review of the award by another special arbitration was proposed. Belgium refused to reopen the case, contending that by reason of the exchange of notes of January 8 and 9, 1903, Venezuela recognized the competence of the commission to settle the claim, and that the objections of Venezuela were considered by the tribunal and disposed of by it. It referred to the rule of the Hague Convention that a tribunal was authorized to determine its own competence and to the rule of the protocol whereby the two parties agreed to consider the decision as definite and final.[11] Venezuela consistently recognized its obligations to the company under the contract, but denied the validity of the award.[12] However, after a final stern note by Belgium,[13] Venezuela announced its "determination to carry out the award . . . in such manner as may be decided by the Permanent Court of Arbitration of the Hague."[14]

34. SAME: PANAMA–COSTA RICA BOUNDARY DISPUTE AND THE AWARDS OF PRESIDENT LOUBET AND CHIEF JUSTICE WHITE.—When Chief Justice White rendered his award of September 12, 1914, in the Pan-

---

11 Baron de Favereau to the Venezuelan Chargé d'Affaires, Aug. 22, 1904, *ibid.*, 279.

12 Minister Ybarra to Chargé Jennsens, Jan. 8, 1906, *op. cit. supra* note 5, at 82.

13 Chargé Wolters to Minister in Charge of Foreign Relations Churlón, July 27, 1909 (1909) *ibid.*, 46.

14 Minister Churlón to Chargé Wolters, July 31, 1909, *ibid.*, 47.

ama–Costa Rica boundary arbitration, holding the earlier award
of President Loubet to be void for excess of jurisdiction, it was a
strange coincidence that Chief Justice White then decided a question not submitted.

Upon the creation of the independent state of Panama, it fell
heir to a boundary dispute with Costa Rica which had persisted
since Colombia and Costa Rica came into separate existence. A
number of unsuccessful attempts to settle the controversy by treaty
arrangements had been made, culminating in the convention of
December 25, 1880.[1] This convention contained no statement of the
claims of either party. Article 1 recited that the parties agreed to
submit to arbitration the question of boundaries existing between
them and the fixing of a line which shall "permanently and clearly"
divide their territories. The king of Spain was selected as arbitrator,
but his death occurred before proceedings were completed. By a
further convention of November 4, 1896, the president of France
was substituted as arbitrator.[2] A supplementary convention of January 22, 1886, had defined the question in dispute as follows:

ARTICLE II

The territorial limit which the Republic of Costa Rica claims, on the
Atlantic side, reaches as far as the Island Escudo de Veraguas, and the River
Chiriqui (Calobebora) inclusive; and on the Pacific side, as far as the River
Chiriqui Viejo, inclusive, to the East of Point Burica.

The territorial limit which the United States of Colombia claim reaches,
on the Atlantic side, as far as Cape Gracias a Dios, inclusive; and on the
Pacific side, as far as the mouth of the River Golfito, in Gulf Dulce.

ARTICLE III

The arbitral award shall confine itself to the disputed territory that lies
within the extreme limits already described and cannot affect . . . any
rights that a third party . . . may set up.[3]

These articles were confirmed by Article 5 of the convention of
November 4, 1896. The finality of the award was stipulated in
Article 4 in the following terms:

[1] STATEMENT ON BEHALF OF PANAMA (before Chief Justice White as arbitrator),
Appendix A, p. 28.

[2] *Ibid.*, Appendix C, p. 34.   [3] *Ibid.*, Appendix B, p. 32.

The award of the Arbitrator, no matter what may be, shall be considered as a perfect and binding treaty as between the High Contracting Parties, and shall not admit of any appeal. Both Parties bind themselves to its faithful fulfillment, and they waive any appeal against the decision pledging thereto their national honor.[4]

On September 11, 1900, President Loubet of France rendered his award, which, so far as here material, defined the boundary as follows:

The frontier between the Republics of Colombia and Costa Rica shall be formed by the counterfort of the cordillera which starts from Cape Mona on the Atlantic Ocean and closes on the north the valley of the Rio Tarire or Rio Sixòla; then by the chain of division of waters between the Atlantic and Pacific to 9 degrees, about, of latitude; it will follow next the line of division of waters between the Chiriqui Viejo and the affluents of Gulf Dulce, to end at Point Burica on the Pacific Ocean.[5]

Shortly after the award was announced the minister of Costa Rica in Paris addressed a note to M. Delcassé, the Minister of Foreign Affairs of France, requesting that a certain line be fixed by the president as an interpretation of his award.[6] To this request, reply was made by M. Delcassé in a note under date of November 23, 1900.[7] M. Delcassé declined so to interpret the award, upon the ground that in the absence of precise geographical data the arbitrator was able to fix the frontier only by general indications and that there would accordingly be difficulty in fixing it on a map. He indicated, however, that it must be traced within the limits of the territory in dispute, which limits were set forth in Articles 2 and 3 of the treaty of January 20, 1886. It remained for Colombia and Costa Rica to proceed "in accordance with these principles" to determine their frontiers.

[4] *Supra* note 2, p. 35.

[5] This translation was taken from the STATEMENT ON BEHALF OF PANAMA, *supra* note 1, Appendix D, 38. A somewhat less precise translation is in (1910) FOR. REL. U.S. 786.

[6] Minister Peralta to M. Delcassé, Sept. 29, 1900, reprinted in PORRAS, LIMITES ENTRE PANAMÁ Y COSTA RICA; PRIMERA EXPOSICIÓN PRESENTADA AL HONORABLE THE CHIEF JUSTICE DE LOS ESTADOS UNIDOS DE AMÉRICA, EN CALIDAD DE ARBITRO (1911) 53.

[7] *Ibid.*, 55. An English translation may be found in the award of Chief Justice White (1914) FOR. REL. U.S. 1000, 1008.

No charge of nullity appears to have been made by Costa Rica after the award. In connection with the abortive Guardia-Pacheco treaty of March 6, 1905, a declaration of the same date was made by both parties in which it was recited that the question of boundaries being settled by the Loubet award by virtue of general indications only, the practical fixing of the same remained to be reached by mutual agreement.[8] It appears that the treaty was accepted by the legislature of Panama, but with certain *aclaraciones* which were unacceptable to the government of Costa Rica, which, on June 15, 1909, informed Panama that in its view the treaty had expired.[9] No question ever arose as to the validity of the award in the boundary established by it on the Pacific side from Punta Burica to the central cordillera; the controversy concerned the Atlantic zone. Objection against that aspect of the award was made in the note of the Costa Rican minister to the Secretary of State of the United States of December 28, 1908, in which certain contentions were advanced which, it was said, if established would bring about the defect of *ultra petita*.[10]

The Secretary of State, whose good offices in the settlement of the controversy had been invoked by Costa Rica,[11] attempted to find a formula for arbitration which would be acceptable to both parties. Panama insisted that the Loubet award must be the starting point for the new arbitration, though it expressed its willingness to submit to arbitration the question which of the two boundary lines was correct if the Loubet award should pass beyond the maximum boundary of Colombia.[12] Costa Rica, in turn, proposed arbitration of, first, which of the two interpretations given by the interested parties to the award was correct and, second, whether the Loubet award was obligatory.[13] When the Secretary of State pro-

---

[8] Enclosure with Minister Calvo of Costa Rica to the Secretary of State, Nov. 26, 1906. Department of State, Numerical File, Case No. 2491/3–7.

[9] Minister Arosemana (Panama) to the Secretary of State, July 30, 1909, Enclosure: Memorandum regarding boundaries (1910) FOR. REL. U.S. 784, 788, 789.

[10] *Ibid.*, 777.

[11] Minister Anderson to the Secretary of State, Dec. 9, 1907, *ibid.*, 772.

[12] Memorandum regarding boundaries, *supra* note 9, at 790.

[13] Minister Anderson to the Secretary of State, Oct. 18, 1909 (1910) FOR. REL. U.S. 795.

posed a formula which, it was hoped, would furnish a means of reconciling the divergent views of the two governments,[14] Minister Anderson, of Panama, stated that "the acceptance of the Loubet award must form the basis of the arbitration."[15] Accordingly, he modified the formula suggested by the secretary to read as follows: "What is the boundary between the Republic of Panama and Costa Rica under and in accordance with the correct interpretation and true intention of the Loubet award?"[16] This question was substantially incorporated in the convention of March 17, 1910, as that to be decided by the arbitrator named by it, the Chief Justice of the United States.[17] A supplementary paragraph was added thereto to the effect that "in order to decide this the arbitrator will take into account all the facts, circumstances and considerations which may have a bearing upon the case, as well as the limitation of the Loubet award expressed in the letter of his excellency M. Delcassé . . . of November 23, 1900." Article 7 provided for the finality of the award of the Chief Justice as follows:

> The award, whatever it be, shall be held as a perfect and compulsory treaty between the high contracting parties. Both high contracting parties bind themselves to the faithful execution of the award and waive all claims against it.
> The boundary line between the two Republics as finally fixed by the arbitrator shall be deemed the true line, and his determination of the same shall be final, conclusive, and without appeal.[18]

The position of Costa Rica before the arbitrator was not altogether clear. On the one hand, it contended that the case was not one of "mere interpretation," but, rather, that it might come to involve "a partial reforming" of the award "to purge it of a certain defect resulting from overstepping of power."[19] On the other, it stated that "the nullification of the Award is not asked for; it will be sufficient that the Honorable the Chief Justice should take into account this excess of power of the French Arbitrator in preparing

---

[14] Memorandum of the Secretary of State of Mar. 1, 1910, *ibid.*, 810, 811.
[15] Minister Anderson to the Secretary of State, Mar. 10, 1910, *ibid.*, 812.
[16] *Ibid.*
[17] (1910) FOR. REL. U.S. 820.
[18] *Ibid.*, 822.
[19] ARGUMENT OF COSTA RICA, 231.

his decision . . . that he decide . . . a boundary that will be more
in accord with justice in the light of the other antecedents, circumstances and considerations to which he must also give weight." [20]
The substance of its argument appears to have been that in view of
the defects existing in the Loubet award the arbitrator was under
no obligation to accept it. His decision should be in accord with the
intention of President Loubet, and that intention "was to adhere
to the historical precedents, to the colonial *uti poseditis* [sic] and to
the fact of present possession." [21] The defects existing in the award
were vagueness and lack of certainty,[22] impossibility, since there was
no counterfort or spur connecting Punta Mona with the main Cordillera,[23] incongruities,[24] and notorious injustice.[25] If interpreted
literally, it invaded territories undisputedly belonging to Costa
Rica [26] and handed to Colombia more than she had claimed.[27] Manifest error was committed in awarding to Colombia the two islands of
Mangle Chico and Mangle Grande. Those islands belonged to a
third party, Nicaragua. Thus, the casual manner in which the award
was prepared was shown.[28]

Panama placed its argument squarely on the immutability of the
Loubet award. It contended that the present arbitration started from
that award "as a fixed datum." It was not to be impeached or questioned, for by the *compromis* both parties had solemnly recorded
their acceptance of it.[29] Not what *should have been* the award of
President Loubet, but what *was* his award, properly construed and
applied, was the question. The request of Costa Rica for a decree
of a line substantially different from that of the Loubet award dif-
fered from annulment only in form.

The result is the same whether the Award be declared void or so defective
as to require a total change in the only parts now under consideration, in
order to avoid *ultra petita*. . . . If the Loubet Award were really so obscure in its terms that it could not be given an intelligible meaning or so at

[20] *Ibid.*, 270.
[21] *Ibid.*, 332, 333.
[22] *Ibid.*, 233.
[23] *Ibid.*, 278–281.
[24] *Ibid.*, 269.
[25] *Ibid.*, 332, 333.
[26] *Ibid.*, 233.
[27] *Ibid.*, 266, 267.
[28] *Ibid.*, 265.
[29] STATEMENT ON BEHALF OF PANAMA, 2.

variance with the natural features of the country that its true intention could not be discerned, then no award would be possible on this arbitration.[30]

Panama pointed out, with considerable reason, that there never had been any doubt as to the meaning of the award or where the line fixed by it lay. The root of all the difficulty was that Costa Rica did not entertain the slightest doubt concerning it. Her real objection was simply that of every defeated litigant, even though she was in honor pledged to accept the award.[31] Less convincing were the arguments designed to meet the Costa Rican objections. It was contended that President Loubet had not exceeded the limitations imposed by Articles 2 and 3 of the treaty of January 22, 1886, since they only defined the terminal points of the boundary claims, while leaving unrestricted his jurisdiction as to the internal lines. The line fixed was not *ultra petita,* because Punta Mona was north of the Chiriqui and south of the northerly limit, and Punta Burica was north of the Chiriqui Viego and south of the Golfito. Thus, it only remained to ascertain the line which Loubet described. This could readily be done by a natural interpretation of its words—a verbal interpretation.[32] Panama further took occasion to warn the arbitrator that in its view he would commit an excess of jurisdiction and his award would be null if he departed from the Loubet award and adopted any other basis for the tracing of the line.[33]

The award rendered by Chief Justice White on September 12, 1914,[34] seems partially to adopt the double line of argument advanced by Costa Rica. The Loubet line on the Atlantic side was discarded because it ran through undisputed territory, and a new line following the Sixaolo and Yorquin rivers was substituted for that beginning at Punta Mona as " 'most in accordance with the correct interpretation and true intention' of the former award." [35] But the preliminary propositions were advanced that "the fundamental question to be decided requires it to be determined whether

[30] ANSWER OF PANAMA, 4, 5. [31] *Ibid.,* 7.
[32] STATEMENT ON BEHALF OF PANAMA, 9, 10.
[33] PORRAS, *op. cit. supra* note 6, at 45.
[34] (1914) FOR. REL. U.S. 1000. [35] *Ibid.,* 1012, 1013, 1015.

the boundary line fixed by the previous arbitration was within the previous treaty or treaties. And if it was not, it must follow that its correction is within the scope of the authority conferred by this treaty" and, again, that "by the terms of the present treaty the previous award was not set aside as a whole, and the power was only given to correct it in so far as it might be found to be without the authority conferred." [36] It was accordingly deduced that "as the line of boundary fixed by the previous award from Punta Mona to the Cordilleras was not within the matter in dispute or within the disputed territory, it results that such award was beyond the submission and that the Arbitrator was without power to make it, and it must therefore be set aside and treated as non-existing." [37]

Costa Rica accepted the award,[38] but Panama declined to accept or to recognize its validity.[39] It submitted that the only question presented to the arbitrator was the " 'correct interpretation and true intention' " of the Loubet award. This the arbitrator had omitted to decide; instead, he had gone into the questions carefully excluded from his jurisdiction, namely, the question of the validity of the Loubet award and the question of what the arbitrator might think to be the proper boundary if that award were disregarded. Panama deemed it hardly necessary to "point out that where an arbitrator, asked only to interpret the description of a boundary in a previous award, renders a purported decision declaring the boundary which he was asked to define 'non-existent,' such a decision is beyond his powers." Still less was it thought necessary "to argue that where an arbitrator, whose only office is to apply the boundary awarded by a former arbitrator, wholly discards that boundary and undertakes to fix one of his own choice, avowedly and intentionally differing from the boundary which he was asked to apply, his decision is *ultra petita,* null and void." [40] With regard to the arbitrator's profession that the line adopted was "most in ac-

36 *Ibid.,* 1010, 1012.

37 *Ibid.,* 1012.

38 President Gonzales of Costa Rica to President Wilson, Sept. 13, 1914, *ibid.,* 993; Minister Mesén to the Secretary of State, Nov. 7, 1914, *ibid.,* 999.

39 Minister Morales to the Secretary of State, Oct. 20, 1914, *ibid.,* 994.

40 *Ibid.,* 996, 997.

cordance with the correct interpretation and true intention" of the Loubet award, it was declared to be belied by the rest of the award which denied legal existence to the Loubet line.

The contentions of Panama were rejected by Costa Rica upon the ground that the necessity of modifying the Loubet line if it trenched upon territory not in dispute was specifically provided for in the treaty of March 17, 1910, in its reference to the note of M. Delcassé, of November 23, 1900, and was admitted by Panama in the statement of its case.[41] The United States supported Costa Rica in its position, the Secretary of State remarking that the department was "convinced that no exception can be taken to the procedure followed, or to the findings of the Arbitrator." [42]

Nothing was done to carry out any part of the award during the ensuing World War I. In February, 1921, when Costa Rica occupied the Coto District on the Pacific which had been given it by the original Loubet award and conceded by Panama, it was expelled by forces of Panama. Costa Rican forces then crossed the Sixaola River into Panama's territory, and war was threatened in both countries. In this situation, immediately after his entry into the office of Secretary of State, Mr. Hughes sent identic notes to Costa Rica and Panama, upholding the White award and calling for a cessation of hostilities. Panama continued to disavow the White award and proposed plebiscites to settle the matter.[43] It also unsuccessfully invited the mediation of Argentina. Finally, on August 18, 1921, Secretary Hughes sent a strong note to the effect that the Costa Rican occupation of the Coto region must proceed and that the United States would not look with favor upon a resumption of hostilities. Panama thereupon abandoned the disputed territory under protest and without its co-operation a delimitation of the boundary was made.[44]

---

[41] Minister Quesada to Minister Lefevre, Oct. 30, 1914, *ibid.*, 1017, citing pages 3, 4, 5 and 10 of Panama's Case.

[42] Secretary of State to Minister Price, Apr. 28, 1915 (1915) *ibid.*, 1147.

[43] DOCUMENTOS RELATIVOS AL CONFLITO DE JURISDICCIÓN TERRITORIAL CON LA REPUBLICA DE PANAMÁ Y SUS ANTECEDENTES, SECRETARIA DE RELACIONES EXTERIORES, COSTA RICA (1921) 4 *et sqq.*, 160 *et sqq.*

[44] SURVEY OF AMERICAN FOREIGN RELATIONS, COUNCIL ON FOREIGN RELATIONS (1929) 211-213.

Though the dispute was the occasion of violent controversy between the parties, it is believed that the legal relations involved are fairly simple. Whatever legal claim Costa Rica had against the validity of the Loubet award was lost by its failure opportunely to raise the objection of nullity. It would also seem to be barred by the waiver clause of Article 4 of the convention of November 4, 1896. It was, of course, privileged to request Panama to make concessions and to readjust the boundary so as not to deprive it of territories undisputedly its own. It could advance in support of such a request arguments with respect to the unsatisfactory and inequitable character of the award and indicate defects which otherwise would have rendered it null.[45] But any readjustment conceded by Panama would have been dictated purely by political motives, not by legal obligations. The convention of May 17, 1910, did represent such a concession by Panama. Though the history of the negotiations preceding that convention as well as the phrasing of the question which was to be arbitrated amply sustains the conclusion that the validity of the Loubet award was not put in issue before the new arbitrator, the arbitration was not devoid of meaning, as it clearly would have been if its sole purpose was to reaffirm in different and perhaps clearer language the Loubet award. In the ascertainment of the true intention of the Loubet award the principle was admitted that the arbitrator could look to the statement of M. Delcassé in his note of November 23, 1900, that it was not intended to trench upon territory not in dispute. Within the limits indicated by that letter, a readjustment by the arbitrator was permissible. It is submitted, therefore, that the award of Chief Justice White was valid and obligatory, since it can reasonably be rested upon this ground as well as upon its statements which cast the odium of nullity upon the Loubet award. In any event, it would seem that when Panama had by Article 7 of the convention of March 17, 1910, expressly

---

[45] For a recapitulation of the Costa Rican arguments concerning the nullity of the Loubet award see ANDERSON, EL LAUDO LOUBET; CONTRIBUCIÓN AL ESTUDIO DE LIMITES ENTRE COSTA RICA Y PANAMÁ (1911) 14–16, 24–25, 46 et sqq.

waived all claims against the award, it would be thereby precluded from attacking the decision.[46]

35. SAME: HONDURAN-NICARAGUAN ARBITRATION UNDER THE TREATY OF CORINTO.—In the arbitration between Honduras and Nicaragua under the Treaty of Corinto of January 20, 1902,[1] the question was presented whether an arbitral tribunal can require one party to perform a treaty obligation owed to the other when no specific authorization had been given it to order such a measure. The Treaty of Corinto established the principle of obligatory arbitration between the signatories—Nicaragua, Honduras, El Salvador, and Costa Rica —for every difficulty or question arising between them. A permanent tribunal was established, the members of which were to be elected annually.[2] Article 13 provided that "the Arbitral Tribunal shall dictate all those dispositions of internal order which it may consider necessary, in order completely to fulfil the high mission which is by this treaty conferred upon it." [3] The material provision in the controversy which subsequently arose was Article 11: "The Governments of the States in dispute solemnly engage not to execute any act of hostility, warlike preparations or mobilization of forces, in order not to impede the settlement of the difficulty or question by the means established in the present convention." [4]

In 1906 and 1907 relations between Nicaragua and Honduras became very strained, and war threatened as the result of charges made by Honduras that revolutionists seeking the overthrow of its government were receiving aid from Nicaragua and allegations by Nicaragua that its territory had been violated by Honduras troops.

[46] Cf. Anderson, *The Costa Rica–Panama Boundary Dispute* (1921) 15 AM. J. INT. LAW 236. De Bustamente advances the novel theory that the convention of March 17, 1910, entailed a certain stage of the proceedings which were in effect the execution of the judgment of President Loubet. Since in adjudging the Loubet award to be void, Chief Justice White exceeded his jurisdiction, the Loubet award still persists. PANAMA–COSTA RICA BOUNDARY CONTROVERSY; OPINION GIVEN BY DR. ANTONIO S. DE BUSTAMENTE (1921) 8, 9, 14.

[1] DOCUMENTOS OFICIALES REFERENTES Á LA GUERRA ENTRE NICARAGUA Y HONDURAS Y Á LA PARTICIPACIÓN DE EL SALVADOR COMO ALIADO DE LA ÚLTIMA, NICARAGUA, MINISTERIO DE RELACIONES EXTERIORES (1907) 46–52.

[2] Art. 2, 3, *ibid.*, 48.

[3] *Ibid.*, 51.   [4] *Ibid.*, 50.

It was agreed to submit the dispute to the tribunal established under the Treaty of Corinto.[5]

At the beginning of the proceedings the tribunal notified Nicaragua that in accordance with Article 11 it must proceed to disarm pending the arbitration.[6] President Zelaya of Nicaragua replied that his government was willing to recognize only the power of the tribunal to allow reparation; any authority to demand disarming was denied.[7] Nicaragua would consider mediation to stop the conflict only if Honduras gave complete satisfaction for its offenses.[8] Honduras, however, expressed its willingness to accept the tribunal's proposal.[9] On February 6, 1907, the tribunal issued an order in which it finally decided that Article 11 of the treaty required disarming and notified the parties that unless such steps were taken it would be necessary for the tribunal to dissolve.[10] The Nicaraguan arbitrator withdrew from the consideration of the question, contending that Article 11 only imposed upon the opposing governments the obligation not to arm in such a manner as to interfere with the functioning of the tribunal.[11] When the powers of the arbitrators of Honduras and El Salvador were withdrawn, the tribunal issued its final protocol closing the arbitration.[12]

In defense of its position Nicaragua addressed a circular note to friendly States,[13] in which it affirmed the general principle that arbitrators may decide only the questions of fact and law submitted to them; otherwise they exceed their powers. In the instant case, Nicaragua charged, the tribunal had arrogated itself to the political power and had dictated orders wholly foreign to its judicial mission.

---

[5] MUNRO, THE FIVE REPUBLICS OF CENTRAL AMERICA (1918) 207.

[6] Undated letter from Central American Tribunal of Arbitration to the Nicaraguan Minister at San Salvador, received Feb. 2(?), 1907, NICARAGUA, MEMORIA DE RELACIONES EXTERIORES (1906–1907) 20.

[7] Telegram from President Zelaya to President Escalon of San Salvador, Feb. 5, 1907, ibid., 23.

[8] Same to same, Feb. 12, 1907, ibid., 24.

[9] Telegram from President Escalon to President Zelaya, Feb. 4, 1907, ibid., 22.

[10] Ibid., 105.

[11] Ibid., 95.

[12] February 8, 1907, ibid., 106–109.

[13] Circular note from the Nicaraguan Minister of Foreign Relations to friendly States, Mar. 30, 1907, ibid., 28.

It had ended by dissolution without having rendered that justice which was the sole object of its creation. It had attempted to ensure the faithful execution of all the provisions of the Treaty of Corinto and had become the censor of the conduct of governments, while it was in international law limited to the consideration of its own judgment.

Costa Rica notified the ministers of El Salvador, Honduras, and Nicaragua by note of February 25, 1907, that it was its opinion that the Treaty of Corinto no longer had legal force in view of Nicaragua's action.[14] By the Treaty of Amapala of April 23, 1907, an agreement was made to call a Central American Conference; [15] the result was that the Central American Court of Justice was established.[16]

The question may be close, but it would seem that the Nicaraguan position was well taken. A more specific conferral of authority than that embodied in Article 13 of the Treaty of Corinto should be deemed necessary to enable a tribunal to order States to take measures so vitally affecting their existence as that of disarming when war is imminent. The obligation set forth in Article 11 was one expressly declared to exist between the signatory governments, and question of its performance does not appear to have been submitted to the tribunal.[17]

36. SAME: JUDGMENTS NOS. 3 AND 4, PERMANENT COURT OF INTERNATIONAL JUSTICE.—It is possible for a tribunal to confuse the process of reasoning by which it arrives at its decree with the scope to be given the decree. Obviously, the permissible limits of the former are largely unrestricted, while the decretal part of its judgment must be directly responsive to the *compromis*. It is elementary that much of what may be said in the course of arriving at a judgment is *dicta* and only the exact point to be decided is the obligatory part of

---

[14] NOTAS CRUZADAS ENTRE LAS CANCILLERIAS DE COSTA RICA Y NICARAGUA RELATIVAS Á LA ABROGACIÓN DEL PACTO DE CORINTO DE 20 DE ENERO DE 1902, SECRETARIA DE RELACIONES EXTERIORES (1907).

[15] *Op. cit. supra* note 6, at 38.

[16] *Cf.* DUMBAULD, INTERIM MEASURES OF PROTECTION IN INTERNATIONAL CONTROVERSIES (1932) 95–99, for a discussion of the exercise by that tribunal of its power to order the preservation of the status quo pending arbitration.

[17] But see *ibid.*, 97.

the judgment. That one of the reasons incident to a judgment may perchance be incorporated in the decree will not make it any the more binding upon the parties. This principle is illustrated in Judgments Nos. 3 and 4 of the Permanent Court of International Justice.

Article 179, Annex, paragraph 4, of the Treaty of Neuilly provided that property of any Bulgarian national within the territory of any Allied or Associated Power and the proceeds of its liquidation could be charged by that power with the payment of claims of its nationals "growing out of acts committed by the Bulgarian Government or by any Bulgarian authorities since October 11, 1915, and before that Allied or Associated Power entered into the war. The amount of such claims may be assessed by an arbitrator appointed by M. Gustave Ador. . . . They may be charged in the second place with payment of the amounts due in respect of claims by the nationals of such Allied or Associated Power with regard to their property, rights and interests in the territory of other enemy Powers, in so far as those claims are otherwise unsatisfied." [1] Bulgaria raised certain objections to the competence of the arbitrator appointed under this article and the dispute was submitted to the summary procedure of the Permanent Court of International Justice (Statute, Article 29) for settlement. The *compromis* provided that the Court was to:

determine the precise meaning of the last sentence of the first sub-paragraph of paragraph 4 of the Annex to Section IV, Part IX of the above-mentioned Treaty, replying in particular to the two following questions:

(1) Does the text above-quoted authorize claims for acts committed even outside Bulgarian territory as constituted before October 11, 1915, in particular in districts occupied by Bulgaria after her entry into the war?

(2) Does the text above-quoted authorize claims for damages incurred by claimants not only as regards their property, rights and interests, but also as regards their person, arising out of ill-treatment, deportation, internment or other similar acts?

It was contended by the Bulgarian government that Article 121 fixed the maximum limits which the Allied Powers and Bulgaria judged that the latter was capable of paying. It was, therefore, neces-

---

[1] 112 BRITISH AND FOREIGN STATE PAPERS (1919) 781, 844, 845.

sary to examine with circumspection any clause of the treaty which would extend the obligations of Bulgaria beyond the global responsibility fixed by that article. Paragraph 4 introduced a new obligation beyond those of Articles 121 and 177.[2] Express words, therefore, should be required to extend this obligation beyond Bulgarian territory.[3] Greece asserted, however, that this argument was false. It replied that because a security had been created for the payment of a debt, it did not follow that the debt existed only in the security.[4]

The Court, in its decision,[5] indicated that nothing in paragraph 4 created any fresh obligations over and above those imposed by the other clauses of the treaty, that the parts of the treaty establishing responsibility for the claims mentioned in paragraph 4 should be ascertained, that Article 121 of the treaty was drawn up in such general terms as to include reparation for losses caused by military operations previous to the declaration of war, and held (i) that the sentence of paragraph in question "should be interpreted as authorizing claims in respect of acts committed even outside Bulgarian territory as constituted before October 11, 1915, and in respect of damage incurred by claimants not only as regards their property, rights and interests but also as regards their person," and (ii) that "reparation due on this ground is within the scope of the reparation contemplated in Article 121 and consequently is included in the total capital sum mentioned in Articles 121 and 122."

A request was made by Greece for an interpretation of its Judgment No. 3, in regard to the question whether the second part of that judgment sanctioned the liquidation by Greece of Bulgarian property in its territory in order to satisfy the sums which might be awarded by the arbitrator referred to in paragraph 4. The request was refused by the Court on the gound that the interpretation desired went beyond the limits of the judgment itself, which were

---

[2] Art. 121 (reparation) *ibid.*, 812; Art. 177 (compensation for exceptional war measures, etc., affecting private property) *ibid.*, 839.

[3] *Mémoire du Gouvernement Bulgare*, 31, 35–42. Ser. C., No. 6, Documents Relating to Judgment No. 3.

[4] *Réplique du Gouvernement Hellenique*, 83, 87, *ibid.*

[5] Interpretation of Treaty of Neuilly, Article 179, Annex, Paragraph 4 (September 12, 1924), Ser. A., No. 3, 6–10.

fixed by the *compromis*. The interpretation desired by the parties to which Judgment No. 3 was addressed related only to the basis and extent of the sentence of paragraph 4 of the Treaty of Neuilly in question, the applicability of which was taken for granted in the *compromis*. The present request was based on a different conception under the agreement, "namely, that there is some doubt as to the applicability of the sentence in question as between the Parties." [6]

M. Yotis, agent for Greece in the case, later advanced the contention that the second part of the decree was *ultra petita*.[7] The argument is a strong one, and in its fundamental thesis that the decree must confine itself to the scope of the *compromis* it would seem to be sustained by Judgment No. 4 of the Court. The Court was, of course, free to reason in such a manner as it deemed necessary to arrive at a conclusion, but its conclusion, or, in other words, the decretal part of its judgment, should contain only a response to the two questions which had been submitted by the *compromis*. It was submitted by M. Yotis that a simple comparison of the *compromis* and of the decree would show that the first section contained an answer fully responsive to all the questions submitted and that the second section was accordingly superfluous and exceeded the terms of the *compromis*.[8] It does not follow, however, that the judgment is not binding upon Greece in view not only of its failure to protest, but also of its request for an interpretation of the second section of the judgment.

37. SAME: HUNGARIAN OPTANTS CASE.—The so-called case of the *Hungarian Optants* is the most discussed case of recent years in which excess of jurisdiction has been alleged. The literature which it has occasioned is voluminous.[1] It has led to the advancement of proposals for the further development of the system of international arbitration which are most significant.[2] The jurisdictional problems

---

[6] Interpretation of Judgment No. 3 (March 26, 1925), SER. A., No. 4, 5–7.

[7] Yotis, *La Question ultra petita à propos d'un Arbitrage entre la Grèce et la Bulgarie* (1926) 53 JOUR. DU DROIT INT. (Clunet) 879.

[8] *Ibid.*, 881, 882, 886.

[1] See the bibliography collected by DEÁK, THE HUNGARIAN-RUMANIAN DISPUTE (1928) 103, n. 132, 263.

[2] See *infra* Ch. VII.

involved in the case are, nevertheless, believed to be relatively simple.

Source of the Controversy.—Rumania was at peace with Austria-Hungary when the Armistice of November 3, 1918, was concluded by the Allied Powers with it. But on November 9, 1918, it re-entered the war against the Central Powers, and occupied Hungarian territory, including Transylvania, until into 1920 and after the signing of the Treaty of Trianon.[3] By that treaty Transylvania was ceded to Rumania.[4] On July 30, 1921, four days after the Treaty of Trianon came into force, Rumania promulgated the third of a series of what purported to be land reform laws, called the Garoflid Law. This law provided for the expropriation of land in Transylvania and other districts. Certain provisions of the law were viewed as objectionable by Hungary as injuring the interests of her nationals. One of these was the absentee clause, which provided that the estate of any person absent from the territory from December 1, 1918, until March 23, 1921, should be expropriated in its entirety. The others related to the method of compensation and the mode of payment.[5] It appears that their effect was to give the expropriated owners something less than one percent of the value of their property.[6]

Treaty Provisions.—Certain articles of the Treaty of Trianon bore directly upon the controversy and, in the opinion of Hungary, sustained her complaint against the Rumanian legislation, as well as the general principles of international law. Those articles have a primary significance in question of jurisdiction which later arose before the Rumanian-Hungarian Mixed Arbitral Tribunal. By Article 232(b)[7] Rumania reserved the power to liquidate all property of Hungarian nationals within its control in order to satisfy its claims against Hungary. Article 250 excepted from this general

[3] DEÁK, *op. cit. supra* note 1, at 3–8.
[4] Art. 27, 113 BRITISH AND FOREIGN STATE PAPERS (1920) 486, 504.
[5] DEÁK, *op. cit. supra* note 1, at 18, 19.
[6] *Cf.* Borchard, *Opinion on the Roumanian-Hungarian Dispute before the Council of the League of Nations,* etc., 2 SOME OPINIONS, ARTICLES AND REPORTS BEARING UPON THE TREATY OF TRIANON AND THE CLAIMS OF THE HUNGARIAN NATIONALS WITH REGARD TO THEIR LANDS IN TRANSYLVANIA 23, 31.
[7] *Op. cit. supra* note 4, at 585.

provision the property of Hungarian nationals situated in territories forming part of old Austro-Hungary, in the following language:

. . . the property . . . shall not be subject to retention or liquidation in accordance with these provisions.

Such property, rights and interests shall be restored to their owners freed from any measure of this kind, or from any other measure of transfer, compulsory administration, or sequestration, taken since the 3d November, 1918, until the coming into force of the present Treaty . . .

Claims made by Hungarian nationals under this article shall be submitted to the Mixed Arbitral Tribunal provided for in Article 239.[8]

Further protection for Hungarian nationals in the annexed territory of old Austro-Hungary was given by Article 63, which enabled them to opt for the retention of their Hungarian nationality and guaranteed that "they will be entitled to retain their immovable property." [9]

Action before the Mixed Arbitral Tribunal.—A Mixed Arbitral Tribunal had been established between Rumania and Hungary under Article 239 of the Treaty of Trianon to decide the various classes of questions designated by the treaty for regulation by it. If a vacancy occurred in its membership which the two States were unable to fill, the Council of the League of Nations was empowered to nominate a new member. The parties agreed to regard the decisions as "final and conclusive, and to render them binding upon their nationals." [10]

A suit brought by Emeric Kulin before the tribunal, praying that it declare the restrictive measures taken against the plaintiff's property by Rumania to be contrary to the provisions of Article 250 of the Treaty of Trianon and that it order Rumania to restore to the plaintiff his property free of all charges and to pay all damages suffered.[11] Rumania objected to the jurisdiction, on the ground that the measures complained of had been taken by virtue of the agrarian law of Transylvania and constituted measures of expropriation to

8 *Ibid.,* 607, 608.   9 Art. 63, Par. (3), *ibid.,* 515.
10 Art. 239, *ibid.,* 599.   11 7 RECUEIL DES DÉCISIONS (1927–1928) 138, 144.

the end of agrarian reform which were applied equally to all lands, whether belonging to nationals or aliens, and, moreover, an indemnity had been provided; and that consequently they were not measures of sequestration in the sense of Article 250 of the Treaty of Trianon.[12] M. Millerand argued for Rumania that the tribunal had jurisdiction only over liquidation as distinguished from expropriation. Liquidation was a measure of war, while expropriation was subservient to the general interests of the state. When applied equally to all, it was permissible under Article 250, since that article and Article 63 related to measures of liquidation.[13] M. Politis added that upon the slightest doubt occurring, the tribunal should hold itself to be without jurisdiction. He submitted that it was "inconceivable that a country can accept to submit itself to a decision eventually capable of provoking in its social and political organism the most serious and dangerous disturbances." Article 250 was to be considered the law of the tribunal as the *compromis* was the law of every arbitrator. If an abusive interpretation of the *compromis* took place, he asserted that the decision would be vitiated by an excess of jurisdiction which authorized the parties to disregard it.[14]

The tribunal held that it possessed jurisdiction to entertain the suit and directed the defendant State to answer to the merits. It declared that by the insertion of Article 250 in the Treaty of Trianon the Allied Powers had the purpose of bringing within its protective measures the property, rights, and interests of Hungarian subjects situated in the territory of the old Austro-Hungarian Empire and that consequently claims founded on Article 250 were to be judged by the principles of international law. The question in the instant case was whether the measures taken by Rumania were comprehended by Article 250; unless they were so comprehended, the tribunal had no jurisdiction. But it was only by entering upon an examination of the case upon the merits that the tribunal could determine what was the nature of these measures and whether

12 *Cf.* RECLAMATIONS DES OPTANTS HONGROIS DE TRANSYLVANIE CONTRE LA REFORME AGRAIRE EN ROUMANIE, PLAIDOIRIES DE MM. MILLERAND, POLITIS ET ROSENTAL (1927).
13 *Ibid.*, 12, 16, 23, 31.
14 *Ibid.*, 51, 64, 65.

they possessed the characteristics contemplated by Article 250. It appeared that the property of Kulin had been formally seized, that a transfer had been made under the agrarian law, and that the name of the Rumanian State had been inscribed as owner in the records of real property. With respect to the sufficiency of the indemnity promised for these acts, that was a matter to be considered on the merits. But the measures taken constituted a violation of the principle of respect for acquired rights, exceeded the limits of international law, and were an expropriation in the sense of Article 250. A reference by Rumania to a position taken by Hungarian representatives at the Brussels Conference and before the Council of the League of Nations in 1923 was rejected as not being an official recognition on the part of the Hungarian government of such a nature as to bind its subjects and preclude them from exercising the rights which Article 250 guaranteed them.[15]

The Rumanian member of the tribunal held in a dissenting opinion [16] that the tribunal was not competent to take jurisdiction for the purpose of examining the case on its merits. International tribunals were tribunals of limited jurisdiction and should exercise the greatest discretion in determining their competence. Measures of retention and liquidation discriminate against ex-enemy property as such and have as their purpose reparation for damages suffered by the Allied Powers and their nationals. But the measures of expropriation here brought in question were enacted as a further incident in a long-adhered-to policy of agrarian reform and applied equally to all landowners of whatever nationality. To assert that the measures taken were indirectly aimed at Hungarian property would be to put in question the good faith of the State, which should always be presumed until the party contesting it has furnished proof. Accordingly, the measures were not incompatible with Article 250 of the Treaty and the tribunal could decline jurisdiction. Even if it were true that Article 250 in annulling the prerogative of

---

[15] *Supra* note 11.
[16] 1 *op. cit. supra* note 6, at 185; also in DEÁK, *op. cit. supra* note 1, at 190.

Article 232 (b) returned Hungarian property in the ceded territories to common international law, it did not follow that the property would have a privileged status, but simply that the property would have the protection accorded to all alien property. Such property was to be considered governed by the principle of equality of treatment with that of nationals and not excluded from expropriation for a public purpose. This principle of equality of treatment, he stated, was inscribed in the Treaty of Trianon. To include the vague concept of international law in Article 250 would involve a radical extension of the jurisdiction of the tribunal. It would follow from it that every violation of international law would be a liquidation and Rumania would be subjected to an oversight by the tribunal more humiliating than the system of capitulations.

After the tribunal pronounced its decision, the Rumanian government announced that its ruling would not be acceded to and that Rumania was withdrawing its arbitrator in the agrarian cases.[17] Thereupon, Hungary addressed an application to the Council of the League of Nations requesting the appointment by it in conformity with Article 239 of deputy arbitrators to fill the office thus vacated.[18] Rumania, on the other hand, submitted a request for the intervention of the Council under paragraph 2 of Article 11 of the Covenant as a matter affecting international relations that threatened to disturb international peace.[19] The positions taken by the two parties before the Council, the action taken by it, and the legal effects of that action will be dealt with later.[20]

The Question of Excess of Jurisdiction.—As stated before, the jurisdictional questions involved in this case seem fairly simple. Whether or not the decision was binding upon the parties is not to be determined by such generic formulas as that in case of doubt a

17 Letter from M. Millerand to the President of the Mixed Arbitral Tribunal, Feb. 24, 1927, APPLICATION BY THE HUNGARIAN GOVERNMENT TO THE COUNCIL OF THE LEAGUE OF NATIONS OF MAY 21, 1927, Annex B. 2, p. 25.
18 *Ibid.*, 3.
19 8 LEAGUE OF NATIONS, OFFICIAL JOURNAL (1927) 350.
20 *Infra* sec. 56.

tribunal should decline jurisdiction.[21] It is solely to be answered upon the criterion of whether a manifest excess of jurisdiction has occurred. As Schiffer [22] remarks in this connection, essential error is not to be confused with "usurpation of jurisdiction." Supplementing this principle is the one that a tribunal is competent to decide questions of its own jurisdiction. On the basis of the firmness with which that principle is established in international arbitral law, Schätzel [23] makes the cogent observation that it is difficult to perceive how anyone could question the decision in this case; analysis of the decision would indicate not only that the fatal defect of nullity did not occur but also that the decision was correct.

The question of the merits of a case should always be distinguished from that of jurisdiction. It is the nature and not the justice of a claim that determines jurisdiction.[24] Generally speaking, to oust jurisdiction it must be shown that the complaint does not on the face of it disclose matter over which the tribunal has jurisdiction.[25] It is, of course, necessary that a possibility exist that the allegations of jurisdiction be sustained by the facts to be proved.[26] Thus, Dupuis [27] states that it was enough that Hungary pled a violation of Article 250. De Lapradelle says:

The jurisdiction of the Mixed Arbitral Tribunals is assured from the moment that it appears from a *prima facie* examination of the case that the property, rights and interests of Hungarian nationals, situated in the territories of the former Austro-Hungarian Monarchy, have been subjected to a measure of retention or liquidation.[28]

[21] This misconception appears in Basdevant, Jèze, and Politis, *Les Principes juridiques sur la compétence des juridictions internationales et, en particulier, des tribunaux arbitraux mixtes organisés par les traités de paix de Versailles, de Saint Germain, de Trianon* (1927) 44 REV. DU DROIT PUB. S.P. 45, 48.

[22] Schiffer, *Opinion on the Roumano-Hungarian Dispute*, 2 *op. cit. supra* note 6, at 109, 116.

[23] SCHÄTZEL, RECHTSKRAFT UND ANFECHTUNG VON ENTSCHEIDUNGEN INTERNATIONALER GERICHTE, 6 FRANKFURTER ABHANDLUNGEN ZUM KRIEGSVERHÜTUNGSRECHT (1928) 88.

[24] Barthélémy, *Opinion in the Matter of the Agrarian Cases of the Hungarian Nationals before the Roumanian-Hungarian Mixed Arbitral Tribunal*, 1 *op. cit. supra* note 6, at 105, 106; Dupuis, *Opinion, ibid.*, 77.

[25] Joint Opinion of Sir Henry Slesser and Mr. Ralph Sutton, *Hungarian Interests in Rumania*, 2 *ibid.*, 3, 4.

[26] Borchard, *supra* note 6, at 34.

[27] Dupuis, *supra* note 24, at 77.

[28] Lapradelle, *Doctrinal Memorandum*, 1 *op. cit. supra* note 6, at 195, 197.

The question whether the measures attacked were in fact forbidden by Article 250 related to the merits.[29]

Upon the issue of the meaning of Article 250, it is the conclusion of Borchard that its text and purport were "unquestionably intended to preserve intact, in accordance with the rules of international law, and thus in contrast to the provisions of Article 232, the property owned by Hungarian nationals in the ceded Hungarian territory." [30] An interpretation converse to that of Rumania is advanced by Brunet,[31] who states that the privilege of liquidation accorded the Allies by the peace treaties is taken away in Article 267 of the Treaty of St. Germain and Article 250 of the Treaty of Trianon and the principle of international law that the private property of aliens must be respected resumes its sway.[32] The contention that the legislation was an economic and a political necessity was irrelevant as far as Rumania's international obligations were concerned.[33] The motives actuating a law have little to do with its legal effects. The argument that the expropriation was effected by an agrarian law and not by legislation against enemies as such was answered correctly by the tribunal when it said that the name assigned to a measure cannot determine its legality.[34] Kaufmann [35] states: "It is by no means a question of the *general* Agrarian reform law, but of a *special* law for the territories ceded by Hungary, consequently in no case of a *general reform scheme.*" The decision of the tribunal was carefully drafted and left open all questions of differential treatment and amount of compensation until the de-

29 Dupuis, *Observations on the Session of the Council of the League of Nations of March 7th, 1927, and on the Roumanian and Hungarian Theses, ibid.*, 241, 243; see also Udina, *The Powers of the Council of the League of Nations in the Appointment of Members of the Mixed Arbitral Tribunals,* 2 *ibid.*, 243, 253: "Now the Tribunal in the judgment on jurisdiction was bound to consider, simply, whether the measures taken . . . could be included among the liquidations referred to in Article 250 of the Treaty of Trianon, not whether they were included without further ado."

30 Borchard, *supra* note 6, at 31.

31 Brunet, *Opinion,* 1 *op. cit. supra* note 6, at 113, 115.

32 As to the appositeness of Article 267 of the Treaty of St. Germain to this case, see DEÁK, *op. cit. supra* note 1, at 13–15.

33 Bellot, *Opinion,* 1 *op. cit. supra* note 6, at 55, 57.

34 *Cf.* Borchard, *supra* note 6, at 23, 41.

35 Kaufmann, *The Hungarian-Roumanian Dispute,* 2 *op. cit. supra* note 6, at 79, 91.

cision on the merits.[36] The conclusion of the tribunal would seem to be further supported by the interpretation of the words "liquidation" and "expropriation" used in Head III of the Geneva Convention, which was adopted by the Permanent Court of International Justice in Judgment No. 7. The Court found that "liquidation" as used in Article 6 of the Convention conveyed the "meaning that, subject to the provisions authorizing expropriation, the treatment accorded to the German private property, rights and interests in Polish Upper Silesia is to be the treatment recognized by the generally accepted principles of international law. . . . The legal designation applied by one or other of the interested Parties to the act in dispute is irrelevant if the measure in fact affects German nationals in a manner contrary to the principles enunciated above." [37] The defense that the legislation in question applied to nationals as well as to foreigners was rejected by the Court with the remark that "a measure prohibited by the Convention cannot become lawful under this instrument by reason of the fact that the State applies it to its own nationals." [38]

38. DECISIONS AFFECTING THE RIGHTS OF THIRD PARTIES.—At the Hague Conference of 1899 Mr. Asser proposed an amendment to the Russian draft of arbitral code,[1] which, with substantially no change in substance, became Article 56 of the Convention of 1899 for the Pacific Settlement of International Disputes [2] and Article 84 of the Hague Convention of 1907. As embodied in the latter convention, it reads:

The award is binding only on the parties in dispute.

When there is a question as to the interpretation of a convention to which Powers other than those in dispute are parties, the latter inform all the signatory Powers in good time. Each of these powers is entitled to intervene in the case. If one or more avail themselves of this right, the interpretation contained in the award is equally binding upon them.[3]

[36] *Ibid.*, 86.
[37] SER. A., No. 7, pp. 21–22.
[38] *Ibid.*, 33.
[1] PROCEEDINGS OF THE HAGUE PEACE CONFERENCES, CONFERENCE OF 1899 (Carnegie trans., 1920) 742.
[2] *Ibid.*, 98.
[3] 1 PROCEEDINGS OF THE HAGUE PEACE CONFERENCES, CONFERENCE OF 1907 (Carnegie trans., 1920) 612–613.

Article 59 of the Statute of the Permanent Court of International Justice provides:

The decision of the Court has no binding force *except between the parties* and in respect to that particular case.[4] (Italics supplied.)

The right of intervention of third parties is permitted in Article 63.

Whenever the construction of a convention to which States other than those concerned in the case are parties is in question the Registrar shall notify all such States forthwith.

Every State so notified has the right to intervene in the proceedings: but if it uses this right, the construction given by the judgment will be equally binding upon it.[5]

It can hardly be questioned that an arbitral award is binding only upon the States which had constituted the tribunal in question.[6] Says Stoykovitch:

All the obligatory force of an award is based on the *compromis* by which the parties obligate themselves to submit their dispute to arbitration and agree in advance to execute the decision rendered within the terms of the *compromis*. Consequently, it is absolutely impossible for the decision to produce effects with regard to states complete strangers to the *compromis*.[7]

If in the course of its opinion it becomes necessary to touch upon legal questions in which other States are directly interested, such as the construction of an international convention to which States other than the parties to the dispute are signatories, its decision would have no obligatory force upon such States. In the cases before the Central American Court of Justice involving the Bryan-Chamorro Treaty,[8] the Court was exceedingly careful not to encroach upon this rule. The treaty was between the United States and

---

[4] STATUTE AND RULES OF COURT (1936) 25.
[5] *Ibid.*, 26.
[6] BALASKO, CAUSES DE NULLITÉ DE LA SENTENCE ARBITRALE EN DROIT INTERNATIONAL PUBLIC (1938) 192; Limburg, *L'Autorité de chose jugée des décisions des juridictiones internationales* (1929) 30 RECUEIL DES COURS 560–561; Scelle, *Une Instance en revision devant la Cour de la Haye, l'affaire de la Orinoco Steamship Company* (1911) 18 REV. GEN. DE DROIT INT. PUB. 164. As to intervention by third party States which are signatories to a multilateral arbitration agreement, see Castberg, *L'Excès de pouvoir dans la justice internationale* (1931) 35 RECUEIL DES COURS 443.
[7] STOYKOVITCH, DE L'AUTORITÉ DE LA SENTENCE ARBITRALE EN DROIT INTERNATIONAL PUBLIC (1924) 109.
[8] *Infra* sec. 40.

Nicaragua. States adjacent to Nicaragua alleged that it violated
duties owed by that State to them. The United States was not a
party to the arbitration. The Court, though it judged Nicaragua's
action in concluding the treaty in the light of what it conceived to
be Nicaragua's international obligations, refrained from rendering
a decree of a form which would indicate an assumption that the
United States was subject to its jurisdiction. In any event, it is not
believed to have been open to Nicaragua to raise the charge of
nullity, because the court decided upon a question affecting the
rights of third parties. That would be for the third parties in question, and upon that issue alone the award would be without force
only with regard to such third parties. In all other respects it would
remain binding upon the parties to the *compromis*.

39. SAME: DISPUTE OF GREAT BRITAIN AND VENEZUELA REGARDING THE
BOUNDARY OF BRITISH GUIANA.—Examination of the award in the
arbitration between Great Britain and Venezuela under the convention of February 2, 1897, indicates that the tribunal entered upon
the decision of matters affecting the rights of Brazil, a stranger to the
arbitration. Though the arbitrators were appointed to determine
the boundary between British Guiana and Venezuela, they did not
restrict their pronouncements to that question but also traced a
line which touched upon the territories of Brazil, who, of course,
was not a party to the arbitration. Apparently they appreciated the
nature of their action, for in so doing they entered the following
reservation.

Provided always that the line of delimitation fixed by this Award shall be
subject and without prejudice to any questions now existing, or which may
arise, to be determined between the Government of Her Britannic Majesty
and the Republic of Brazil, or between the latter Republic and the United
States of Venezuela.[1]

The writer of an unsigned note in the *Revue Générale de Droit
International Public* [2] proffers in explanation of the tribunal's action
that it encountered in its studies the facts necessary to enable it to

[1] Award of October 3, 1899, 92 BRITISH AND FOREIGN STATE PAPERS (1899–1900)
160, 161.
[2] (1901) 71.

propose an equitable delimitation of the lands of Great Brazil and set it forth in the hope that these parties would adhere to it. He is, nevertheless, compelled to admit that the tribunal exceeded its mandate.[3]

40. SAME: CASES BEFORE THE CENTRAL AMERICAN COURT OF JUSTICE INVOLVING THE BRYAN-CHAMORRO TREATY.[1]—The protests of Nicaragua against the validity of the decisions of the Central American Court of Justice in the actions brought against it by Costa Rica and El Salvador involving the Bryan-Chamorro treaty between the United States and Nicaragua are believed to possess little merit. The Court, in its decision, refrained from holding the treaty void, as requested by Costa Rica, since the United States, which was a party to the treaty, was not subject to the jurisdiction of the Court. Nevertheless, Nicaragua charged that the Court exceeded its authority and rendered a decision which was unjust and impossible of execution. The cases illustrate the unfortunate results consequent upon the present system of international arbitration which leaves claims of nullity to regulation between the parties.

The jurisdiction of the Central American Court of Justice was set forth in Article 1 of the convention of December 20, 1907, by which it was established.[2] The contracting parties thereby bound themselves to submit "all controversies of questions which may arise among them, of whatsoever nature," to the Court, "in case the respective Departments of Foreign Affairs should not have been able to reach an understanding." By Article 21 it was provided that the Court should be governed by its free judgment in deciding points of fact and by the principles of international law with respect to points of law.[3] Its competence to determine its own jurisdiction was affirmed.[4] With respect to the finality of its judgments, it was stated that the "interested parties solemnly bind themselves to submit to

3 *Ibid.*, 80.
1 With regard to the history of the Central American Court of Justice see Hudson, *The Central American Court of Justice* (1932) 26 AM. J. INT. LAW 759. These cases are there briefly reported at pp. 773–781.
2 (1907) FOR. REL. U.S., Part 2, 697.
3 *Ibid.*, 700.
4 Art. 22, *ibid.*, 700.

said judgments, and all agree to lend all moral support that may be necessary in order that they may be properly fulfilled." [5]

Certain cases were brought before the Court, based on the effects of the Bryan-Chamorro Treaty of August 5, 1914, between the United States and Nicaragua.[6] In Article 1 of this treaty Nicaragua purported to make the following grant.

The Government of Nicaragua grants in perpetuity to the Government of the United States . . . the exclusive proprietary rights necessary and convenient for the construction, operation and maintenance of an interoceanic canal.[7]

The conclusion of the treaty was protested by Costa Rica,[8] El Salvador,[9] and other States [10] as affecting their rights, but the Department of State reiterated the views which it had previously expressed in the same relation that the treaty did not in fact infringe upon any rights of the States adjacent to Nicaragua,[11] and in addition invited attention to the resolution of ratification of the United States Senate.[12] In its declaration advising ratification the Senate stated that it was given with the understanding that nothing in the treaty was intended to affect any right of Costa Rica, El Salvador, or Honduras.

Costa Rica v. Nicaragua.—A complaint was thereafter filed by Costa Rica against Nicaragua in which the Court was asked to declare that the treaty violated the complainant's rights in certain respects and that the treaty was void for the want of capacity of Nicaragua to enter into it. It also requested an interlocutory decree for the preservation of the *status quo ante.*[13] At the outset Nicaragua notified the Court that it would not permit discussion of the sub-

---

[5] Art. 25, *ibid.,* 700.
[6] (1916) *ibid.,* 849.
[7] *Ibid.,* 850.
[8] Minister Quesada to the Secretary of State, Feb. 8, 1916, *ibid.,* 814.
[9] Minister Zaldwar to the Secretary of State, Feb. 9, 1916, *ibid.*
[10] See Hudson, *supra* note 1, at 778–780.
[11] Secretary of State to the Minister of Costa Rica, Aug. 1, 1914 (1914) FOR. REL. U.S. 964.
[12] Same to same, Mar. 1, 1916 (1916) *ibid.,* 820.
[13] Hudson, *supra* note 1, at 774.

ject and that any proceedings by it in the matter would be considered void.[14]

The Court admitted the complaint by order of May 1, 1916, enjoining both parties to maintain the *status quo* existing between them prior to the treaty.[15] The magistrate for Nicaragua dissented.[16] His opinion summarized the arguments advanced by the Nicaraguan government in its previous communications to the Court. It was asserted that the requirement of Article 1 of the Convention of 1907 that the Court could consider a case only when diplomatic action had failed was not fulfilled. No attempt had been made by Costa Rica to come to an understanding with Nicaragua. The treaty Costa Rica attacked left for a later convention the details concerning the construction of the canal, and no decision had been made to carry out work injurious to Costa Rica's rights.

Costa Rica contended in its case [17] that, so far as possible, it had protested the canal treaties of 1913 and 1914 and that the jurisdictional requirement of Article 1 was therefore satisfied. It stated that in April, 1913, it had become aware of the conclusion of the Chamorro-Weitzel treaty of February 8, 1913, between the United States and Nicaragua for the opening of an interoceanic canal. Since Nicaragua had refused to disclose the contents of the treaty, Costa Rica was unable to make specific charges against it. When notice was received of the conclusion of the Bryan-Chamorro Treaty, Costa Rica protested it to the United States both before and after ratification.

To sustain its action, Costa Rica relied on the Cañas-Jerez Treaty of April 15, 1858, and the Cleveland award of March 22, 1888.[18] Under the Cañas-Jerez Treaty it was provided that Nicaragua should have the dominion over the San Juan River and that Costa

---

[14] Nicaraguan Minister for Foreign Affairs to the Secretary of the Central American Court of Justice, Apr. 1, 1916 (1916) FOR. REL. U.S. 842; see also telegram of Nicaragua to the Court, Apr. 26, 1916, *ibid.*, 864.

[15] 5 ANALES (Nos. 14 to 16) 87. Also in (1916) FOR. REL. U.S. 841.

[16] 5 ANALES (Nos. 14–16) 90; (1916) FOR. REL. U.S. 843.

[17] (1916) FOR. REL. U.S. 865–873.

[18] (1888) *ibid.*, Part 1, 458.

Rica should have perpetual rights of free navigation from the mouth up to three English miles before reaching Castillo Viejo. Nicaragua agreed not to conclude any future contract of canalization without first hearing the opinion of Costa Rica. This treaty was interpreted by the Cleveland award. It was there declared that Nicaragua was under an obligation not to make any concessions for canal purposes without first asking the opinion of Costa Rica. The "natural rights" of Costa Rica were defined to include rights in the ports of San Juan del Norte and Bahia de Salinas and in that part of the San Juan River which lies three English miles below Castillo Viejo. Those rights were to be considered injured when anything injurious to Costa Rica was done in the ports or when there occurred such an obstruction or deviation of the San Juan River as seriously to impede its navigation where Costa Rica had a right of navigation.

Costa Rica agreed that the treaty did not give it the right to be a party to any concessions which Nicaragua might make for an interoceanic canal. However, in cases in which the construction of the canal involved injury to its "natural rights," it submitted that its opinion must be more than a mere consulting voice. Its consent was necessary in such cases, and it was therefore privileged to exact compensation for any concessions which it might be asked to grant. It seemed impossible to Costa Rica that a third party could construct a canal without injuring its contractual and natural rights. The allegation was made that Nicaragua had sold the San Juan River as if she were its absolute owner, without taking into account Costa Rica's rights. The latter accordingly repeated the request for relief which had been made in its complaint.

Nicaragua replied that the convention said nothing about a sale of the San Juan River, but was merely an option to conclude a canal treaty. It again affirmed that Article 1 of the treaty of 1907 had not been complied with. With respect to Costa Rica's contention that all possible steps had been taken to meet that article, Nicaragua observed that the Chamorro-Weitzel Treaty of 1913 must be eliminated from the discussion, since it had become ineffective. No steps had been taken by Costa Rica as regards the Bryan-Chamorro Treaty.

Therefore it could not be said that it was impossible to reach an agreement. It was essential that jurisdiction be proved in connection with the Bryan-Chamorro Treaty. If the Court disregarded this requirement, it would exceed the limits of its mission, and everything that it might decide would be void.[19]

At its session of September 22, 1916, the Court considered some fourteen questions propounded by the President and decided that it possessed jurisdiction; that Nicaragua had violated, to the detriment of Costa Rica, the rights granted to the latter by the treaty of 1858 and the Cleveland award; but that it could make no declaration that the Bryan-Chamorro Treaty was void owing to the fact that the government of the United States was not subject to its jurisdiction.[20]

Its opinion and award were rendered on September 30, 1916.[21] The Court remarked that the pretext of Nicaragua that its acts were performed in the exercise of its sovereignty would not exclude the jurisdiction of the Court, since Article 1 gave it competence over all classes of disputes. The fact that the treaty was concluded with a State not within the jurisdiction of the Court, did not prevent it from examining the legal relations between the Central American nations. The Chamorro-Weitzel and the Bryan-Chamorro treaties were declared to be two stages in the same transaction. The Costa Rican complaint was viewed as one not based on the Bryan-Chamorro Treaty, but on the fact that that compact related to concessions for an interoceanic canal against which it had protested as early as 1913. The arguments then made by Nicaragua, that its sovereignty and the necessity of maintaining secrecy precluded it from making public the provisions of the treaty, applied as a necessary consequence to the second treaty. It must therefore be considered that Costa Rica had exhausted all available diplomatic negotiations. The Court felt that the final requirement of Article 1 should not be understood "as meaning that the High Contracting

19 (1916) *ibid.*, 873–875; see Message of Nicaragua to the Court, Aug. 1, 1916, 5 ANALES (Nos. 14–16) 122.
20 (1916) FOR. REL. U.S. 875–877.
21 5 ANALES (Nos. 14–16) 130–176; (1916) FOR. REL. U.S. 862.

Parties are obliged to insist on steps as being taken which, besides being useless as regards the object of securing an agreement, are incompatible with their interests and honor." Upon these grounds Costa Rica held that it possessed jurisdiction.

With regard to the merits of the case, the Court reasoned that the treaty embodied "a perfect sale of the property rights necessary for the construction of an inter-oceanic canal by way of the San Juan River or the Great Lake of Nicaragua or by any other route in Nicaraguan territory." If the canal were to be constructed by way of the San Juan River, the opinion of Costa Rica ought to have been heard, under the Cañas-Jerez Treaty, as " 'to the disadvantages which the deal may have for the two countries.' " In the alternative of construction by any other route, her opinion should also have been heard, but only as a consulting voice. The Court remarked that it was not necessary to wait "until the site of the proposed work is located and until the 'natural rights' of Costa Rica have suffered concrete and material injury before deeming it appropriate to give a hearing to the High Complainant Party." With regard to the reservation of the United States Senate, it was considered as being without effect upon the legal relations between the nations at dispute. The injury against Costa Rican rights was consummated, and the amendment did not produce the effect of restoring matters to the legal status created by the treaty of 1858. The Court refrained from declaring the treaty void, because, as before stated, the United States was not subject to its jurisdiction. Its final award reaffirmed its holding of September 22, 1916.

A dissent was entered by the Nicaraguan judge, Gutierrez Navas.[22] It was his view that the two treaties were not two aspects of the same international negotiation. Their stipulations were different. The Chamorro-Weitzel Treaty was simply a project not carried to completion, while the Bryan-Chamorro Treaty had a legal existence. He contended that the Court should not extend its jurisdiction to the consideration of rights acquired by a State which had not delegated any authority to it. This case involved contractual

[22] 5 ANALES (Nos. 14–16) 177.

interests of the United States. For the Court to interfere therewith exceeded the powers which the convention of 1907 had granted to it. The treaty of 1858 gave Costa Rica the right to discuss the inconveniences which a definitive canal treaty might occasion. It was not, therefore, violated, inasmuch as the Bryan-Chamorro Treaty granted only a simple option or right of preference. That treaty envisaged only the *possibility* of the construction of the canal. It did not require the voice of the Costa Rican government, because there would be lacking fixed data to judge the inconveniences of the plan. No natural right of Costa Rica had been injured; if the canal were not constructed, its rights remain unchanged. If it were determined to construct the canal, a new treaty would be necessary. There would then be ample opportunity for Costa Rica to protect its rights. The Nicaraguan judge pointed out that it remained for engineers to fix the route and make studies of excavations. A judgment as to whether the work would occupy or inundate Costa Rican territory or affect its natural rights should be based upon the decision of engineers. The holding that Costa Rica has a decisive vote had no such data to support it.

The Nicaraguan government informed the Court that it refused to abide by its award, upon the ground that it lacked jurisdiction and had committed grave error.[23] This statement was affirmed in its note to the Secretary of the Court of October 21, 1916.[24] It was there stated that the treaty of 1907 contained nothing which touched upon the sovereignty and local integrity of the Central American Republics. Nicaragua did not admit that the power granted to the Court should extend to controversies relating to matters prior to the treaty of 1907 or that it could revise an award accepted by the parties—as it did in respect of the award of President Cleveland, when it declared that a joint ownership existed in Salinas Bay and San Juan del Norte. Article 1 of the treaty operated to exclude the case because the requirement had not been fulfilled that the respective foreign offices must have failed to come to an agreement.

[23] Telegram from the Nicaraguan Minister of Foreign Affairs to the Secretary of the Court, Oct. 14, 1916, *ibid.*, 232.
[24] *Ibid.*, 234; (1916) FOR. REL. U.S. 888.

A defense of its judgment was made by the Court in a communication addressed to the Central American Republics other than Nicaragua.[25] For the consideration of those governments, an analysis was made of the arguments whereby the decision was impugned. It stated that the convention of 1907 had previously been regarded as unrestricted with respect to the scope of questions to be arbitrated. Nor was it limited to disputes arising subsequent to its creation. No revision of the Cleveland award had taken place, only the interpretation necessary in the case. In considering the grounds of the complaint, the Court had simply exercised the proper judicial function of inquiring into the spirit and scope of the Cañas-Jerez Treaty. If on this point, which was of secondary importance, Nicaragua had had a different criterion, it should have presented its argument. Having failed to do so, its censures must be held to be without effect. With respect to the argument that Costa Rica failed to fulfill the requirement of taking steps through the diplomatic channel, the Court answered that it had considered all the facts thereon and had carefully reached its conclusion and that under Article 21 it was given free judgment in deciding points of fact. Nicaragua ignored the circumstances that the 1913 and 1914 compacts were fundamentally the same and that she had closed the door to subsequent diplomatic settlement by her declarations that she could not reveal the terms of the treaty. It should, moreover, be observed that the government of Nicaragua had never brought before the Court any action based on the violation to which it alluded.

A final exposition of its position was made by the Nicaraguan government to the Central American governments in a communication of November 24, 1917.[26] It was there pointed out that, despite the fact that the Bryan-Chamorro Treaty had been fully carried out, the natural rights of Costa Rica remained on the same footing. The execution of the treaty involved no canal construction, which was the only way in which the natural rights of Costa Rica could be in-

[25] Communication of the Central American Court of Justice to the Governments of Costa Rica, Salvador, Honduras, and Guatemala, Nov. 9, 1916 (1916) FOR. REL. U.S. 893.
[26] (1917) FOR. REL. U.S. 1104.

jured. By the treaty, Nicaragua had transferred her sovereign rights to construct a canal through her territory. Those rights existed in Nicaragua without affecting the natural rights of Costa Rica. Similarly, by their transfer no injury could be caused to Costa Rica. The decision of the Court assumed as a certainty that the canal would be constructed via the San Juan River. The treaty, however, granted the right to construct a canal indeterminately and did not have as its immediate object the construction of the canal. The Court, therefore, did not decide "according to truth and justice" when it held that the treaty violated the rights of Costa Rica.

El Salvador v. Nicaragua.—In its complaint against Nicaragua,[27] El Salvador adverted to specific measures taken by it to obtain redress through the diplomatic channel. It stated that it had addressed a note on the matter concerning which the complaint was filed to the Nicaraguan Foreign Office, but that no reply thereto had been received from that office. The complaint petitioned first, that the suit be admitted and considered by the Court; secondly, that the Court issue an appropriate decree fixing the situation to be maintained by Nicaragua in order that the *status quo ante* be preserved; thirdly, that Nicaragua be compelled to abstain from fulfilling the Bryan-Chamorro Treaty; and, fourthly, that the Court grant all other appropriate relief. The petition was based on the allegations that the treaty was an official act of Nicaragua that placed in danger the national security of El Salvador, violated her rights of co-ownership in the Gulf of Fonseca, and prejudiced the fulfillment of her aspirations for the creation of a Central American union. It was further alleged that the treaty was not validly concluded, since it was in violation of the constitutional powers of the Nicaraguan government. Certain additional points were later added to the complaint on which judgment was asked.[28]

In its argument Nicaragua stated that in answering the complaint it had not admitted that the Court had jurisdiction. It asserted that the Court could not take cognizance of the complaint, because the

[27] (1916) *ibid.*, 853.
[28] (1917) 11 AM. J. INT. LAW 685; see order of Court of Oct. 2, 1916, provisionally admitting additions, 6 ANALES (Nos. 16–18) 10.

controversy did not involve a purely Central American question, but rather a mixed question which depended upon the rights of a third State which had not submitted to the authority of the Court. The negotiations between the foreign offices on the subject had not been exhausted, because El Salvador had introduced a new claim in its complaint that had not previously been discussed between the foreign offices. The material allegations of El Salvador's complaint were denied, and arguments were produced against them.[29]

The contentions of Nicaragua were rejected by the Court,[30] which held that it was competent to take cognizance of the action. The concession of the naval base in the Gulf of Fonseca by the Bryan-Chamorro Treaty was held to menace the national security of El Salvador and to violate her rights of ownership in the gulf, within the limitations set forth in its opinion. The Court further held that the treaty violated Articles 2 and 9 of the treaty of December 20, 1907, and that "the Government of Nicaragua *is under the obligation*—availing itself of all possible means provided by international law—to reestablish and maintain the legal status that existed prior to the Bryan-Chamorro Treaty between the litigant republics in so far as relates to the matters considered in this section." The Court considered itself without power to declare the treaty null, because that would involve judging the rights of the other signatory power, which had neither been heard by or submitted to the jurisdiction of the Court. The argument that the efforts towards settlement were made solely in connection with the additions to the complaint was stated not to be well founded, inasmuch as those additions did not involve a new controversy. The diplomatic efforts resorted to were directed against the entire legal structure of the Bryan-Chamorro Treaty. That a third nation was involved was no reason to refuse jurisdiction. The jurisdiction of the Court was general and covered all questions of whatever nature and origin. The fact that the United States had interests connected with Nicaragua did not justify Nicaragua's evasion of its obligation to submit to the Court. The

---

[29] See opinion of Court, *ibid.*, 96, 112 *et seq.*; (1917) 11 Am. J. Int. Law 674, 686 *et sqq.*
[30] *Ibid.*

Bryan-Chamorro Treaty related to the legal order created in Central America and contracts concerning property located there. To admit lack of jurisdiction would render almost negligible the Court's judicial power, for questions of transcendental importance to the Central American States having their origin in treaties would be excluded. It was sufficient that the Court render a decision embracing solely the rights in litigation between El Salvador and Nicaragua.

Having sustained its jurisdiction to consider the complaint, the Court recognized the Gulf of Fonseca to be in the category of historic bays, possessed of the characteristics of a closed sea. It declared that a community of interests existed in the bay and that Nicaragua, El Salvador, and Honduras were co-owners of the waters of the bay, as well as of those portions necessary for police inspection and for purposes of national security. Nicaragua as a coparcener could not alienate to or share with a third party the use of such waters without the consent of all. The Court stipulated the proviso, however, that the rights of Honduras as a coparcener were not to be affected by its decision. The establishment of a naval base at any point on the borders of the gulf was thought to menace the security of El Salvador and to endanger its national integrity. The Bryan-Chamorro Treaty was viewed as violative of Articles II and IX of the treaty of December 20, 1907. It altered the constitutional order of Nicaragua in contravention of Article II, because Nicaragua supplanted its own sovereignty in part of its territory by that of a foreign country. Article IX was violated, because by granting to the United States sovereign authority over the territory leased and granted it had given the United States power to disrupt the equality of treatment accorded to vessels of the signatory powers by Article IX.

As in the case of Costa Rica against Nicaragua, the Nicaraguan judge entered a dissenting opinion.[31] He again made the point that the plaintiff had not adequately carried out its duty of attempting to arrive at a diplomatic agreement and added that the general terms of Article 1 of the treaty of 1907 could not be legally interpreted to give the Court power to prevent the fulfillment of a solemn treaty

[31] 6 ANALES (Nos. 16–18) 171.

celebrated by one of the signatory powers thereto. Any other holding would be a grave interference with its sovereignty. El Salvador had from October 21, 1913, to April 14, 1916, confined its protests to the United States. Not until the latter date did it direct a protesting note to its sister State, Nicaragua. Such a measure was wholly insufficient for the conciliation of the important interests at stake and did not establish that a settlement was impossible. Another reason advanced as prohibiting the Court from taking jurisdiction over the complaint was that the rights of a third State would be materially affected without a hearing on its part.

The Nicaraguan representative before the Court duly entered a protest against its decision.[32] He stated that the tribunal, passing beyond the limits of the function imposed by the pact creating it, without subjecting itself to the precepts of international law, without the views of experts which were necessary for the case, and without proof or any base, had rendered a decision which it was his painful duty to reject. In this refusal he was confirmed by a note addressed by the Nicaraguan Minister of Foreign Relations to the Court.[33] Arguments essentially similar to those advanced by Judge Navas and noted above were set forth in this communication. A reply was made by the secretary of the Court [34] that the matter of jurisdiction had been fully argued before the Court and carefully studied by it. In order to decide the question of jurisdiction, it had been necessary for the Court to consider the pertinent treaties and conventions, of which the Bryan-Chamorro Treaty was the most pertinent. The Court was privileged to consider the injuries caused the plaintiff by the treaty, and the fact that its decision would have no legal effect as regards the United States did not diminish the fact that it was *res judicata* for Nicaragua. Sovereignty was not unrestricted and could not be invoked by Nicaragua in order to injure rights which she was obligated by treaties to respect. The text of the treaty of 1907 gave to the Court jurisdiction over all questions of

[32] *Ibid.*, 199.
[33] Minister Urtecho to the Secretary of the Court, Apr. 16, 1917, 7 ANALES (Nos. 19–20) 18.
[34] Secretary of the Court to the Nicaraguan Minister, July 14, 1917, *ibid.*, 22.

whatever nature and was the only instance of absolute obligatory arbitration in the world. Formulas such as "national honor," "absolute honor," "unrestricted sovereignty," "vital interests" were banished from the chambers of the Court. A State causing damage to another was obligated to repair it by appropriate means sanctioned by international law. What those means were and the manner in which the *status quo ante* decreed by the Court was to be obtained, were to be determined by the interested parties. In this part of its decision the Court had not exceeded its functions, but had only issued a resolution upon a request of the complainant. The secretary of the Court also addressed to the foreign offices of the other Central American States a request that they lend their moral influence to the end that Nicaraguan government should accept and respect the judgment of the Court.

As a final statement of its position, Nicaragua, in a communication to the Central American governments, criticized the award in this case as also involving excess of authority,[35] asserting that it had opportunely informed the tribunal that the treaty did not come under the Court's jurisdiction because no purely Central American question was involved. Moreover, it was impossible to render an award against the Nicaraguan government without at the same time affecting the rights of a third nation. The arrogation to itself of jurisdiction by the tribunal on the ground that otherwise its work would be rendered nugatory was unjustifiable. It was not subversive of arbitration that a tribunal should take cognizance of matters not within its jurisdiction. The award was either manifestly impossible of execution or, if capable of execution, injurious to the interests of a third party. Nicaragua alleged that the award was unjust and stated that there was no joint dominion over the Gulf of Fonseca and that the three States bordering it had uniformly recognized that the waters of the gulf were prolongations of their respective territories. El Salvador had no common boundary with Nicaragua, and the Court could not, without exceeding its powers, declare that there

[35] Minister of Foreign Affairs of Nicaragua to the Central American Governments, Nov. 24, 1917 (1917) FOR. REL. U.S. 1104.

was a joint dominion, since it would then follow that the boundaries were common. In any event, the concession of the naval base was made within its own maritime territory, over which Nicaragua had exclusive sovereignty. If violation of rights by Nicaragua existed, it would have been proper to decree that Nicaragua was under obligations to make reparation, but the award imposed the obligation of restoring the status prior to the treaty, which would be tantamount to abrogating the treaty at the cost of Nicaragua's national honor.

41. DECISIONS FAILING TO APPLY THE LAW PRESCRIBED BY THE COMPROMIS.—A decision which manifestly fails properly to apply a rule for decision laid down in the *compromis* or an applicable rule of international law having a material bearing upon the outcome of the case involves an excess of jurisdiction and is therefore void. For, unless the *compromis* stipulates otherwise, it is either an express or an implied term that the arbitrator should apply international law as the basis of his decision. Consequently, a decision which manifestly ignores a rule of international law that has a decisive bearing upon the outcome of the case or patently fails to apply the special conventional rules of decision laid down in the *compromis* exceeds the limits of the arbitrator's powers and is therefore void.[1]

Such a departure from the terms of submission is not to be confused with essential error. The latter involves an erroneous appreciation of the facts or law, resulting possibly in an unjust or unsound decision, but one that does not ignore the rule of decision enjoined upon the arbitrator by the *compromis*.[2] A number of writers have identified an error of law with excess of power. States Audry: [3]

The error of law, in effect, arises always from the fact that the principles of international law have been ill interpreted and consequently identifies itself with excess of jurisdiction, since the latter consists in the arbitrator not observing the principles prescribed for him in the *compromis*.

[1] *Supra* secs. 26 and 27, and cases under this title *infra*.
[2] *Infra* Ch. iv.
[3] AUDRY, LA REVISION DE LA SENTENCE ARBITRALE (1914) 76–77.

Hoijer [4] reaffirms this view in almost identical language. The reasoning of Stoykovitch [5] is more accurate:

As to the error of law, we believe that it ought to be considered a defect of the award only when it constitutes an excess of jurisdiction. The error of law will be a cause of nullity when the arbitrator has disregarded a principle of international law expressly or implicitly mentioned in the *compromis*.

Hertz [6] states:

The *compromis* constitutes a particular type of legislation; the arbitrator finds himself, as the judge, in the presence of a law. The *excès de pouvoir* is nothing other than an infraction of the law, an infraction as to jurisdiction.

It would, therefore, seem elemental that if an arbitrator is instructed to decide according to international law, he cannot decide contrary to a fundamental rule of international law.[7] If he is restricted to the measurement of damages, he cannot enter upon the question of legal liability.[8] If special conventional rules are decreed for his decision, he cannot ignore them.[9]

42. SAME: PELLETIER CASE.—The Pelletier case is one of the best-known illustrations of the manner in which a departure from the terms of submission may occur in the decision on the merits, rather than in the decision of the preliminary jurisdictional question whether the tribunal has jurisdiction over the parties and the subject matter. There was no question that the arbitrator lacked the power to decide the case; the objection raised was that his construction of the *compromis* as to the manner in which the case was to be disposed of was erroneous and thereby resulted in an excess of jurisdiction.

---

[4] HOIJER, LA SOLUTION PACIFIQUE DES LITIGES INTERNATIONAUX (1925) 279–280.

[5] STOYKOVITCH, DE L'AUTORITÉ DE LA SENTENCE ARBITRALE EN DROIT INTERNATIONAL PUBLIC (1924) 214.

[6] Hertz, *Essai sur le problème de la nullité* (1939, 3d ser.) 20 REV. DE DROIT INT. L.C. 450, 465. See also Borel, *Le Voies de recours contre les sentences arbitrales* (1935) 52 RECUEIL DES COURS 37; Castberg, *L'Excès de pouvoir dans la justice internationale* (1931) 35 RECUEIL DES COURS 420.

[7] *Infra* sec. 42.

[8] *Infra* sec. 43.   [9] *Infra* secs. 44 and 45.

In 1861 one Pelletier, master of the bark *William,* was found within Haitian waters under circumstances indicating an attempt at slave trading. The laws of Haiti assimilated his acts to those of piracy. In pursuance of those laws, he was arrested, tried, and condemned to imprisonment for five years, and his vessel was confiscated. Pelletier made representations to the Department of State which finally prompted it to submit his claim to Haiti. An arbitration agreement was concluded with Haiti on May 28, 1884, to settle the claim, and also the claim of Lazare, which was pending between the two States. It was provided that the arbitrator was to decide "according to the rules of International Law existing at the time of the transactions complained of." [1] The parties agreed "to accept the decision of said Arbitrator in each of said cases, as final and binding, and to give to such decision full effect and force, in good faith, and without unnecessary delay or any reservation or evasion whatsoever." [2] In an award under date of June 13, 1885,[3] the arbitrator held that Pelletier was undoubtedly in Haitian waters for the purpose of there engaging in the slave trade, but that in trying him the Haitian courts should not have applied their municipal law as to what constituted piracy, but international law. Since according to that law in 1861 slave trade was not piracy, an award of $57,-250 was rendered in favor of Pelletier.

The Haitian minister protested that the arbitrator had mistaken his jurisdiction under the protocol. In a report to the President of the United States, the Secretary of State, Mr. Bayard, concurred in the view that the award should not be enforced. Mr. Bayard stated that the arbitrator had apparently misconstrued the rule of decision as laid down in the protocol, in that he had declared that by it he was precluded from any consideration of Haitian law, but was limited to the question of the status of Pelletier's acts under international law. He considered such a construction to be wrong, because under international law the jurisdiction of the sovereign extended to offenses committed in territorial waters. He noted that

---

[1] Art. IV, 1 MALLOY, TREATIES 932, 934.
[2] Art. VI, *ibid.*   [3] 2 MOORE, INT. ARB. 1757.

Pelletier had in fact made an attempt to carry on the slave trade in Haitian waters, had been fairly tried therefor by Haitian courts, and had received a lenient punishment and that the advancement of the claim by the United States did not bar the examination of these matters by the arbitrator. He continued that the United States had acted on what seemed to be a *prima facie* case and its presentment of the claim was not a prejudgment of it. He concluded that the United States could not honorably press for the enforcement of an award which was *ultra vires*. The indemnity was, therefore, not exacted from Haiti.[4]

43. SAME: CLAIM OF THE UNITED STATES AND PARAGUAY NAVIGATION COMPANY.—The question whether a commission created to fix the amount of damages payable in a claim for which responsibility was admitted, can render an award allowing no damages whatever was presented in the decision of the commission created under the convention of February 4, 1859, between the United States and Paraguay.

The United States and Paraguay Navigation Company was an American corporation created for the purpose of developing commercial enterprises in Paraguay. It established in 1853 a cigar factory and a sawmill and purchased other property in Paraguay. The company's agent soon abandoned the business, alleging that he was expelled; but his departure in fact appears to have been impelled by the withdrawal from the undertaking of the friendly aid and support of the government, owing to the overbearing attitude which he had assumed. In 1855 the affair of the *Water Witch* occurred.[1] Both incidents prompted President Buchanan to send a naval force to Paraguay. A special commissioner was appointed to procure payment of the company's claims. He was instructed that if no agreement could be reached as to the amount of the indemnity, that question could be left for arbitration, but that it was an indispensable prerequisite that the Paraguayan government should acknowledge its liability to the company. A convention was concluded on February 4, 1859, in which Paraguay bound itself "for the responsibility

[4] *Ibid.*, 1793 *et sqq.*   [1] 7 MOORE, DIG. 109.

in favor of the 'United States and Paraguay Navigation Company' which may result from the decree of commissioners," [2] the appointment of which was provided for in Article II. That commission was constituted in order "to determine the amount of said reclamations." [3] The only provisions relating to the basis of the decision and its finality were that the commissioners were to render a "just decision" and that Paraguay bound itself to pay the draft which the United States should issue for the amount of the award.[4] After the submission of proofs and the hearing of argument, the commissioners rendered a decision that upon the proofs submitted the company had not established any right to damages.[5] The grounds of the award were stated in a separate opinion by Mr. Johnson, the United States commissioner.[6] On the question of jurisdiction, it set forth the view that the commissioners were required to make "a full and unrestricted examination of the claim," and that "to ascertain the 'amount' of the claim necessarily obliged them to determine between o and the highest amount which figures could express, according to the exigencies of the proofs." It observed that the liability which Paraguay had admitted was only that " 'which may result from the decree of the commissioners.' " [7]

Unquestionably, it was incumbent upon the company to furnish proofs of its damages, and the interpretation of their *compromis* to that effect by the commissioners cannot be said to involve a departure from its terms. Insofar as their decision professed to rest on that basis, no excess of jurisdiction could reasonably have been alleged, though question of the good faith of the arbitrators or essential error might have arisen if the record patently failed to sustain their conclusion that no damages were proved. An examination of the opinion indicates its correctness as to most of the items of damages claimed, but its denial of an award for the sawmill and the cigar factory seems to be based on the failure of the company to comply

---

[2] Art. I, Convention of Feb. 4, 1859, between the United States and Paraguay, 2 MALLOY, TREATIES 1362.
[3] Art. II, *ibid.*, 1363.
[4] Art. III, V, *ibid.*   [5] 2 MOORE, INT. ARB. 1501.
[6] *Ibid.*, 1502.   [7] *Ibid.*, 1507.

with a local license law rather than the lack of satisfactory proofs of value. In this respect President Buchanan's statement that it was not "competent for commissioners authorized to ascertain the indemnity for the injury to go behind their authority and decide upon the original merits of the claim" [8] seems correct. The decision upon its face departed from the limits within which it was recognized that the arbitrators were to act. The substantial character of this injury having been established, it was not within their powers to refuse an indemnity upon the ground that the claim therefor was ill-founded.[9] Nevertheless, the veiled animadversions upon the sending of a naval mission to Paraguay to collect the claims which were made at the close of Mr. Johnson's opinion [10] were probably not without some influence upon President Buchanan's outspoken dissatisfaction with the decision.

From time to time the claim was thereafter brought up by the Department of State. On August 12, 1887, and again on May 21, 1888, a protocol was agreed upon between the two governments settling the claim for $90,000, but upon both occasions it failed approval by the Paraguayan legislature, and there the matter ended.

44. SAME: ORINOCO STEAMSHIP COMPANY CASE.—In the Orinoco Steamship Company case before the Hague Tribunal under the *compromis* of February 13, 1909, an award of an international tribunal was for the first time formally annulled and modified by the decision of a second tribunal.[1] In so doing, although a certain doubt exists as to the basis of its holding, the tribunal admitted that:

Excessive exercise of power may consist, not only in deciding a question not submitted to the arbitrators, but also in misinterpreting the express provisions of the agreement in respect of the way in which they are to reach their decisions, notably with regard to the legislation or principles of law to be applied.[2]

[8] *Ibid.*, 1539.
[9] *Cf.* Doctrinal note in 2 LAPRADELLE ET POLITIS, RECUEIL DES ARBITRAGES INTERNATIONAUX (1905) 53; BALASKO, CAUSES DE NULLITÉ DE LA SENTENCE ARBITRALE EN DROIT INTERNATIONAL PUBLIC (1938) 292–293.
[10] 2 MOORE, INT. ARB. 1528.
[1] Dennis, *The Orinoco Steamship Company Case before the Hague Tribunal* (1911) 5 AM. J. INT. LAW 35, 36.
[2] SCOTT, HAGUE COURT REPORTS (1916) 228, 232.

In 1894 the Venezuelan government entered into a contract with one Grell, whereby it granted the exclusive right to the navigation of a portion of the Orinoco River in steam vessels for a period of fifteen years. There was included in the contract the so-called Calvo clause providing that questions arising out of the contract were to be settled by the municipal courts and not made the subject of international claims. This contract was transferred to the Orinoco Shipping and Trading Company, a British corporation. Ninety-nine percent of its stock was owned by American citizens. The company became the creditor of the Venezuelan government for services rendered and damages sustained in the sum of about half a million dollars. On May 10, 1900, a settlement was made of these claims by which the Venezuelan government agreed to extend the Grell concession for a period of six years, to pay down 100,000 bolivars ($19,-219.19) in cash, and to pay a second 100,000 bolivars at a future date. This contract also contained a Calvo clause. Later in the same year the Venezuelan government by decree threw open to the world the navigation of the Orinoco, and in 1901 it cancelled by decree the six-years extension of the 1900 contract. Thereafter the stockholders of the company formed an American corporation, the Orinoco Steamship Company, which took over the business, assets and liabilities of the Orinoco Shipping and Trading Company.

The resulting claims of the Orinoco Steamship Company were heard by the United States and Venezuelan Mixed Commission, sitting under the protocol of February 17, 1903. The protocol laid down that all claims should be decided "upon a basis of absolute equity, without regard to objections of a technical nature, or of the provisions of local legislation." It further provided that "the decisions of the commission . . . shall be final and conclusive." [3] The umpire, Dr. Barge, disallowed the claim almost in its entirety. The claim of $1,209,700.05 as damages for the annulment of the concession was rejected on the grounds that the contract of 1894 did not confer a concession for the exclusive navigation of the Orinoco, that recourse to the local courts had not been had, as the contract re-

[3] Art. I, RALSTON'S REPORT (1904) 2.

quired, and that the transfer of the contract to the American corporation had been made without notice to the Venezuelan government. The claim for the unpaid $19,219.19 (100,000 bolivars) was rejected because of the company's failure to go to the Venezuelan courts and the lack of notification of the transfer of the credit to the new corporation. Of a claim for $147,638.79 for damages sustained and services rendered, $28,224.93 was allowed. A claim of $25,000 for counsel fees was disallowed.[4]

When this award was rendered, the commission was no longer in session and the American agent was not at Caracas.[5] In this situation, the claimant company addressed a protest to Secretary of State Hay,[6] in which it invited his attention to the award and protested against "the acceptance and acquiescence therein" by the United States. It was contended that the award was not in accordance with the evidence and documents submitted and was "founded upon mistakes of fact and law apparent upon the face of the Umpire's decision," that the principles of decision upon which it was professed to be based contravened the express terms of the protocol, and that if it were accepted and sustained it would constitute "a flagrant denial of justice." The company's protest was considered by the Department of State, which, on February 28, 1907, requested of Venezuela a re-examination of the award by a new tribunal.[7] The department contended that the arbitrator had shown "a disregard of the express terms of the protocol" in not deciding upon a basis of absolute equity and had committed "gross errors of law and fact." Equity meant "not local equity, that is, not necessarily the equity of the United States or the equity of Venezuela, but the spirit of justice applied to a concrete question irrespective of local statute, ordinance, or interpretation." It did not require the creditor

---

[4] *Ibid.*, 83.

[5] ARGUMENT OF THE UNITED STATES OF AMERICA ON BEHALF OF THE ORINOCO STEAMSHIP COMPANY; PERMANENT COURT OF ARBITRATION AT THE HAGUE; UNITED STATES–VENEZUELA ARBITRATION (1910) 33.

[6] PROTEST OF THE ORINOCO STEAMSHIP COMPANY, A CORPORATION, LATELY A CLAIMANT BEFORE THE UNITED STATES AND VENEZUELAN MIXED COMMISSION, AGAINST AN AWARD OF THE UMPIRE, FILED AT CARACAS, FEBRUARY 22, 1904.

[7] Secretary of State to Minister Russell, Feb. 28, 1907 (1908) FOR. REL. U.S. 774.

to notify the debtor of the transfer of a debt if it did not injuriously affect the debtor's rights. It did not mean the technical provisions of the Venezuelan law or of the contract. It assimilated knowledge to specific notice, and of the transfer the Venezuelan government had actual knowledge.[8] In 1908 the United States was finally constrained to sever diplomatic relations with Venezuela, owing to its refusal to grant redress in this and other matters.[9]

In the following year, with a new Venezuelan government in power, a protocol was signed on February 13, 1909, in which it was agreed to submit the case to a tribunal constituted under the Hague Convention.[10] The question for arbitration was defined as follows:

The arbitral tribunal shall first decide whether the decision of Umpire Barge, in this case, in view of all the circumstances and under the principles of international law, is not void, and whether it must be considered so conclusive as to preclude a reexamination of the case on its merits. If the arbitral tribunal decides that said decision must be considered final, the case will be considered by the United States of America as closed; but on the other hand, if the arbitral tribunal decides that said decision of Umpire Barge should not be considered as final, said arbitral tribunal shall then hear, examine and determine the case and render its decision on the merits.[11]

It has been thought preferable to deal later herein with the arguments of the respective counsel before the Hague Tribunal.[12] The award, which was rendered on October 25, 1910, substantially sustained the position of the United States and held the Barge decision void on four points.[13] It recognized that in principle an arbitral judgment should be respected and carried out by the parties. But, it said, by the protocol of February 13, 1909, the parties had submitted the binding character of the Barge decision to the tribunal to be decided "in accordance with the principles of international law" and, by their agreement, had "implicitly admitted, as vices involving the nullity of an arbitral decision, excessive exercise of juris-

---

8 *Ibid.*, 783–785.
9 Secretary of State to Chargé Sleeper, June 13, 1908, *ibid.*, 820.
10 2 MALLOY, TREATIES 1881.   11 *Ibid.*, 618.
12 *Infra* sec. 58.   13 SCOTT, *op. cit. supra* note 2, at 234.

diction and essential error in the judgment." It was pointed out that the Barge award need not be void as an entirety. When several independent claims are put forward for decision in one award, the decision upon one is without influence upon the others, particularly when the integrity and good faith of the arbitrator are not questioned. The Barge decision on the claim for the cancellation of the concession, therefore, was held valid. His ruling was found to be based on the appreciation of facts and the interpretation of documents, matters which were within his competence, and it was, therefore, not open to review. In the view of the Tribunal, the issue was not whether the case were well or illy judged, but whether it should be annulled. "If an arbitral decision could be disputed on the ground of erroneous appreciation, appeal and revision, which the Conventions of The Hague of 1899 and 1907 made it their object to avert, would be the general rule." The Barge decision on the claim for the unpaid $19,200 (100,000 bolivars) was held void. The protocol of February 17, 1903, was considered not to invest the arbitrators with discretionary powers.

Excessive exercise of power may consist, not only in deciding a question not submitted to the arbitrators, but also in misinterpreting the express provisions of the agreement in respect of the way in which they are to reach their decisions, notably with regard to the legislation or principles of law to be applied.

By the agreements of 1903 and 1909 Venezuela had renounced invoking the Calvo clause, upon which Barge had relied. Secondly, equity did not require notice of transfer, as Barge assumed, when the debtor actually possessed knowledge of the transfer. The holding of the Barge award on two other items of claim was declared void because based on the omission of notice to Venezuela of transfer of the credit, a defense eliminated by the protocol. Except as modified, the Barge award was expressly preserved in "its full force and entire effect."

It will be observed that the tribunal refrained from expressing any opinion upon the point of essential error as argued before it and confined its decision to three points. First, that irrespective of customary international law the parties themselves had by the protocol of February 13, 1909, implicitly admitted that the Barge award might be null and had submitted this question to the tribunal; secondly, that departure from the terms of submission is a cause of nullity; and, thirdly, that a failure to apply the law decreed by a *compromis* to be the basis of decision of a case was such a departure, but that mistakes of fact were not. The first point of the opinion may seem somewhat to qualify the subsequent two,[14] but it would seem related to the question of jurisdiction of the Hague Tribunal to hear the case, not to the substantive law of nullity of awards.

In its statement that erroneous appreciation of fact was not a ground for nullity, the tribunal stated nothing that was not admitted by both parties.[15] As a statement of substantive law no criticism can be voiced against it.[16] But to invoke this rule in regard to its own jurisdiction and to hold that by the rule it was precluded from entering into an examination of a portion of the Barge award upon the merits may justly be criticized.[17] The inadmissibility of the principle of appeal relied upon by it was beside the point. The principle of appeal was admitted by the fact that the tribunal had been instituted to reconsider the Barge award. That protocol did not contemplate the severability of the award. It was first to decide whether the entire award was to be considered final and conclusive. In so doing, the rule announced by it was unquestionably applicable in reaching its decision, and if the only bases of nullity found were mistakes of fact, the case would properly have remained closed. But if substantial grounds of nullity were found, as they were, the case as a whole was to be examined anew on its merits. Both agents pleaded the entire validity or nullity of the award.[18] It would seem, therefore, that the tribunal erred in interpreting the rule as one partially *limiting* its jurisdiction, whereas that jurisdiction was con-

---

[14] *Cf.* Dennis, *supra* note 1, at 54.

[15] ARGUMENT OF THE UNITED STATES, *supra* note 5, at 18.

[16] Scelle, *Une Instance en revision devant la Cour de la Haye, l'affaire de la Orinoco Steamship Company* (1911) 18 REV. GEN. DE DROIT INT. PUB. 189.

[17] *Ibid.*, 190, 194, 196; *cf.* Dennis, *supra* note 1, at 44–47.

[18] See discussion in Scelle, *supra* note 16, at 196; Dennis, *supra* note 1, at 44–45.

clusively governed by its protocol. The rule was one only of substantive law to be resorted to in determining the first of the two
questions submitted to it, namely, whether the award was binding
upon the parties under the principles of international law.

45. SAME: CHAMIZAL ARBITRATION.[1]—The award of the tribunal in
the *Chamizal* arbitration of 1910 between the United States and
Mexico was charged by the American commissioner and the American agent with having exceeded the terms of submission in failing
to apply the conventional rules prescribed as the basis of decision
in the *compromis*. The award was also charged with having decreed as boundary a line which it would be impossible to locate.

By the Treaty of Guadalupe Hidalgo of 1848 [2] and the Gadsden
Treaty of 1853,[3] a portion of the boundary line between the United
States and Mexico was fixed at the middle of the Rio Grande River,
following the deepest channel. In 1884 another boundary convention was concluded, defining the rules which should govern
changes in the river. Articles I and II of that convention read as
follows:

> The dividing line shall forever be that described in the aforesaid Treaty
> and follow the center of the normal channel of the rivers named, notwith-
> standing any alterations in the banks or in the course of those rivers,
> provided that such alterations be effected by natural causes through the
> slow and gradual erosion and deposit of alluvium and not by the abandon-
> ment of an existing river bed and the opening of a new one.
>
> Any other change, wrought by the force of the current, whether by the
> cutting of a new bed, or when there is more than one channel by the
> deepening of another channel than that which marked the boundary at
> the time of the survey made under the aforesaid Treaty, shall produce no
> change in the dividing line as fixed by the surveys of the International
> Boundary Commission in 1852, but the line then fixed shall continue to

[1] See editorial *"El Chamizal" Dispute between the United States and Mexico*
(1910) 4 AM. J. INT. LAW 925; editorial, *The Chamizal Arbitration Award* (1911) 5
ibid., 709.

[2] Art. V: "up the middle of that river following the deepest channel," 1 MALLOY,
TREATIES 1107, 1110.

[3] Art. I: "Beginning in the Gulf of Mexico, three leagues from land, opposite
the mouth of the Rio Grande, as provided in the fifth article of the treaty of
Guadalupe Hidalgo; thence, as defined in the said article, up the middle of that
river," *ibid.*, 1121, 1122.

follow the middle of the original channel bed, even though this should become wholly dry or be obstructed by deposits.[4]

An International Boundary Commission, composed of a representative of each government, was created by a convention of 1889.[5] All differences and questions arising out of changes in the river were to be submitted to this body for examination and decision. Article IV provided that:

When, owing to natural causes, any change shall take place in the bed of the Rio Grande . . . it shall be the duty of the said Commission . . . to decide whether it has occurred through avulsion or erosion, for the effects of Articles I and II of the convention of November 12, 1884 [i.e., the above-quoted articles].

A dispute later arose as to the ownership of the Chamizal tract, an area of about 600 acres lying south of the channel of the Rio Grande as it was in 1852 and north of the channel of 1910 and of a number of years prior thereto. It was contiguous with the city of El Paso, Texas, and was regarded as a part of the city by its inhabitants. When neither the Boundary Commission nor diplomatic negotiation could arrive at a settlement of the question, it was agreed in 1910 to submit the matter to the Boundary Commission, enlarged by the addition of one member. The commission was required under Article 3 to decide "solely and exclusively as to whether the international title to the Chamizal tract is in the United States of America or Mexico." The boundaries of the tract had been very carefully defined in Article 1. The only provision relating to finality was that of Article 8, which required the award to be executed within two years if favorable to Mexico.[6]

The presiding commissioner and the Mexican commissioner joined in an award to the United States of that portion of the tract lying between the boundary of 1852 and the middle of the river as it existed before a flood that occurred in 1864, and the remainder was awarded to Mexico.[7]

[4] Convention of Nov. 12, 1884, *ibid.*, 1159, 1160.
[5] Convention of Mar. 1, 1889, *ibid.*, 1167.
[6] Convention of June 24, 1910, 3 TREATIES (Malloy Supp. 1923) 2729–2732.
[7] Award of June 15, 1911 (1911) FOR. REL. U.S. 572, 573, 587.

It was the view of the presiding commissioner that the treaties of 1848 and 1853 established a fluvial, not a fixed and invariable boundary. The treaty of 1884 applied to all changes in the river subsequent to 1852. The changes in the river from 1852 to 1864 "were caused by slow and gradual erosion and deposit of alluvium within the meaning of Article I of the convention of 1884," and the boundary moved with the river. Moreover, all changes which took place since 1852 up to the time of the award "have not resulted from any change of bed of the river." But the changes of 1864 caused by a flood of that year were not "slow and gradual erosion and deposit of alluvium" within the convention of 1884. The evidence tended to show that the cutting away of the Mexican bank could be observed with the eyes, that pieces of earth of a yard or more square were constantly being torn away. Consequently, the accretions to the Chamizal tract in 1864 should be awarded to Mexico. It was not within the province of the commission to relocate the line of 1864, since the parties had offered no evidence to enable it to do so. Finally, the United States had not established a title to the tract by prescription.

The validity of the award in attempting to divide the Chamizal tract was vigorously attacked by the American commissioner in a dissenting opinion upon the following bases: (1) It clearly departed from the terms of reference in deciding a question not submitted by the parties. Article I of the convention of 1910 bounded the tract with technical accuracy; Article III provided that the commission was to decide solely whether the title to the tract was in the United States or in Mexico. Neither government, in its diplomatic correspondence or in its arguments before the tribunal, took any other position than that the question was as to the ownership of the tract in its entirety. (2) It departed from the terms of submission by failing to apply the rules of the convention of 1884. In the language of the Hague Court in the *Orinoco Steamship Company Case*, " 'excessive exercise of power may consist . . . in misinterpreting the express provisions of the agreement in respect of the way in which they are to reach their decisions, notably with regard to the legislation or the principles of law to be applied.' " That convention classed all changes either as slow and gradual erosion and accretion or the cutting of a new bed. The decision imported into the treaty a rule unknown to it as well as to international law—rapid and violent erosion. (3) It was "equivocal and uncertain in its terms and impossible of accomplishment." It would be impossible to locate the channel of 1864.[8]

The American agent entered, subject to the consideration of his government, his protest against the award, based upon similar grounds and, in addition, that it failed to " 'state the reasons upon which it is based,' " because it failed to state specifically whether the alleged rapid and violent erosion came within the terms of the treaty or is governed by international law and failed to state the reasons for the inferential finding that it came within the provisions of the treaty of 1884. He also submitted that the award involved "essential error of law and fact." [9]

The Department of State advised the government of Mexico that "although profoundly convinced of the invalidity of the award," it was "loath to press this view so long as it may properly be avoided," and suggested a new boundary convention to settle the matter through direct agreement between the two States.[10] Mexico, however, did not prove amenable to the suggestion, and so far as is known the case remains in status quo.[11]

It is believed that the American commissioner was correct in his criticism of the award. The tribunal decided a question not submitted when it attempted to divide the territory in dispute. The treaty very carefully defined the exact limits of the Chamizal tract and then stipulated that the tribunal was "solely and exclusively" to decide whether the title of the tract was in the United States or Mexico. An intention that the tribunal was solely to decide whether the tract as a whole was to go to Mexico or was to be retained by the United States could hardly have been more clearly expressed. It

[8] *Ibid.*, 587.
[9] *Ibid.*, 597.
[10] Department of State to the Mexican embassy, Aug. 24, 1911, *ibid.*, 598.
[11] *Ibid.*, 605.

further ignored Articles I and II of the convention of 1884, which were decreed by Article IV of its constitutive convention of 1889 as the basis for its decision. Those articles were not only misapplied, but were applied in a manner for which there appears to have been no precedent in international law.

46. DECISIONS "EX AEQUO ET BONO"; EXCESS OF JURISDICTION UPON THE GROUND OF EQUITY.—In his concurring opinion in the case of the *Diversion of Water from the Meuse* before the Permanent Court of International Justice, Judge Hudson said: "What are widely known as principles of equity have long been considered to constitute a part of international law." [1] This does not mean equity in the sense of a particular form of law or law of a particular branch of the courts; rather, it means equity in the sense of universally recognized principles of law. The role of equity in the international tribunal is to lead to a decision consistent with justice in the particular circumstances of the case, but, nevertheless, within a faithful application of legal principles.[2] A tribunal may not rest its decision solely on the grounds of equity, and particularly so in the face of established rules of law, unless the parties have given a clear and express authorization to that effect.[3] Nevertheless, equity may be resorted to in order to supplement and fulfill the law.[4]

Neither conscience nor his subjective views of equity should be the guide of the arbitrator.[5] The contention that the clause "abso-

---

[1] Judgment of June 28, 1937. SER. A./B., Fascicule No. 70; see Jenks, *Equity as a Part of the Law Applied by the Permanent Court of International Justice* (1937) 53 L.Q. REV. 519, 523; (1937) ANNUAIRE 271.

[2] (1934) ANNUAIRE 214, 300–301.

[3] BALASKO, CAUSES DE NULLITÉ DE LA SENTENCE ARBITRALE EN DROIT INTERNATIONAL PUBLIC (1938) 158; Strupp, *Le Droit du juge international de statuer selon l'équité* (1930) 33 RECUEIL DES COURS 469, 470; (1937) ANNUAIRE 271; (1934) ANNUAIRE 300–301; Art. 38 of the Statute of the Permanent Court of International Justice provides that the statement of the rules of law to be applied by the Court made in that article "shall not prejudice the power of the Court to decide a case *ex aequo et bono*, if the parties agree thereto." STATUTE AND RULES OF COURT (1936) 21.

[4] HABICHT, THE POWER OF THE INTERNATIONAL JUDGE TO GIVE A DECISION "EX AEQUO ET BONO" (1935) 68; Strupp, *supra* note 3, at 470; (1934) ANNUAIRE 224; *cf.* Mouskhéli, *L'Equité en droit international moderne* (1933) 40 REV. GEN. DE DROIT INT. PUB. 345, 349, 373.

[5] LAMMASCH, DIE LEHRE VON DER SCHIEDSGERICHTBARKEIT IN IHREM GANZEN UMFANGE (1914) 180, 181, distinguishing the case of the *amiable compositeur*; *cf.* MÉRIGNHAC, TRAITÉ THEORIQUE ET PRATIQUE DE L'ARBITRAGE INTERNATIONAL (1895)

lute equity" in the protocol of the American-Venezuelan Mixed Claims Commission invested it with unlimited powers was expressly overruled by the Hague tribunal in the *Orinoco Steamship Company Case* in its statement that the protocol "did not invest the arbitrators with discretionary powers." [6] The arbitrator is not privileged to disregard a legal obligation resting upon the parties in the name of "equity." [7] When the American and British Claims Tribunal in the *Cayuga Indians* case [8] resorted to equity as a basis of its decision, it then assumed that no legal obligations existed on the part of the United States to compensate the claimants. When it took this step, it was on the ground that it was confronted with "an anomalous and hard situation." [9] And in deciding according to equity, it held that it must be "guided by legal analogies and by the spirit and received principles of international law." [10] Though a somewhat contrary view appears to have been taken by the recent German-Mexican Claims Commission, the basis of liability admitted by Mexico in the convention of March 16, 1925, under which the commission sat, was *ex gratia*.[11] The proper sphere of an arbitral judge is that described by Lammasch: "He must not correct the law governing between the parties according to his subjective views of equity, but he may and should fill the gaps of the law according to equity, that is, in the spirit of the law, according to legal analogy." [12]

---

297 (arbitrator privileged to decide according to his personal conscience when "the *compromis* remits the decision to the absolute liberty of the arbitrator"); Fiore, *La Sentence arbitrale du président de la Republique Argentine dans le conflit de limites entre la Bolivie et le Pérou* (1910) 17 Rev. Gen. Droit Int. Pub. 225, 245.

6 Scott, Hague Court Reports (1916) 228, 232.

7 Lammasch, Die Rechtskraft internationaler Schiedssprüche (1913) 38.

8 American and British Claims Arbitration under the Special Agreement of August 18, 1910, Report of Fred K. Nielsen (1926) 306. See *infra* sec. 49.

9 *Op. cit. supra* note 8, at 313.

10 *Ibid.*, 314, 315. *Cf.* the strict interpretation of the equity clause adopted by the same tribunal in Eastern Extension, Australasia and China Telegraph Company, Ltd. (Great Britain) v. United States (1923), *ibid.*, 73; William Hardman (Great Britain) v. United States (1913), *ibid.*, 495.

11 *Cf.* Feller, *The German-Mexican Claims Commission* (1933) 27 Am. J. Int. Law 62, 64, 65.

12 Lammasch, *op. cit. supra* note 5, at 181; *cf.* Mérignhac, *op. cit. supra* note 5, at 295: "Thus, in international law, there exists no contradiction between conforming to that law and judging according to equity; and the formula which seems to us really exact, is that which leads us to say that *international law is*

This is also the conclusion of Orfeld, who lucidly defines equity as a basis for arbitral decision as follows:

> Equity is not the subjective views of the individual arbitrator. . . . Equity, it appears, is the compound of legal and semi-legal materials used to fill the gaps in international law. It is based largely on analogy. This analogy is to be drawn from legal science or jurisprudence as developed in close connection with the actually existing and accepted rules of international law. The scope of equity must not be too broadly stated. It will not alter positive rules of international law. Equity is not contrary to international law, but instead follows it to the extent of its existence. The theory is that international law is based in part at least on consent, and this would no longer be true if the tribunal could alter the rules.[13]

Their view is sustained by the reasoning of the American and British Claims Tribunal, which cites Lammasch with approval in the *Cayuga Indians* case [14] and by the Hague tribunal in the *Norwegian Claims Case*.[15] In the last-mentioned case the tribunal, in interpreting the clause of its *compromis* that it was to decide "in accordance with the principles of law and equity," said that it was "a regular legal institution" and that it was "at liberty to examine if these [American] Statutes are consistent with the equality of the two Contracting Parties, with Treaties passed by the United States, or with well established principles of international law." [16] The words " 'law and equity' " were, it said, in the opinion of the "majority of international lawyers . . . understood to mean general principles of justice as distinguished from any particular system of jurisprudence or the municipal law of any State." [17]

Not even if the *compromis* be silent as to the basis upon which the arbitrator is to decide the case is he unrestrained in his power

---

applied with equity"; Reinsch, The Concept of Legality in International Arbitration (1911) 5 AM. J. INT. LAW 604, 612: "The concept of legality is and must remain the center of international judicature, though it will be interpreted in a broad and equitable fashion."

[13] Orfeld, *Equity as a Concept of International Law* (1929) 18 KY. L.J. 31, 126, 127.

[14] *Op. cit. supra* note 8, at 320.

[15] SCOTT, HAGUE COURT REPORTS (2d ser., 1930) 40, 64.

[16] *Ibid.*, 65, 66.

[17] *Ibid.*, 65.

of decision. It is fairly to be implied that it was intended by the parties that he should resort to international law as the basis of his decision. An express statement that the case is left to his absolute liberty of decision seems necessary to the grant of purely discretionary powers to him.[18] Thus, in order to settle finally the Alsop claim against Chile, which once had been dismissed by an international tribunal as being outside its jurisdiction, the United States and Chile conferred upon King George V the power of *amiable compositeur*.[19] Unless such a power is conferred upon him, it is the duty of an arbitrator to pronounce a *non liquet* whenever the absence of law or the impossibility of legal analogy and reasoning force him to his personal conception of justice as the only basis of decision.[20]

In determining the question whether a tribunal has, through invoking equity, committed an excess of jurisdiction, recourse must be had, as always, to the particular *compromis*. It alone determines the capacity in which he is to act. Attempts to classify the various phrases which parties have used in arbitration treaties and to draw deduction therefrom as to the meaning of "equity" in a particular treaty [21] are believed to serve little purpose.[22] The role of the arbitrator in any one case is to be ascertained from the normal meaning of the words used in the *compromis* and, if necessary, from such extrinsic evidence bearing upon the intention of the parties as is discoverable. When he is directed to act in the capacity of "judge of law," he obviously has no power to act as "judge of equity." [23] When it is permissible for him to frame his decision in terms of equity, it should be grounded on legal reasoning, not upon his subjective appreciation of the case. It should not be resorted to as a device to

[18] MÉRIGNHAC, *op. cit. supra* note 5, 295–297.
[19] Protocol of December 1, 1909. 3 TREATIES (Malloy Supp., 1923) 2508.
[20] POLITIS, LA JUSTICE INTERNATIONALE (1924) 84–85.
[21] E.g., the classification made in Cayuga Indians (Great Britain) v. United States, AMERICAN AND BRITISH CLAIMS ARBITRATION UNDER THE SPECIAL AGREEMENT OF AUGUST 18, 1910, REPORT OF FRED K. NIELSEN (1926) 314–319, and reported *infra* sec. 49.
[22] *Cf.* Orfeld, *supra* note 13, at 39, 41.
[23] Boundary dispute between Bolivia and Peru *infra* sec. 48.

evade an obligation resting upon a State under international law.[24] If, however, under the name of equity a decision is rendered that is in fact inequitable,[25] the issue of nullity thereby raised is believed to involve essentially the question of *essential error,* not of excess of jurisdiction.[26]

47. SAME: CASE OF THE CARACAS GENERAL WATERWORKS COMPANY.— This case has already been discussed,[1] but comment was then reserved as to the validity of the award under the provisions of the protocol requiring the decisions of the tribunal to be based upon "absolute equity." It will be recalled that the bonds there in suit were taken by the claimant company at 40 percent of their nominal value. In regard to this fact, the Venezuelan commissioner commented that in taking the bonds the company entered into a speculation in which they hoped that if the bonds did not reach par at least they would be quoted at from 50 to 70 percent, if the claim advanced by the company were paid in full, its transaction would be more profitable than ever dreamed of by it. The commissioner said:

That it would be a scandalous violation of the protocol, by virtue of which this Commission is constituted, to oblige Venezuela to redeem in gold at its normal value the waterworks debt, which was issued at 40% of said value by an agreement between the Government of Venezuela and the company.[2]

The only statement of the umpire with regard to this contention was that "the argument . . . is contradicted by the text itself of the contract, in which it has been formally stipulated that these bonds were delivered at par." [3]

In its protest against the award Venezuela pointed out that by condemning her to pay substantially the entire sum at par it threw

---

[24] *Cf.* the position of the United States in the Norwegian Claims Case *infra* sec. 50.

[25] Case of the Caracas General Water Works Company *infra* sec. 47.

[26] *Cf.* Orinoco Steamship Company Case *infra* sec. 58.

[1] *Supra* sec. 33.

[2] RALSTON'S REPORT (1904) 288.

[3] *Ibid.,* 290.

upon her an additional debt, for which she had not received an equivalent.[4]

Disregarding the jurisdictional questions raised by the rendering of any award in favor of the claimant, it would seem that a certain lack of equity existed in compelling the respondent government to pay the bonds in full well in advance of their due date. An award more nearly approaching proper compensation could have been computed on the basis of the then-present value of the bonds. It is not believed, however, that in rendering an award computed as it was the commission committed an excess of jurisdiction serious enough to give rise to nullity.

48. SAME: BOUNDARY DISPUTE BETWEEN BOLIVIA AND PERU.—A general arbitration agreement was entered into between Peru and Bolivia on November 21, 1901, in which they agreed to submit to arbitration all disputes arising between them.[1] It provided that the arbitrator should decide strictly according to international law and, in boundary cases, on the principle of *uti possidetis* as of 1810. Scientific or technical questions were to be referred to stated technical societies. A careful regulation was made in the treaty of the finality of awards. Article 10 provided that "the Award, legally pronounced, decides within the limits of its compass the dispute between the Parties." [2] Under Article XII the award was "unappealable," but the recourse of revision was permitted if the decision were reached by a false or altered document or if the decision were totally or partially the consequence of an error of fact resulting from the documents in the cause.[3]

A dispute as to their boundary having arisen between the two States, a special arbitration convention was made on December 30, 1902, referring the dispute to the decision of the Argentine government in the "capacity of arbitrator, judge of law." The arbitrator's decision was to be "final and unappealable" and was to allot to

---

[4] Minister Paul to Baron de Favereau, Mar. 7, 1904 (1905) VENEZUELA. EXPOSICIÓN. MINISTRO DE RELACIONES EXTERIORES 256, at 269.

[1] (1901) DESCAMPS ET RENAULT, RECUEIL INTERNATIONAL DES TRAITÉS DU XXE SIÈCLE 453.

[2] *Ibid.*, 455.   [3] *Ibid.*, 455–456.

Bolivia those territories that belonged in 1810 to the Audiencia de Charcas within the Vice-Royalty of Buenos Aires and to Peru those territories that at the same date belonged to the Vice-Royalty of Lima.[4] If the various applicable Spanish laws and documents should not be found sufficient to fix any portion of the territory, the arbitrator was allowed by Article IV to decide the question "equitably, approximating, as far as possible, their sense and the spirit which they manifested." It was ordered that possession of a territory exercised by one of the parties should never in any case prevail against royal acts establishing the contrary.[5]

On July 9, 1909, the Argentine president rendered his award.[6] It stated that the arbitrator had confined his study to the respective territorial rights of the two parties, for if he were called upon to determine the full boundaries of either Vice-Royalty, the rights of third parties would be touched upon. The proofs submitted were found to be insufficient to enable *either* of the two lines advanced by the parties to be considered the boundary. The authority of Article 4 was accordingly invoked to fix a boundary in the spirit of the various royal acts relied on by the parties.

The decision provoked intense resentment on the part of Bolivia. The Bolivian minister to Argentina announced that conformably to instructions from his government he would not be present at its reading. The Argentine legation in La Paz was stoned. The Bolivian attitude eventually compelled Argentina to break off diplomatic relations on July 20.[7] The dispute appears to have been finally settled by the negotiation of the treaty of September 17, 1909, defining the boundaries to be established between the two countries, which, in Bolivia's opinion, guarded its interest and security.[8]

The factor most influencing the Bolivian attitude was probably

---

[4] Art. 1 (1902) *ibid.*, 428, 429.

[5] Art. V, *ibid.*, 429.

[6] ARBITRAJE ARGENTINO EN LA CUESTIÓN DE LÍMITES ENTRE LAS REPÚBLICAS DEL PERÚ Y DE BOLIVIA; LIBRO AZUL (Ministerio de Relaciones Exteriores y Culto de la República Argentina, 1909) 96.

[7] *Ibid.*, 108, 127, 128, 159, 166–169.

[8] EL ARBITRAJE ENTRE LAS REPÚBLICAS DE BOLIVIA Y EL PERÚ Y SU ULTIMA NEGOCIACIÓN SOBRE FRONTERAS; DOCUMENTOS DIPLOMATICOS (Ministerio de Relaciones Exteriores de la República de Bolivia, 1909) 19.

the circumstance that the award handed over to Peru regions which had been populated and developed by Bolivia and were under her dominion. Thus, the Bolivian minister, in his note of protest against the decision, contended that equity did not exist in a decision despoiling it of such territories, in the absence of a definite legal right. He submitted that it was difficult to reach a solution founded in equity without an examination of the territory in relation to its topography, importance, and the interests vested in it.[9] Bolivia rested its legal position on the failure of the arbitrator to conform to Articles I and V of the treaty of December 30, 1902, and his misinterpretation of Article IV. Under Article I he had the restricted capacity of a "judge of law," and his decision was lacking in this essential condition of the treaty.[10] He had, while ostensibly acting under Article IV, only carried out his particular appreciation of equity, for he had not subjected himself to the letter of the documents and neither had he observed the spirit of them. The truth was, said Bolivia, that he had divided in two the territory in dispute, with the good intentions of a mediator.[11] Article V of the treaty, in stating that possession could not be opposed to titles, implicitly recognized the fundamental rule that possession constituted a right. The arbitrator had exceeded the limitations of the treaty, since, on the one hand, his line did not follow an express title and, on the other, it failed to maintain possession, the only right in the absence of title.[12]

Weiss [13] and Fiore [14] in their studies of the case are both of the opinion that the decision was manifestly rendered in excess of the terms of the *compromis*.[15] Their view seems sound, that the arbi-

---

[9] Minister Escalier to the Minister of Foreign Affairs of Argentina, July 19, 1909, LIBRO AZUL, *op. cit. supra* note 6, at 159, 161–166.

[10] *Ibid.*, 160.

[11] DOCUMENTOS DIPLOMÁTICOS, *op. cit. supra* note 8, at 9, 13; but see LIBRO AZUL, *op. cit. supra* note 6, x–xi.

[12] *Supra* note 9, at 161.

[13] Weiss, *L'Arbitrage de 1909 entre la Bolivie et le Pérou* (1910) 17 REV. GEN. DE DROIT INT. PUB. 135.

[14] Fiore, *La Sentence arbitrale du président de la République Argentine dans le conflit de limites entre la Bolivie et le Pérou* (1910) 17 REV. GEN. DE DROIT INT. PUB. 245–247.

[15] But *cf.* Renault, *Le Différend entre la Bolivie et le Pérou et l'arbitrage international* (1909) 16 REV. GEN. DE DROIT INT. PUB. 368, 370, 371.

trator was constituted a "judge of law," not an *amiable compositeur*, and in assuming the power of an equity judge he arrogated himself to a jurisdiction that was not his. A legal, not an equitable, decision was apparently the desire of the parties as expressed in the *compromis* as a whole.[16] In any event, criticism may be made of the decision as a decision of equity in its failure to allot to a State territories which it had long occupied.[17] He seems to have failed to conform to the treaty in two respects. He was required first to examine the applicable laws and documents and to fix the boundary as they showed it to be. The circumstance that the territories were unexplored, that the documents did not support the contentions of either party, did not prevent him from carrying out this duty. If he were in fact unable to decide the boundary from the proofs submitted, he should have referred to one of the designated learned societies. If it, in turn, were unable to form a scientific judgment, a *non liquet* should have been pronounced.[18]

49. SAME: CAYUGA INDIANS CASE.—Though he did not take the final step of refusing to accept as valid the decision of the American and British Claims Tribunal under the agreement of August 18, 1910, in the *Cayuga Indians* case, the agent of the United States asserted in no uncertain manner that the decision had departed from the terms of submission,[1] which he supported by a comprehensive analysis and criticism of the decision.[2] It further appears that the decision was rested upon a theory of liability which the United States had had no opportunity to argue; though this would seem to be only a cause for a request for reargument and not of itself to affect the validity of the decision.

The original source of the claim lay in certain treaties negotiated by the State of New York with the Cayuga Indians in 1789,

---

16 Fiore, *supra* note 14, at 245–247; Weiss, *supra* note 13, at 130.
17 Fiore, *supra* note 14, at 255; Weiss, *supra* note 13, at 133; *cf.* MOORE, MEMORANDUM ON UTI POSSIDETIS; COSTA RICA–PANAMA ARBITRATION (1913) 14 *et sqq.*
18 Fiore, *supra* note 14, at 244, 245; Weiss, *supra* note 13, at 135.
1 AMERICAN AND BRITISH CLAIMS ARBITRATION UNDER THE SPECIAL AGREEMENT OF AUGUST 18, 1910, REPORT OF FRED K. NIELSEN (1926) 304. The award appears at p. 307.
2 *Ibid.*, 267–306.

1790, and 1795. Before the treaties were made the Cayuga tribe had split, and the greater part had removed to Canada. Representatives of both branches entered into the last treaty, by which New York agreed to pay the "Cayuga Nation" $1,800 a year in return for certain cessions of land. As the result of the War of 1812 a change in the mode of payments of annuities was made which deprived the Canadian Cayugas of any share. In 1849 they presented their claim to the New York legislature, but they were denied. In 1899 the British minister at Washington presented the claim to the United States.

Though an elaborate discussion was made by the tribunal of the equitable features of the claim and of its validity under the power of the tribunal to decide cases in accordance with "equity," it said that it was "not necessary to rest the case upon this proposition." The tribunal's legal argument rested upon the following propositions: (1) by Article IX of the Treaty of Ghent closing the War of 1812 the United States engaged to restore to the Canadian Cayugas their share of the annuities. In this article the United States agreed to restore to the Indian tribes with which they had been at war "all the possessions, rights, and privileges which they may have enjoyed . . . previous to such hostilities"; [3] (2) this claim was not barred by Article V of the Claims Convention of 1854,[4] because the claim did not arise at least until 1860. It did not arise until then because the treaty of 1795 was a New York treaty, not a Federal contract, and the United States, therefore, would not be liable under international law for its breach by New York. Not until 1860 could it be said that "the matter was brought to the attention of the authorities of the United States, and that Government did nothing to carry out the treaty provision"; (3) the claim should not be deemed barred by laches, in view of the facts that the Canadian Cayugas occupied a dependent position and were unable to act except through their sovereign and had pressed their claim persistently since 1860, and that the State of New York was not prejudiced by the delay after 1849. An award of $100,000 was rendered, which was said to embrace the two elements of "(1) an amount equal to a just share in the pay-

[3] 1 MALLOY, TREATIES 612, 618.   [4] Ibid., 667.

ments of the annuity from 1849; (2) a capital sum which at five per
cent interest will yield half of the amount of the annuity for the
future."

The equity argument of the tribunal rested on that clause in its
protocol by which it was authorized to decide the claims before it
in accordance with "the principles of international law and of
equity." [5] It declared that the equity clause was not meaningless
and cited the views of Mérignhac [6] with approval. It submitted that
there are cases in which arbitral tribunals "must find the grounds
of decision, must find the right and the law, in general considerations of justice, equity, and right dealing guided by legal analogies
and by the spirit and received principles of international law."
After an examination of the facts of the case, it was constrained to
conclude that the "Cayuga Nation" with which New York had contracted in 1789, 1790, and 1795 was a legal unit of New York, so far
as it possessed legal personality. The legislature of New York was
recognized as competent to decide what constituted the "Nation,"
"for the purposes of the prior treaties made by the State with an
entity in a domestic sense of its own law and existing only for its own
municipal purposes." In turn, the "Cayuga Nation" could not change
its national character without concurrence by New York and become a legal unit of British law while preserving its identity as the
covenantee in the treaty. "The legal character and status of the
New York entity with which New York contracted was a matter of
New York law." But, the tribunal said, Great Britain could nevertheless press a claim on behalf of the Cayugas in Canada. The legal
obstacles which, the tribunal had admitted, existed against the advancement of any such claim were made by it to serve the purpose
of justifying its validity as a claim in equity. It was an "anomalous
and hard situation," according to the tribunal, that as to the annuities the Cayugas were still a unit of New York law after the tribe
divided. This situation "gave rise to obvious claims according to

5 Art. 7, 3 TREATIES (Malloy Supp., 1923) 2621.
6 MÉRIGNHAC, TRAITÉ THEORIQUE ET PRATIQUE DE L'ARBITRAGE INTERNATIONAL
(1895) 295: "International law is applied with equity."

universally recognized principles of justice." This conclusion, together with the analogy of corporate law that courts would occasionally in the interests of justice look behind the legal personality of a corporation, were deemed to be sufficient to entitle the Canadian Cayugas to their proportionate share of the annuity since 1810.

The equity argument of the tribunal seems to ignore what is believed to be a fatal objection to it, an objection later recognized in the opinion, that the contract upon which it is founded was a contract, not of the United States, but of the State of New York. Moreover, even if the argument be admitted in its full strength, there remains to be considered the effect of the barring clause of the treaty of 1853. If the Canadian Cayugas were entitled to the annuities since 1810, as the tribunal found that they were, then their claim would seem to be barred. The American agent made the outright charge that "the Tribunal had no power under the terms of submission, properly construed, particularly as construed by the parties to the arbitration, and by the Tribunal in other decisions, to fix liability on the United States by the application of its theory of *ex aequo et bono*." [7] Certainly, the tribunal's construction of the equity clause seems to be at variance with the strict interpretation which it adopted in the *Hardman* case [8] and the cable-cutting cases.[9] Likewise, the tribunal's statement that the Cayugas had had a valid claim in equity since 1810 would seem to be not entirely reconcilable with its prior statements that the British nationality of the claim for the *whole* annuity since 1810 could not be established because the obligee was an Indian tribe. So far as it existed as a legal unit, it was "by virtue of the domestic law of the sovereign nation within whose territory the tribe occupies the land."

The American agent made a number of additional charges with respect to the opinion. In point of fact, he noted that the tribunal did not undertake to explain what event it may have had in mind which

[7] *Op. cit. supra* note 1, at 305.
[8] Hardman (Great Britain) v. United States (Decision June 18, 1913), *ibid.*, 495.
[9] Eastern Extension, Australasia and China Telegraph Company, Ltd. (Great Britain) v. United States (Decision November 9, 1923), *ibid.*, 73. *Cf.* Orfeld, *Equity as a Concept of International Law* (1929) 18 KY. L.J. 122–124.

caused the claim to originate in 1860 and that "it seems to be useless to speculate what the Tribunal may have had in mind." [10] In
the matter of procedure, he charged that in fixing this date the
tribunal disregarded the contentions of both parties and denied
counsel any opportunity to argue the question. The argument on
the barring clause was said, therefore, to have taken on a farcical
aspect.[11] In this connection, it may be observed that while the circumstance that a tribunal places its decision upon a point not argued
by the parties would not seem to be of itself a cause of nullity, it
might well serve as a ground for rehearing. As additional departures
from the terms of submission, he alleged that the tribunal failed to
make a preliminary ruling conformably to Article 1 of the agreement
of August 18, 1910, on whether the claim was excluded by the barring
clause of the treaty of 1853.[12] Its failure to give reasons for its decision on the point when the claim arose, as required by the Hague
Convention of 1907, which was incorporated into the *compromis*,
was also charged to be a departure.[13]

50. SAME: NORWEGIAN CLAIMS CASE.—In the arbitration before the
tribunal created under the Permanent Court of Arbitration of the
claims of Norwegian subjects for losses incident to the requisition by
the United States of contracts for the construction of ships in the
United States held by such subjects, the United States advanced a
position as to the meaning of "equity" somewhat at variance with
the meaning of the term which it had supported in the *Orinoco
Steamship Company Case*. In this it was not sustained by the tribunal and, it is believed, correctly so. Yet the United States refused
to accept the award as a precedent, though the damages allowed
were paid by it.

In 1917 the United States requisitioned from all shipyards in the
country all ships of more than 2,500 tons, including as well material
and contracts. Norwegian owners of construction contracts for fifteen
ships were thereby deprived of their contract rights. When it appeared that they could not reach an agreement with the United

10 *Op. cit. supra* note 1, at 269.   11 *Ibid.*, 267–268.
12 *Ibid.*, 304, see 291–297.   13 *Ibid.*, 304.

States Shipping Board as to the compensation to be allowed them, a *compromis* was entered into between the United States and Norway, on June 30, 1921, whereby the two States agreed to submit the claims to an arbitral tribunal constituted in accordance with the Hague Convention of 1907. Article I stated that "the tribunal shall examine and decide the aforesaid claims in accordance with the principles of law and equity and determine what sum if any shall be paid in settlement of each claim." It was agreed in Article IV that "the decision shall be accepted as final and binding." [1]

The United States contended that the use of the phrase "principles of law and equity" made it the duty of the tribunal to apply the municipal law of the United States to matters within the jurisdiction of the United States which were before the tribunal for decision. The tribunal held that the phrase meant "general principles of justice," that it was at liberty to examine the statutes of the United States in the light of international law, that the United States had taken the contracts, and that these contracts were property. After stating generally the bases by which it had determined just compensation, the tribunal set forth in terms of thousands of dollars the amounts to be allowed each of the claimants. [2]

The American agent stated in open court that he reserved all the rights of the United States arising from the departure of the award from the terms of submission and from the " 'essential error' " by which it was invalidated. [3] The American member of the tribunal, Chandler P. Anderson, notified the Secretary General of the Permanent Court of Arbitration by letter of October 13, 1922, that in his opinion the members rendering the award had disregarded the terms of submission and exceeded the authority conferred upon them by the *compromis* and that he accordingly refused to be present when the award was announced. [4] The reasons for the attitude of the American government towards the award were set forth in a letter by Secretary of State Hughes to the Norwegian minister, dated February

[1] 3 Treaties (Malloy Supp., 1923) 2749–2751.
[2] Decision of October 13, 1922, Scott, Hague Court Reports (2d ser., 1932) 40.
[3] (1923) 17 Am. J. Int. Law 399.
[4] *Ibid.*

26, 1923, with which he enclosed a draft for $12,239,852.47 in full
payment of the award as proof of his government's desire to respect
arbitral awards. He stated that certain bases of the award could not
be accepted as a binding precedent, that international law imposed
no duty to favor neutral aliens in the requisition of property such
as was concerned in the case, and that the award had failed "to give
a satisfactory explanation of the manner in which the Tribunal has
arrived at the amounts awarded," thereby not meeting the requirement of Article 79 of the Hague Convention of October 18, 1907.[5]

It is somewhat difficult to accept in full measure the protest of
the United States. In its determination of what constituted just compensation to foreign owners of expropriated property from the
standpoint of international law, it cannot be said to have failed to
apply or to have misapplied any rule of international law in such
a clear manner as to lead to the nullity of the award. Rather, such
error as it may have committed was error of law. It is interesting
to note that in connection with the *Orinoco Steamship Company
Case,* the United States had denied that the use of equity in a
protocol of arbitration meant "equity of the United States." Instead, it then stated that equity was "the spirit of justice applied
to a concrete question irrespective of local statute, ordinance, or
interpretation." [6] With respect to its attack upon the award for its
failure to show the manner in which damages were computed, it
would seem that that alone would not be sufficient to invalidate the
award.[7] The measurement of damages becomes necessary only after
liability has been established. Errors in their computation would
not affect the authority of the decision. The appropriate remedy
in such case, if the tribunal has not become *functus officio,* is a request to the tribunal that it rectify its award.

51. EFFECT OF FAILURE TO RAISE IN A TIMELY MANNER JURISDICTIONAL
OBJECTIONS.—A tribunal's jurisdiction may in certain circumstances
be derived from sources other than the *compromis.* The *compromis* is
the best evidence of the scope of the powers intended to be conferred

[5] (1923) FOR. REL. U.S., Part 2, 626.   [6] *Supra* p. 147.
[7] See 23 Decisions of the Comptroller of the Treasury (1916–1917) 692, 697.

upon the tribunal by the parties, but it is not the only means for
the conferment of jurisdiction; for by their conduct the parties can
by tacit consent enlarge the powers of the tribunal.[1] Accordingly, objection should promptly be made to departures from the course of
procedure stipulated for the tribunal if a State desires to avoid the
otherwise reasonable inference that its inaction is to be viewed as
acquiescence.[2] Some question may arise as to whether the agents of
the State or the executive branch would constitutionally have the
power to bind the State by their waiver.[3] This would be true with
respect to a case involving a tacit conferral of jurisdiction to decide
a question not included in the *compromis*. Even this question, however, will liquidate itself if eventually the State should take no exception to the question action, for some agent or organ of the State
is presumed to be empowered to act, and the constitutional question
is essentially whether that agent or organ has tacitly ratified.

To be distinguished from tacit acquiescence in or waiver of errors
made by a tribunal during the course of the hearings is the effect
of laches upon the privilege of a State to attack an arbitral award. In
the *Pious Fund Case* [4] the agent of the United States contended before the Hague Tribunal that since Mexico had not immediately
upon its rendering opposed the validity of the award of the Mixed
Commission of 1868, which was under consideration by the tribunal,
it should not, after a lapse of twenty-six years and without the discovery of any new fact affecting the sanctity of the former adjudication, which new fact was not at that time discoverable, be permitted

---

[1] SCHÄTZEL, RECHTSKRAFT UND ANFECHTUNG VON ENTSCHEIDUNGEN INTERNA-
TIONALER GERICHTE, 6 FRANKFURTER ABHANDLUNGEN ZUM KRIEGSVERHÜTUNGSRECHT
(1928) 82, 83; see discussion *supra* sec. 22 and case *supra* sec. 23.

[2] Permanent Court of International Justice, "Rights of Minorities in Upper
Silesia" (Apr. 26, 1928) SER. A., No. 15, at 25; see BALASKO, CAUSES DE NULLITÉ DE LA
SENTENCE ARBITRALE EN DROIT INTERNATIONAL PUBLIC (1938) 107–108, 142; Hertz,
Essai sur le problème de la nullité (1939, 3d ser.) 20 REV. DE DROIT INT. L.C. 468–
469; Morelli, *La Théorie générale du procès international* (1937) 61 RECUEIL DES
COURS 330; Rolin-Jaequemyns, *Quelques mots sur la phase nouvelle du Différend
Anglo-Américain* (1872) 4 REV. DE DROIT INT. L.C. 127, 139; 3 CALVO, LE DROIT
INTERNATIONAL (5th ed., 1896) 474.

[3] BALASKO, *op. cit. supra* note 2, at 108.

[4] REPORT OF JACKSON H. RALSTON, AGENT OF THE UNITED STATES (1902) FOR. REL.
U.S. (App. 2).

to attack that adjudication as invalid.[5] Mexico had at no time subsequent to the award questioned the validity of the treaty or the jurisdiction of the commission to decide the case. It was its laches which should have prevented any such issue from being revived.

52. SAME: NICARAGUA-HONDURAS BOUNDARY DISPUTE.—When a State has not only failed to object to the authority of a particular arbitrator but also actively pressed its case before him and apparently accepted his judgment when rendered, it clearly should not thereafter be open to it to impugn the judgment upon the ground that the modalities for the naming of the arbitrator prescribed in the *compromis* were not followed. Its action fairly implies a recognition of the arbitrator's competence to decide the dispute litigated before him and consent to be bound by his award. Yet just such a position was assumed by Nicaragua during its boundary dispute with Honduras.

The facts of the case as relating to this point have heretofore been set forth.[1] In this relation it was the contention of Nicaragua that the powers of the arbitrators were limited and that their failure strictly to follow the procedure indicated in the treaty rendered invalid the appointment of the king of Spain as single arbitrator. Nor was that appointment to be deemed validated by the irregular participation of the executive of Nicaragua in the arbitration. In further detail, Nicaragua's position was that the rules of a treaty should strictly be followed. Its contentions were that the national arbitrators did not represent their country with full powers, that their authority was limited by the treaty. They had failed to follow Articles 3 and 5 of the treaty by naming the king of Spain arbitrator without having sought to exhaust the members of the diplomatic corps in Guatemala. They had failed to follow Article 5 of the treaty when they sought directly to procure through his minister the acceptance by the king of Spain of the post of arbitrator. The governments were thereby deprived of the power which they had reserved

[5] Brief of the United States, *ibid.*, 229. For possible comment of tribunal on this point see *ibid.*, 17.
[1] *Supra* sec. 23.

under that article. Even if the nomination of the king be assumed to have been valid, it was an arbitrary assumption of power to convert him into a single arbitrator. It was contemplated that the arbitration would be "tripersonal," and in voluntarily resigning their powers in favor of the king they dissolved *ipso facto* the arbitral tribunal which they had just constituted and abrogated in fact the treaty which was the source of their jurisdiction and deprived the king of the legitimate power to judge. Finally, Nicaragua contended, the prohibition of Article 11 upon any modification in the terms of the treaty made it clear that the participation of the executive as well as the irregular action of the arbitrators could not constitutionally impose any obligation on Nicaragua.[2]

Judge Moore, in examining these contentions of Nicaragua, pointed out that the treaty must be interpreted reasonably. It was unreasonable to suppose that the two governments intended the exhaustion of the diplomatic corps one by one. A certain discretion was contemplated. The protocol of the arbitrators indicated that they fulfilled their duty in accordance with the treaty, and such was the view of their governments as shown by their participation in the arbitration. It was practically an impossibility to require the exhaustion of the category of "any public personage" before having recourse to the government of Spain. The governments were deprived of no right by the naming by the arbitrators of the king of Spain. The treaty did not prescribe how the Spanish government was to be notified. It was only if that government should default that the foreign offices were themselves to choose a South American government as arbitrator. That stage was never reached. With respect to the objection of authority, it could not under the treaty reasonably be considered otherwise than that a government would act as the *only* arbitrator. Finally, it had not heretofore been supposed that a treaty would be abrogated because the subordinate agents of a government had failed to observe its stipulations.[3]

[2] 1 Mediación del Secretario de los Estados Unidos en la controversia de límites entre la República de Nicaragua y la República de Honduras (1920). Exposición de Nicaragua 40–42, 57–58, 60, 76.
[3] Opinion of John Bassett Moore, Counsellor for Honduras, Honduras-

In addition to Judge Moore's remarks, it may be observed, with reference to Nicaragua's contention that the participation of its executive in the arbitration was of no legal effect, that it is quite usual for the executive branch of a government to settle by executive agreement disputes with other States by arbitration. No question of ratification was here involved. The arbitration went forward under an existing treaty. If constitutional limitations there were upon the course which that arbitration took, cognizance of them cannot reasonably have been expected from Honduras. In any event, the failure opportunely to raise the objection of the irregularity of the form of the appointment was fatal. It should have been raised when known.

53. RESPECT FOR TRIBUNAL'S JURISDICTION BY OTHER INTERNATIONAL BODIES.—When acting within the scope of the powers conferred upon the tribunal by the parties, other international bodies should refrain from interfering with the tribunal's proceedings and should respect the authority of its judgments properly rendered.[1] This is not to say that they should consider themselves bound by such judgments. It is rather to recognize that in the international order each body will have its specific role, whether it be political, administrative, or judicial, and should confine itself to its role. A number of episodes occurring in connection with the League of Nations illustrate the tendency of losing parties to an arbitration to seek political recourse when legal means fail and demonstrate that a harmonious functioning of the various international organizations requires respect for each other's proper sphere of action.[2]

It is recognized that provisions such as paragraph 4 of Article 13 of the Covenant, empowering the Council to propose what steps should be taken to give effect to an arbitral award in the event of

Nicaragua Boundary Mediation before the Secretary of State of the United States, 1920–1921. 5 COLLECTED PAPERS OF JOHN BASSETT MOORE (1944) 161–162.

[1] In its Judgment of June 15, 1939, the Permanent Court of International Justice stated that it "can neither confirm nor annul . . . either wholly or in part" the valid decisions of another tribunal. SER. A./B., Fascicule No. 78, "Société Commerciale de Belgique," at 174.

[2] SCHÄTZEL, RECHTSKRAFT UND ANFECHTUNG VON ENTSCHEIDUNGEN INTERNATIONALER GERICHTE, 6 FRANKFURTER ABHANDLUNGEN ZUM KRIEGSVERHÜTUNGSRECHT (1928) 89.

the failure of a party to carry it out, might, for example, require an examination into the validity of an award. But such a review would not be a judicial process or result in an arbitral judgment of an obligatory character, even though the opinion reached by the Council might have been coupled with proposals whereby such opinion could be made effective.[3]

54. SAME: THE SALAMIS CASE.—The principle that the League could not intervene in a question pending before another and competent international body was established in the case of the cruiser *Salamis*. The Greek government had contracted in 1912 with the Vulcan Company in Germany for the construction of the armored cruiser *Salamis*. The cruiser was not completed. The Vulcan Company contended that work was dropped owing to the failure of the Greek government to make the stipulated progress payments. Greece alleged that the failure of completion was due to the intervention of the war and the later prohibition of Article 192 of the Treaty of Versailles against the construction and exportation of naval war material by Germany. In 1923 suit was brought by the Greek government against the Vulcan Company before the Greco-German Mixed Arbitral Tribunal, asking that it declare the contracts void and order the defendant to return the sums already advanced in payment. Upon objection by the defendant, the tribunal rendered an interlocutory judgment sustaining its jurisdiction. While it reserved final decision as to the application of Article 192, it noted that the clause did not "prohibit the export of an uncompleted and unarmed cruiser."[1]

The Greek government thereafter requested the Council of the League by letter of June 24, 1927, to make an official interpretation of Articles 190 and 192 of the Treaty of Versailles as to whether they prohibited the export of vessels contracted for before August 1, 1914. The Council referred the matter to a committee of jurists

[3] *Cf.* Castberg, *L'Excès de pouvoir dans la justice internationale* (1931) 35 RECUEIL DES COURS 462. See concerning this and following sections of this chapter the author's article *Conflits de compétence entre les organismes internationaux* 67–72 JOUR. DU DROIT INT. (Clunet) 730.

[1] Greece v. Vulcan Werke (Decision August 12, 1925) 5 RECUEIL DES DÉCISIONS (1925) 887.

headed by M. Urrutia, which reported on September 28, 1927, that the request involved the preliminary question of the Council's own competence to hear it and suggested that an advisory opinion be asked of the Permanent Court of International Justice.[2] No decision was reached by the Council and the question was adjourned until December.[3] A second report of the jurists was then submitted and approved.[4] That report laid down the principle that the Council should not intervene in a question pending before another international body, such as a Mixed Arbitral Tribunal, when the request for intervention is made by one of the parties and the case was being dealt with by that international organ with the consent of both parties and was regarded by it as being within its jurisdiction. This principle, however, would not apply if both parties to the case joined in asking the Council to intervene or if the Mixed Arbitral Tribunal itself did so. It was accordingly suggested that "it would be courteous for the Council to address a communication to the Mixed Arbitral Tribunal informing the Tribunal that, if it should judge it to be desirable that an interpretation of Article 192 (and 190, if that article is considered relevant) should be obtained by way of an advisory opinion by the Permanent Court of International Justice and should address a communication to the Council to that effect, the Council would defer to such a desire."[5]

55. SAME: QUESTION OF THE MARITZA.—An interpretation of the conditions under which the Council could intervene in the decision of a matter pending before another international body was made in the *Maritza* controversy before the Council. This matter arose under paragraph 2 of Article 11 of the Covenant permitting each member to bring to the attention of the Assembly or of the Council any circumstance threatening to disturb international peace.

The Treaty of Lausanne provided in Article II that for a certain distance the boundary between Turkey and Greece should be "the course of the Maritza" River. Article V established a boundary commission to trace the frontier defined in Article II. An official map

[2] 8 LEAGUE OF NATIONS, OFFICIAL JOURNAL (1927) 1456.
[3] *Ibid.*, 1475.
[4] 9 *ibid.* (1928), 178.   [5] *Ibid.*, 180.

was annexed to the treaty. Turkey contended that there was a divergence between this map and the text of the treaty and that on the basis of the map the commission should choose the greater of the two arms of the river. Greece, while relying on the text of the treaty, requested the Council of the League to ask the Permanent Court of International Justice to give an advisory opinion on the interpretation of the treaty, asserting that the Council should consider the affair as a circumstance threatening to disturb international peace within paragraph 2 of Article 11 of the Covenant. The matter was referred to a committee of jurists, who reported [1] that it was for the boundary commission to delimit the frontier in accordance with the treaty, regarding in so doing the map as important, but not conclusive, evidence. Only when the commission had exhausted all sources of information and announced that it was unable to decide the questions or if it had "flagrantly exceeded its powers" would the parties be justified in attempting to reach a settlement in accordance with international law. In the absence of such circumstances, the Council could not deal with the question under the authority of Article XI, paragraph 2, invoked by Greece.[2]

56. SAME: HUNGARIAN OPTANTS CASE.—The facts of this matter and the question of excess of jurisdiction of the tribunal here involved have already been discussed.[1] The case is further significant, however, because of the eventual recognition given by the Council of the League to the jurisdiction of the Mixed Arbitral Tribunal. In view of the historical importance of the episode and the personalities involved, as well as the various aspects of the principle of respect for jurisdiction which were there so ably discussed, the circumstances will be reviewed in some detail.

Positions Taken by Hungary and Rumania before the Council of the League of Nations.—Hungary applied to the Council under Article 239 of the Treaty of Trianon, which empowered the Council to appoint a substitute arbitrator to the Mixed Arbitral Tribunal created under the treaty, and remarked that Rumania

[1] 7 LEAGUE OF NATIONS, OFFICIAL JOURNAL (1926) 511, 516.
[2] *Ibid.*, 529.   [1] *Supra* sec. 37.

apparently did not take seriously the argument advanced by it as to an excess of jurisdiction, because it would not enter into judicial proceedings on the point. Hungary pointed out that it had already offered before the Council, in connection with the request of Rumania, to arbitrate the question before the Permanent Court of International Justice. Any further expression of generosity by Hungary would involve its consent to the revision of the Treaty of Trianon itself. The further tenor of the Hungarian argument ran as follows: Rumania, because of its actions, was charged with having attacked the fundamental principles that no appeal existed from arbitral awards, that judicial bodies are independent of political bodies, that judicial decisions should be secured against arbitrary action on the part of losing parties, that in matters concerning liquidation differential treatment of enemies or exenemies was not an essential point, and that an alien cannot be deprived of his property without suitable compensation. The alleged defect that the award did not settle such essential points as the difference between liquidation and expropriation was asserted to be in reality a virtue, because this question related to the merits. The action before the tribunal was not concerned with the agrarian reform itself, but only with those portions of the measures adopted which were contrary to the treaty. The agrarian legislation complained of was said to be but a cloak for liquidation. It embodied special provisions, ministerial decrees, rules and instructions which were directed against Hungarians and applied to the detriment of Hungarians by the executive organs, so that almost all the Hungarian property had been confiscated on one pretext or another. As against the request of the Rumanian government under paragraph 2 of Article 11 of the Covenant,[2] Hungary argued that the mere words "agrarian reform" could not divest the tribunal of its jurisdiction. The facts, in their objective aspects, must be examined by the tribunal. Hungary inquired whether the losing party would not always be able in a doubtful case to protest that there was an abuse of powers by the court in rendering its decision. It stated that the accusation of

[2] 8 LEAGUE OF NATIONS, OFFICIAL JOURNAL (1927) 350 et sqq.

abuse of powers could be seriously considered only if Rumania should consent to submit the question to the Permanent Court.[3]

Rumania requested the intervention of the Council under Article 11, paragraph 2, of the Covenant, on the ground that the matter affected international relations and threatened to disturb international peace.[4] In support of Rumania's request, M. Titulesco in large part repeated the arguments made by its representatives and judge in connection with the proceedings before the tribunal. He submitted that the purpose of the measures should always be considered. The distinction between liquidation and expropriation was again advanced, and the contention was made that only as to liquidation—discriminatory measures applied to exenemy property as such—was the tribunal competent. He argued that if liquidation meant any violation of international law, it was a violent extension of the tribunal's jurisdiction. A violation of the treaty was said to be prerequisite to recourse to the international jurisdiction, for otherwise the essential condition of consent would be lacking. He concluded that there was no violation of the treaty here, and this had been recognized by Hungary in 1923.[5]

Action by the Council of the League of Nations; Report of the Committee of Three.—The questions thus raised were referred by the Council to the Committee of Three for report. Sir Austin Chamberlain was appointed reporter. The other two members were Viscount Ishii of Japan and Mr. Villegas of Chile.[6] In September of 1927 the committee made its report,[7] stating that it had considered the following questions:

1. Is the Roumano-Hungarian Mixed Arbitral Tribunal entitled to entertain claims arising out of the application of the Roumanian Agrarian Law to Hungarian optants and nationals?

2. If the answer to that question be in the affirmative, to what extent and in what circumstances is it entitled to do so? [8]

[3] *Ibid.*, 369. See in connection with the above, APPLICATION BY THE HUNGARIAN GOVERNMENT TO THE COUNCIL OF THE LEAGUE OF NATIONS OF MAY 21, 1927, reprinted in DEÁK, THE HUNGARIAN-RUMANIAN LAND DISPUTE (1928) 1904.
[4] *Supra* note 2.   [5] *Ibid.*, 354–355, 357.   [6] *Ibid.*, 372.
[7] *Ibid.*, 1379, 1381.   [8] *Ibid.*, 1381.

The committee admitted that:

If it could be established in any particular case that the property of a Hungarian national suffered retention or liquidation or any other measure of disposal under the terms of Articles 232 and 250 as a result of the application to the said property of the Roumanian Agrarian Law and if a claim were submitted with a view to obtaining restitution, it would be within the jurisdiction of the Mixed Arbitral Tribunal to give relief.

. . . the claim of a Hungarian national for restitution of property in accordance with Article 250 might come within the jurisdiction of the Mixed Arbitral Tribunal even if the claim arises out of the application of the Roumanian Agrarian Law.[9]

Upon the basis of its study it submitted that the following principles were obligatory for Hungary and Rumania under the Treaty of Trianon:

1. The provisions of the peace settlement . . . do not exclude the application to Hungarian nationals . . . of a general scheme of agrarian reform.

2. There must be no inequality between Roumanians and Hungarians, either in the terms of the Agrarian Law or the way in which it is enforced.

3. The words "retention and liquidation" mentioned in Article 250, which relates only to the territories ceded by Hungary, apply solely to the measures taken against the property of a Hungarian in the said territories and in so far as such owner is a Hungarian national.[10]

Action Taken by the Council and the Parties on the Report of the Committee of Three.—Count Apponyi for Hungary informed the Council that his government could not accept the suggestions of the Committee of Three.[11] He remarked that after an examination of the report he found nothing in the three principles laid down which had any connection with the Treaty of Trianon. It seemed difficult to him to prove an abuse of powers when the decision of the tribunal was in harmony with the opinions of eminent jurists. Nevertheless, Hungary had proposed to submit the question to the Permanent Court.[12] Rumania, on the other hand, stated

9 *Ibid.*, 1382. 10 *Ibid.*
11 *Ibid.*, 1389. 12 *Ibid.*, 1383 *et sqq.*

that it would accept the solution proposed by the Council, provided that Hungary would also accept it.[13]

The Council adopted a proposal of the President that the parties be requested to conform to the three principles of the committee and to delay their final opinion on the report until December.[14]

The legal objections of the Hungarian government upon which it founded its refusal to accept the three principles of the jurists were set forth in a strong and convincing memorial addressed to the Council, November 29, 1927.[15] It was submitted therein that the statements of the jurists that the tribunal might have jurisdiction even if the claim arose out of the application of the agrarian laws was in contradiction with the tendency of the report to admit an excess of jurisdiction. The jurists were said to have recognized that the tribunal was always competent to discover in concrete cases prohibited measures, even if they were hidden under the aspect of agrarian reform. It was pointed out that the claims before the tribunal did not demand the examination of the reform as such; no decision would be made on this question. The award was said to have rightly reserved for the examination upon the merits whether there existed the prohibited measures, whereas the jurists had confused matters of merit with those of jurisdiction, requiring the claimants to establish their case on the merits before they could have the right to sue. It was said to be the very object of the suit to examine the justice and substance of the allegation that the measures complained of were prohibited measures, and to accomplish this the tribunal "should open its door and not close it in advance." [16] Hungary contended that decisions upon questions arising under Articles 250 and 232 belonged exclusively to the tribunal and could not be taken from it without violating the treaty. It noted that the treaty was multilateral and that the case therefore was not a matter of a *compromis* between two parties which they could modify, even with the invitation of the Council. Article 248 so decreed, as well as international law. Principle No. 1 sought to eliminate completely the question of indemnification, whereas No. 2 made differentiation an indispensable characteristic of the prohibited measure. One or the other of these theses were said to be erroneous. International law prohibited expropriation without compensation, and Rumania's sovereignty was accordingly to be considered as limited in this respect. Hungary urged that seizure without compensation and differential treatment were included in the measures prohibited by Articles 232 and 250. Judgment No. 7 of the Permanent Court was cited as supporting this conclusion. The question of the existence of an indemnity was said to be an integral part of the problem of liquidation or of a prohibited measure. A number of acts which would not be prohibited in themselves would become so by virtue of an insufficient indemnity. The principle that indemnification had no importance from the point of view of liquidation, while differentiation was indispensable, was opposed to the treaty and to international law. Hungary read the comment of the jurists on Principles No. 2 and No. 5 as requiring the claimant to prove not only differentiation but also the intention of the Rumanian government to injure him because he was a Hungarian. This, it was said, would make the treaty a penal code and the tribunal a criminal court and would impose insurmountable difficulties of proof before the claimant could get a hearing.

The contentions of Hungary eventually prevailed. At its meeting of March 9, 1928, the Council submitted to the parties for their acceptance the recommendation that it name two persons who should be added to the Mixed Arbitral Tribunal—which would have restored to it the arbitrator appointed by Rumania—to which would be submitted the claims filed under Article 250 by Hungarian nationals whose property had been expropriated under the Rumanian agrarian laws.[17] This resolution was adopted by Count Apponyi, the Hungarian representative, and the Council. M. Titulesco, for Rumania, refrained from voting. The two governments there-

17 9 LEAGUE OF NATIONS, OFFICIAL JOURNAL (1928) 446.

after concerned themselves with direct negotiations in an effort to
reach a settlement. At its meeting of May 12, 1930, their representatives requested the Council to withdraw the question from
the agenda, subject to the entry into force of the agreements concluded at The Hague and signed at Paris, April 28, 1930. The question was withdrawn.[18]

Criticism of Report of Committee of Three.—Bruns,[19] in an admirable analysis of the question as it involved action by the Council
of the League, points out that the proceedings initiated by Hungary
under Article 239 of the Treaty of Trianon required a purely
juridical solution, while those initiated by Rumania required a
political solution. He submits that Article 239 constitutes a legal
obligation which could not be evaded and that Article 11 of the
Covenant applies only to those situations to which international
law is not applicable.

His distinction is valuable, but it requires further analysis as to
the authority of the Council in either situation. As previously shown,
the Council was not empowered to act, under Article 11, while the
tribunal possessed jurisdiction; and, under Article 239, if the tribunal possessed jurisdiction, the Council would apparently be
obliged to appoint substitute judges.[20] Under either article it would
be necessary for the Council to inquire into the question of whether
or not the tribunal had acted within its jurisdiction.

It would seem that the scope of that inquiry by the Council would
need to be sharply limited. It should inquire only whether a clear

[18] 11 *ibid.*, (1930) 498. A special "Agrarian Fund" was created for the
payment of claims arising out of the agrarian legislation of Rumania, Czecho-
slovakia and Jugo-Slavia, see AGREEMENTS CONCLUDED AT THE HAGUE CONFERENCE,
JANUARY, 1930 (1930) 373 *et sqq.* See also Permanent Court of International Justice,
"The Pajzs, Czáky, Esterházy Case," Judgment of December 16, 1936, SER. A./B.,
Fascicule No. 68.

[19] Bruns, *An Opinion on the Questions Connected with the Appointment of Sub-
stitute Arbitrators to the Roumano-Hungarian Mixed Arbitral Tribunal by the
Council of the League of Nations*, 2 SOME OPINIONS, ARTICLES AND REPORTS BEAR-
ING UPON THE TREATY OF TRIANON AND THE CLAIMS OF THE HUNGARIAN NATIONALS
WITH REGARD TO THEIR LANDS IN TRANSYLVANIA 147, 158.

[20] *Cf.* Appointment of substitute members for the Franco-German, Franco-
Austrian, Franco-Hungarian and Franco-Bulgarian Tribunals, 4 LEAGUE OF NA-
TIONS, OFFICIAL JOURNAL (1923) 242-243.

usurpation of jurisdiction had taken place so that the tribunal's decision was not obligatory upon the parties under the principles of international law.[21] Its decision on that point should be based solely on legal criteria and should not go beyond the single issue of whether manifest excess of jurisdiction had occurred. But, though based on legal reasoning, the opinion of the Council thus reached of itself would not possess the binding force of a judgment of a court duly instituted between the parties to decide upon the question of excess of jurisdiction. The Council had no *judicial* power to decide such a question.[22] A specific *compromis* or other conferment of authority would be required to confer such power upon it. In connection with the proceedings under Article 239, if it should have decided the preliminary question of excess of jurisdiction to the effect that none had occurred, it might then have proceeded to the nomination of arbitrators—as it, in fact, contemplated doing—and presumably even applied sanctions towards securing the appearance of the parties before the newly constituted tribunal. But the decision upon the preliminary question of jurisdiction so rendered would be a judicial decision having the binding force of an arbitral decision. As to the action of the Council under Article 11, clearly it would not have been binding upon the parties. Thus, in the report on the Geneva Protocol submitted to the Assembly it is stated that this article "confers no right on the Council or the Assembly to impose any solution of a dispute without the consent of the parties. Action taken by the Council or the Assembly to impose any solution under this article cannot become binding on the parties to the dispute in the sense in which recommendations under Article 15 become binding, unless they have themselves concurred in it." [23]

Furthermore, it seems clear that the Council would have no authority to inquire into the form which the decision of the tribunal on

21 Kaufman, *The Hungarian-Rumanian Dispute,* etc., 2 *op. cit. supra* note 19, at 79, 81.
22 Unden, *Le Différend roumano-hongrois devant le Conseil de la Société des Nations en septembre 1927* (1927) 1 REV. DE DROIT INT. 746, 754.
23 LEAGUE OF NATIONS, OFFICIAL JOURNAL, SPECIAL SUPP. NO. 24 (1924) 126.

the merits should take, and it is here that criticism has centered upon the action of the Committee of Three. Fachiri [24] finds that the fundamental error of their report is that, while finding that the tribunal had jurisdiction to entertain the claims, it proceeded to lay down the tests by which the decision on the merits should be governed. Kaufmann [25] remarks that while Sir Austin Chamberlain, the reporter, states that the whole question turns on whether excess of jurisdiction had occurred, he never answers this in the affirmative. Kaufman submits that the only question raised was whether the jurists would *affirm* the jurisdiction of the tribunal, an entirely different question from whether an excess of jurisdiction had occurred. Not even a plain "yes" or "no" had been given in answer to that question. Had the Council accepted the viewpoint of the jurists as correct, it would only have followed that in the opinion of the Council the tribunal had committed an error of judgment. He points out that either the question of usurpation of jurisdiction should have been clearly put and plainly answered—and if it were found that none had occurred, then substitute judges would have had to be appointed—or an attempt should have been made to avoid the question altogether, thereby leaving unsettled the essential element of the dispute, whether the Rumanian action was right or wrong. Borchard [26] states that whether the "liquidation" prohibited by Article 250 applies only to measures directed against exenemies as such is a question of the interpretation of a treaty. Since the interpretation of treaties was a legal, not a political, function, in his view it should, if possible, be left to the courts.

[24] Fachiri, *The Present Position of the Hungarian Optants Case, 2 op. cit. supra* note 19, at 229, 234; *cf.* Borchard, *Opinion on the Roumanian-Hungarian Dispute before the Council of the League of Nations, ibid.,* 23, 36.

[25] *Supra* note 21, at 82–83, 85, 86.

[26] *Supra* note 24, at 41, 42.

CHAPTER 4

DOCTRINE OF ESSENTIAL ERROR

57. DOCTRINE OF ESSENTIAL ERROR AND THE PROBLEM OF MISTAKE.—
Up to this point we have been concerned with the procedural and
jurisdictional aspects of an international arbitration and the legal
effect of departures by the tribunal from the terms of submission,
express or implied. The rules discussed in the two preceding
chapters may be considered to be fundamental rules of procedure
and jurisdiction, the violation of which by the tribunal or the
parties will lead to the nullity of the ensuing award. There remain the questions of the effect of mistake of fact or law by the
tribunal in its award and the means available for its correction.
While the tribunal is still in being and before it becomes *functus
officio,* the procedure of rehearing for the correction of such a mistake is available to the parties in accordance with the rules later
discussed herein.[1] The problem with which we are now concerned
is whether, in addition to the fundamental rules of procedure and
jurisdiction previously formulated in this text, there are circumstances of mistake or error in the award which will lead to its nullity.

Writers since the time of Grotius have concerned themselves
with the question of what action a State should be privileged to
take if an unjust award or an award vitiated by "essential error" were
rendered against it. Their method of analysis has justly been criticized by Judge Moore as "emanating from the desire to round out
or to develop symmetrically some a priori conception rather than
from an effort to meet any conditions that actually exist." [2] Their
discussion has ranged from the effects of a "denial of justice" by

[1] *Infra* Ch. VI.
[2] Opinion of John Bassett Moore, Counsellor for Honduras, Honduras-Nicaragua
Boundary Mediation before the Secretary of State of the United States, 1920–1921.
5 COLLECTED PAPERS OF JOHN BASSETT MOORE (1944) 154.

the tribunal[3] to the consequences of "material error."[4] The term "essential error" has also been used to indicate error caused by the production of false evidence.[5] To those possessing the background of the English common law, however, the term seems to suggest more aptly judicial error in the appreciation of the facts or law of a case than fraud. It is believed that clearer thinking would be aided if the term were no longer used to indicate cases involving fraud in the production of evidence; such cases involve more properly a violation of a fundamental rule of procedure.[6] Little purpose is served in continuing to consider such cases as involving "essential error," when in the minds of many that term is suggestive of an unconscionable decision.

Historically, the use of the term to cover cases of the fraud of the parties seems to have had its origin in the projected code of arbitral procedure of Goldschmidt. Section 32 (11) thereof provided that a decision could be attacked, among other grounds, if it were established that "the arbitral tribunal had been deceived by the adverse party, for instance, by means of false or altered documents or of corrupted witnesses."[7] His project was considered by the Institute of International Law at its session of Geneva of 1874. Mancini there proposed in committee as a substitute the following article:

The arbitral award is null in case of an invalid *compromis*, or of excess of jurisdiction, or of corruption proved against one of the arbitrators, if it has influenced the majority, or of essential error caused by the production of false documents.[8]

---

[3] *Infra* p. 189. The American agent in the Orinoco Steamship Company Case *infra* p. 183 said that the term "essential error" referred to "that situation, admittedly varying in its facts, but reasonably well understood by lawyers and jurists, and described with legal certainty by the phrase 'denial of justice.'"

[4] *Infra* this section note 12.

[5] *Infra* this section note 9.

[6] *Cf.* SCHÄTZEL, RECHTSKRAFT UND ANFECHTUNG VON ENTSCHEIDUNGEN INTERNATIONALER GERICHTE, 6 FRANKFURTER ABHANDLUNGEN ZUM KRIEGSVERHÜTUNGSRECHT (1928) 19–20, affirming that a case of this nature justifies a refusal to proceed further in the arbitration.

[7] Goldschmidt, *Projet de règlement pour tribunaux internationaux, présenté à l'Institut de Droit International* (Session de Genève, 1874) (1874) 6 REV. DE DROIT INT. L.C. 447.

[8] *Ibid.*, 595–596.

At the session of the Institute of International Law of 1875, Rivier, the reporter, said that the committee considered essential error to involve error caused by false documents or false testimony,[9] in which view Goldschmidt seems to concur.[10]

Probably since the development of this branch of the law of nullity by writers has largely been based upon a priori reasoning—rarely is an actual case cited by them—a considerable range of opinion exists as to the scope and meaning of the concept of "essential error." Some content themselves with merely mentioning "essential error" [11] or "material error" [12] as a cause of nullity, without making clear its meaning. Others apparently conceive of "essential error" in the sense of the definition of the project of the Institute of International Law.[13] Another and very considerable group of writers have addressed themselves to the question of what consequences should follow from an unjust decision. Says Grotius:

Although municipal law may make provision for arbitrators to whom resort is had under promises on both sides, and in some places has provided that it shall be lawful to appeal from them and to make complaint of injustice, nevertheless such a procedure cannot become applicable in relation to kings and peoples. For here there is no higher power, which can either hold fast or loosen the bond of the promise. Under such conditions, therefore, the decision of arbitrators, whether just or unjust, must stand absolutely.[14]

Pufendorf [15] held a similar view.

Vattel, however, seems to have been of a contrary opinion, though his exact meaning is somewhat difficult to ascertain. He states that:

---

[9] (1877) ANNUAIRE 87.
[10] Goldschmidt, *Observations supplémentaires relatives aux réglement pour tribunaux internationaux* (1875) 7 REV. DE DROIT INT. L.C. 423, 426.
[11] BISHOP, INTERNATIONAL ARBITRAL PROCEDURE (1930) 242; 2 DE LOUTER, LE DROIT INTERNATIONAL PUBLIC POSITIF (1920) 155.
[12] BRY, PRÉCIS ÉLÉMENTAIRE DE DROIT INTERNATIONAL PUBLIC (1910) 491; ROUARD DE CARD, DROIT INTERNATIONAL; L'ARBITRAGE INTERNATIONAL DANS LE PASSÉ, LE PRÉSENT ET L'AVENIR (1877) 53 ("evident injustice or material error").
[13] 2 OPPENHEIM, INTERNATIONAL LAW (4th ed. 1928) 28; Lisboa, *Revision de sentences arbitrales* (1902, 2d ser.) 4 REV. DE DROIT INT. L.C. 64; Nys, *La Revision de la sentence arbitrale* (1910, 2d ser.) 12 *ibid.*, 621.
[14] 3 GROTIUS, DE JURE BELLI AC PACIS (Kelsey trans., 1925, Vol. 2) 823–824.
[15] 2 PUFENDORF, LE DROIT DE LA NATURE ET DES GENS (1734) 176.

. . . if the arbitrators should render a decision which is evidently unjust and unreasonable, they would thereby divest themselves of their character as arbitrators and their decision would have no weight since they were only chosen to decide doubtful questions.[16]

He then proceeds to the definition and regulation of his rule, as follows:

Suppose that arbitrators should condemn a sovereign State, in reparation for an offense, to become subject to the offended State; would any sensible man say that the State should submit to the decision? If the injustice is of little moment it must be put up with for the sake of peace; and if it is not absolutely evident it should be borne with as an evil to which the State voluntarily exposed itself; for if it were necessary to be convinced of the justice of a sentence before submitting to it, it would be quite useless to appoint arbitrators.[17]

He then takes up the relation of such an "evidently unjust" decision to the obligation to conform to the arbitral agreement.

. . . in the case of a vague and indefinite agreement. . . . It may then happen, as in the example just cited, that the arbitrators will exceed their powers and decide points which have not really been submitted to them. Having been appointed to decide what satisfaction a State owes for an offense, they condemn it to become subject to the offended State. Clearly the offending State never gave them such extensive power, and their absurd sentence is in no way binding upon it.[18]

It would seem from the last-quoted statement that Vattel may have had in mind a decision so absurd as to be beyond the bounds of submission properly construed. But his concluding remarks, though at first tending to bear out the inference just noted, make clear that he admits that a decision may be invalid even though it be upon a subject clearly submitted to the arbitrators. He states that:

In order to avoid all difficulties and to leave no foothold for bad faith it is necessary that the agreement to arbitrate should state the precise subject in dispute, the respective and conflicting claims of the parties, the demands made on the one side and the defense offered on the other. What is thus defined constitutes the subject-matter submitted to the arbitrators and the

---

[16] 2 VATTEL, LE DROIT DE GENS (ed. 1758, Fenwick trans., 1916) sec. 329, p. 223.
[17] Ibid., 223–224.   [18] Ibid., 224.

points on which it is agreed to submit to their decision. Under such conditions, if their decision is within the limits prescribed, the parties must submit to it. It cannot be said that the decision is manifestly unjust, since it is given upon a *question rendered doubtful by the disagreement of the parties and submitted as such*. In order to invalidate a decision of this kind it must be shown that it was the result of corruption or of *obvious partiality*.[19] [Italics supplied.]

Stemming from these ideas a number of writers have said that the performance of an award may be refused if it is "unjust" [20] or "absolutely contrary to the rules of justice" [21] or "manifestly contrary to all reasonable justice" [22] or an "open denial of justice" [23] or "inequitable or unconscionable" [24] or "in absolute conflict with the rules of justice and therefore incapable of being the subject of a valid international compact," [25] or if "manifestly unjust and contrary to reason," [26] or if there is "glaring partiality" [27] or "evident injustice" [28] or "a flagrant denial of justice." [29]

With a similar point of view, some affirm that the award is null if contrary to international law.[30] The conception lying behind this generalization has been variously expressed. Bluntschli says "an arbitral award cannot decree that which the parties themselves would not have been able to establish by a treaty." [31] Pradier-Fodéré states that it is intended to refer to a case in which the award "would order

19 *Ibid.*, 224.
20 BULMERINCQ, VÖLKERRECHT (1887) 352.
21 3 CALVO, LE DROIT INTERNATIONAL (5th ed., 1896) 486.
22 2 FERGUSON, MANUAL OF INTERNATIONAL LAW (1884) 207.
23 HALL, INTERNATIONAL LAW (8th ed., 1924) 420.
24 2 HYDE, INTERNATIONAL LAW CHIEFLY AS INTERPRETED AND APPLIED BY THE UNITED STATES (2d ed., 1945) 1640.
25 2 TWISS, THE LAW OF NATIONS (2d ed., 1875) 8. He gives as an illustration: "that decision of the Roman people, which Livy narrates with very strong reprobation, when the cities of Ardea and of Aricium having deferred their dispute in regard to the sovereignty over a certain country to the arbitration of the Roman people, the Assembly of the Roman Tribes adjudged the territory in controversy to be the property of the Roman State" (citing Livii Historia, L. III, c. 71), *ibid.*, 9.
26 Weiss, *L'Arbitrage de 1909 entre la Bolivie et le Pérou* (1910) 17 REV. GEN. DE DROIT INT. PUB. 119.
27 3 PHILLIMORE, COMMENTARIES UPON INTERNATIONAL LAW (1857) 5.
28 *Ibid.;* ROUARD DE CARD, *op. cit. supra* note 12, at 53.
29 TAYLOR, A TREATISE ON INTERNATIONAL LAW (1901) 380.
30 2 FIORE, NOUVEAU DROIT INTERNATIONAL PUBLIC (Antoine trans., 1885) 643.
31 BLUNTSCHLI, LE DROIT INTERNATIONAL CODIFIÉ (1895) 281.

an immoral act or one contrary to the laws of humanity; in which it would impair the absolute rights of the nations, and could not, consequently, serve as the basis of a valid international convention." [32] Carnazza-Amari [33] refers to the violation by the arbitrators of a primitive right of the States.

From the foregoing review of authorities one can only conclude with Mérignhac that the concept of "essential error" is vague.[34] Yet it is believed that a certain legal analysis of the problem can be made with a view to clarifying and restricting the issues involved. No one would gainsay that merely a mistake or a questionable application of the law would not give rise to nullity.[35] Accordingly, the exception has been advanced that the error must relate to the principal object of the *compromis,* not merely an accessory error which can be readily corrected by the parties requesting a modification of the award on that point.[36] Balasko [37] classifies essential error as a "gross error of fact or of law." Hall remarks, in this connection, that there is "ample room for the commission, under the influence of sentiment, of personal or national prejudices, or erroneous theories of law, and views unconsciously biased by national interests, of grave injustice, for which the injured state has no remedy." [38] Occasion has already been taken to distinguish essential error from cases involving fraud of the parties. The problem, therefore, narrows to the status of those arbitral opinions which are based upon an erroneous appreciation by the arbitrators of the facts or of the law.[39] If the error of fact were owing to the fact that both the tribunal and

[32] 6 Pradier-Fodéré, Traité de droit international public (1894) 435.

[33] 2 Carnazza-Amari, Traité de droit international public (1882) 564.

[34] Mérignhac, L'Arbitrage international (1895) 314; 2 De Louter, Le Droit international public positif (1920) 158; see also Lammasch, Die Rechtskraft internationaler Schiedssprüche (1913) 204.

[35] Taylor, op. cit. supra note 29, at 379.

[36] 2 Fiore, op. cit. supra note 30, at 644.

[37] Balasko, Causes de nullité de la sentence arbitrale en droit international public (1938) 133.

[38] Hall, op. cit. supra note 23, at 420.

[39] See analysis of Schätzel, Rechtskraft und Anfechtung von Entscheidungen internationaler Gerichte, 6 Frankfurter Abhandlungen zum Kriegsverhütungsrecht (1928) 93, 108; Scelle, Une Instance en revision devant la Cour de la Haye, l'affaire de la Orinoco Steamship Company (1911) 18 Rev. Gen. de Droit Int. Pub. 190.

the parties were ignorant of evidence later discovered, the procedure of revision would be open to them.[40] With regard to the error of law, there is much force in the view of Ulloa that:

The *error of law* should be discarded, because its appreciation cannot be left to the appreciation of the prejudiced State, which will always discover allegations on which to base it. The error of law is only a manifestation of the incapacity of the arbitrator, imputable to the parties who have selected him and must suffer the consequences.[41]

But if the error in law should consist in a failure to apply an applicable rule of law stipulated in the *compromis*, nullity may result.[42] The reasoning of the tribunal in the *Trail Smelter* case [43] is pertinent in this connection:

The formula "essential error" originated in a text voted by the International Law Institute in 1876. From its inception, its very authors were divided as to its meaning . . .

The Tribunal is of the opinion that the proper criterion lies in a distinction not between "essential" errors in law and other such errors, but between "manifest" errors, such as that in the Schreck case or such as would be committed by a tribunal that would overlook a relevant treaty or base its decision on an agreement admittedly terminated, and other errors in law.[44]

The ramification of the views of writers as to the meaning of essential error demonstrates the looseness, vagueness, and lack of legal exactness of the term. It is a phrase of the pleader or the advocate rather than that of the judge. Even considered as referring to a denial of justice or a failure to afford a minimum of justice, it is subjective rather than objective in nature. It is a conclusion based upon other and preceding legal steps in the analysis of an award, steps embracing questions such as aspects of departure from terms of submission, express or implied, and failure to apply applicable rules of international law. When the arbitral award is lacking in one or more of the conditions required for its validity, as estab-

40 *Infra* sec. 75.
41 2 ULLOA, DERECHO INTERNATIONAL PÚBLICO (1929) 202–203.
42 *Supra* sec. 41.
43 *Infra* sec. 70.   44 (1941) 35 AM. J. INT. LAW 707.

lished by the practice of States, the tribunal may be said to have committed an essential error. For essential error, if it is to serve any useful purpose, should be deemed to refer to the absence of one or more of the various objective, definite, established legal conditions necessary for the validity of the award. If essential error is to be considered in any other light, that is, as referring to error or mistake generally, the ascertainment of its existence would require not only an examination of the tribunal's action and its award in the light of the *compromis,* as does excess of jurisdiction, but an examination of the intrinsic merit of the reasons which dictated the award, an examination of the facts and documents submitted, in short, a new examination of the case on the merits.[45]

58. SAME: ORINOCO STEAMSHIP COMPANY CASE.—In the *Orinoco Steamship Company Case*[1] extended arguments were made before the Hague Tribunal as to the meaning of the term "essential error." The remarks of the American agent furnish a particularly illuminating and thoughtful discussion of the subject, and occasion will, therefore, be taken to quote extensively from them. He noted that both the United States and Venezuela were in agreement that mere mistake was not a ground for revision.[2] He stated that he also was of the opinion, with the Venezuelan agent, that the stipulation ordinarily contained in arbitral conventions—which was included in the protocol of 1903 between the United States and Venezuela —providing that awards shall be final is entirely superfluous. With or without the stipulation, governments must abide by an arbitral decision unless it be subject to a defect which justifies revision.[3] In regard to the view of the Venezuelan agent that essential error is

---

[45] Castberg, *L'Excès de pouvoir dans la justice internationale* (1931) 35 RECUEIL ᴅES COURS 420: "of a different nature is the defect which consists, not in the use of a wrong category of rules, but in the application in an erroneous manner of the appropriate category of rules. Such a defect is not an excess of jurisdiction. It is not an excess of jurisdiction if a tribunal pronounces a decision erroneous as to the merits. It is necessary to distinguish between an error as to the merits and an excess of jurisdiction." See also Scelle, *supra* note 39, at 190; GUERMANOFF, L'EXCÈS DE POUVOIR DE L'ARBITRE (1929) 63.

[1] *Supra* sec. 44.

[2] ARGUMENT OF THE UNITED STATES OF AMERICA ON BEHALF OF THE ORINOCO STEAMSHIP COMPANY; PERMANENT COURT OF ARBITRATION AT THE HAGUE; UNITED STATES–VENEZUELA ARBITRATION (1910) 18.   [3] *Ibid.,* 29.

error caused by false evidence, it was submitted that the weight of authority opposed this interpretation.[4] The thesis was offered that:

. . . three fundamental ideas appear to underlie the views of the writers of international law on this topic:—First, Vattel's idea that a decision might be so "manifestly unjust and unreasonable," or "flagrantly partial," as to render it invalid. Vattel evidently had in mind a very extreme case, such as would instantly appeal to any unprejudiced observer. Second, the idea that an award is of the same dignity as a treaty, and that anything which "cannot be stipulated by treaty can also not be embodied by an arbitral award" (Bluntschli). Presumably these authors have in mind a decision decreeing something immoral or against public policy. Third, the general conception that an arbitral decision becomes invalid when it violates international law. This conception is naturally somewhat indefinite and elastic, in view of the many unsettled questions of international law. However, out of these three general conceptions and their variations, and partaking of them all, there has gradually grown up a general conception, which is perhaps as definitely understood and expressed as could be expected as regards a point of this difficulty.

It is submitted that the fundamental idea of all these authors is that which is perhaps expressed as clearly as the nature of the case permits of by Hall in the words "an open denial of justice," and by the Institute in the words "essential error." It is believed that the conception of all these authors and of the Institute is the same. It is submitted that they refer in general to that kind of patent injustice and outrageous error which constitutes a denial of justice in municipal courts, and which justifies a claimant suffering therefrom in appealing to an international tribunal. This conception differs only in degree from the original concept of Vattel. It does not require such an extraordinary aberration as Vattel apparently had in mind, such, for instance, as the case which he uses in the earlier portion of his section by way of illustration of arbitrators condemning a sovereign State to become a subject of the State it has offended. It does not require such a vagary on the part of the court as would attract the instant attention of the ordinary layman. It merely requires that situation, admittedly varying in its facts, but reasonably well understood by lawyers and jurists, and described with legal certainty by the phrase "denial of justice." As this differs only in degree from the original idea of Vattel, so also it differs only in degree from ordinary error, which by the great weight of authority furnishes no ground for attacking an award; but the importance which sometimes attaches to a difference in degree is familiar to every lawyer.[5]

[4] *Ibid.*, 83, 90.   [5] *Ibid.*, 81–83.

On behalf of Venezuela it was contended that a decision duly rendered was *res judicata* for the matters decided. International law recognized certain causes of nullity.[6] Errors of fact or of law and errors consisting in an inexact appreciation of fact or mistaken application of law were not among these.[7] Authors were unanimous that the infraction of the principles of equity was not a cause of nullity.[8] Essential error consisted in the production of false proofs.[9]

As noted in connection with the previous discussion of this case, the tribunal refrained from commenting upon the points so argued. It merely reaffirmed that upon which both agents agreed, namely, that mere mistake was not a basis of nullity.

59. SAME: BERMUDEZ LAND CLAIM AND ORA MILLER CLAIM BEFORE THE JOINT LAND COMMISSION, UNITED STATES AND PANAMA.—Merely a questionable interpretation of provisions of the *compromis* defining the law to be applied by the tribunal or a simple mistake such as an erroneous computation of damages does not justify an allegation of nullity. Under such conditions and if the tribunal be not *functus officio*, the losing State may ask for a reargument or a rectification of the award. Otherwise the State should address its request for correction to the other party. If the mistake be manifest, that State could hardly refuse to accede to its correction. These principles are believed to be illustrated in the controversy between the United States and Panama concerning the interpretation given by the joint land commission to certain treaty provisions existing between them.

By Article VI of the convention of November 18, 1903,[1] a joint commission was created to determine the compensation to be paid to owners of land included in the canal zone, which Panama had granted to the United States under Article II. It further provided that the appraisal of such properties "shall be based upon their value before the date of this convention." Expressly excepted from the grant in Article II were "the cities of Panama and Colon and the

6 ALEGATOS DEL REPRESANTE DE VENEZUELA, DR. CARLOS F. GRISANTI (1910) (Caracas, 1930) 14, 16–17.

7 *Ibid.*, 20; VENEZUELA, PRIMER CONTRA-ALEGATO, *ibid.*, 85–86.

8 *Op. cit. supra* note 6, at 18.

9 *Ibid.*, 21.   1 2 MALLOY, TREATIES 1349, 1351.

harbors adjacent" thereto, which were within the boundaries of the zone.[2] By Article XV all decisions of the commission or of the umpire were to be "final." [3]

In the award by the commission to Ora Miller of April 21, 1917, damages were allowed for land in Panama City as of the date of expropriation, which was not until 1912, instead of before the date of the treaty of 1903. Counsel for the United States moved for a rehearing, upon the grounds that it was greatly in excess of the value of the property and based upon erroneous conclusions of law and fact. The American and Panamanian commissioners disagreed upon the granting of the motion, but it was not referred to the umpire, since after some correspondence the Department of State announced that it was not "disposed to obstruct the payment of the award." [4] But the governor of the Panama Canal Zone submitted to the comptroller of the Treasury an application for the revision of the allowance of the award by the auditor of the War Department. It was alleged that the record in the case showed upon its face that the award was not made upon the basis prescribed in the treaty and was therefore void. The application was rejected by the comptroller. In his opinion he noted that the question was whether the commission had gone beyond its jurisdiction clearly enough to justify his rejection of the award. "No fraud is alleged, and the contention is one involving the meaning of the treaty, and as to that meaning there has been some difference of opinion." [5] It was held that it was not "the duty of his office to go behind the award and determine what was the value in 1905, just before the date of the treaty, and if that be less than the award to declare the award void because the joint land commission exceeded its jurisdiction." [6] To require the accounting officers of this government to "review the action of the joint land commission as to the amount of its awards would involve an examination of the evidence and a decision would

2 *Ibid.*, 1350.
3 *Ibid.*, 1354.
4 See Decision of May 28, 1917, 23 Decisions of the Comptroller of the Treasury (1916–1917) 692, 693–695.
5 *Ibid.*, 697.   6 *Ibid.*, 698.

be rendered without viewing the property and with none of the ordinary facilities for reaching a proper conclusion. Such a procedure would give no weight to the finality of decision accorded to the commission's awards by both Articles VI and XV of the treaty." [7] After an unusually well-conceived analysis of the legal status of a decision of an international tribunal, he held that the commission had not so clearly exceeded its jurisdiction as to justify him in declaring its award void. In the analysis to, the comptroller said:

I think it is well settled that an international tribunal is vested with broad powers to determine its own jurisdiction, and that when a treaty provides that its awards shall be final it is but the customary way of settling disputed questions. When a tribunal is composed of two representatives of each country it is to be expected that in reaching an agreement as to the value of some property mutual concessions will be involved and a procedure will be adopted in the nature of a compromise. If practical results are to be obtained, the necessity is apparent for making the conclusion reached final on both parties.

If one party to the treaty is dissatisfied with the action of its representatives, the remedy as to future cases appears to be clear, but an allegation of error of judgment as to the law or the facts (*the tribunal having jurisdiction of the subject matter and the parties*) is not sufficient ordinarily to render void the award or to require other officers of one of the Governments to review the facts and the law to determine whether or not the allegation is well founded. A deliberate departure from the rules laid down in a treaty to govern a tribunal might justify a refusal to pay the award but that is not the situation here.[8] (Italics supplied.)

The *Bermudez* land claim involved the expropriation by the United States of a certain tract known as Punta Paitilla. This was located on the shore opposite Panama City and in the vicinity of its residential section. Possession of it was taken by the United States in October, 1913. The exact area taken was not known until 1918, when the governor of the Canal Zone informed the secretary of foreign affairs of Panama that the United States would require 50.6 hectares. In addition to the area thus expropriated, the United

7 *Ibid.*, 697.   8 *Ibid.*, 699.

States occupied an area of about 100 hectares during the first World War.[9]

Counsel for the government admitted the validity of the claimant's title, but the commission disagreed on the question of value. The American commissioners, in their opinion, referred to the agreement of June 15, 1904,[10] which located the 50.6 hectares within the Canal Zone, and to the treaty of September 2, 1914,[11] by which certain modifications of the boundary were made and the 50.6 hectares were ceded back to Panama. It was their contention that Article X of the treaty of 1914 [12] embodied the intention to make Article VI of the treaty of 1903 controlling upon any expropriation and that damages should, therefore, be fixed as of before 1903. Since the evidence showed that the tract was but little developed prior to 1903 and was difficult of access, damages were fixed by them at $3,795, and $300 were allowed for the occupation during the war. The Panamanian members of the commission, taking into consideration that the land was within the limits of the City of Panama when the United States government decided upon the area to be taken, appraised its value at $101,200, and estimated damages for occupation at $1,200.[13]

The umpire referred to his award No. 199 relating to a portion of 12 hectares of the estate "San Juan Caballero," located outside the Canal Zone at the time of its expropriation, in which he had held that Article VI of the treaty of 1903 should not be applied for

---

9 See Award of the Umpire in Julia Bermudez de Aleman, et al. v. United States (Decision May 8, 1920), enclosure with Secretary Bliss of the Joint Commission, United States and Panama, to the Secretary of State, May 8, 1920 (411. 19 L 22/936).

10 3 TREATIES (Malloy Supp., 1923) 2752.

11 Ibid., 2770.

12 This article provided that the "Convention shall not diminish, exhaust or alter any rights acquired by them [the Contracting Parties] heretofore in conformity with the Canal Treaty of November 18, 1903; and it is further expressly agreed that the United States, in the exercise of the rights granted to it under articles II and III of the said Canal Treaty and subject to article VI of said Treaty" may at any future time enter upon, occupy and control any of the Sabanas land or any territory transferred by the convention to Panama. It was the contention of counsel for claimant that since the words "subject to article VI" were used instead of "in conformity with," the United States incurred the obligation imposed by Article VI but forfeited all benefits conferred by it.

13 Supra note 9.

purposes of valuation, since Article II of the treaty excepted from the grant to the United States the cities of Panama and Colon, which were within the zone.[14] He concluded that the general principles of law relative to forcible expropriation were applicable and concurred with the Panamanian commissioners in their award.[15]

The special attorney of the Panama Canal refused to attach his certificate to the award upon the ground that the umpire had "exceeded his authority and that the award is therefore void, and because the award is grossly excessive." The ruling of the umpire was declared to be "a departure from the instructions contained in Article VI," while the American valuation of $75 a hectar was asserted to be a liberal valuation even as of the time of the award. He therefore deemed it his "duty to submit the case to the Department of State, through proper channels, for its resolve." [16]

The United States, upon consideration, informed Panama that it protested the award and regarded it as without binding force, since statements in the decision of the umpire contravened Article VI of the convention of 1903.[17] Panama at first replied that in other cases it had interpreted Article VI differently, but had refrained from protesting those cases, that the decisions which the umpire dictated were final in accordance with Article XV, and that it hoped that the United States would reconsider and pay the award.[18] Its position was later amplified in the note of February 10, 1921.[19] It was there admitted that an *ultra vires* award may be void, but, it was stated,

---

[14] It appears that the San Juan Caballero property was *outside* the Canal Zone in 1903, and hence in accordance with the proviso of Articles 2 and 7 of the treaty of 1903, it would not be within the stipulation of the last sentence of Article 6, and that the umpire was right in assessing damages as of the time of expropriation. It was included in the transfer of September 2, 1914. But the Bermudez land was originally a part of the Canal Zone but excepted therefrom by the convention of September 2, 1914.

[15] *Supra* note 9.

[16] The Secretary of War to the Secretary of State, June 14, 1920, enclosing copy of letter from Special Attorney of the Panama Canal Feuille to Acting Governor Morrow, May 21, 1920 (411. 19 L 22/941).

[17] Chargé d'Affaires *ad interim* Hewes to the Acting Secretary of Affairs Hazera, Aug. 30, 1920, enclosure with Minister Price to the Secretary of State, Sept. 28, 1920 (411. 19 L 22/948).

[18] Secretary Hazera to Minister Price, Sept. 28, 1920, *ibid.*

[19] Chargé d'Affaires Lefevre to the Secretary of State, Feb. 10, 1921 (411. 19 L 22/958).

"no party may allege, without infringing the fundamental principles of arbitration, that the award is void, because the arbitrator, proceeding under the rules of existing law and the powers conferred upon him by the agreement, nevertheless viewed in an erroneous manner the questions of fact upon which the award is based." When Panama suggested payment as an act of grace as a solution,[20] Secretary Hughes replied that a more favorable consideration to such a payment might be given if it did not appear that the award was excessive, even if the value at the time of taking be considered.[21]

An amicable settlement finally appears to have been reached, upon Minister Davis's suggestion that the United States acquire the land by direct purchase, for approximately the amount of the award with interest, without making any reference to the award in the documents transferring the property.[22]

It will be observed that the property involved in the *Ora Miller* case was at no time within the limits of the Canal Zone and that the United States consequently could not take advantage of Article VI of the treaty of 1903. On the other hand, the land involved in the *Bermudez* claim was embraced in the Canal Zone, as measured by the agreement of 1904. But the expropriation did not take place until after the treaty of 1914, and hence the question before the umpire was the interpretation of Article X of the treaty of 1914. The umpire failed even to mention Article X in his decision, though its construction appears to have been argued by counsel and made the subject of discussion by the American commissioners. The "San Juan Caballero" award cited by him afforded no support for his decision, for that involved property which, like the Ora Miller property, was outside the Canal Zone in 1903. Moreover, the sum awarded may reasonably have been believed to be excessive.

60. SAME: TACNA-ARICA ARBITRATION.—In its case before the arbitrator of the Tacna-Arica dispute between Peru and Chile, Chile made the rather remarkable statement that even if the arbitrator

---

[20] Minister Alfaro to the Secretary of State, Mar. 5, 1923 (411. 19 L 22/981).

[21] Secretary of State to Minister Alfaro, Oct. 15, 1923 (411. 19 L 22/981).

[22] Minister Davis to the Secretary of State, Apr. 11, 1930 (411. 19 L 22/1038). See Second Deficiency Act of July 3, 1930, 46 STAT. 860, 888, appropriating $160,000 in payment for the land.

should decide in answer to the first question submitted to him that no plebiscite should be held, Chile would nevertheless still be compelled to insist upon the application of the principle of the right of the inhabitants of the territory to a plebiscite in any negotiations which might result from the arbitrator's decision.[1] Such an eventuality fortunately never arose, because the arbitrator held in favor of a plebiscite.[2]

After the publication of the award, the Peruvian government, through the president of the Peruvian Defense Commission, informed the president of the United States, as arbitrator, that, before consenting to participate in the plebiscite, it desired to submit certain requests.[3] It declared that the arbitrator had been led into "a substantial error" in translating certain words in the Treaty of Ancon from which the decision in favor of the plebiscite was derived. It further alleged that the arbitrator failed to give weight to proofs offered by it as to violent acts of Chile which would prevent a fair plebiscite. The assertion was made that there had been a violation of the essential conditions for a plebiscite which would justify Peru in refusing to accept the decision. It would, however, carry out the award, notwithstanding the errors which it had indicated.[4] Certain guarantees were requested as a condition for assuring fair voting.[5]

The Arbitrator ruled that:

The Award was the result of a careful examination of the elaborate record submitted by the parties. This record fully covered all the questions treated in the views now submitted on behalf of the Government of Peru and argued all the questions which it is now sought to reargue. Under the Terms of Submission agreed to by both parties as well as by the general principles of International Law these questions have been decided by the Award "finally and without appeal."

. . . In deference, however, to the great nations who are the parties to this arbitration, and keeping in mind the importance of a correct understand-

---

[1] CASE OF THE REPUBLIC OF CHILE, 182.

[2] Award of March 4, 1925 (1925) 19 AM. J. INT. LAW 393.

[3] Communication of S. Polo, President, Peruvian Defense Commission, to the President of the United States, April 2, 1925, THE MEMORIAL OF PERU AND THE RULING AND OBSERVATIONS OF THE ARBITRATOR (1925) 3. Printed also in (1925) 19 AM. J. INT. LAW 633.

[4] Ibid., 7–9.   [5] Ibid., 9–12.

ing of the Arbitrator's Award, and the proper procedure thereunder, the Arbitrator deems it advisable to make certain additional observations.[6]

He stated that the offending translation fairly interpreted the passage referred to by Peru and that the problem before him was one of construction rather than of translation. He had weighed the proofs of intimidation offered by both parties. The conditions under which the plebiscite was to be held constituted one of the questions submitted to him. Peru had made no requests for findings thereon before the award, yet the arbitrator had fixed conditions after a careful study.[7] "Orderly procedure and the agreement under which this Arbitration was held forbid that a party to the arbitration should wait until after the Award is rendered before making requests for findings."[8] Nevertheless, he examined the requests for the several guarantees, rejected each, and gave reasons for his action.[9]

61. SAME: NORD RAILWAY COMPANY CASE.—Niedermayer, in a study of the Nord Railway Company decision of the Franco-German Mixed Arbitral Tribunal,[1] contended that it played lightly with every judicial analysis and evidenced a purposeful manipulation of the law by the tribunal. He charged that a trained lawyer could hardly have made unconsciously such legal errors as were made and that the reasoning did not represent the judicial convictions of a judge.[2] A formal excess of jurisdiction is alleged to have occurred in that the tribunal failed to accord a fair hearing to the defendant, by not giving it an opportunity to state its argument.[3]

The plaintiff company operated railway lines in Belgium which had been operated by Germany during its occupation of Belgium in the war. It had obtained from Belgium compensation for the material damage done to its property, but also filed a complaint with

---

[6] Ibid., 12–13.
[7] Ibid., 13–15.
[8] Ibid., 15.
[9] Ibid., 16–20.
[1] Compagnie des Chemins de Fer du Nord (France) v. Germany (Decision of Apr. 8, 1929) 9 RECUEIL DES DÉCISIONS (1930) 67.
[2] NIEDERMAYER, DAS VÖLKERRECHTLICHE NICHT-URTEIL, NORMEN UND METHODE SEINER FESTSTELLUNG, 26 FRANKFURTER ABHANDLUNGEN ZUM MODERNEN VÖLKERRECHT (1931) 40.
[3] Ibid., 30, 32.

the Mixed Arbitral Tribunal for nearly 150 million francs for the loss of expected profits. This was later amended to a claim of 78,-812,296.59 francs, which was alleged to represent the sum of the "net benefits" resulting from the transportation by Germany of civilians and merchandise during the occupation. Germany objected to the jurisdiction of the tribunal to entertain the claim. It alleged that the claim was already pending before the Reparations Commission and was of a nature to fall within its jurisdiction. It contended that the claimant's reliance on Article 297(e) of the Treaty of Versailles as a source of jurisdiction was without merit, since that article contemplated exceptional war measures taken "in German territory as it existed on August 1, 1914," [4] while the damages claimed, on the face of the complaint, were caused on Belgian territory.

The tribunal affirmed its jurisdiction to hear the case and awarded damages in the sum of 52,699,872 francs and 25,000 francs for costs. It reasoned that the pendency of the case before the Reparations Commission was not a cause for the dismissal of the complaint, for if the fact that the claim was pending before both bodies was alone sufficient to justify either in dismissing it, a denial of justice might result. It referred to Article 53 of the Fourth Hague Convention respecting the laws of war on land, which authorizes the seizure by an occupying army of means of transport, with the proviso that they be restored and compensation fixed when peace is made.[5] The action of Germany in using the railway for military purposes was recognized as an exercise of a public right on its part in conformity with Article 53, but in its commercial exploitation of the railway Germany was considered by the tribunal not to be acting in its public capacity. The tribunal found that the necessary elements for a quasi-contract existed, that cases of quasi-contracts were within Article 304 of the Treaty of Versailles conferring jurisdiction upon the tribunal to decide "questions . . . relating to contracts concluded . . . between nationals of the Allied and Associated Powers and

---

[4] 112 BRITISH AND FOREIGN STATE PAPERS (1919) 147.
[5] 1 PROCEEDINGS OF THE HAGUE PEACE CONFERENCES, CONFERENCE OF 1907 (Carnegie trans., 1920) 631.

German nationals," [6] and concluded that since Germany in operating the railway commercially "had acted as its own subject in the sense of article 304," the tribunal was competent to decide the difference as arising out of a quasi-contract between the parties.

It is the opinion of Niedermayer that since the concession was revocable Germany was privileged to take it over and that international law did not prohibit Germany from taking the profits of management. Article 53 of the Hague Convention was deemed by him not to change present international law, which neither authorized nor prohibited an occupying power to manage commercial railways.[7] The flexible interpretation which the tribunal gave to the treaty could not be considered judicial reasoning.[8] If no relation whatever existed to an actual contract, it was his view, which he believed the jurisprudence of the Mixed Arbitral Tribunals to support, that a quasi-contract falls outside Article 304 of the treaty.[9] In fact, he states that the court was in error even under the Belgian civil code when it held that a quasi-contract existed.[10] He noted that the plaintiff had rested its case on Article 297(e) and did not consider Article 304 as a basis of jurisdiction, and the latter article was not mentioned during the rest of the case except by the defendant as supplementary to Article 53. He concluded that the tribunal therefore committed a formal excess of jurisdiction when it failed to give the defendant a fair hearing and an opportunity to state its case.[11] He called attention to the fact that under the rules of procedure a decision could not increase the claim or change its nature. If it did so, the decision would be *ultra petita*.[12]

According to Niedermayer, Germany nevertheless regarded the decision as final under Article 304(g) of the Treaty of Versailles.[13]

---

[6] See *op. cit. supra* note 4, at 161.
[7] NIEDERMAYER, *op. cit. supra* note 1, at 10–11.
[8] *Ibid.*, 17.
[9] *Ibid.*, 19.
[10] *Ibid.*, 12, 13.
[11] *Ibid.*, 32.
[12] *Ibid.*, 36, citing Articles 71 (2).
[13] *Ibid.*, 43. That article reads: "The High Contracting Parties agree to regard the decisions of the Mixed Arbitral Tribunal as final and conclusive, and to render them binding upon their nationals." *Op. cit. supra* note 4, at 161.

It must be said that it is difficult to find in the reasoning of the tribunal justification for the severe charges of Niedermayer; a decision can hardly be said to be void because it rests on grounds not argued by the parties. His complaints would justify a petition for rehearing, but would fail to demonstrate nullity of the award.

CHAPTER 5

FINALITY OF THE AWARD

62. LEGAL EFFECTS OF THE AWARD.—By entering into the arbitration agreement and participating in the proceedings before the tribunal, the parties impliedly engage to execute the award when rendered.[1] Although the British arbitrator, Six Alexander Cockburn, dissented in vigorous terms from the decision of the tribunal in the *Geneva Arbitration,* at the close of his opinion he expressed the hope that it would be accepted "by the British people . . . with the submission and respect which is due to the decision of a tribunal by whose award it has freely consented to abide." [2] The decision of the international tribunal has obligatory force; States are required to take all necessary measures to carry it into effect.[3] In the terms of Article 59 of the Statute of the Permanent Court of International Justice, it has "binding force . . . between the parties and in respect of that particular case." [4] It becomes *res adjudicata* between the parties, and ordinarily the same question may not be submitted to a new tribunal unless the parties both renounce the first decision.[5] Article 37 of the Hague Convention of 1907 provides that "recourse to arbitration implies an engagement to submit in good faith to the award," [6] while Article 81 states that "the award, duly

---

1 BONDE, TRAITÉ ÉLÉMENTAIRE DE DROIT INTERNATIONAL PUBLIC (1926) 371; CREASY, FIRST PLATFORM OF INTERNATIONAL LAW (1876) 394; FUNCK-BRENTANO ET SOREL, PRÉCIS DU DROIT DE GENS (3d ed., 1930) 459; MÉRIGNHAC, TRAITÉ THEORIQUE ET PRATIQUE DE L'ARBITRAGE INTERNATIONAL (1895) 298; 1 PLANAS SUÁREZ, TRATADO DE DERECHO INTERNACIONAL PÚBLICO (1916) 439; Goldschmidt, *Projet de règlement pour tribunaux arbitraux internationaux, présenté à l'Institut de Droit International* (Session de Genève, 1874) (1874) 6 REV. DE DROIT INT. L.C. 446 (Section 30).

2 4 PAPERS RELATING TO THE TREATY OF WASHINGTON (1872) 544.

3 WITENBERG, L'ORGANISATION JUDICIAIRE, LA PROCÉDURE ET LA SENTENCE INTERNATIONALES (1937) 352–353; Limburg, *L'Autorité de chose jugée des décisions des juridictions internationales* (1929) 30 RECUEIL DES COURS 566.

4 STATUTE AND RULES OF COURT (1936) 25.

5 Limburg, *supra* note 3, at 536.

6 1 PROCEEDINGS OF THE HAGUE PEACE CONFERENCES, CONFERENCE OF 1907 (Carnegie trans., 1920) 605.

pronounced and notified to the agents of the parties, settles the dispute definitively and without appeal." [7] Limburg [8] considers that the binding force of the award to derive from the treaty of submission and to partake of a treaty. Morelli,[9] apparently thinking primarily of the decretal portion of the award, states that "the effect of the award is to oblige the parties to consider the decision as a definitive regulation of the conflict of interests which comprise the dispute . . . it indicates the attitude which the parties should adopt *vis-à-vis* the decision and not the rights and obligations."

In the event of failure of a party to carry out an award duly rendered, any means taken to procure enforcement of the award must be limited strictly to the terms of the exact decision. If political means are not sufficient, it is the view of some writers that coercive means short of war may be used, such as reprisals and retorsions and pacific blockade.[10] Mérignhac [11] goes so far as to state that failure to carry out an award is a violation of a treaty and therefore a *casus belli;* but the categorical character of this statement is later qualified by his comment with regard to the *Weil* and *La Abra* cases that Mexico could have refused to execute the arbitral judgments in question by affirming and proving in a memorial addressed to the United States that they were the result of fraud. In the absence of express authorization by the parties, the tribunal may not itself decree penalties for failure to comply with its award.[12]

The award must, of course, be made on the merits of the case. A decision that a case is beyond the jurisdiction of a particular tribunal will not bar the claimant government from bringing it before an-

[7] *Ibid.,* 612.

[8] Limburg, *supra* note 3, at 530–535.

[9] Morelli, *La Théorie générale du procès international* (1937) 61 RECUEIL DES COURS 318.

[10] Dumas, *Sanctions of International Arbitration* (1911) 5 AM. J. INT. LAW 941, 955–957; *cf.* LAMMASCH, DIE RECHTSKRAFT INTERNATIONALER SCHIEDSSPRÜCHE (1913) 212, 225, 226 (winning party has no right to intervene but may use reprisals). See generally DUMAS, LES SANCTIONS DE L'ARBITRAGE INTERNATIONAL (1905).

[11] Mérignhac, *De l'autorité de la chose jugée en matière de sentence arbitrale* (1898) 5 REV. GEN. DE DROIT INT. PUB. 606, 622.

[12] Permanent Court of International Justice, Judgment No. 1 (Aug. 17, 1923) SER. A., No. 1, at 32.

other. Thus, in the *Alsop* case the United States pointed out in the arbitration before King George V that a prior arbitral decision of 1901, by which the tribunal then instituted held that it did not have jurisdiction to hear and determine the case on its merits under its *compromis,* could not be regarded "as a bar to the negotiation of a further organic act which should . . . provide for the consideration of the merits." [13]

63. SAME: PERU-ECUADOR BOUNDARY DISPUTE.—The requirement of good faith, that a State shall not captiously attack the validity of an award for the purpose of escaping its obligations, is illustrated in the history of the Peru-Ecuador boundary dispute.

The sensitiveness of States in boundary controversies, touching, as they do, a vital source of state power, renders exceedingly difficult the task of an arbitrator of such a controversy. It is believed that this factor of sensitiveness is in large part the cause of the recurrence of boundary arbitrations in the several instances in which the validity of an award has been attacked. States in such disputes are least likely to be conciliatory and most likely to be insistent upon the preservation of their every legal right. On the other hand, an arbitrator may well be here most prone to indulge in compromise, to seek for a solution which in his view will afford an equitable and satisfactory settlement of the conflict. In this he is aided by the circumstances that the decision of such cases is largely dependent upon analysis of fact and evidence and that the applicable legal rules are relatively simple and broad, affording wide scope for their interpretation.

Most significant in this relation are the outspoken comments of Peruvian representatives made in the course of the boundary dispute of their government with that of Ecuador. Some of these, apparently originally intended to be confidential and not to go beyond the Peruvian foreign office, have been made public by Ecuador.

---

[13] ALSOP CLAIM; COUNTER CASE OF THE UNITED STATES VERSUS CHILE UNDER PROTOCOL OF DECEMBER 1, 1909 (1910) 60. King George in his award adverted to this failure of the prior tribunal to settle the dispute and stated that it was now before him to determine the amount equitably due the claimants (1911) 5 AM. J. INT. LAW 1079, 1085.

The attitude of the two countries as revealed in the history of this dispute lends further support to the view expressed in the preceding paragraph.

For many years, even before the revolution of 1830, by which Ecuador separated from Colombia, the ownership of the rich and undeveloped territory known as the Oriente has been in dispute. This territory forms the upper part of the Amazon basin and reaches from the cordilleras of the Andes to the eastern boundary of Ecuador, including the provinces of Mainas, Tumbez, and Jaen.[1] An arbitration agreement for the settlement of the question was finally reached on August 1, 1887.[2] It was recited therein that the two governments, desirous of terminating "the pending questions of boundaries between both Nations," have agreed "to submit said questions to His Majesty the King of Spain, in order that he may decide them as Arbitrator of law in a definitive manner and without appeal."

Peru apparently realized that conceivably it might be deprived of the provinces of Tumbez and Jaen, which it had occupied for more than seventy years, if the award were confined to the legal rights of the parties.[3] Thus, its minister in Ecuador suggested to the Peruvian foreign office that a friendly settlement might be preferable since "the arbitral award, whether favorable to Peru or to Ecuador, and based on proof and on valid judicial reasons, will not and can not be accepted by the country to which it may be unfavorable, and as the Arbitrator will not have the authority or means to enforce it, an inevitable struggle will arise, which can only be settled by force."[4]

[1] FLORES, HISTORY OF THE BOUNDARY DISPUTE BETWEEN ECUADOR AND PERU (1921) 23, 41, 45, 49; SANTAMARÍA DE PAREDES, A STUDY OF THE QUESTION OF BOUNDARIES BETWEEN THE REPUBLICS OF PERU AND ECUADOR (1910) 65 et sqq.

[2] 5 ARANDA, COLECCIÓN DE LOS TRATADOS (1895) 803.

[3] Private Memorandum of Dr. Jose Pardo, counsel for Peru, to the Ministry of Foreign Relations of Perú, July 28, 1888, Informe presentado á la nación por el Ministerio de Relaciones Exteriores del Ecuador, June 30, 1921 (1921) 1 THE REPUBLIC OF ECUADOR 9, at 14.

[4] Minister Bonifaz to Ministry of Foreign Relations of Peru, July 10, 1888, ibid., 12 (writer's translation).

In a particularly illuminating memorial of a Señor Arturo Garcia to the Peruvian chancellery the following statement appears.

Arbitration still goes on. But the arbitration means war, however paradoxical it may seem. Arbitration, in the absolute, unrestricted form in which it is covenanted and being strictly legal in its character, will not permit of anything but radical solutions of the great dispute which we are discussing. If the Arbitrator is simply to stick to the proved rights of the parties, his award may deprive us of two populous provinces of some thousands of Peruvians and a vast extent of country to the south of the Marañon or carry our boundary not only to the center but to the northern part of Ecuador, establishing our frontier within two days of the capital. Would there, in either case, be sufficient moral power on the part of the losing party that would prejudice the interests and wound the most sacred feelings of the nation? . . . These questions are so grave that it is worth while to consider them at length before rejecting all idea of settlement simply to await an arbitral award that will incur such risks of strong opposition to its execution. And supposing that it were carried out in its entirety, the question of the boundaries would be settled, but the peace of both countries far from being established on firm foundations would be broken forever. The party thus greatly injured would forever be on the lookout for an opportunity to recover all or a part of what he had lost, and by settling one difficulty we would be creating a hot bed of others. This has not been the case in other boundary disputes submitted to arbitration. In none has such a large extent of territory been involved; in none have such vital interests been endangered. For this reason, arbitration, which is the best method of solution of matters of this character, is the worst for the present case.[5]

The insistence of Peru upon the importance of the fact of its possession of the territory is made evident from the statements in its *Memoria* presented to the arbitrator that any power which would seek to interrupt a century of possession by alleging casuistic interpretations would encounter a most categorical refusal and that "if Peruvians occupy all the Eastern territory, those lands are and shall remain Peruvian, in spite of all the declarations of the world." [6]

The case never approached decision until about 1910, when rumors circulated as to the probable nature of the award produced

[5] Memorial of August 9, 1890, *ibid.*, 12 (writer's translation).
[6] 4 MEMORIA DEL PERÚ PRESENTADA Á S.M. REAL ARBITRO 24, 52.

an agitation in both countries that led to preparations for war.[7] In this state of affairs a joint offer of mediation was made by the United States, Argentina, and Brazil,[8] which was accepted by both Ecuador [9] and Peru.[10] The king of Spain withdrew from his office as arbitrator, believing that "a prolongation of the present situation will not bring about the desired conciliation." [11] However, the advisers of the king appear to have written an opinion concerning the dispute from which Román, counsellor of state, dissented upon the ground that the arbitrator should hold himself without jurisdiction to decide it.[12] In his opinion the *compromis* was too vague to submit a specific matter for the decision of the arbitrator. The declaration of the governments that it was their desire to put an end to the questions of boundaries pending between them failed to set forth the exact legal questions which an "Arbitrator of law" should decide. Any award which might be rendered under such circumstances would be vitiated by nullity, because of lack of jurisdiction over the subject matter.[13] In other words, any decision whatever would be beyond the bounds of submission because no case had been submitted.

Peru proposed arbitration by the Hague Tribunal,[14] but Ecuador declined, preferring direct negotiation.[15] A compromise of the two views was finally reached in the protocol of June 21, 1924.[16] It was there announced that the two governments would send to Washing-

[7] Memorandum enclosed with note of the Secretary of State to Chilean Chargé Yoachim, June 9, 1910 (1910) FOR. REL. U.S. 468; see also *ibid.*, 430, 433; (1911) *ibid.*, 176; *op. cit. supra* note 3, at 10, 15.

[8] Acting Secretary of State Wilson to Minister Combs, May 18, 1910 (1910) FOR. REL. U.S. 454.

[9] Minister Carbo to the Secretary of State, May 23, 1910, *ibid.*, 456.

[10] Minister of Foreign Affairs Porras to Minister Combs, May 23, 1910, *ibid.*, 458.

[11] Spanish Minister of State Prieto to the Ecuadorian Minister of Foreign Relations, Nov. 24, 1910, enclosure with Minister Fox to the Secretary of State, Nov. 28, 1910, *ibid.*, 503, 504.

[12] Separate opinion of Jan. 21, 1909, COLOMBIA. BOLETÍN DEL MINISTERIO DE RELACIONES EXTERIORES (1910) 183.

[13] *Ibid.*, 190.

[14] Minister for Foreign Affairs Althaus to the American Minister, Jan. 2, 1911 (1911) FOR. REL. U.S. 177.

[15] Minister for Foreign Affairs Peralta to the American Minister, Jan. 16, 1911, *ibid.*, 177; Message of President Alfaro to Congress, Aug. 10, 1911, *ibid.*, 176–177.

[16] 27 LEAGUE OF NATIONS, TREATY SERIES, 347.

ton their respective delegations to discuss the matter of boundaries. If they failed to fix a definite line, they were to determine by agreement the zone which each of the parties recognized as belonging to the other and that zone in respect of which the president of the United States would be invited to render an arbitral award. The two governments also pledged themselves to seek a solution of the difficulty through their respective ministers.

Not until January 29, 1942, however, with the signature of the Protocol of Rio de Janeiro, was provision made for the definitive demarcation of a new boundary between the two countries.[17]

64. EFFECT OF THE FINALITY CLAUSE IN THE COMPROMIS.—No special clause in the *compromis* that the award shall be binding upon the parties is necessary in order that the award shall have obligatory force. If such a clause is inserted, it is but declaratory of existing law. The recurrent affirmation of the clause in arbitration treaties, the thousands of instances in which international arbitral awards have been respected and faithfully carried out, as well as reason and authority, support this view.[1]

An examination of various cases in which nullity of the award has been alleged reveals that its presence has not prevented States from making such a charge.[2] It did not prevent the Hague Tribunal from holding the award of the United States–Venezuelan Mixed

---

[17] (1942) 6 DEPARTMENT OF STATE BULLETIN 496.

[1] GUERMANOFF, L'EXCÈS DE POUVOIR DE L'ARBITRE (1929) 31; KAMAROWSKY, LE TRIBUNAL INTERNATIONAL (1887) 346; MÉRIGNHAC, L'ARBITRAGE INTERNATIONAL (1895) 299; Hertz, *Essai sur le problème de la nullité* (1939, 3d ser.) 20 REV. DE DROIT INT. ET DE L.C. 461.

[2] Bermudez and Ora Miller land claims, sec. 59 at n. 3: "final"; Caracas General Waterworks Company, sec. 33 at n. 2: "final and conclusive"; Hungarian Optants case, sec. 37 at n. 10: "final and conclusive"; Northeastern Boundary dispute, sec. 29 at n. 2: "final and conclusive"; Orinoco Steamship Company Case, Barge award, sec. 44 at n. 3: "final and conclusive"; Pelletier case, sec. 42 at n. 2: "final and binding"; Umpire Cases, sec. 10 at n. 3: "final and conclusive"; United States–Venezuelan Claims Commission of 1866, sec. 17 at n. 1: "final and conclusive"; Weil and La Abra cases, sec. 19 at n. 7: "absolutely final and conclusive"; Norwegian Claims Case, sec. 50 at n. 1: "final and binding"; Cerruti case, sec. 31 at n. 8: "final and conclusive and not subject either to discussion or appeal"; Central American Court of Justice, sec. 5: "parties solemnly bind themselves to submit to said judgments"; Bolivia-Peru boundary dispute, sec. 48 at n. 4: "final and unappealable"; Nicaragua-Honduras boundary dispute, sec. 23 at n. 2: "unappealable arbitration"; East Griqualand arbitration, sec. 24 at n. 11: "to execute faithfully"; Panama–Costa Rica boundary dispute: Loubet award, sec. 34

Claims Commission in the *Orinoco Steamship Company Case* void in part.[3] It did not prevent Costa Rica from attacking and Chief Justice White from holding the Loubet award null;[4] nor, when Panama wished to attack Chief Justice White's decision, did it prevent her from so doing.[5] In justification of its action, Panama stated that its pledge to consider the White award final was under the condition that it fulfill the essential terms of the arbitral agreement. It affirmed that "declarations of this kind, which are customary in arbitration conventions, are not construed with prejudice to the legitimate rights of the contracting parties, nor can they be alleged to justify a denial of justice by reason of exceeding of powers or of any other legal fault which carries with it the nullity of the decision."[6] When the United States requested that the *Orinoco Steamship Company Case* be submitted anew to a different tribunal for re-examination, Venezuela set up as a bar the allegation that to do so would be to disregard the finality of the decision of the first tribunal. In answer, the United States stated that "to this there is an obvious and very reasonable reply, namely, that a decree of a court of arbitration is only final provided the court acts within the terms of the protocol establishing the jurisdiction of the court, and that a disregard of such terms necessarily deprives the decision of any claim to finality."[7] A protocol was agreed upon by Venezuela pro-

---

at n. 4: "The award of the Arbitrator, no matter what may be, shall be considered as a perfect and binding treaty as between the High Contracting Parties and shall not admit of any appeal. Both Parties bind themselves to its fulfillment, and they waive any appeal against the decision pledging thereto their national honor." Panama–Costa Rica boundary dispute: Award of Chief Justice White, sec. 34 at n. 17: "The award, whatever it be, shall be held a perfect and compulsory treaty between the high contracting parties. Both parties pledge themselves to the faithful execution of the award and waive all claims against it.

"The boundary line between the two Republics as finally fixed by the arbitrator shall be deemed the true line, and his determination of the same shall be final, conclusive, and without appeal."

[3] *Supra* sec. 44.   [4] *Supra* sec. 34.   [5] *Ibid.*

[6] Secretary of Foreign Relations of Panama to Minister Price, Mar. 18, 1921, DOCUMENTOS RELATIVOS AL CONFLITO DE JURISDICCIÓN TERRITORIAL CON LA REPÚBLICA DE PANAMÁ Y SUS ANTECEDENTES; SECRETARIA DE RELACIONES EXTERIORES, COSTA RICA (1921) 156, 161 (writer's translation).

[7] Secretary of State Root to Minister Russell, Feb. 28, 1907 (1908) FOR. REL. U.S. 774, 783.

viding for the resubmission of the claim to the Permanent Court of Arbitration. In the light of the foregoing, it is submitted that the intention of a State to give an arbitrator an unrestrained power of decision and to deny itself the privilege of objecting to a decision rendered in excess of jurisdiction must clearly appear. Even then it cannot be admitted that by such declarations States intend to confer upon an arbitrator arbitrary powers, such as, for example, of authority to decide *any* dispute pending between them.

65. EFFECT OF HAGUE CONVENTION UPON THE PRINCIPLE OF FINALITY.— In the *Orinoco Steamship Company Case,* the Permanent Court of Arbitration made certain remarks respecting the finality of arbitral awards and the relation thereto of Article 81 of the Hague Convention for the Pacific Settlement of International Disputes of 1907. Those remarks are somewhat vague and inconclusive but tend to deny the right of appeal under the Convention. The umpire of the tribunal in question was Heinrich Lammasch, and the views which he presumably then held found expression in a work later written by him on the binding force of international arbitral decisions.[1] Probably they had their origin in the writings of certain commentators upon the Hague Conferences.[2] The views of Lammasch will shortly be further examined; their purport is that the Hague Convention ruled out the concept of nullity in the sense that a State was no longer privileged to disregard an award of the Hague Tribunal by alleging nullity.

It is significant that until 1928 such a construction of the Convention has never occurred to any other writer dealing with the topic of the nullity of arbitral awards. No State has ever invoked such a construction, though reliance has been placed upon the rule embodied in Article 48 of the Convention of 1899 that an arbitral tribunal is authorized to determine questions of its jurisdiction.[3] On the contrary, allegations of nullity have continued to be raised

---

[1] LAMMASCH, DIE RECHTSKRAFT INTERNATIONALER SCHIEDSSPRÜCHE (1913).

[2] E.g., NIPPOLD, DIE FORTBILDUNG DES VERFAHRENS IN VÖLKERRECHTLICHEN STREITIGKEITEN (1907) 359 *et sqq.*

[3] Baron de Favereau (Belgium) to the Venezuelan Chargé d'Affaires, Aug. 22, 1904 (1905) VENEZUELA. EXPOSICIÓN. MINISTRO DE RELACIONES EXTERIORES 279.

by States and have found judicial recognition.[4] But in 1928, following the famous *Hungarian Optants* case, De Lapradelle, in an article in the *Revue de droit international*,[5] again raised and further elaborated the views of Lammasch. In the following year a doctoral dissertation at the University of Paris was published in which similar conclusions were reached.[6] While to dispose of their argument it would perhaps be sufficient to remark that such a revolutionary change in the settled doctrine of international arbitrations could hardly be inferred from the silence of the Hague Conventions upon the question of nullity,[7] occasion will be taken to review the history of the conventions upon this point and to analyze the conclusions which these writers draw from it.

Origin of Article 81 of the Hague Convention of 1907.—Article 81 of the Hague Convention of 1907, regulating the finality of awards, reads as follows: "The award, duly pronounced and notified to the agents of the parties, settles the dispute definitively and without appeal." [8] The history of this article may be traced back to the draft project of arbitral code submitted by Goldschmidt to the Institute of International Law at its session in Geneva in 1874 and to the *projet* adopted by the Institute in 1875. Section 30 of Goldschmidt's draft reads: "The award duly pronounced (Sections 24 to 29) decides, within the limits of its scope, the dispute between the parties." [9] The sections referred to by him related to the procedure to be followed by the tribunal in its deliberations and in its publication of the award. This reference was omitted by the Institute in its final *projet,* but otherwise Article 25 adopted by it was identical with the section drafted by Goldschmidt.[10]

---

[4] *Supra* secs. 34 and 44.

[5] Lapradelle, *L'Excès de pouvoir de l'arbitre* (1928) 2 REV. DE DROIT INT. 5.

[6] GUERMANOFF, L'EXCÈS DE POUVOIR DE L'ARBITRE (1929).

[7] Brierly, *The Hague Conventions and the Nullity of Arbitral Awards* (1928) 9 BRITISH YEARBOOK 114, 116.

[8] 1 PROCEEDINGS OF THE HAGUE PEACE CONFERENCES, CONFERENCE OF 1907 (Carnegie trans., 1920) 612.

[9] Goldschmidt, *Projet de règlement pour tribunaux arbitraux internationaux* (1874) 6 REV. DE DROIT INT. L.C. 446.

[10] (1877) ANNUAIRE 133: "The award duly pronounced decides, within the limits of its scope, the dispute between the parties."

It will be observed that two concepts are embodied in that article. One is contained in the words "duly pronounced," which relate to the procedure of rendering the award. The other involves the meaning to be given to the word "decides,"—whether the award creates a moral or a legal obligation upon the parties. At that time there were apparently still some who adhered to the view that an international arbitral award had no obligatory force. In the words of Thonissen, "each nation is always considered perfectly free not to submit to an arbitral award." [11]

It was this latter question which was settled in Article 54 of the Hague Convention of 1899, the predecessor of Article 81 of the Convention of 1907. In the report of Chevalier Descamps to the Conference it is stated that this article "insists upon the decisive and unappealable character of the arbitral award." [12]

The genesis of Article 83, relating to revision, will elsewhere be set forth.[13] We are here concerned with the effect of the suppression of Article 25 of the Russian draft of an arbitral code, relating to nullity. The probable inspiration of that article was Article 27 of the *projet* of the Institute, which reads: "The arbitral award is null in case of an invalid *compromis*, or of excess of jurisdiction, or of proved corruption of one of the arbitrators or of essential error." [14] Article 26 of the Russian draft code reads: "The arbitral award is void in case of a void *compromis* or exceeding of power, or of corruption proved against one of the arbitrators." [15] When this article was considered in the Committee of Examination, Asser expressed the view that it should be suppressed unless some authority could be found on which would devolve the duty of declaring the award null. Its appreciation, he said, should not be left to the arbitrary action or initiative of the losing State.[16] Bourgeois, the president of

---

[11] Reported by Rolin-Jaequemyns, *Chronique du droit international* (1875) 7 Rev. de Droit Int. L.C. 70, 83.

[12] Proceedings of the Hague Peace Conferences, Conference of 1899 (Carnegie trans., 1920) 149.

[13] *Infra* sec. 76.

[14] *Op. cit. supra* note 10, at 133.

[15] *Op. cit. supra* note 12, at 804.

[16] The original report reads: "M. Asser demande, si on ne pourrait trouver un pouvoir à qui incomberait la mission de déclarer nulle la sentence, à fin de ne pas

the committee, stated that it was not possible to provide for cases of nullity without knowing who would be the judge to pass upon such cases. The committee could not think of imposing the decision of the permanent tribunal upon the parties "in the instances which they have not intended to submit to this jurisdiction." [17]

Neither the committee nor the Third Commission took final action upon the Russian proposal. The reporter, Chevalier Descamps, explained that the committee had gone no farther in the examination of this question "in view of the difficulties of providing for cases of nullity without at the same time deciding who would be the judge to decide these cases. It should be observed, however, that the Permanent Court of Arbitration could guide States to a solution of this order." [18]

The Doctrine of Lammasch and De Lapradelle.—It is the argument of Lammasch that the Conferences recognized that no appeal existed against an arbitral award, that for the lack of an instance of appeal the bases for nullity contained in the Russian proposal were rejected, and that only for special reasons was Article 83, relating to revision, adopted. The effect of Article 83, he states, was to exclude every attack upon a decision except that based upon the discovery of new facts. The Conferences, in other words, did not leave the question of nullification in *status quo,* but really decided it negatively. The privilege of a single State to disregard a decision upon grounds of nullity had been rejected. But it was still open to States to provide by agreement for the revision or appeal of an award.[19]

In the *Orinoco Steamship Company Case,* the tribunal stated that it was essential that:

---

laisser cette appréciation si grave à l'arbitraire ou à l'initiative de l'État qui aura perdu. Si, comme il le croit, on n'arrive pas à trouver ce pouvoir, alors M. Asser est d'avis de supprimer l'art. 26." CONFÉRENCE INTERNATIONALE DE LA PAIX; MINISTÈRE DES AFFAIRES ÉTRANGÈRES (1899) Part IV, Third Commission, p. 149.

[17] *Ibid.*

[18] *Ibid.,* Part I, *Procès-Verbaux,* p. 139: "Le Comité s'est arrêté, dans l'examen de cette question, devant les inconvénients de prévoir des cas de nullité sans déterminer en même temps qui sera juge d'apprécier ces cas. On a fait observer toutefois que la Cour permanente d'arbitrage pouvait mettre les États sur la voie d'une solution dans cet ordre."

[19] *Op. cit. supra* note 1, at 161–163.

. . . a decision be accepted, respected and carried out by the parties without any reservation, as it is laid down in Article 81 of the Convention . . . and besides no jurisdiction whatever has been instituted for reconsidering similar decisions . . .

. . . if an arbitral decision could be disputed on the ground of erroneous appreciation (of facts and documents) appeal and revision, which the Conventions of The Hague of 1899 and 1907 made it their object to avert would be the general rule . . .[20]

The foregoing arguments were elaborated into a consistent whole by De Lapradelle in the article referred to above.[21] The thesis advanced by him is ingenious and somewhat involved. Its fundamental proposition is that an arbitral award is binding, even upon jurisdictional questions; that excess of power is a cause of nullity, but not of nonexistence; and that whoever alleges nullity has the duty of proposing arbitration of the issue.[22] He believed that of the various solutions of the question of nullity open to the Conference of 1899, it adopted the one which permitted "the winning state to refuse all manner of discussion upon the question, entrenching itself behind the definitive character of the award." [23] It was erroneous to interpret the words "duly pronounced" in Article 54 of 1899 as implying the fact that the arbitrator had not exceeded his jurisdiction, because those words related to matters of form and procedure.[24] From Article 48, empowering an arbitrator to determine his jurisdiction, it resulted that if the arbitrator declared in his award that he was interpreting the *compromis,* it was not open to attack on the ground of excess of jurisdiction.[25] "From the suppression of Article 26 of the Russian plan, it did not follow that the award alleged to involve excess of power would be left to the *arbitrary action* of a state, as the partisans of lack of existence asserted, but instead to the *initiative* of the party who alleges it." [26] To such a party "it is not permitted to contend the existence of excess of power without offering a new court for its determination, but to this offer the other party is not required to respond." [27] Guermanoff held a similar view.[28] Independently of the

---

20 Scott, Hague Court Reports (1916) 230, 231. 21 *Supra* note 5.
22 Lapradelle, *supra* note 5, at 32. 23 *Ibid.,* 35.
24 *Ibid.,* 31, 36. 25 *Ibid.,* 37. 26 *Ibid.,* 39.
27 *Ibid.,* 43–44. 28 Guermanoff, *op. cit. supra* note 6, at 23, 24, 86.

Hague Convention, De Bustamente has also reached a somewhat similar conclusion.[29]

Analysis and criticism of the Lammasch–De Lapradelle doctrine.— The rules of Goldschmidt, of the Institute of International Law, and of the Hague Convention relied upon by De Lapradelle do not seem to sustain the construction which he places upon them. Those articles, generally embodying the rule that an award "duly pronounced" is binding upon the parties, were not intended to cover cases of nullity. "Duly pronounced" admittedly related to procedure; but for the rest, those articles were intended to settle the question whether an award had obligatory or moral force. Expressly included in the draft of Goldschmidt and the *projet* of the Institute were articles governing nullity. Such articles were not deemed inconsistent with the rule of finality. Nor is there anything in the language of Article 54 of the Hague Convention of 1899 or the reports of the Conference to indicate that that article was intended to exclude nullity. It did not touch upon the question. It only embodied the rule of the legal effect ordinarily to be attributed to arbitral awards. Article 48 of the Convention of 1899 is likewise entirely consistent with the existence of nullity.[30] It is merely declaratory of the general rule of international law that arbitrators have the power to determine questions of their jurisdiction. The meaning and scope of that rule have already been discussed.[31] It has never meant that arbitrators can thereby assume powers not conferred upon them. All that the history of Article 26 of the Russian draft shows is that the committee, considering it impracticable to provide a procedure—"a judge"—for adjudicating on allegations of nullity, left the matter unsettled. Those who spoke concerning the matter

[29] PANAMA–COSTA RICA BOUNDARY CONTROVERSY, OPINION GIVEN BY DR. ANTONIO S. DE BUSTAMENTE (1921) 13: "Although it may appear evident in the rational order of things that the Arbiter has exceeded his powers and that his award is objected to as null and void, until a declaration to that effect is made in a manner binding upon all the litigant parties, this cannot be held as a definite fact. It is a unilateral aspiration which under the realm of Law has before it different means to become effective or to be dismissed."

[30] *Cf.* Verdross, *L'Excès de pouvoir du juge arbitral dans le droit international public* (1928, 3d ser.) 9 REV. DE DROIT INT. L.C. 225, 234–236, analyzing the effect of corresponding Article 73 of the Hague Convention of 1907.

[31] *Supra* sec. 25.

apparently fully appreciated that under the present system the final resolution of cases of nullity was left to the unregulated action of States. The Conference, therefore, left the law of nullity in *status quo*.[32] Brierly quite properly remarks that: "International conferences pass *sub silentio* over matters on which they are unable to agree far too commonly for it to be permissible to deduce positive, and in this case revolutionary, innovations from the omission."[33] The distinction between nullity and nonexistence which De Lapradelle advances independently of his arguments concerning the Hague Conference is not sustained by theory or practice. The distinction, in both municipal and international law, has meaning only when an organized judicial machinery for the review of judgments exists. A court to which all claims of nullity must be brought for decision before they will be entitled to legal weight is lacking in international law. In its absence, this distinction and similar concepts of private law have no place.[34] The individual judgment of States rather than the judgment of a court, in international law, determines questions of nullity. International law does not permit their decision to be arbitrary, but by definite rules regulates it in an objective manner. The judgment of a State, as well as a judgment of a court, must rest on legal grounds if its refusal to perform an award is to be sanctioned by international law. With relation to the *Orinoco Steamship Company Case*, it is sufficient here to remark that the Tribunal seems to have erroneously conceived its position. By virtue of its *compromis*, it occupied the very position of an appellate tribunal which Chevalier Descamps hoped the Permanent Court of Arbitration would provide for cases of nullity.[35]

---

[32] 1 Mérignhac, Traité de droit public international (1905) 539; 1 Fauchille, Traité de droit international public (1926) Part III, 565, 566; Schätzel, Rechtskraft und Anfechtung von Entscheidungen internationaler Gerichte, 6 Frankfurter Abhandlungen zum Kriegsverhütungsrecht (1928) 12; Castberg, *L'Excès de pouvoir dans la justice internationale* (1931) 35 Recueil des cours 357, 430; Nys, *La Revision de la sentence arbitrale* (1910, 2d ser.) 12 Rev. de Droit Int. L.C. 595, 619.

[33] Brierly, *supra* note 7, at 116.

[34] 6 Pradier-Fodéré, Traité de droit international public (1894) 432.

[35] *Supra* p. 216. *Cf.* Scelle, *Une Instance en revision devant la Cour de la Haye, l'affaire de la Orinoco Steamship Company* (1911) 18 Rev. Gen. de Droit Int. Pub. 164, 194. For report of case see *supra* sec. 44.

66. PRIVATE LAW ANALOGIES.—Under municipal law in arbitration of controversies between individuals it has been found necessary to provide judicial means for the control of arbitrators. The granting of legal sanctions to arbitral awards is conditioned by certain procedures designed to protect the individual from excessive action on the part of arbitrators. Arbitrators do not possess the judicial character of a court, and such protection is, therefore, even more necessary than those guarantees which are always provided against error on the part of courts of law of first instance.

Arbitration in the international sphere is a proceeding instituted by the will of the parties and limited to the sphere which they assign it. The arbitral tribunal possesses, not a general, but a special jurisdiction. It is not a court with a continuing life, but a body which dissolves upon the completion of the task assigned to it. Uncontrolled power is not and cannot be vested in it. International law may require the fulfillment of its decisions, but at the same time it recognizes the exceptional character of the proceeding. It provides States with a protection similar to that afforded individuals. It does not require them in all circumstances to perform the orders of arbitrators. It permits States to disregard the awards of arbitrators when rendered under certain conditions, which, it will be observed, are remarkably identical with the guarantees provided by municipal law systems.

Though in Roman law the awards of arbitrators were, in principle, final, the maxim persists to the present day, *arbiter nihil extra compromissum facere potest.*[1]

Under French law parties are permitted, through the procedure of *opposition à l'ordonnance d'exequatur* before the tribunal which rendered the award, to demand the nullification of the award in the following cases:

1. If the judgment had been rendered without a *compromis,* or beyond the terms of the *compromis;*
2. If it had rested upon a *compromis* which was null or terminated;

[1] For a short historical summary see GUERMANOFF, L'EXCÈS DE POUVOIR DE L'ARBITRE (1929) 40, 41.

3. If it had been rendered by certain arbitrators not authorized to judge in the absence of others;

4. If it had been rendered by a third member without having conferred with the other arbitrators;

5. Finally, if it had decided upon matters not requested.[2]

German law permits the parties to request the extinguishment of arbitral decisions if the procedure followed were illegal, if a party were represented according to the code of civil procedure, except where he had expressly or impliedly consented to such lack of representation, if the party were not accorded a fair hearing, or if there were no reasons given for the decision. With regard to the last two cases, it seems that the parties are privileged to agree that extinguishment shall not take place if such a violation of the code occurs and that such agreements will be given precedence over the rules of the code.[3]

Under United States law, it may generally be stated that arbitrators are required to pursue their authority as provided in the submission in order that their awards may be valid and capable of enforcement.[4] When they depart from the submission and fail to decide the questions submitted to them, their award is of no effect.[5] An award obtained by fradulent misrepresentations [6] or through the corruption of the arbitrator [7] is likewise void.

67. LEGAL POSSIBILITY OF NULLITY.—It is believed that the foregoing discussion has amply demonstrated that an arbitral award may under certain conditions be null. This is supported by the practice of States and the views of writers.[1] In the words of Judge Moore, the finality of awards "does not mean that in no case whatsoever, no

---

[2] Section 1028, Code of Civil Procedure. *Cf.* 4 DALLOZ, NOUVEAU CODE DE PROCÉDURE CIVILE (1922) 742.

[3] Section 1041, Code of Civil Procedure.

[4] Tucker v. Page, 69 Ill. 179 (1873).

[5] Consolidated Water Power Company v. Nash, 109 Wis. 490, 85 N.W. 485 (1901); *cf.* Colombia v. Cauca Company, 190 U.S. 524 (1903) (arbitration award between Colombia and a private corporation set aside in part as beyond scope of submission).

[6] Cox v. Fay, 54 Vt. 446 (1882).

[7] Worley v. Moore, 77 Ind. 567 (1881).

[1] For a collection of authorities in addition to those cited herein see MALAUZAT, LA COUR DE JUSTICE ARBITRALE (1914) 154.

matter what the circumstances may be, an award cannot be attacked on the ground of its character or the means by which it may have been obtained." [2] Borel [3] concludes:

It may be said that by the outbreak of the World War, the doctrine and practice of international law recognized that an arbitral award could be considered as without effect by reason of the lack of jurisdiction of the arbitrator or of an excess of jurisdiction committed by him.

68. LEGAL STATUS OF A NULL AWARD.—A null award is considered to be wholly lacking in legal effect and existence and to have no effect upon the status of the parties.[1] If it is practicable to separate the valid from the invalid parts of a decision, the whole award need not necessarily fall.[2] The award is not in itself executory, and the contention has accordingly been advanced that if its validity be attacked, its obligatory force is suspended.[3] The doctrine is clearly inadmissible and unsound. The mere objection of a dissatisfied litigant State will not suffice to free it from its obligation to carry out the award.[4] Though the State may *in fact* have the power to refuse to execute the award, whether it will be privileged in the exercise of that power will depend upon the merits of its contentions as to the invalidity of the award. Ordinarily, awards are binding upon the parties and the mere motion of one of the parties will not serve to destroy the obligation which they create. If a State should refuse to execute the award, it would do so at its own risk, and to maintain

[2] Opinion of John Bassett Moore, Counsellor for Honduras, Honduras-Nicaragua Boundary Mediation before the Secretary of State of the United States, 1920–1921. 5 COLLECTED PAPERS OF JOHN BASSETT MOORE (1944) 126.

[3] Borel, *Les Voies de recours contre les sentences arbitrales* (1935) 52 RECUEIL DES COURS 5, 11.

[1] Morelli, *La Théorie générale du procès international* (1937) 61 RECUEIL DES COURS 327, 329–330; Rundstein, *La Cour Permanente de Justice Internationale comme instance de recours* (1933) 43 RECUEIL DES COURS 16, 81–82; *cf.* Limburg, *L'Autorité de chose jugée des décisions des juridictions internationales* (1929) 30 RECUEIL DES COURS 615, raising the problem of restoring the parties prior to the decision when that decision has been *annulled* by formal procedure.

[2] BALASKO, CAUSES DE NULLITÉ DE LA SENTENCE ARBITRALE EN DROIT INTERNATIONAL PUBLIC (1938) 203; *cf.* Orinoco Steamship Company Case *supra* sec. 44.

[3] GUERMANOFF, L'EXCÈS DE POUVOIR DE L'ARBITRE (1929) 3, 32, 33; see also Verzijl, *La Validité et la nullité des actes juridiques internationaux* (1935) 15 REV. DE DROIT INT. 284, 338.

[4] *Cf.* GUERMANOFF, *op. cit. supra* note 3, at 84, 85.

that the award is null will not of itself free the State from the responsibility which it incurs by its action or inaction. Only if the award is null in fact and law will the State be free from such responsibility. In such a case the award never had an obligatory force to be suspended. In theory, it was void *ab initio*.[5] So far as the State ostensibly the gainer is concerned, says Bruns, "a state which, by exploiting a wrongful declaration of jurisdiction, endeavored to enforce an unjustifiable arbitral award in its own favour on the merits, would act in 'dolos.'" [6] International practice sustains his statement. The objecting State, of course, would be ill-advised to assert its claim of nullity without setting forth reasons in support of its contention, and no State has ever failed so to do. A regulation or some final settlement of the dispute becomes necessary simply as a matter of preserving the existence of good relations between the states. In the Panama–Costa Rica controversy the intransigeance of the parties almost led to war. [7] But whether the claim of nullity be admitted or denied by the other State, in contemplation of law the award remains without legal effect and meaning. If the parties agree to submit the dispute of nullity to a new arbitral tribunal, then new conventional arrangements supervene the legal relations previously existing between the parties. The exact question of the validity of the decision is to be submitted to the new tribunal, and whether it affirm or reverse the prior decision, its jurisdiction or power to decide the disputed question may not ordinarily be impugned, and by its determination of the issue of validity the parties agree to be bound, irrespective of their prior contentions and legal relations.

5 Castberg, *L'Excès de pouvoir dans la justice internationale* (1931) 35 RECUEIL DES COURS 357, 448–449.
6 Bruns, *An Opinion on the Questions Connected with the Appointment of Substitute Arbitrators to the Roumano-Hungarian Mixed Arbitral Tribunal by the Council of the League of Nations (Hungarian Optants Case)* 2 SOME OPINIONS, ARTICLES AND REPORTS BEARING UPON THE TREATY OF TRIANON AND THE CLAIMS OF THE HUNGARIAN NATIONALS WITH REGARD TO THEIR LANDS IN TRANSYLVANIA 147, 150.
7 *Supra* sec. 34.

CHAPTER 6

REHEARING

69. CORRECTION OF MISTAKE IN THE AWARD AND THE PRINCIPLE OF
FINALITY.—Occasionally tribunals have fallen into error as to the
proper scope and application of the principle of finality and have
applied rules applicable to their *power* to reopen a decision to questions concerning the *propriety* of their reconsidering a former decision.[1] Until the tribunal has finally adjourned, it is not lacking in
jurisdiction to re-examine and correct its decision upon a proper
showing by a party. While the error should be clear, substantial,
and of prejudice in order for it so to act, it should not dismiss any
petition for rehearing upon the ground of lack of authority and
res adjudicata.

Hyde [2] states:

Upon the rendition of its award a court of arbitration is said to become
functus officio, and thereafter to be unable to re-open the case or re-consider
its decision. . . . The tribunal may, nevertheless, without lack of deference
for the design of the contracting parties, defer the taking of the last step
that shall cause the termination of its life, by declining to permit the rendition of its award to be final or unsusceptible to change until it shall have
had opportunity to revise or correct or even interpret its own achievement.
The extent of what a court of arbitration may do in this regard, during the
continuance of its life as such, yet after the rendition of its award, must of
course depend upon the terms of the *compromis;* it raises a question of which
the solution is not found in implications derived from situations where a
tribunal has in fact become *functus officio*. It may be contended that where
the agreement to arbitrate provides for the establishment of a court which
is to adjudicate with respect to a large group of cases and for a protracted
period of time, authority is by implication conferred to exercise a measure

[1] *Infra* sec. 70.
[2] 2 HYDE, INTERNATIONAL LAW CHIEFLY AS INTERPRETED AND APPLIED BY THE
UNITED STATES (2d ed., 1945) 1628–1629; see also 1 SCHWARZENBERGER, INTERNATIONAL
LAW (1945) 428–429.

of control over cases in which an award has been rendered even after the occurrence of that event, and within a limited period of time such as may be fixed by the tribunal under the rules thereof, as a possible incident of such power as may have been given it to prescribe rules for its procedure.

Sandifer [3] points out the circumstances to be considered as follows:

In considering the authority of international tribunals to revise their awards, it is essential to make two general distinctions. First, revision should be clearly distinguished from the correction of errors or mistakes in awards arising from slips, accidental omissions, etc. In the second place, as in the case of rehearings, it is important to separate the three different situations in which revision may be sought, that is after the close of the hearings but before a decision, after a decision but before the adjournment of the tribunal, and after adjournment and dissolution of the tribunal.

On the one hand, one rule applies when the tribunal has become *functus officio:*

after a tribunal has rendered its decision and been discharged of the duties imposed upon it by the arbitral agreement, it has no authority to entertain a petition for rehearing.[4]

On the other hand, a different rule applies when the tribunal is still in being:

In the instances in which a number of cases have been submitted to a tribunal, and a rehearing on the basis of new evidence is sought before the tribunal has closed its work . . . it is to be doubted whether a tribunal is discharged of jurisdiction and responsibility in these cases until the date of its final award and adjournment *sine die.* . . .

The conclusion seems warranted that, in the absence of a specific provision to the contrary, a tribunal has jurisdiction to grant a rehearing upon the basis of newly discovered evidence of a decisive character at any time before its final adjournment.[5]

70. SAME: TRAIL SMELTER CASE.—In the *Trail Smelter* case the tribunal sustained its power to reconsider its decision before final adjournment, but held, and it is believed mistakenly so in the circumstances of the case, that "mere error in law is no sufficient ground for

---

[3] SANDIFER, EVIDENCE BEFORE INTERNATIONAL TRIBUNALS (1939) 321.
[4] *Ibid.,* 297.
[5] *Ibid.,* 297–298, 299.

a petition tending to revision." [1] This is sound law, when applied to a case in which the tribunal had become *functus officio*. It is also sound law even when the tribunal is still in being but a reasonable time for the filing of a petition for rehearing has lapsed. But the tribunal mistakenly conceived cases applicable to the principle of *res adjudicata* as permitting it to set aside its decision on the ground of "error of law."

The questions of the responsibility and extent of liability in damages of Canada for injury to the United States occasioned by fumes from the Trail Smelter in Canada were submitted to an arbitral tribunal under the convention of April 15, 1935.[2] A partial decision was rendered on April 16, 1938, awarding damages in the sum of $78,000 for the period from January 1, 1932, to October 1, 1937, which the tribunal declared to be "not subject to alteration or modification hereafter." [3] The period for rendering the full and final decision was thereafter extended by agreement of the two governments, the final decision of the tribunal awarding further damages to the United States being rendered March 11, 1941.

The United States petitioned the tribunal to reconsider a denial of an allowance of interest which it had made in the 1938 decision. The tribunal denied the petition on the ground that its prior decision was *res adjudicata* and not to be reopened for "mere error in law." No comment was made that the United States did not present its petition in a timely manner. Jurisdiction to reconsider was acknowledged to exist. But on the basis of holdings affirming the status of *res adjudicata* possessed by decisions which, for the most part, were beyond the *power* of the tribunal to review—being decisions of a different tribunal or decisions which had otherwise come to possess a final character—the tribunal held that the 1938 decision should not be reopened for an error of law. In so doing it applied rules relating to jurisdiction as rules of practice. If the tribunal had power to reconsider its decision, the petition for reconsideration

---

[1] (1941) 35 Am. J. Int. Law 684, 706.
[2] 49 Stat. 3245.
[3] (1939) 33 Am. J. Int. Law 182, 209.

should have been considered on its merits, particularly so in view of the direction in its *compromis* that the tribunal "shall give consideration to the desire of the High Contracting Parties to reach a solution just to all parties concerned." The tribunal, however, rightly recognized that in order to reopen its decision the error must be "manifest," but this is a rule of sound practice, not a jurisdictional limitation.

71. SAME: SABOTAGE CASES.[1]—On May 4, 1933, the American agent filed a petition for a rehearing of the so-called *Sabotage Cases* alleging that "certain important witnesses for Germany, in affidavits filed in evidence by Germany, furnished fraudulent, incomplete, collusive and false evidence which misled the Commission and unfairly prejudiced the cases of the claimants."[2] Upon a certificate of disagreement of the two national commissioners as to their power to reopen the 1930 decision of the commission on the merits, the umpire sustained the jurisdiction of the commission to reopen in a decision of December 15, 1933, as follows:

The petition, in short, avers the Commission has been misled by fraud and collusion on the part of witnesses and suppression of evidence on the part of some of them. The Commission is not *functus officio.* It still sits as a court. To it in that capacity are brought charges that it has been defrauded and misled by perjury, collusion, and suppression. No tribunal worthy of its name or of any respect may allow its decision to stand if such allegations are well-founded. Every tribunal has inherent power to reopen and to revise a decision induced by fraud. If it may correct its own errors and mistakes, *a fortiori* it may, *while it still has jurisdiction of a cause,* correct errors into which it has been led by fraud and collusion.

I am of the opinion, therefore, that the Commission has power to reopen these cases, and should do so, in order that it may consider the further evidence tendered by the American Agent and, dependent upon its findings from that evidence and any that may be offered in reply on behalf of Germany, either confirm the decisions heretofore made or alter them as justice and right may demand.[3] [Italics supplied.]

1 See history of these cases *supra* sec. 14.
2 MIXED CLAIMS COMMISSIONS, UNITED STATES AND GERMANY, ADMINISTRATIVE DECISIONS AND OPINIONS OF A GENERAL NATURE (1933–1939) 1118.
3 *Ibid.,* 1127–1128.

The remarks of the umpire that *any* tribunal may reopen a decision induced by fraud are to be read in conjunction with his later words, "while it still has jurisdiction of a cause." After an international tribunal has become *functus officio* it is without power to reconvene even for the correction of fraud.[4] In the instant case, however, the tribunal functioned as a continuing body and had not then ceased to exist under its *compromis*.[5]

On June 15, 1939, the umpire found "material fraud in the proofs submitted by Germany" and ruled that the petitions for rehearing should be granted.[6]

72. RECTIFICATION OF AWARDS.—Practice has shown that, prior to final adjournment, any tribunal possesses the power to reconsider decisions made by it. The exercise of such a power is often necessary and desirable, though, as tribunals have fully appreciated, it must be kept within strict limits. Its use is clearly demanded to correct errors of calculation in the award.[1] Accordingly, the rules of procedure of the Franco-German[2] and of the Belgo-German Mixed Arbitral Tribunal[3] distinguish between the interpretation or rectification of judgments and their revision or amendment.[4] In pursuance of these rules, the existence of an error of writing or calculation, or of an obscurity or omission in the decretal part of the judgment has been held necessary to justify the correction of a judgment.[5] The rectification of errors of this description is admittedly

4 2 HYDE, INTERNATIONAL LAW CHIEFLY AS INTERPRETED AND APPLIED BY THE UNITED STATES (2d ed., 1945) 1628; see also Hill, *The Interpretation of the Decisions of International Courts* (1934) 22 GEORGETOWN L.J. 535–536.

5 See *supra* sec. 14 as to jurisdictional questions raised by later withdrawal of German Commissioner.

6 MIXED CLAIMS COMMISSION, UNITED STATES AND GERMANY, OPINIONS AND DECISIONS IN THE SABOTAGE CLAIMS HANDED DOWN JUNE 15, 1939, AND OCTOBER 30, 1939, 312.

1 Thadeus Amat (U.S.) v. Mexico (1868) 2 MOORE, INT. ARB. (1898) 1358; Mrs. Dewhurst et al. v. German Government (English-German Mixed Arbitral Tribunal) 4 RECUEIL DES DÉCISIONS (1925) 1; Max Byng v. Der Anker Gesellschaft für Lebens und Rentenversicherungen, Vienna (English-Austrian Mixed Arbitral Tribunal) *ibid.*, 297.

2 Art. 78, 1 *ibid.* (1922), 54.

3 Art. 75, *ibid.*, 43.

4 See *infra* sec. 78.

5 Itzig v. Bauer and Germany (Franco-German Mixed Arbitral Tribunal) 8 RECUEIL DES DÉCISIONS (1928–1929) 130; Daville v. Germany (Franco-German Mixed Arbitral Tribunal) 2 *ibid.* (1923), 429.

proper. No more is involved than causing the opinion as written to conform to the judgment in fact reached by the court. The problem lies in keeping within reasonable limits attempts to have an international commission reverse its prior holding. Obviously a tribunal will not sanction efforts to reintroduce under a new number and upon a different legal basis claims resting on the same injuries previously made the subject of claim and considered and rejected by the tribunal.[6] In the *Rietsch* cases [7] before the Franco-German Mixed Arbitral Tribunal two identical claims for the sequestration of his property were made by Jules Rietsch against Germany, one being for 3,324 francs and one for 900 francs. Adjustment of the first claim was reached by the two governments in 1924, of the second in 1925, the tribunal affirming the adjustments reached. When this fact was discovered the German agent presented a request for annulment, in which the French agent joined. The tribunal annulled the decision of 1925 and held as valid only the decision of 1924.

73. OVERRULING OF DECISIONS.—To be distinguished from a rehearing of the same case is the perfectly proper practice of raising subsequently in different cases important points of law previously decided by the tribunal with a view to their reconsideration and possible overruling.[1] The practice is familiar in municipal courts, where further argument and reflection convinces the court of the desirability of overruling itself. No less instrumental in achieving the ends of justice is the similar practice before international tribunals. In the case of *Gunn* v. *Gunz* [2] before the English-German Mixed Arbitral Tribunal the British agent objected to the admissibility of an argument made by the German Clearing Office upon the ground

6 John F. Machado (U.S.) v. Spain (1871), (United States and Spanish Claims Commission under Convention of Feb. 12, 1871) Claim No. 3, 1 MS OPINIONS AND PAPERS, 1 JOURNAL OF COMMISSION 104, Claim No. 129, 50 MS OPINIONS AND PAPERS, see also 3 MOORE, INT. ARB. 2193; Danford Knowlton & Company and Peter V. King & Company (U.S.) v. Spain (1871), Claim Nos. 97 and 131, *ibid.*, 2194.

7 SCHÄTZEL, RECHTSKRAFT UND ANFECHTUNG VON ENTSCHEIDUNGEN INTERNATIONALER GERICHTE, 6 FRANKFURTER ABHANDLUNGEN ZUM KRIEGSVERHÜTUNGSRECHT (1928) Appendix, p. 169.

1 International Fisheries Company (U.S.) v. Mexico (1923) OPINIONS OF COMMISSIONERS, GENERAL CLAIMS COMMISSION, UNITED STATES AND MEXICO (1931) 207; *cf.* Von Tiedemann v. Poland (German-Polish Mixed Arbitral Tribunal) 7 RECUEIL DES DÉCISIONS (1927–1928) 704 (reversal of an interlocutory decision on jurisdiction).

2 2 *ibid.* (1923) 202.

that it impugned a prior decision of the tribunal and thus reopened a question finally solved. The tribunal stated:

With regard to this objection, the Tribunal are of opinion that considering the nature of their task and their position as a final Arbitral Court created by the Peace Treaty, a decision given by them in a case cannot be deemed as unreservedly binding for future cases. They must reserve to themselves the right of reconsidering in a new case, a legal question dealt with by them in a former decision. Likewise, any of the parties may not only bring before the Tribunal a new case which they consider as not identical with a former case already decided, but also request the Tribunal with regard to the new case to reconsider a legal question on which a former decision has been grounded. The Tribunal trust that this will not be done without serious reasons.[3]

74. CORRECTION OF MISTAKE AS TO THE APPLICABLE LAW.—Tribunals will also, within limits, correct decisions based on misapprehensions as to the applicable law. In the case of *Young, Smith & Company* against Spain [1] the claimants tried to obtain a further award of interest, the umpire's decision having made no mention of it. In this they were supported by the American arbitrator, who argued that owing to a mistake on his part as to the law of Cuba he had omitted any mention of interest and that this omission might have misled the umpire. The arbitrator for Spain did not oppose a reference of the matter to the umpire in order that the latter could correct his decision, "lest there should be a failure of justice from any mere mistake." [2] The umpire nevertheless reaffirmed his award, stating that in not allowing interest he had acted on full consideration. In the *Schreck* case [3] before the United States–Mexico Claims Commission of 1868, the umpire reversed a prior decision disallowing the claim and entered an award for the claimant, when the agent for the United States produced a law of Mexico not previously con-

---

[3] *Ibid.*, 203, 204.

[1] (1871), Claim No. 96, United States and Spanish Claims Commission under the Convention of Feb. 12, 1871, 3 MOORE, INT. ARB. 2184.

[2] *Cf.* F. M. de Acosta y Foster (U.S.) v. Spain (1871) 3 MOORE, INT. ARB. 2187, where as an act of courtesy the arbitrator for Spain consented to the reopening of the commission's decision of dismissal, when the American arbitrator stated that his first examination of the case was hasty.

[3] 2 MOORE, INT. ARB. 1357, Claim No. 768.

sidered by the commission according to which it appeared that the commission was in error in its assumption that because the claimant had been born in Mexico he was a Mexican citizen.

The final disposition of cases cannot, of course, be interminably dragged out through continued petitions for rehearings. The American agent in the case of *Young, Smith & Company* above referred to,[4] challenged the umpire's second decision, alleging errors of fact therein. His motion for a second rehearing was summarily refused by the two national arbitrators. The American arbitrator, in his opinion, stated:

> It is an award made after a rehearing upon the precise question for which a second rehearing is now asked. . . .
> There is no lack of precision in the terms employed by the umpire in making his award; it appears to contain his honest decision after a full and fair hearing; and therefore belongs to that class of awards which a court of equity will not set aside for error in law or fact.[5]

It appears that in the case of the *North American Dredging Company*[6] before the General Claims Commission, United States and Mexico, the American agent presented a petition for rehearing.[7] Of the propriety of this action, an American member of the Commission later remarked: "Motions for re-hearing have been presented to and entertained by other international tribunals. Such a motion of course in no way involves the repudiation by a Government of a final decision."[8] To justify modifying a prior decision 'on this ground, the error alleged must not be frivolous, it must involve substantial prejudice, and it must be manifest.[9]

75. REVISION BASED UPON NEW EVIDENCE.—The term "revision" has been used variously to designate a type of rehearing in which a modification of a decision is sought before the same tribunal before it has become *functus officio* and also to indicate a ground for re-

---

[4] *Supra* note 1.
[5] 3 MOORE, INT. ARB. 2187.
[6] North American Dredging Company (U.S.) v. Mexico (1923) OPINIONS OF COMMISSIONERS, GENERAL CLAIMS COMMISSION, UNITED STATES AND MEXICO (1927) 21.
[7] See International Fisheries Company (U.S.) v. Mexico (1923) *ibid.* (1931) 232.
[8] *Ibid.*
[9] Trail Smelter case *supra* sec. 70.

opening a final award upon certain specific grounds after the tribunal has dissolved. The cases are quite different; the first is addressed to the discretion of the tribunal, in the second the tribunal is powerless to act. Sandifer,[1] who has a most careful treatment of this topic, notes the varying uses of this term and that of rehearing as follows:

A rehearing is somewhat analogous to appeal or cassation, as it involves first a finding that there is sufficient new evidence or sufficient evidence of fraud to warrant reopening the case for a retrial or reargument on the merits. Revision, however, as the term has come to be generally used, is more limited in scope, consisting of an amendment of the award without a reargument. The term is usually used with reference to an amendment upon the basis of new evidence but does not necessarily exclude an amendment upon the basis of a showing of fraudulent evidence. It must be added, however, that strictly speaking neither of these terms are words of art as they are not infrequently used loosely in an interchangeable sense to denote any procedure in which it is sought to obtain the reopening of an award for the purpose of amending it.

Strictly speaking, the term "revision" should be limited to cases in which a reopening of an award is sought while the tribunal still possesses jurisdiction, upon the ground of the discovery of new evidence of such a nature that it would have produced a change in the tribunal's views had it known thereof.[2] So considered, revision is but a special application of the power of rehearing. Thus, even though the treaty or the rules made no provision for such a procedure, it has been held that the presentation of evidence of this important nature constitutes grounds for the reopening of a case, provided that there has been no laches of the claimant.[3] Where, however, full opportunity has been given a claimant to litigate his case and submit evidence and the decision has been against him,

---

[1] SANDIFER, EVIDENCE BEFORE INTERNATIONAL TRIBUNALS (1939) 284.

[2] *Supra* note 1; WITENBERG, L'ORGANISATION JUDICIAIRE, LA PROCÉDURE ET LA SENTENCE INTERNATIONALES (1937) 371–372; GUERMANOFF, L'EXCÈS DE POUVOIR DE L'ARBITRE (1929) 35; see also remarks of Mr. Rolin (Belgium) LEAGUE OF NATIONS, OFFICIAL JOURNAL (Spec. Supp. No. 76), Records of the Tenth Ordinary Session of the Assembly, Minutes of the First Committee (1929) 18, and *infra* secs. 76–79.

[3] George Moore (U.S.) v. Mexico (1868), 2 MOORE, INT. ARB. 1357; Alfred A. Green (U.S.) v. Mexico (1868), *ibid.* 1358. But *cf.* refusal of Umpire Thornton to grant a rehearing upon allegations of perjury in La Abra Silver Mining Company (U.S.) v. Mexico (1868) *ibid.*, 1329.

he may not thereafter, without alleging special grounds, obtain a rehearing merely by presenting additional evidence.[4]

76. REVISION IN THE HAGUE CONVENTIONS.—The use of the term "revision" in the sense of reconsideration of an award on the ground of new evidence apparently stems from a proposal of Professor Corsi incorporated in Article 13 of the Permanent Treaty of Arbitration between Italy and the Argentine Republic of July 23, 1898.[1] Professor Corsi distinguished between the causes of nullity or injustice which the same judge could be trusted to correct and those which must necessarily be reserved for the decision of some other independent tribunal. In the former category were defects, such as were stipulated in the treaty, arising from circumstances which if known to the judge before rendering his decision would have led him to a different decision. On the other hand, where the cause of nullity arose from circumstances which the judge could have prevented or lay in the appreciation of facts or law for which he would be morally or intellectually responsible, it could not well be expected that he, as the author of the decision, would correct it.[2]

At the Hague Conference of 1899 in the Committee of Examination of the Third Commission, Holls, the American delegate, submitted an amendment of Article 24 of the Russian draft of an arbitral code [3] to the effect that each litigant should be allowed the privilege

[4] José G. Delgado (U.S.) v. Spain (1871) 3 ibid., 2196; cf. the refusal of the motion of the Agent of Mexico for a rehearing of the Weil and La Abra cases, accompanied with some additional evidence and containing a re-examination of the old, 2 ibid. 1329.

[1] "The revision of the Award before the same tribunal which has pronounced it may be asked before the execution of the sentence: First, if the judgment has been based on a false or erroneous document; second, if the decision in whole or in part has resulted from an error of fact, positive or negative, resulting from the acts or documents of the trial." DARBY, INTERNATIONAL TRIBUNALS (3d ed., 1899) 219, 222. Cf. Art. 40 of Professor Corsi's proposal printed in Corsi, Un Nouveau Traité d'arbitrage permanent (1899) 64 REV. GEN. DE DROIT INT. PUB. 26, n. 1. See also Art. XII, arbitration convention of November 21, 1901, between Peru and Bolivia, supra p. 160. The same distinction and substantially the same arguments in support of it were advanced by DE LAPRADELLE, L'Arbitrage international en 1897 (Chronique Internationale) (1898) 10 REV. DU DROIT PUB. S.P. (Part 2) 523, 525.

[2] Corsi, supra note 1, at 26, 27; see also STOYKOVITCH, DE L'AUTORITÉ DE LA SENTENCE ARBITRALE EN DROIT INTERNATIONAL PUBLIC (1924) 224.

[3] This article read: "The arbitral award, duly pronounced . . . settles the dispute definitely and without appeal." PROCEEDINGS OF THE HAGUE PEACE CONFERENCES; CONFERENCE OF 1899 (Carnegie trans., 1920) 804.

of re-examination of a case by the same judges within three months after notification of the decision, if it could invoke new evidence or questions of law.[4] The resulting discussion centered about the objections that the proposal was opposed to the principle of arbitration, which was to end disputes, and was dangerous to international peace.[5] Chevalier Descamps remarked that the possibility of injustice was inherent in all courts.[6] Bourgeois, apparently relying on the distinction advanced by Corsi, suggested a means of reconciliation in his remarks that the committee should "carefully distinguish between the discovery of an *error* and the discovery of a *new fact*." In the latter case only was the conscience of the judge not put in question. Accordingly, he submitted a new draft, which was accepted by a majority vote, that revision be allowed upon the discovery of a new fact of a nature to exercise a decisive influence on the award which at the time of the award was unknown to the tribunal and to the parties.[7]

This last proposal was referred by the committee to the Third Commission as Article 54 of the draft Convention,[8] where it created an even more vigorous discussion. Martens, adhering to his previous views, was answered by Holls. The latter stated that there was a limit to the principle invoked by Martens and that that limit had been well expressed by the American statesman Abraham Lincoln when he said, "Nothing is settled until it is settled right." Injustice should not be perpetuated. It need not be feared that new facts would be forged or manufactured by any civilized government. Rather than being impaired, the moral authority of a judgment would be enhanced by a provision that an opportunity has existed for correcting errors and achieving substantial justice.[9] The proposal was finally adopted and became Article 55 of the Convention for the Pacific Settlement for International Disputes of 1899.[10] At the

[4] *Ibid.*, 749, at 834.
[5] Remarks of Johkheer van Karnebeek, Mr. Martens, *ibid.*, 750, 753, 754.
[6] *Ibid.*, 754.
[7] *Ibid.*, 753, 754, 755.
[8] *Ibid.*, 593, 617.
[9] *Ibid.*, 618–619, 621–622.
[10] *Ibid.*, 625, 91, 98. "The parties can reserve in the *compromis* the right to demand revision of the award."

second Hague Peace Conference of 1907, Martens unsuccessfully proposed the suppression of Article 55 of the Convention of 1899.[11] The article became Article 83 of the Convention as adopted by the First Commission [12] and by the Plenary Conference.[13]

The rule of the Hague Convention recognizes that it is necessary for the parties to make a reservation in the *compromis* in order to avail themselves of the privilege of revision. In view of this fact and of the further fact that the demand for revision can be addressed only to the tribunal which pronounced the award, and then in accordance with the period fixed by the *compromis,* the Hague formula involves a type of *rehearing* rather than *appeal.* The tribunal established to decide the particular dispute is vested with a jurisdiction continuing after the decision of the case to revise its award. Not until the additional period stipulated in the *compromis* has expired does the tribunal become *functus officio.* Thus, in the *North Atlantic Coast Fisheries* arbitration each party reserved the right to demand a revision of the award within five days after its promulgation. That demand was required to be heard by the tribunal within ten days thereafter and, if allowed, the tribunal was to afford opportunity for such further hearings and arguments as it should deem necessary.[14] But the absence of such a reservation in the *compromis* does not mean that the parties are entirely without remedy if a revision of a judgment is desired. Its only effect would be to vary the procedure for the reopening of the decision. Since the jurisdiction over the case granted to the original tribunal would have expired with its decision, it would be necessary to arrive at a new *compromis* of arbitration. This the parties would be free to do.[15]

---

[11] Meetings of the First Subcommission of the First Commission, 2 PROCEEDINGS OF THE HAGUE PEACE CONFERENCES; CONFERENCE OF 1907 (Carnegie trans., 1921) 369.
[12] *Ibid.,* 131.
[13] 1 *ibid.,* 330, 604, 612.
[14] Art. X, Special Agreement of January 27, 1909, United States and Great Britain, 1 MALLOY, TREATIES 835, 840. Art. XIII, Protocol of May 22, 1902, between the United States and Mexico, for the submission to the Permanent Court of Arbitration of the Pious Fund Case, also permitted proceedings for revision, *ibid.,* 1194, 1198.
[15] Thus, Mérignhac, in criticizing Article 55 of the Convention of 1899, states: "Firstly, why require that the *compromis* expressly reserve the right to demand revision? Revision, at least to the extent the parties have not expressly excluded it,

77. SAME: VENEZUELA-COLOMBIA BOUNDARY ARBITRATION.—The construction placed upon Article 83 of the Hague Convention of 1907 by Venezuela in its boundary arbitration with Colombia under the convention of November 3, 1916, hardly seems sound; it referred to Article 83 as justifying a right of revision when the *compromis* had failed to reserve such a right.

The questions of boundaries pending between the two States had previously been submitted to arbitration. The execution of the resulting award encountered difficulties which were in effect impossible of solution. The award had confused certain provinces and had, by reason of imperfect description, rendered it impossible to trace the boundary at a number of points.[1] Since Colombia maintained that it could enter upon the possession of territories which had been clearly recognized as belonging to it, the question was submitted to the arbitrator under the treaty of 1916 to decide whether the execution of the award should proceed partially or should take place as an entirety. The arbitrator was further required to complete the delimitation of the boundary fixed by the award.[2] In this second arbitration it was contended by Venezuela that because it was impossible of execution, the award contained errors which fell within the category of facts discovered subsequent to its publication and according to Article 83 of the Hague Convention, would be sufficient to justify its revision. There is certainly little in the language of Article 83 to sustain this construction. It looks only to facts not disclosed to the tribunal because they were unknown to the parties themselves. The article contemplates a limited form of rehearing and in no sense is intended to authorize appeal.[3] The

---

should be a right, just as appeal is in internal legislation, in the absence of an express prohibition of positive law. It is only by virtue of an express prohibitory clause that one of the parties would be justified in refusing the revision claimed by the other." 1 MÉRIGNHAC, TRAITÉ DE DROIT PUBLIC INTERNATIONAL (1905) 535.

[1] AFFAIRE DE LIMITES ENTRE LE VÉNÉZUELA ET LA COLOMBIE; PREMIÈRE MÉMOIRE DU VÉNÉZUELA (1918) 22–23.

[2] SENTENCE ARBITRALE DU CONSEIL FÉDÉRAL SUISSE SUR DIVERSES QUESTIONS DE LIMITES PENDANTES ENTRE LA COLOMBIE ET LE VÉNÉZUELA, BERNE, 24 mars 1922 (1922) 27–28.

[3] *Cf.* Remarks of Mr. Asser, PROCEEDINGS OF THE HAGUE PEACE CONFERENCES; CONFERENCE OF 1899 (Carnegie trans., 1920) 753.

arbitration now under discussion was essentially an instance of appeal, for the award was submitted to a new and independently created tribunal. No reservation of the privilege of revision was made in the original *compromis,* nor, even if such a reservation had been made in terms similar to those employed by the then-unwritten Article 83,[4] would it authorize the reopening of the award when no new facts relating to the merits of the dispute were shown and only the mistakes made by the original arbitrator were invoked.

Such is the strictness of language in which Article 83 is couched that considerable doubt exists whether it is intended to cover the discovery that the award was based on fraudulent documents produced by one of the parties. Fauchille urges that it is.[5] The question was directly raised by Sir Julian Pauncefote during the Conference of 1899 in the Committee of Examination, to which Holls replied "that fraud evidently constitutes a case of nullification and of a *new fact.*"[6] But the sentiment of subsequent speakers seems to be opposed to this view. Thus, when Sir Pauncefote referred to the text of the Italian treaty[7] as a useful precedent on the point which he had raised, Asser stated that the article of the Italian treaty was too broad, in that it provided not only for revision but also for appeal. In this view he was sustained by Léon Bourgeois, the president of the committee, and finally by the committee itself in its decision not to adopt the text of the Italo-Argentine treaty.[8] On the other hand, Count Nigra, the Italian representative, shortly thereafter presented the question of what tribunal would be competent to declare the fraud if a government had produced a forged document. Asser categorically replied that "the arbitration tribunal itself would decide whether it is false or not."[9] However, it is difficult to discover any logical inconsistency in the position that the discovery of the falsity of the documents relied on in an arbitration is one of a new fact and that that fact is certainly of such a nature as profoundly

---

[4] The original arbitration was under treaty of September 14, 1881, *op. cit. supra* note 2, at 11.
[5] 1 FAUCHILLE, TRAITÉ DE DROIT INTERNATIONAL PUBLIC (1926) Part IV, at 567.
[6] *Op. cit. supra* note 3, at 753.
[7] *Supra* p. 233, n. 1, for the text of the pertinent article of this treaty.
[8] *Op. cit. supra* note 3, at 753.   [9] *Ibid.,* 753, 754.

to influence the decision of the tribunal. Whether the desire of the conference to limit the application of the principle of revision is to be given effect to the extent of denying revision in the case of the discovery of fraud, as against its apparent inclusion in the language of the article governing revision, will eventually have to be tested by judicial decision.

78. REVISION BEFORE THE EUROPEAN MIXED ARBITRAL TRIBUNALS.—The rules of the Mixed Arbitral Tribunals created under the treaties of peace closing the first World War usually provided a definite procedure for the revision of decisions. Under the regulations of the Franco-German Mixed Arbitral Tribunal a request for revision could be presented if based upon the discovery of a new fact which might exercise a decisive influence upon the award and at the close of argument was unknown to the tribunal and to the party making the request. The procedure of revision was to be fixed by the tribunal and could only be opened by a preliminary decision expressly deciding that the new fact existed and possessed the stipulated characteristics.[1] To similar effect were the rules of the Belgian-German Mixed Arbitral Tribunal.[2] Such proceedings are not regarded as in conflict with the engagement of the parties to consider the decisions of the tribunal as "final and conclusive."[3] That clause is deemed to mean the impossibility of any general right of appeal or revision and not to contravene "the admissibility of this action for restitution mildly termed revision."[4] The scope of the application of these rules has been decisively limited by the tribunals upon such occasions as it has been invoked. The procedure which they set up provides no means of ordinary rehearing, permitting the parties to question the legal reasoning on which the decision was based.[5] The

---

[1] Art. 79–81, 1 RECUEIL DES DÉCISIONS (1922) 55.

[2] Art. 76, ibid., at 43.

[3] Art. 304 (g), Treaty of Versailles, 112 BRITISH AND FOREIGN STATE PAPERS (1919) 161.

[4] Strupp, The Competence of the Mixed Arbitral Courts of the Treaty of Versailles (1923) 17 AM. J. INT. LAW 661, 683, 684.

[5] Epoux Ventense v. Jugoslavia (German-Jugoslav Mixed Arbitral Tribunal) 7 RECUEIL DES DÉCISIONS (1927–1928) 79; but cf. the statement of the Franco-German Mixed Arbitral Tribunal that, in general, a fact would be of such a nature as to exercise a decisive influence on an award when it was a fact giving rise to the application of a rule of law or of the proof of the existence of a law which the

term "fact" has been strictly construed. The case of *Baron de Neuflize* v. *Deutsche Bank and Germany* [6] involved a suit by owners of coupons of the Ottoman Public Debt to compel the payment of coupons maturing during the period from 1915 to 1920 from blocked funds deposited in the German banks. The tribunal disallowed the suit on the ground, among other grounds, that no contractual relation between the parties existed, remarking in so doing that prejudice would result to the plaintiffs only if it should develop that Turkey would not fulfill its obligations to the holders of the coupons. The plaintiffs later requested the revision of the award [7] on the ground that loss was actually threatened, contrary to the assumption in the award. The arbitration partitioning the debt of the original Turkish State between its successor and the States to whom went the territories detached from it, had fixed a sum for payments during 1915 to 1920 which was *less* than those already made by Turkey. It would follow, plaintiffs contended, that no more payments could be expected from Turkey. The tribunal held that the fact advanced failed to meet the requirements of its rules governing revision. The ground for revision raised by the plaintiffs simply concerned the question whether the plaintiffs had suffered prejudice and left unaffected the reasons of law and fact upon which it had reached its former decision. The rules required (*a*) the discovery of a new fact (*b*) unknown at the time of the closing of argument either to the tribunal or to the party raising it (*c*) which was of such a nature as to exercise an important influence on the award. Revision in this sense should not be confused with appeal. Only the insufficiency of the information as to the facts of a case would give rise to it, not that the decision was illy judged in failing to consider a doctrine of law or to appreciate in an exact manner the facts presented. The sole task of the tribunal in a case of revision was to determine whether the new fact, when placed with the original group of facts, would

---

judge could not be presumed to know and which one of the parties had to prove as a fact, Heim and Chamant v. German Government (Franco-German Mixed Arbitral Tribunal) 3 *ibid.* (1924) 50; Strupp, *supra* note 4, at 685.

[6] (Franco-German Mixed Arbitral Tribunal) 4 RECUEIL DES DÉCISIONS (1924) 792.

[7] 7 *ibid.* (1927–1928) 629.

materially modify their structure and the conclusions which had first been drawn from them.[8] The requirement that the fact be *unknown* at the time of the closing of argument and subsequently discovered, has been construed to exclude petitions based on facts occurring *subsequently* to the rendering of the decision of the tribunal.[9]

79. REHEARING AND REVISION BEFORE PERMANENT INTERNATIONAL TRIBUNALS.—It is significant that in those international courts which have been created with a view to a continuing existence provision has been made for the rehearing, within certain limits, of decided cases. Any established judicial body necessarily must possess such a power. Under the Ordinance of Procedure of the now-defunct Central American Court of Justice, revocation of orders or decrees upon the ground of error was permitted upon the petition of any of the parties filed within five days after the notification of their issuance.[1] The parties could also request the interpretation of a judgment within thirty days following its notification.[2] The convention for the establishment of an International Central American Tribunal adopts the familiar clause that amendment of the decision is permissible on the discovery of a new fact calculated to exercise a decisive influence upon the award which was unknown at the time the discussion was closed.[3] Similarly, the project of the American Institute of International Law for a Pan American Court of Justice stipulates that an "application for a revision" can be made within not later than six months after the discovery of such a fact, provided that the ignorance of the fact by the party claiming revision was not owing to its negligence.[4]

Article 61 of the Statute of the Permanent Court of International Justice was in the matter of rehearings consciously based on the pat-

---

[8] *Ibid.*

[9] Créange v. Busch (Franco-German Mixed Arbitral Tribunal) 5 *ibid.* (1925) 114; Krichel v. France and Germany (Franco-German Mixed Arbitral Tribunal) 8 *ibid.* (1928–1929) 757, 764.

[1] Art. 45 (1914) 8 AM. J. INT. LAW, SUPP. 204.

[2] Art. 48, *ibid.*

[3] Convention of February 7, 1923, Art. 1, par. 4, (1923) 17 AM. J. INT. LAW, SUPP. 85.

[4] Project No. 28, Art. 43 (1926) 20 AM. J. INT. LAW, SUPP. (special numbers) 380.

tern of the Hague Conventions of 1899 and 1907 for the Pacific Settlement of International Disputes, though the requirement was
added that the ignorance of the party requesting revision must not
be due to its negligence.[5] Otherwise, it restricts proceedings for the
modification of judgments to *revision,* for which applications may
not be filed after the lapse of six months from the date of the discovery of the new fact or ten years from the date of the sentence.[6]
It is, perhaps, advisable to point out in this connection that the
Hague Convention establishes, of course, no continuing court in the
sense of the Permanent Court of International Justice. It is based
on the system of occasional arbitration through special treaties and
only provides a permanent panel of judges for selection as arbitrators of individual disputes. Essentially Article 83 contemplates
a system of arbitration no different from that assumed in Article 11,
of similar tenor, in the German-Swiss treaty of conciliation and arbitration of December 3, 1921.[7]

80. INTERPRETATION OF DECISIONS.—The statement has often been
made that a tribunal is powerless to interpret its final decision once
rendered.[1] As stated by the Permanent Court of International Justice: "in the absence of an express agreement between the parties, the
Arbitrator is not competent to interpret, still less to modify his award
by revising it." [2] The rule is but an application of the principle that
the tribunal loses all power with respect to its judgment once it has
become *functus officio.* So considered, a new *compromis* becomes the
only means for submitting such a dispute to the tribunal. Thus,
Article 82 of the Hague Convention of 1907, providing that "any
dispute arising between the parties as to the interpretation and execution of the reward shall, in the absence of an agreement to the

---

[5] COUR PERMANENTE DE JUSTICE INTERNATIONALE, COMITÉ CONSULTATIF DE JURISTES,
PROCÈS-VERBAUX DES SÉANCES DU COMITÉ, 16 JUIN–24 JUILLET 1920, p. 744.

[6] STATUTE AND RULES OF COURT (1936) 25.

[7] 12 LEAGUE OF NATIONS, TREATY SERIES 281, 287.

[1] HUDSON, INTERNATIONAL TRIBUNALS (1944) 123; Hill, *The Interpretation of the
Decisions of International Courts* (1934) 22 GEORGETOWN L.J. 535; *contra* WITEN-
BERG, L'ORGANISATION JUDICIAIRE, LA PROCÉDURE ET LA SENTENCE ARBITRALE INTER-
NATIONALES (1937) 361–362 (states that since interpretation does not involve judg-
ing, tribunal may interpret its decision even after dissolution).

[2] Delimitation of the Polish-Czechoslovak Frontier (Question of Jaworzina), SER.
B., No. 8 (1923) 38.

contrary, be submitted to the tribunal which pronounced it," [3] would require a new *compromis* for this purpose after the tribunal had finally adjourned.[4] In the case of the Permanent Court of International Justice the power to construe its judgments upon the request of a party was expressly reserved.[5] But the Court has held, and rightly, that it would be without jurisdiction to respond to a request for an interpretation which went "beyond the limits of that judgment itself, which are fixed by special agreement." [6]

81. MODIFICATION OF AWARDS BY DIPLOMATIC MEANS.—It is, of course, unnecessary that a new tribunal be established to require a party to relinquish the advantage of a void award; the other party is under a direct obligation not to take advantage of such an award, whether procured through fraud [1] or rendered in a manner departing from the terms of submission.[2] Accordingly, upon the discovery of new evidence indicating that a claim is in fact without foundation, a State wrongfully ordered by a tribunal to pay it has the right to expect that the interposing State will not compel that payment to be made.[3]

82. SAME: LAZARE CASE.—Quite apart from specific treaty clauses looking towards revision, governments have recognized the propriety and desirability of the procedure of revision. Particularly is this shown in the action taken by the United States following the decision in the *Lazare* case.[1] The claim was based on an alleged wrongful violation and annulment by the Haitian government of a contract granting Lazare a concession for the establishment of a national bank. The arbitrator, Judge Strong, found that on the day when the bank was to go into operation Lazare stood ready to pay in his share of the capitalization in drafts on reputable English

---

[3] SCOTT, REPORTS TO THE HAGUE CONFERENCES OF 1899 AND 1907 (1917) 306.
[4] Hill, *supra* note 1, at 539.
[5] Art. 60, STATUTE AND RULES OF COURT (1936) 25: "In the event of dispute as to the meaning or scope of the judgment, the Court shall construe it upon the request of any party."
[6] Interpretation of Judgment No. 3, SER. A., No. 4 (March 26, 1925) 7.
[1] See cases under secs. 17, 19, 20 *supra*.
[2] See *supra* sec. 42.
[3] *Infra* sec. 82.
[1] Lazare (U.S.) v. Haiti (1884), 2 MOORE, INT. ARB. 1749, 1779.

bankers. The government, however, the arbitrator found, had violated the contract by diverting customs receipts pledged as security and by depositing its quota only partly in currency. Lazare was not obligated to pay until the government had done so. The arbitrator accordingly held that the government was not justified in annulling the contract and awarded damages for the value of the concession.

After the award Secretary of State Bayard reported in favor of reopening it upon the ground, among other reasons, of newly discovered evidence and the existence in the Department of State of certain papers which did not appear to have been laid before the arbitrator. Both tended to establish Lazare's inability to comply with the contract. The newly discovered evidence tended to show that Lazare was insolvent at the time of the transactions in Haiti, that the London firms with which he had negotiated for funds had little or no standing, and that he was wholly unprepared to furnish the funds which he had engaged to provide for the opening of the bank. In further support of his recommendation Mr. Bayard referred to a letter from Judge Strong to the Haitian minister in which he stated that after his office as arbitrator had ceased, the newly discovered evidence was presented to him by the counsel for Haiti with an application for a rehearing. It was stated that the application had been denied verbally on the ground that his power over the award had terminated, but the new evidence was said to be of such strength that it would "materially have affected" his decision had it been presented to him during the hearing of the case. The award was never paid by Haiti, nor was Mr. Bayard's disposition of the case disturbed.[2]

[2] *Ibid.*, 1793, 1800–1805.

CHAPTER 7

APPEAL

83. JUDICIAL REGULATION OF THE RIGHT TO CONTEST VALIDITY OF THE AWARD.—If the development of international arbitration as a judicial system is to be fostered and strengthened, means should be established whereby claims of nullity of awards can be judicially determined. The present system of leaving the regulation of such questions to the parties themselves has been criticized as anarchic, war-provoking, and tending to create doubt in the authority of international tribunals.[1] The establishment of a means of judicial review would go far towards eliminating many of the ills of the present system. It would then be easier to distinguish between the case in which a refusal to carry out an award on the pretext of its nullity is a true international fault and the situation in which such a refusal is reasonable and legitimate.[2] Moreover, if it should be possible to establish some time limit within which the right to contest validity must be exercised or otherwise be waived, the long-drawn-out arguments as to nullity now possible would be eliminated.[3]

The primary concern of States in submitting their disputes to arbitration is that their legal rights shall be respected. It is their desire that the settlement of disputes between them shall proceed upon the basis of the fullest respect for their legal rights, that ample opportunity shall be afforded to present their legal position to the

---

[1] Garner, *Appeal in Cases of Alleged Invalid Awards* (1932) 26 AM. J. INT. LAW 126, 132; Erich, *Le Projet de conférer à la Cour Permanente de Justice Internationale des fonctions d'une instance de recours* (1931, 3d ser.) 12 REV. DE DROIT INT. L.C. 268, 270; *cf.* Mérignhac, *De l'Autorité de la chose jugée en matière de sentence arbitrale* (1898) 5 REV. GEN. DE DROIT INT. PUB. 606, 623.

[2] Rundstein, *La Cour Permanente de Justice Internationale comme instance de recours* (1943) 43 RECUEIL DES COURS 109.

[3] Borel, *Les Voies de recours contre les sentences arbitrales* (1935) 52 RECUEIL DES COURS 81.

tribunal, and that the judgment shall not through error or conscious compromise sacrifice any of their legal privileges. Each of these motivating factors is better safeguarded through a system of appellate review than under the present system. With a permanent international tribunal established to regulate the various acts of doubtful validity which may occur in the international order, and with States prepared to accept its decisions, the problem of nullity would be much simplified.[4]

It is not necessary at this stage to go so far as to establish a conventional obligation to submit all charges of invalidity to judicial examination.[5] The recognition of the existence of such an obligation on the part of States can be better achieved through the inclusion at an appropriate time in the Statute of the International Court of Justice of authority to review the decisions of arbitral tribunals to the extent that States may by special agreement confer such jurisdiction upon it. A draft clause for that purpose for insertion in arbitration conventions would be most helpful. An approach of this nature, which would be *optional* rather than compulsory, would permit a system of appeal in international arbitration to grow as needed and out of its own vitality. Such a system would involve appeal in the true sense of the term, for arbitration of the question of whether a prior decision is void, such as took place in the *Orinoco Steamship Company Case*, for example, is not, strictly speaking, an example of appeal, but only a new arbitration under a new *compromis*. A right of appeal necessarily presupposes the existence of an established and permanent judicial body for that purpose.[6]

84. EXTENT TO WHICH A SYSTEM OF APPEAL SHOULD BE ESTABLISHED.—
In last analysis the extent to which the principle of appeal shall be established in international arbitration is dependent upon the objectives of the parties.[1] If the dispute is of sufficient importance to

---

[4] Verzijl, *La Validité et la nullité des actes juridiques internationaux* (1935) 15 REV. DE DROIT INT. 284, 339.

[5] *Cf.* WITENBERG, L'ORGANISATION JUDICIAIRE, LA PROCÉDURE ET LA SENTENCE INTERNATIONALES (1937) 369–370. See also *infra* sec. 87.

[6] Rundstein, *La Cour Permanente de Justice Internationale comme instance de recours* (1933) 43 RECUEIL DES COURS 78.

[1] Hill, *Influence of Disputants over Procedure in International Courts* (1934) 21 VA. L. REV. 205.

their national interests, if their pre-eminent desire is that the dispute shall be well-judged, they then will be the more ready to establish a right of appeal in its broadest form. To what extent, however, is it desirable as a general rule that means of appeal be established?

If questions of nullity are to be subjected to judicial regulation instead of being left to the decision of the parties, it is obvious that means of appeal must be provided, at least to the extent of correcting violations of minimum procedural standards and departures from terms of submission. But appeal to correct error *in judicando* is very difficult to apply in the system of international justice.[2] International law has numerous fields in which legal rights are in process of growth and clarification and authoritative conclusion as to the applicable principles of law cannot readily be reached. In such cases, it will often not be possible to assert that international law has been misapplied in the award in the clear and certain manner which would be required to support a charge of nullity. Although the criticism that the recognition of any right of appeal whatever would tend to weaken the authority of arbitrators and faith in their decisions[3] is not believed to be sound, it must be admitted that, insofar as national interests are involved, the recognition of a right of appeal on grounds of mistake would lead losing States only too often to attack the decision.[4] In the present stage of development of international arbitration it is the more practicable course to let the creation of a means of appeal for error of law occur as a natural step in the growth of the system of *ad hoc* arbitrations, to be availed of by the parties whenever desired, than to establish such a right of appeal for all cases.

85. RUNDSTEIN'S PROPOSAL TO CONFER APPELLATE JURISDICTION UPON THE PERMANENT COURT OF INTERNATIONAL JUSTICE.—The Statute of

2 Rundstein, *La Cour Permanente de Justice Internationale comme instance de recours* (1933) 43 RECUEIL DES COURS 5, 91–92.

3 Caballero de Bedoya, *État actuel de la question de la Cour Permanente de Justice Internationale considérée comme instance de recours* (1932) 10 REV. DE DROIT INT. 142, 156.

4 Borel, *Les Voies de recours contre les sentences arbitrales* (1935) 52 RECUEIL DES COURS 5, 85–87.

the Permanent Court of International Justice did not include any provision for regulating questions of excess of jurisdiction. Article 60 permitted a motion for the interpretation of a judgment, and Article 61 allowed revision because of the discovery of a new fact. But except for a few special instances, to be discussed below,[1] no specific means were provided either for the Court to review its own decisions when it was contended that they were *ultra petita*[2] or to review the decisions of arbitral tribunals upon similar grounds.

In connection with the study of the revision of the Statute of the Court which was made by the committee appointed by the Council of the League of Nations under the resolution of December 13 and 14, 1928, Rundstein, the Polish member of the Committee, submitted a memorandum suggesting an extension of the jurisdiction of the Court. The committee, while taking no action thereon, considered it desirable to include the memorandum with its final report transmitted to the Secretary-General on March 20, 1929, and suggested that it be brought to the attention of the Council.[3]

Rundstein's proposal took the form of a draft declaration for signature by States. The declaration announced the principle that where a dispute arising between the signatory States was submitted to arbitration outside the jurisdiction of the Permanent Court of International Justice, recourse could be had by each party to the Court as a jurisdiction of appeal. The appeal was permitted to lie in regard to the "exceeding of its competence by the tribunal" or to the "violation of a rule of international law," but its exercise was limited to two months after the notification of the award. After it had been decided by the Permanent Court, the case was to be remanded to the original arbitral tribunal for correction, unless the parties had expressly conferred on the Court jurisdiction as a tribunal for revision. The dignity and position of the tribunal whose decision was under review was thereby preserved.

An interpretation of the proposal, including argument in its sup-

---

[1] See *infra* sec. 88.

[2] Yotis, *La Question ultra petita à propos d'un arbitrage entre la Grèce et la Bulgarie* (1926) 53 JOUR. DU DROIT INT. (Clunet) 879, 889.

[3] 10 LEAGUE OF NATIONS, OFFICIAL JOURNAL (1929) 1113, 1125.

port, was communicated to the Secretary-General on June 13, 1929.[4]
It was pointed out that the declaration was designed to have a
strictly optional character and that it would operate only if the
parties accepted it for all disputes which, under the relevant conventions, were not within the jurisdiction of the Permanent Court.
Even if they have accepted the declaration, States would remain free
to agree to exclude the appellate jurisdiction of the Court for particular disputes or classes of disputes.

It will be observed that both this proposal and the Finnish proposal discussed in the following section did not purport to cure the
omission of the Statute of the Court to enable a *rehearing* by the
Court of its own decisions upon the grounds of excess of jurisdiction.
The proposals are limited to cases of appeal from other tribunals.
But their study is helpful in exploring the problems incident to
establishing a system of review for the decisions of international
tribunals.

86. FINNISH PROPOSAL TO CONFER APPELLATE JURISDICTION UPON THE
PERMANENT COURT OF INTERNATIONAL JUSTICE.—It will be observed
that Rundstein's proposal purposely avoided the inclusion of a system of procedure for the appeal which he proposed. The formulation of a procedure under which appeal to the Court could take
place became one of the outgrowths of a proposal made by the government of Finland at the Assembly of the League of Nations in
1929.

A draft resolution was submitted by Finland for the consideration
of the First Committee—the committee on constitutional and legal
questions—in which it was stated that the Council was requested
to consider whether, and "to what extent, there might be conferred on the Permanent Court of International Justice jurisdiction
as a court of review in respect of arbitral tribunals established by
States." [1] Erich, the representative of Finland, stated that the pur-

[4] LEAGUE OF NATIONS, OFFICIAL JOURNAL (Spec. Supp. No. 76) Records of the
Tenth Ordinary Session of the Assembly, Minutes of the First Committee (1929) 85.
[1] LEAGUE OF NATIONS, OFFICIAL JOURNAL (Special Supp. No. 76) Records of the
Tenth Ordinary Session of the Assembly, Minutes of the First Committee (1929)
82, 83.

pose of the proposal was "to confer on the Court jurisdiction in respect of disputes relating to the absolute incompetence of another tribunal, or the case of a tribunal which had exceeded its jurisdiction." It concerned arbitral tribunals in general, and its aim was to widen the sphere in which review could take place. It was deemed to involve no sacrifice of either Article 83 of the Hague Convention of 1907 or Article 41 of the General Act of Geneva of 1928.[2]

On the basis of criticism voiced by Raestad, representative of Norway, an amendment suggested by the Norwegian delegation was adopted by the committee, with some changes.[3] Raestad remarked that the Finnish draft proposed that specific jurisdiction be given the Court. This implied that the jurisdiction had not previously been possessed by the Court. But it was the view of Raestad—occasion will later be taken herein to discuss the merits of this view—that the jurisdiction was already vested in the Court in relation to States bound by Article 36 of the Statute. In any event, it was not for the League to decide whether each of the parties to an international arbitration should be permitted to submit the award to the Court on the plea that the tribunal was without jurisdiction. Its only preoccupation would be to create a suitable procedure for those States desiring to make use of it.[4] The amended resolution of the committee was adopted by the Assembly.[5] It read in part:

> The Assembly invites the Council to submit to examination the question: What would be the most appropriate procedure to be followed by States desiring to enable the Permanent Court of International Justice to assume in a general manner as between them, the functions of a tribunal of appeal from international arbitral tribunals in all cases where it is contended that the arbitral tribunal was without jurisdiction or exceeded its jurisdiction? [6]

---

[2] *Ibid.*, 12, 16. Art. 83 of the Hague Convention of 1907 provided for revision upon the discovery of a new fact. Art. 41 of the General Act of Geneva would empower the Permanent Court of International Justice disputes "relative to the admissibility of suits and the scope of reservations" in respect of the international tribunals proposed by the Act.

[3] *Ibid.*, 48–50.

[4] *Ibid.*, 48.

[5] LEAGUE OF NATIONS, OFFICIAL JOURNAL (Spec. Supp. No. 75) Records of the Tenth Ordinary Session of the Assembly, Plenary Meetings (1929) 174.

[6] *Op. cit. supra* note 1, at 97.

The Council thereupon invited certain of its members to ask their legal advisors to form a committee to make a preliminary study of the question. The task was entrusted to Messrs. Erich (Finland), Basdevant (France), Gaus (Germany), Pilotti (Italy), and Rundstein (Poland).[7] The report of the committee was submitted to the Council on September 8, 1930, and was by the Council forwarded to the Assembly.[8] The committee's report contained a draft recommendation and two draft resolutions. These documents proposed nearly identical systems of procedure to be followed by States seeking the annulment of an arbitral award before the Permanent Court of International Justice, but varied in their suggestions as to the attitudes which the Assembly might adopt in making the procedure available for States. In general, the procedure was applicable to disputes in which the parties had been in conflict as to their legal rights as contrasted with their political interests. A party alleging that an award was null "because the tribunal had no jurisdiction, or exceeded its jurisdiction, or on the ground of a fundamental fault in the procedure" was declared to be under the obligation to submit its claim to the Permanent Court. The definition of the meaning of these stipulations was left to the Court.[9] The proceeding of appeal was required to be instituted within sixty days from the notification of the award. The Court could declare the award to be void, in whole or in part, and could order appropriate provisional measures. The decision of the Court was regarded as binding upon the parties, and, upon annulment, they were considered to be replaced in their prior legal position. The draft recommendation [10] recommended that the members of the League recognize as between themselves a compulsory jurisdiction of the Court to annul arbitral awards and that they insert in their arbitration treaties provisions of the tenor outlined above. In regard to this recommendation the committee commented that it was modest and made it easier that justice be done for the various types of cases, but expressed a doubt that it

[7] 11 LEAGUE OF NATIONS, OFFICIAL JOURNAL (1930) 86, 101, 1359.
[8] *Ibid.*, 1301, 1359.
[9] *Ibid.*, 1362.
[10] *Ibid.*

would have practical consequences.[11] The first draft resolution [12] made a similar recommendation that a compulsory jurisdiction of the Court be recognized in the annulment of awards and proposed a protocol whereby the signatories would be bound to submit all such disputes to the Court. It was the view of the committee that, while such a proposal possessed the merits of simplicity and uniformity, it might well tend to increase this class of cases.[13] The second draft resolution [14] suggested a declaration by the Assembly that a member contesting the obligatory character of an award "has the duty to propose to the other party the conclusion of a special agreement for the submission of this question to the Permanent Court of International Justice." The member should make its proposal within sixty days from the notification of the award and should be regarded as plaintiff in the action. Such a declaration, in the opinion of the committee, would impose upon the objecting State a method of procedure difficult to avoid. In principle, it stated, an arbitral award was deemed to be regular and binding. A State disputing its validity introduced a new factor into the case. It followed that such a State ought to take the initiative, submit its claim to the Court, and bear the consequences of its action.[15]

The Assembly seems to have taken no other definitive action on the Finnish proposal.[16] The report of the committee of the Council was, however, discussed in the First Committee, which in turn authorized the appointment of a subcommittee to report on the question.[17] The subcommittee submitted a report on September 22, 1931, to which a further draft recommendation and draft protocol was attached.[18] The draft recommendation not only embodied the declara-

[11] Ibid., 1361.
[12] Ibid., 1363.
[13] Ibid., 1360.
[14] Ibid., 1364.
[15] Ibid., 1361, 1362.
[16] Cf. Resolution adopted September 25, 1931, deferring this question for examination at a later session, LEAGUE OF NATIONS, OFFICIAL JOURNAL (Spec. Supp. No. 93) Records of the Twelfth Ordinary Session of the Assembly of the League of Nations, Plenary Meetings (1931) 137.
[17] Ibid. (Spec. Supp. No. 94) Records of the Twelfth Ordinary Session of the Assembly, Minutes of the First Committee (1931) 10–15.
[18] Ibid., 59, 140.

tion suggested in the second draft resolution of the committee of the Council that any State contesting the validity of an arbitral award is obliged to submit its contention to further judicial proceedings but also sought to invoke the authority of the Council to the end that this obligation would be respected. It was recommended that whenever the Council found that the validity of an arbitral award is disputed by one of the parties, it should invite the parties to conclude a special agreement for the submission of this contention to the Permanent Court. If it were unsuccessful in procuring this result, it was recommended that the Council ask the Court for an advisory opinion. The draft protocol was carefully designed to prevent to the utmost degree any interruption in the execution of the award by an allegation of its invalidity. Thus, if the party claiming that an award was vitiated by a defect rendering it invalid failed to submit its claim to the Permanent Court, the other party was not left remediless, since it was independently empowered to bring the case by application before the Court. The filing of the application was limited to within sixty days after the receipt of the award or "the discovery of a new fact." During the period within which recourse to the Court was permitted, the operation of the award would not be suspended, though the Court could order its suspension or other interim measures of protection. The Court was to decide whether and in what measure the award was vitiated by the defects alleged and only insofar as the award was declared to be vitiated by such defects would the parties be permitted to treat the award as not binding.

It will be observed that this last proposal is a distinct refinement on the view taken by the committee of the Council that upon annulment the parties were to be regarded as being replaced in their prior legal position. Moreover, if within three months from the publication of a judgment of the Court declaring the existence of a defect affecting the validity of the award the parties had failed to agree upon a submission to arbitration, either party was authorized to bring the substance of the case by application before the Court for decision. In its comment upon its two proposals, the subcommittee stated that it felt that any appearance of the subordination of tribunals to the Permanent Court should be avoided. The use of the word nullity had been deliberately avoided. The Court should not function in the manner of a court of cassation. It was not to annul the award, but merely to confine itself to declaring the defects which rendered it invalid.[19]

87. SCOPE AND MERIT OF THE PROPOSALS TO CONFER APPELLATE JURISDICTION UPON THE PERMANENT COURT OF INTERNATIONAL JUSTICE.— Recourse to the Permanent Court of International Justice under the proposals of Rundstein and of the committee of the Council was not an unlimited right of appeal. Definite jurisdictional requirements were established which the Court must consider satisfied in any one case which had been appealed to it before entering upon the decision on the merits. The proposal of the committee substantially limited the appellate powers of the Court to cases in which there was excess of jurisdiction or a fundamental fault in the procedure. That of Rundstein substituted for the latter category cases in which a violation of a rule of international law has occurred. While both plans contemplated that the further definition and application of their respective categories in specific cases would be the task of the Court, neither in terms covered all categories of nullity. But whether the categories set forth in the proposals are to be narrowly or broadly construed and whether in any one case they are satisfied, it is for the Court to decide. On the other hand, the draft protocol of the subcommittee completely avoided all jurisdictional questions. Each State seeking to contest or to avoid an international arbitral award is left to carry out the obligation declared to rest upon it of submitting its allegations to the judicial decision of the Permanent Court. The Court's sole task was to determine whether the award was, under customary international law, vitiated by any defects rendering it wholly or in part invalid.

It is somewhat difficult to perceive a material difference between the concepts of absence of jurisdiction and of excess of jurisdiction advocated by the committee of the Council as grounds for appeal.

[19] *Ibid.*, 140 *et sqq.*

In international arbitrations the terms of the *compromis* constitute the bounds of the jurisdiction of a tribunal, and if they have been violated or exceeded, all that can be said is that the tribunal has acted without jurisdiction. Further refinement of terms seems unnecessary. It is thought that this attempt to introduce into international law distinctions arising out of and only having value in municipal law systems is not to be encouraged.[1]

A considerable body of opinion exists to the effect that the proposed extensions of the Statute of the Permanent Court were unnecessary in view of Article 36 of its Statute and Article 41 of the General Act of Geneva of 1928.[2] The report of the subcommittee of the Assembly, however, doubted the possibility of such a construction of Article 36, and Raestad, who was a member of the first committee, has since taken a contrary position.[3] Under Article 36 the compulsory jurisdiction of the Court includes legal disputes concerning "any question of international law" or "the interpretation of a treaty." The thesis that the question whether an arbitral tribunal had exceeded its jurisdiction would fall under either of these categories possesses some plausibility if only the language of the article be considered. That the article, however, was intended to have the effect of creating an appellate jurisdiction is extremely doubtful. It may well be presumed that the Court would not act in an appellate capacity unless its competence were clearly defined and without

[1] Sec. 28 *supra; cf.* remarks of Raestad (Norway), LEAGUE OF NATIONS, OFFICIAL JOURNAL (Spec. Supp. No. 94) Records of the Twelfth Ordinary Session of the Assembly, Minutes of the First Committee (1931) 13.

[2] Remarks of Rundstein (Poland), LEAGUE OF NATIONS, OFFICIAL JOURNAL (Spec. Supp. No. 76) Records of the Tenth Ordinary Session of the Assembly, Minutes of the First Committee (1929) 13; Politis (Greece) and Limburg (Netherlands), the latter referring to Article 13, paragraph 4, of the Covenant, concerning the duties of the Council in the event of the failure of a member of the League to carry out an arbitral award, *op. cit. supra* note 1, at 13, 61; Caballero de Bedoya, *État actuel de la question de la Cour Permanente de Justice Internationale considérée comme instance de recours* (1932) 10 REV. DE DROIT INT. 145, 146, 158 (*contra* as to Art. 41); *cf.* Report of E. Borel, Reporter of the 15th Commission, Institute of International Law (1929) 1 ANNUAIRE 489.

[3] Raestad, *Le Recours à la Cour Permanente de Justice Internationale contre les sentences des tribunaux d'arbitrage internationaux pour cause d'incompetence ou excès de pouvoir* (1932, 3d ser.) 13 REV. DE DROIT INT. L.C. 302, 303.

ambiguity or doubt.[4] Certainly Article 36 affords no solution for the States not bound by it. Article 41 of the General Act establishing a system of international arbitration requires that there shall be submitted to the Permanent Court disputes relating to its "interpretation or application . . . including those relative to the admissibility of suits and the scope of reservations." [5] If, in the course of an arbitration nominally proceeding under the General Act, a State desired to raise the objection that the adverse party had wrongly invoked the jurisdiction of the arbitral tribunal instead of that of the Permanent Court, such an objection would clearly be one for consideration by the Court. But it is hardly likely that the article is intended to authorize appeal to the Court on such grounds after the tribunal has rendered judgment.[6]

The course of the debates upon the Finnish proposal have afforded considerable illumination upon the problem of creating a procedure for the review of decisions of arbitral tribunals. It was affirmed that no steps should be taken which might diminish the prestige and value of the present system of arbitration [7] and that the proposal in effect created in international arbitration a system of a hierarchy of courts long familiar in municipal systems of procedure.[8] In form, at least, the final proposal of the subcommittee largely avoids the criticism that arbitral tribunals will be placed in an inferior position. Thus, the Court is to refrain from entering any new judgment in conformity with what it conceives to be the applicable law, but is merely to confine itself to pointing out the defects existing in the award, remanding the case to the original tribunal for the issuance of the final judgment. An attempt was made by Hoffinger, the rep-

[4] Cf. Erich, Le Projet de conferer à la Cour Permanente de Justice Internationale des fonctions d'une instance de recours (1931, 3d ser.) 12 REV. DE DROIT INT. L.C. 273; Raestad, supra note 3, at 303.

[5] LEAGUE OF NATIONS, OFFICIAL JOURNAL (Spec. Supp. No. 63) Resolutions and Recommendations adopted by the Assembly during its Ninth Ordinary Session (1928) 25.

[6] References supra note 4.

[7] Remarks of Hoffinger (Austria), op. cit. supra note 1, at 61.

[8] Remarks of D'Avila Lima (Portugal), ibid., 14; Politis (Greece), ibid., 13; Hoffinger (Austria), ibid., 11.

resentative of Austria, to formulate a theoretical reconciliation of
the two divergent conceptions in relation to the proposal. It was
stated by him that arbitral tribunals were equally with the Court
supreme judicial tribunals. The powers of these tribunals and of the
Court were co-ordinated and did not represent different degrees of
judicial hierarchy in which arbitral tribunals would occupy an inferior position. It was not the intention of the Finnish proposal to
place arbitral tribunals in a position of inferiority to the Court or to
reduce their status by creating a channel of redress on the lines of
national judicial systems. Its aim was simply to prevent an arbitral
tribunal set up between States from exercising its powers beyond the
limits fixed by such States.[9] But, as Hoffinger himself recognized and
made the basis of his argument of the moment, the thesis is not
sustained when review is permitted upon any grounds except jurisdictional grounds. And in practical effect the position of the Court
is appellate.

If the movement to set up judicial procedures for the review of
arbitral awards be considered upon the basis of its real merits, a
system of judicial review would seem greatly preferable to the present
legal impasse created when the objection of nullity is voiced. The
danger to the system of international arbitration lies, not in any
possible abuses which may grow out of permitting review, but in
the unregulated refusal of States to carry out judicial decisions.[10]

88. PROVISIONS FOR APPELATE REVIEW.—To a limited extent States
have already conferred appellate jurisdiction upon the Permanent
Court of International Justice.[1] Thus, in its Judgment of December
15, 1933, the Court sustained its jurisdiction to hear an appeal from
a judgment on jurisdiction and merits of the Hungarian-Czechoslovak
Mixed Arbitral Tribunal when the parties had by treaty agreed to a

---

[9] *Ibid.*, 11.

[10] Caballero de Bedoya, *supra* note 2, at 157; Erich, *supra* note 4, at 269–270. See
also, in connection with this section, Blanco, *La Validez de las sentencias arbitrales
y el Tribunal Permanente de Justicia Internacional* (1932) 21 REVISTA DE DERECHO
INTERNACIONAL 50.

[1] See Jacoby, *The Permanent Court of International Justice as a Court of Appeals* (1936) 22 VA. L. REV. 405; Rundstein, *La Cour Permanente de Justice Internationale comme instance de recours* (1933) 43 RECUEIL DES COURS 5.

right of appeal to the Court from "all judgments on questions of jurisdiction or merits." [2] The Court also considered in its Judgment of December 16, 1936, the right of appeal to its jurisdiction provided for in Article X of Agreement II of the Young Plan agreements signed at Paris on April 28, 1930. By this article Czechoslovakia, Yugoslavia, and Rumania, on the one hand, and Hungary, on the other hand, recognized "a right of appeal to the Permanent Court of International Justice from all judgments on questions of jurisdiction or merits which may be given henceforth by the Mixed Arbitral Tribunals in all proceedings other than those referred to in Article I of the present Agreement." The appeal was dismissed as falling within the excluded category.[3]

The treaty between Norway and Luxemburg of February 12, 1932, contained a series of articles under which a party raising a question of nullity of an award could bring its contention before the Court, notwithstanding a failure by the other party to concur in such appeal.[4] It provided that if within forty days from the decision of an arbitral tribunal one of the parties should contend that it is null, the resulting dispute could be submitted to the Court. If within three months from the publication of the decision in question the parties should fail to agree on a new *compromis*, either party would be permitted to move the Court to take jurisdiction of the question. The Court was directed to determine the extent to which the decision was void and the further measures to be taken. In the treaty of commerce between Denmark and Lithuania of November 3, 1924, decisions of an arbitral tribunal, which was to regulate disputes arising under the treaty, were permitted to be submitted within a one-month period to the Court "for revision." [5]

The Institute of International Law at its session in New York of

---

[2] Appeal from a Judgment of the Hungarian-Czechoslovak Mixed Arbitral Tribunal (Peter Pázmány University v. Czechoslovakia), Judgment of December 15, 1933, SER. A./B., Fascicule No. 61, p. 221.

[3] "The Pajzs, Czáky, Esterházy Case," Judgment of December 16, 1936, SER. A./B., Fascicule No. 68.

[4] LEAGUE OF NATIONS, TREATY SERIES, Vol. 142, No. 3277, Art. 19–21.

[5] COLLECTION OF TEXTS REGULATING THE JURISDICTION OF THE PERMANENT COURT OF INTERNATIONAL JUSTICE, SER. A., No. 6, 582–583.

1929 adopted a resolution that the powers in their arbitral conventions agree to submit to the Court all differences as to the jurisdiction of the tribunal or of an excess of jurisdiction alleged by one of the parties.[6]

In the Convention instituting the Statute of the Danube, a provision that a State desirous of alleging that a decision of the International Commission of the Danube is *"ultra vires* or violates the Convention may, within six months, submit the matter to the special jurisdiction set up for that purpose by the League of Nations." [7] Reference to the Permanent Court of questions of jurisdiction arising before the tribunal created under the Young Plan was permitted.[8]

Both the system of appeal and that of revision are recognized in the Pan American Court of Justice proposed by the American Institute of International Law.[9] Article 3 of its project contemplates the establishment of a Court of First Instance and of a Court of Appeal. Appeals were allowed on the ground of "non-application or error in the application of a principle of law." [10] Though the judgment of the Court of Appeal was itself to be considered final, interpretation by the Court of the meaning or scope of its judgment was permitted. The possibility of revision of the judgment on the discovery of a new fact was also recognized, provided that the ignorance of such fact by the moving party was not due to its negligence.[11]

In the abortive Olney-Pauncefote Treaty of arbitration of January 11, 1907, between the United States and Great Britain, a request for re-submission of a dispute to a newly constituted tribunal was permitted when the decision on such dispute by a tribunal which had previously been created under the treaty was not unanimous.[12]

---

[6] (1929) ANNUAIRE (Vol. 2) 178–179, 303–304.

[7] Art. 38, Convention instituting the Definitive Statute of the Danube, July 23, 1921, 26 LEAGUE OF NATIONS, TREATY SERIES 175, 193.

[8] Art. 15, par. 8, Agreement with Germany of January 20, 1930, AGREEMENTS CONCLUDED AT THE HAGUE CONFERENCE, JANUARY, 1930 (1930) 13, at 20. *Cf.* references of questions to the Permanent Court of International Justice permitted under Art. 22, Convention on the International Régime of Maritime Ports, December 9, 1923, 2 HUDSON, INTERNATIONAL LEGISLATION (1922–1924) 1156, 1170, 1171; Art. 36, Convention on the International Régime of Railways, December 9, 1923, 47 LEAGUE OF NATIONS, TREATY SERIES 57, 87.

[9] Project No. 28 (1926) 20 AM. J. INT. LAW SUPP. (special numbers) 374.

[10] *Ibid.*, 380 (Art. 41).

[11] *Ibid.* (Art. 42, 43).   [12] (1896) FOR. REL. U.S. 238–239 (Art. V).

CHAPTER 8

FUTURE PROGRESS

89. INTERNATIONAL ARBITRATION AS A JUDICIAL PROCESS.—Despite criticisms against international arbitration upon the ground of its tendency to compromise,[1] it remains a judicial process characterized by a respect for law and legal processes.[2] Judge John Bassett Moore early wrote:

Mediation is an advisory, arbitration a judicial, function. Mediation recommends, arbitration decides.[3]

Later in his address before the Academy of Political Science in 1917 he said:

I venture to assert that the decisions of those international tribunals are characterized by about as much consistency, by about as close an application of principles of law, and by perhaps as marked a tendency on the part of one tribunal to quote the authority of tribunals that preceded it, as you will find in the proceedings of ordinary judicial tribunals.[4]

Thus, Judge Kellogg rightly regarded the Permanent Court of International Justice as a judicial, not a political, institution, "competent to decide only such questions as are susceptible of solution by the application of rules and principles of law." [5]

When all the implications of the fact that international arbitration

[1] Dennis, *Compromise—The Great Defect of Arbitration* (1911) 11 COL. L. REV. 493, 494–495: "The most striking characteristic of arbitration as it exists today between individuals . . . is the almost irresistible tendency shown by arbitration to compromise and split the difference instead of doing justice though the heavens fall."

[2] Balch, *"Arbitration" as a Term of International Law* (1915) 15 COL. L. REV. 590 and 662; see references *supra* p. 80, n. 10.

[3] 7 MOORE, DIG. sec. 1069.

[4] Moore, *International Arbitration* 4 COLLECTED PAPERS OF JOHN BASSETT MOORE (1944) 200, 201.

[5] Observations by Judge Kellogg in Case of the Free Zones of Upper Savoy and the District of Gex, Order of December 6, 1930, SER. A., No. 24, p. 38.

is inherently a judicial process are realized, its extraordinary value as a means for the peaceful settlement of disputes between nations will become apparent. At each step of the process—the formulation and execution of the *compromis*, the establishment of the tribunal, the conduct of hearings before it, the mode of rendering the award, the form and substance of the award—assurances exist for the protection of the parties that they shall not be deprived of their fundamental legal rights or subjected to arbitrary action. In embarking upon an arbitration, a State may rely on the principle that the tribunal will be required to confine itself to the sphere of action defined in the *compromis* and to conduct itself with due regard for law and universally accepted legal procedures. Yet withal international arbitration is an infinitely flexible process; its procedures can ever be adapted to the demands made upon it. The form of the tribunal and the type of the procedure can always be adjusted to the complexity and volume of the litigation to be submitted for decision. This fact renders it essential that the door always be kept open to States to resort to a form of arbitration and arbitrators of their own choosing for the settlement of their controversies.

90. GROWTH OF A SYSTEM OF INTERNATIONAL JURISPRUDENCE AND COURTS.—The flexibility of the system of international arbitration and the rich lore of tradition and experience which has developed out of the thousands of disputes which have been settled through arbitral means require that the conduct of international arbitrations at all times be entrusted to the hands of experts. If full advantage is to be taken of the experience of the past, international arbitration must go forward under the hands of those trained in its problems and technique. Only the carefulness of the approach of experts can make international arbitration fully respond to the demands of justice. Thus, if care and skill are exercised in drafting the *compromis*, defining the task of the tribunal, and establishing its procedural rules, many of the difficulties which have arisen in the past will tend to be eliminated.[1]

---

[1] *Cf.* BALASKO, CAUSES DE NULLITÉ DE LA SENTENCE ARBITRALE EN DROIT INTERNATIONAL PUBLIC (1938) 105; see FOSTER, 2 DIPLOMATIC MEMOIRS (1909) 194: "Experience had shown that the work of courts of arbitration and international com-

It is not sufficient, however, to rely on the *ad hoc* procedures of
the past. Murdock, in an address before the American Bar Association in 1944, said:

> It is manifest that the present improvised methods of adjudication are
> wholly inadequate as to both accessibility and continuity. In relation to
> violation of international law by governments to the injury of individuals
> there can be said to be at present no adequate administration of justice.
> A court which, like the World Court, operates on the basis of hearing three
> or four cases a year or, at its highest peak of activity, hands down a total
> of eleven judgments, orders, and advisory opinions in a year, is not organ-
> ized in such a manner as to provide a continuous administration of justice
> for the thousands of cases which arise annually involving alleged violations
> of international law and treaties. With the increased tempo of international
> transactions that will follow the war, there will be even greater need for
> adequate means of adjudication.[2]

The American Bar Association accordingly adopted in 1944 a
resolution proposing the creation of a system of International Cir-
cuit Courts, sitting in regular terms in the capital of each member
nation of an International Judicial System.[3]

The facilities for international arbitration must be greatly expanded, and elastic systems of procedure must be provided which
can quickly be adapted to the requirements of the particular dispute. Notwithstanding the strictures previously made in these pages
concerning the unworkability of a universal code of international
arbitration procedure,[4] progress can be made in the formulation of
a series of draft arbitration conventions and procedural rules which,
with such further refinements in each individual arbitration as may
be required, could serve as a basis for future arbitration proceedings. These could include recommended procedures for the solution

---

missions is not infrequently nullified or impaired by their members exceeding
their powers in rendering their decisions, or by a departure from the terms of
reference. In framing this treaty, we sought to avoid all error in this direction by
the careful manner in which the points at issue were set forth."

[2] Murdock, *International Judicial Organization* (1944) 69 ANNUAL REPORT OF
THE AMERICAN BAR ASSOCIATION 373, 378–379.

[3] *Op. cit. supra* note 2, at 165, 169; see Carroll, *Postwar International Organization and the Work of the Section of International and Comparative Law of the
American Bar Association* (1945) 39 AM. J. INT. LAW 20, 24.

[4] *Supra* sec. 6.

of such typical controversies as boundary disputes, accumulations of international claims of varied character, war damage claims and the like. Study along these lines would be productive of forms of arbitration treaties and rules which would tend to reduce to a minimum the causes of dissatisfaction with international arbitration which have occurred in the past.

Every effort should be made to establish accessible and convenient arbitration facilities, with simple, flexible procedures, to which parties can readily resort for the settlement of their disputes. Not all international controversies are important enough to justify the weighty and expensive procedures of the International Court of Justice or of its predecessor, the Permanent Court of International Justice. International claims based on injuries to citizens, for example, can still best be handled by special tribunals. These and similar disputes should not be allowed to rankle, but should rather be quickly settled so as to eliminate all causes of dissension between States. This will require established or readily created tribunals which can promptly dispose of such disputes without cumbersome or expensive proceedings.

At the same time, the procedure and functions of the Permanent Court of Arbitration should be re-examined with a view to its integration into a comprehensive system of international arbitration. The Court has been a most important instrument of international arbitration but its usefulness in the settlement of postwar controversies can be greatly enhanced if its constitutive convention, untouched since 1907, were amended and enlarged in scope. The suggestion has been made that a committee be designated to examine the procedures and administration of the Court and to make recommendations concerning its reconstruction as a continuing instrumentality of international arbitration.[5]

The carrying forward of such a program will require public edu-

---

[5] See KELLOR AND DOMKE, ARBITRATION IN INTERNATIONAL CONTROVERSY 88–89. For a comprehensive program of "future policies and machinery" see pp. 83–98; see also Kellor, *A Science of Arbitration* (1946) 1 (New Series) THE ARBITRATION JOURNAL 19, 22–23.

cation in the value of international arbitration as a means for the settlement of international controversy and will also require in our schools and colleges a much expanded program for the study of international law and organization. Our only hope for the future lies in co-operation through various international organizations and in the settlement of controversies, to the fullest extent possible, by judicial means. It is earnestly hoped that the future will bring forth many and varied international bodies. Their successful functioning will require a skilled and trained personnel. Particularly, education and training in the technique of international arbitration should be provided by educational institutions. It seems shocking that an instrument so valuable to the preservation of peace between States and the promotion of their welfare should be practiced without educational facilities devoted to its instruction and improvement.

If we are to have a fully developed system of international jurisprudence for application by international tribunals, we must establish a means for a uniform publication of their decisions. Cases still lie buried in the unpublished archives of Governments, limited and sporadic printings of others are made, with the result that the few repositories of precedents gathered together by scholars such as John Bassett Moore and De Lapradelle become the handbooks of advocates. It is somewhat as if a lawyer in the United States were compelled to search for the decisions of the courts of the forty-eight states in the publications of each jurisdiction without an index and in a variety of languages. How can there be a common international law in the full sense of that term when parties labor in ignorance of all its applicable precedents? Under the present system we must look to chance and the industry and learning of counsel and the members of the court as our only surety that the court will be well advised. This is not to deny, but rather to emphasize, the value of the individual efforts that have been made in this direction. The task is, however, more than an individual one. Means should be provided whereby governments may register copies of arbitral decisions with some international body under the United Nations as they have in the past registered their treaties with the League of

Nations. It is submitted that the pronouncements of international tribunals are of equal value from the standpoint of the development of a system of international jurisprudence.

A universal digest of the past decisions of international tribunals should also be prepared under the joint direction of scholars. The voluminous body of decisions of international tribunals must be brought together in an ordered system which will enable them to be later readily found by tribunals and advocates. This step is essential to the creation of a system of international jurisprudence.[6]

The settlement of disputes between States through arbitration comprises the only means for the elimination of international controversy through resort to law and judicial procedures. In a world which has too long and too often had recourse to force to settle conflicts it furnishes the avenue whereby States may bring themselves under a reign of law in the solution of their disputes. Not political persuasion or coercion through the use of power in whatever form, but the application of legal principles in a judicial manner is the strength of international arbitration. Not negotiation and compromise, but reason and justice constitute its appeal to States. Its further development as a legal science should be one of the first tasks before us.

---

[6] *Cf.* 1 SCHWARZENBERGER, INTERNATIONAL LAW (1945), reviewed by the present author in (1946) 46 COL. L. REV. 156.

APPENDIX

COMPARATIVE ANALYSIS OF STATUTE OF THE
INTERNATIONAL COURT OF JUSTICE AND OF THE
PERMANENT COURT OF INTERNATIONAL JUSTICE

Inasmuch as this work was completed before the publication of the new Statute of the International Court of Justice, the following comparative analysis of this Statute and the Statute of the Permanent Court of International Justice is included in order that the references in the text to the latter Statute may readily be examined in the light of any amended language of the new Statute. The source of this analysis is Dr. Manley O. Hudson's article "The Twenty-Fourth Year of the World Court," in the *American Journal of International Law,* Vol. 40, pp. 1, at 15 *et sqq.* (January, 1946). Permission for its use extended by Dr. Hudson and the *Journal* is gratefully acknowledged. Variations between the two Statutes are indicated below as follows: The matter in brackets represents those parts of the Statute of the Permanent Court of International Justice (1936 text) which are dropped from the new Statute; the italicized matter represents those parts of the new Statute which find no place in the Statute of the Permanent Court.

ARTICLE 1

[A Permanent Court of International Justice is hereby established, in accordance with Article 14 of the Covenant of the League of Nations. This Court shall be in addition to the Court of Arbitration organized by the Conventions of The Hague of 1899 and 1907, and to the special Tribunals of Arbitration to which States are always at liberty to submit their disputes for settlement.]

The International Court of Justice established by the Charter of the United Nations as the principal judicial organ of the United Nations shall be constituted and shall function in accordance with the provisions of the present Statute.

Chapter I: Organization of the Court

ARTICLE 2

The [Permanent] Court [of International Justice] shall be composed of a body of independent judges, elected regardless of their nationality from [amongst] *among* persons of high moral character, who possess the qualifications required in their respective countries for appointment to the highest judicial offices, or are jurisconsults of recognized competence in international law.

ARTICLE 3

1. The Court shall consist of fifteen members, *no two of whom may be nationals of the same state.*

2. *A person who for the purposes of membership in the Court could be regarded as a national of more than one state shall be deemed to be a national of the one in which he ordinarily exercises civil and political rights.*

ARTICLE 4

1. The members of the Court shall be elected by the *General* Assembly and by the *Security* Council from a list of persons nominated by the national groups in the *Permanent* Court of Arbitration, in accordance with the following provisions.

2. In the case of Members of the [League of] *United* Nations not represented in the Permanent Court of Arbitration, [the lists of] candidates shall be [drawn up] *nominated* by national groups appointed for this purpose by their governments under the same conditions as those prescribed for members of the Permanent Court of Arbitration by Article 44 of the Convention of The Hague of 1907 for the pacific settlement of international disputes.

3. The conditions under which a [State] *state* which [has accepted] *is a party to* the *present* Statute [of the Court] but is not a Member of the [League of] *United* Nations [,] may participate in electing the members of the Court shall, in the absence of a special agreement, be laid down by the *General* Assembly [on the proposal] *upon the recommendation* of the *Security* Council.

ARTICLE 5

1. At least three months before the date of the election, the Secretary-General of the [League of] *United* Nations shall address a written request to the members of the *Permanent* Court of Arbitration belonging to the [States] *states* [mentioned in the Annex to the Covenant or to the States which join the League subsequently,] *which are parties to the present Statute,* and to the [persons] *members of the national groups* appointed under [paragraph 2 of] Article 4, *paragraph 2,* inviting them to undertake, within a given time, by national groups, the nomination of persons in a position to accept the duties of a member of the Court.

2. No group may nominate more than four persons, not more than two of whom shall be of their own nationality. In no case [must] *may* the number of candidates nominated *by a group* be more than double the number of seats to be filled.

ARTICLE 6

Before making these nominations, each national group is recommended to consult its [Highest] *highest* [Court] *court* of [Justice] *justice,* its [Legal] *legal* [Faculties] *faculties* and [Schools] *schools* of [Law] *law,* and its [National] *national* [Academies] *academies* and national sections of [International] *international* [Academies] *academies* devoted to the study of [Law] *law.*

ARTICLE 7

1. The Secretary-General [of the League of Nations] shall prepare a list in alphabetical order of all the persons thus nominated. Save as provided in Article 12, paragraph 2, these shall be the only persons eligible [for appointment].

2. The Secretary-General shall submit this list to the *General* Assembly and to the *Security* Council.

ARTICLE 8

The *General* Assembly and the *Security* Council shall proceed independently of one another to elect the members of the Court.

ARTICLE 9

At every election, the electors shall bear in mind [that] not only *that* [should all] the persons [appointed as members of the Court] *to be elected should individually* possess the qualifications required, but *also that in* the [whole] body *as a whole* [also should represent] *the representation of* the main forms of civilization and *of* the principal legal systems of the world *should be assured.*

ARTICLE 10

1. Those candidates who obtain an absolute majority of votes in the *General* Assembly and in the *Security* Council shall be considered as elected.

2. Any vote of the Security Council, whether for the election of judges or for the appointment of members of the conference envisaged in Article 12, shall be taken without any distinction between permanent and non-permanent members of the Security Council.

3. In the event of more than one national of the same [Member of the League being elected by] *state obtaining an absolute majority of* the votes [of] both *of* the *General* Assembly and *of* the *Security* Council, the eldest of these only shall be considered as elected.

ARTICLE 11

If, after the first meeting held for the purpose of the election, one or more seats remain to be filled, a second and, if necessary, a third meeting shall take place.

ARTICLE 12

1. If, after the third meeting, one or more seats still remain unfilled, a joint conference consisting of six members, three appointed by the *General* Assembly and three by the *Security* Council, may be formed[,] at any time [,] at the request of either the *General* Assembly or the *Security* Council, for the purpose of choosing *by the vote of an absolute majority* one name for each seat still vacant, to submit to the *General* Assembly and the *Security* Council for their respective acceptance.

2. If the *joint* [Conference] *conference* is unanimously agreed upon any person who fulfils the required conditions, he may be included in its list, even though he was not included in the list of nominations referred to in [Articles 4 and 5] *Article 7.*

3. If the joint conference is satisfied that it will not be successful in procuring an election, those members of the Court who have already been [appointed] *elected* shall, within a period to be fixed by the *Security* Council, proceed to fill the vacant seats by selection from [amongst] *among* those candidates who have obtained votes either in the *General* Assembly or in the *Security* Council.

4. In the event of an equality of votes [amongst] *among* the judges, the eldest judge shall have a casting vote.

1. The members of the Court shall be elected for nine years[.] *and* [They] may be re-elected[.]; *provided, however, that of the judges elected at the first election, the terms of five judges shall expire at the end of three years and the terms of five more judges shall expire at the end of six years.*

2. The judges whose terms are to expire at the end of the above-mentioned initial periods of three and six years shall be chosen by lot to be drawn by the Secretary-General immediately after the first election has been completed.

3. [They] *The members of the Court* shall continue to discharge their duties until their places have been filled. Though replaced, they shall finish any cases which they may have begun.

4. In the case of the resignation of a member of the Court, the resignation [will] *shall* be addressed to the President of the Court for transmission to the Secretary-General [of the League of Nations]. [   ] This last notification makes the place vacant.

Vacancies [which may occur] shall be filled by the same method as that laid down for the first election, subject to the following provision: the Secretary-General [of the League of Nations] shall, within one month of the occurrence of the vacancy, proceed to issue the invitations provided for in Article 5, and the date of the election shall be fixed by the *Security Council* [at its next session].

A member of the Court elected to replace a member whose [period] *term* of [appointment] *office* has not expired [, will] *shall* hold [the appointment] *office* for the remainder of his predecessor's term.

1. [The members] *No member* of the Court may [not] exercise any political or administrative function, [nor] *or* engage in any other occupation of a professional nature.

2. Any doubt on this point [is] *shall be* settled by the decision of the Court.

1. No member of the Court may act as agent, counsel, or advocate in any case.

2. No member may participate in the decision of any case in which he has previously taken [an active] part as agent, counsel, or advocate for one of the [contesting] parties, or as a member of a national or international [Court] *court*, or of a commission of enquiry, or in any other capacity.

3. Any doubt on this point [is] *shall be* settled by the decision of the Court.

ARTICLE 18

1. [A] *No* member of the Court [cannot] *can* be dismissed unless, in the unanimous opinion of the other members, he has ceased to fulfil the required conditions.

2. Formal notification thereof shall be made to the Secretary-General [of the League of Nations,] by the Registrar.

3. This notification makes the place vacant.

ARTICLE 19

The members of the Court, when engaged on the business of the Court, shall enjoy diplomatic privileges and immunities.

ARTICLE 20

Every member of the Court shall, before taking up his duties, make a solemn declaration in open [Court] *court* that he will exercise his powers impartially and conscientiously.

ARTICLE 21

1. The Court shall elect its President and Vice-President for three years; they may be re-elected.

2. [It] *The Court* shall appoint its Registrar *and may provide for the appointment of such other officers as may be necessary.*

[The duties of Registrar of the Court shall not be deemed incompatible with those of Secretary-General of the Permanent Court of Arbitration.]

ARTICLE 22

1. The seat of the Court shall be established at The Hague. *This, however, shall not prevent the Court from sitting and exercising its functions elsewhere whenever the Court considers it desirable.*

2. The President and *the* Registrar shall reside at the seat of the Court.

ARTICLE 23

1. The Court shall remain permanently in session, except during the

judicial vacations, the dates and duration of which shall be fixed by the Court.

2. Members of the Court [whose homes are situated at more than five days' normal journey from The Hague shall be] *are* entitled [, apart from the judicial vacations,] to [six months'] *periodic* leave, [every three years, not including the time spent in travelling] *the dates and duration of which shall be fixed by the Court, having in mind the distance between The Hague and the home of each judge.*

3. Members of the Court shall be bound, unless they are on [regular] leave or prevented from attending by illness or other serious [reason] *reasons* duly explained to the President, to hold themselves permanently at the disposal of the Court.

ARTICLE 24

1. If, for some special reason, a member of the Court considers that he should not take part in the decision of a particular case, he shall so inform the President.

2. If the President considers that for some special reason one of the members of the Court should not sit [on] *in* a particular case, he shall give him notice accordingly.

3. If in any such case the member of the Court and the President disagree, the matter shall be settled by the decision of the Court.

ARTICLE 25

1. The full Court shall sit except when it is expressly provided otherwise *in the present Statute.*

2. Subject to the condition that the number of judges available to constitute the Court is not thereby reduced below eleven, the Rules of *the* Court may provide for allowing one or more judges, according to circumstances and in rotation, to be dispensed from sitting.

3. [Provided always that a] *A* quorum of nine judges shall suffice to constitute the Court.

ARTICLE 26

[Labour cases, particularly cases referred to in Part XIII (Labour) of the Treaty of Versailles and the corresponding portions of the other treaties of peace, shall be heard and determined by the Court under the following conditions:

[The Court will appoint every three years a special Chamber of five judges, selected so far as possible with due regard to the provisions of

Article 9. In addition, two judges shall be selected for the purpose of replacing a judge who finds it impossible to sit. If the parties so demand, cases will be heard and determined by this Chamber. In the absence of any such demand, the full Court will sit. In both cases, the judges will be assisted by four technical assessors sitting with them, but without the right to vote, and chosen with a view to ensuring a just representation of the competing interests.

[The technical assessors shall be chosen for each particular case in accordance with rules of procedure under Article 30 from a list of "Assessors for Labour Cases" composed of two persons nominated by each Member of the League of Nations and an equivalent number nominated by the Governing Body of the Labour Office. The Governing Body will nominate, as to one-half, representatives of the workers, and, as to one-half, representatives of employers from the list referred to in Article 412 of the Treaty of Versailles and the corresponding articles of the other treaties of peace.

[Recourse may always be had to the summary procedure provided for in Article 29, in the cases referred to in the first paragraph of the present Article, if the parties so request.

[In Labour cases, the International Office shall be at liberty to furnish the Court with all relevant information, and for this purpose the Director of that Office shall receive copies of all the written proceedings.]

1. The Court may from time to time form one or more chambers, composed of three or more judges as the Court may determine, for dealing with particular categories of cases; for example, labor cases and cases relating to transit and communications.

2. The Court may at any time form a chamber for dealing with a particular case. The number of judges to constitute such a chamber shall be determined by the Court with the approval of the parties.

3. Cases shall be heard and determined by the chambers provided for in this Article if the parties so request.

ARTICLE 27

[Cases relating to transit and communications, particularly cases referred to in Part XII (Ports, Waterways and Railways) of the Treaty of Versailles and the corresponding portions of the other treaties of peace, shall be heard and determined by the Court under the following conditions:

[The Court will appoint every three years a special Chamber of five judges, selected so far as possible with due regard to the provisions of

Article 9. In addition, two judges shall be selected for the purpose of replacing a judge who finds it impossible to sit. If the parties so demand, cases will be heard and determined by this Chamber. In the absence of any such demand, the full Court will sit. When desired by the parties or decided by the Court, the judges will be assisted by four technical assessors sitting with them, but without the right to vote.

[The technical assessors shall be chosen for each particular case in accordance with rules of procedure under Article 30 from a list of "Assessors for Transit and Communications Cases" composed of two persons nominated by each Member of the League of Nations.

[Recourse may always be had to the summary procedure provided for in Article 29, in the cases referred to in the first paragraph of the present Article, if the parties so request.]

A judgment given by any of the chambers provided for in Articles 26 and 29 shall be considered as rendered by the Court.

ARTICLE 28

The [special] chambers provided for in Articles 26 and [27] 29 may, with the consent of the parties [to the dispute], sit *and exercise their functions* elsewhere than at The Hague.

ARTICLE 29

With a view to the speedy despatch of business, the Court shall form annually a [Chamber] *chamber* composed of five judges [who] *which*, at the request of the [contesting] parties, may hear and determine cases by summary procedure. In addition, two judges shall be selected for the purpose of replacing [a judge] *judges* who [finds] *find* it impossible to sit.

ARTICLE 30

1. The Court shall frame rules for [regulating] *carrying out* its [procedure] *functions*. In particular, it shall lay down rules [for] *of* [summary] procedure.

2. The Rules of the Court may provide for assessors to sit with the Court or with any of its chambers, without the right to vote.

ARTICLE 31

1. Judges of the nationality of each of the [contesting] parties shall retain their right to sit in the case before the Court.

2. If the Court includes upon the Bench a judge of the nationality of one of the parties, [the] *any* other party may choose a person to sit as judge. Such person shall be chosen preferably from among those persons who have been nominated as candidates as provided in Articles 4 and 5.

3. If the Court includes upon the Bench no judge of the nationality of the [contesting] parties, each of these parties may proceed to [select] *choose* a judge as provided in [the preceding] paragraph 2 *of this Article.*

4. The [present provision] *provisions of this Article* shall apply to the case of Articles 26 [, 27] and 29. In such cases, the President shall request one or, if necessary, two of the members of the Court forming the [Chamber] *chamber* to give place to the members of the Court of the nationality of the parties concerned, and, failing such, or if they are unable to be present, to the judges specially [appointed] *chosen* by the parties.

5. Should there be several parties in the same interest, they shall, for the purpose of the preceding provisions, be reckoned as one party only. Any doubt upon this point [is] *shall be* settled by the decision of the Court.

6. Judges [selected] *chosen* as laid down in paragraphs 2, 3, and 4 of this Article shall fulfil the conditions required by Articles 2, 17 (paragraph 2), 20, and 24 of [this] *the present* Statute. They shall take part in the decision on terms of complete equality with their colleagues.

ARTICLE 32

1. [The] *Each* [members] *member* of the Court shall receive an annual salary.

2. The President shall receive a special annual allowance.

3. The Vice-President shall receive a special allowance for every day on which he acts as President.

4. The judges [appointed] *chosen* under Article 31, other than members of the Court, shall receive [an indemnity] *compensation* for each day on which they [sit] *exercise their functions.*

5. These salaries, allowances, and [indemnities] *compensation* shall be fixed by the *General* Assembly [of the League of Nations on the proposal of the Council]. They may not be decreased during the term of office.

6. The salary of the Registrar shall be fixed by the *General* Assembly on the proposal of the Court.

7. Regulations made by the *General* Assembly shall fix the conditions under which [retiring] *retirement* pensions may be given to members of the Court and to the Registrar, and the conditions under which members of the Court and the Registrar shall have their [travelling] *traveling* expenses refunded.

8. The above salaries, [indemnities and] allowances, *and compensation* shall be free of all taxation.

The expenses of the Court shall be borne by the [League of] *United* Nations [,] in such a manner as shall be decided by the *General* Assembly [upon the proposal of the Council].

Chapter II: Competence of the Court

1. Only [States] *states* [or Members of the League of Nations can] *may* be parties in cases before the Court.

2. The Court, subject to and in conformity with its Rules, may request of public international organizations information relevant to cases before it, and shall receive such information presented by such organizations on their own initiative.

3. Whenever the construction of the constituent instrument of a public international organization or of an international convention adopted thereunder is in question in a case before the Court, the Registrar shall so notify the public international organization concerned and shall communicate to it copies of all the written proceedings.

1. The Court shall be open to the [Members of the League and also to States] *states* [mentioned in the Annex to the Covenant] *parties to the present Statute.*

2. The conditions under which the Court shall be open to other [States] *states,* shall, subject to the special provisions contained in treaties in force, be laid down by the *Security* Council, but in no case shall such [provisions] *conditions* place the parties in a position of inequality before the Court.

3. When a [State] *state* which is not a Member of the [League of] *United* Nations is a party to a [dispute] *case,* the Court shall fix the amount which that party is to contribute towards the expenses of the Court. This provision shall not apply if such [State] *state* is bearing a share of the expenses of the Court.

1. The jurisdiction of the Court comprises all cases which the parties refer to it and all matters specially provided for in *the Charter of the United Nations or in* treaties and conventions in force.

2. The [Members of the League of Nations and the States] *states* [mentioned in the Annex to the Covenant] *parties to the present Statute* may [, either when signing or ratifying the Protocol to which the present Statute is adjoined, or at a later moment,] *at any time* declare that they recognize as compulsory *ipso facto* and without special agreement, in relation to any other [Member or State] *state* accepting the same obligation, the jurisdiction of the Court in all [or any of the classes of] legal disputes concerning:

[(a)] *a.* the interpretation of a treaty;

[(b)] *b.* any question of international law;

[(c)] *c.* the existence of any fact which, if established, would constitute a breach of an international obligation;

[(d)] *d.* the nature or extent of the reparation to be made for the breach of an international obligation.

3. The [declaration] *declarations* referred to above may be made unconditionally or on condition of reciprocity on the part of several or certain [Members or States] *states,* or for a certain time.

4. Such declarations shall be deposited with the Secretary-General of the United Nations, who shall transmit copies thereof to the parties to the Statute and to the Registrar of the Court.

5. Declarations made under Article 36 of the Statute of the Permanent Court of International Justice and which are still in force shall be deemed, as between the parties to the present Statute, to be acceptances of the compulsory jurisdiction of the International Court of Justice for the period which they still have to run and in accordance with their terms.

6. In the event of a dispute as to whether the Court has jurisdiction, the matter shall be settled by the decision of the Court.

ARTICLE 37

[When] *Whenever* a treaty or convention in force provides for [the] reference of a matter to a tribunal to [be] *have been* instituted by the League of Nations, *or to the Permanent Court of International Justice,* the [Court will be such tribunal] *matter shall, as between the parties to the present Statute, be referred to the International Court of Justice.*

ARTICLE 38

1. The Court, *whose function is to decide in accordance with international law such disputes as are submitted to it,* shall apply:

[1] *a.* [International] *international* conventions, whether general or particular, establishing rules expressly recognized by the contesting [States] *states;*

[2] *b.* [International] *international* custom, as evidence of a general practice accepted as law;

[3] *c*. [The] *the* general principles of law recognized by civilized nations;

[4] *d*. [Subject] *subject* to the provisions of Article 59, judicial decisions and the teachings of the most highly qualified publicists of the various nations, as subsidiary means for the determination of rules of law.

2. This provision shall not prejudice the power of the Court to decide a case EX AEQUO ET BONO, if the parties agree thereto.

Chapter III: Procedure

ARTICLE 39

1. The official languages of the Court shall be French and English. If the parties agree that the case shall be conducted in French, the judgment [will] *shall* be delivered in French. If the parties agree that the case shall be conducted in English, the judgment [will] *shall* be delivered in English.

2. In the absence of an agreement as to which language shall be employed, each party may, in the pleadings, use the language which it prefers; the decision of the Court [will] *shall* be given in French and English. In this case the Court [will] *shall* at the same time determine which of the two texts shall be considered as authoritative.

3. The Court [may] *shall,* at the request of any party, authorize a language other than French or English to be used *by that party.*

ARTICLE 40

1. Cases are brought before the Court, as the case may be, either by the notification of the special agreement or by a written application addressed to the Registrar. In either case the subject of the dispute and the [contesting] parties [must] *shall* be indicated.

2. The Registrar shall forthwith communicate the application to all concerned.

3. He shall also notify the Members of the [League of] *United* Nations through the Secretary-General, and also any *other* [States] *states* entitled to appear before the Court.

ARTICLE 41

1. The Court shall have the power to indicate, if it considers that circumstances so require, any provisional measures which ought to be taken to [reserve] *preserve* the respective rights of either party.

2. Pending the final decision, notice of the measures suggested shall forthwith be given to the parties and *to* the *Security* Council.

1. The parties shall be represented by agents.

2. They may have the assistance of counsel or advocates before the Court.

3. The agents, counsel, and advocates of parties before the Court shall enjoy the privileges and immunities necessary to the independent exercise of their duties.

1. The procedure shall consist of two parts: written and oral.

2. The written proceedings shall consist of the communication to the [judges] *Court* and to the parties of [Cases, Counter-Cases] *memorials, counter-memorials* and, if necessary, [Replies] *replies;* also all papers and documents in support.

3. These communications shall be made through the Registrar, in the order and within the time fixed by the Court.

4. A certified copy of every document produced by one party shall be communicated to the other party.

5. The oral proceedings shall consist of the hearing by the Court of witnesses, experts, agents, counsel, and advocates.

1. For the service of all notices upon persons other than the agents, counsel, and advocates, the Court shall apply direct to the government of the [State] *state* upon whose territory the notice has to be served.

2. The same provision shall apply whenever steps are to be taken to procure evidence on the spot.

The hearing shall be under the control of the President or, if he is unable to preside, of the Vice-President; if neither is able to preside, the senior judge *present* shall preside.

The hearing in Court shall be public, unless the Court shall decide otherwise, or unless the parties demand that the public be not admitted.

1. Minutes shall be made at each hearing [,] and signed by the Registrar and the President.

2. These minutes *alone* shall be [the only] authentic [record].

ARTICLE 48

The Court shall make orders for the conduct of the case, shall decide the form and time in which each party must conclude its arguments, and make all arrangements connected with the taking of evidence.

ARTICLE 49

The court may, even before the hearing begins, call upon the agents to produce any document [,] or to supply any explanations. Formal note shall be taken of any refusal.

ARTICLE 50

The Court may, at any time, entrust any individual, body, bureau, commission, or other organization that it may select, with the task of carrying out an enquiry or giving an expert opinion.

ARTICLE 51

During the hearing any relevant questions are to be put to the witnesses and experts under the conditions laid down by the Court in the rules of procedure referred to in Article 30.

ARTICLE 52

After the Court has received the proofs and evidence within the time specified for the purpose, it may refuse to accept any further oral or written evidence that one party may desire to present unless the other side consents.

ARTICLE 53

1. Whenever one of the parties [shall] *does* not appear before the Court, or [shall fail] *fails* to defend [his] *its* case, the other party may call upon the Court to decide in [favour] *favor* of [his] *its* claim.

2. The Court must, before doing so, satisfy itself, not only that it has jurisdiction in accordance with Articles 36 and 37, but also that the claim is well founded in fact and law.

ARTICLE 54

1. When, subject to the control of the Court, the agents, [advocates and] counsel, *and advocates* have completed their presentation of the case, the President shall declare the hearing closed.

2. The Court shall withdraw to consider the judgment.

3. The deliberations of the Court shall take place in private and remain secret.

ARTICLE 55

1. All questions shall be decided by a majority of the judges present [at the hearing].

2. In the event of an equality of votes, the President or [his deputy] *the judge who acts in his place* shall have a casting vote.

ARTICLE 56

1. The judgment shall state the reasons on which it is based.

2. It shall contain the names of the judges who have taken part in the decision.

ARTICLE 57

If the judgment does not represent in whole or in part the unanimous opinion of the judges, *any* [dissenting Judges] *judge* [are] *shall be* entitled to deliver a separate opinion.

ARTICLE 58

The judgment shall be signed by the President and by the Registrar. It shall be read in open [Court] *court,* due notice having been given to the agents.

ARTICLE 59

The decision of the Court has no binding force except between the parties and in respect of that particular case.

ARTICLE 60

The judgment is final and without appeal. In the event of dispute as to the meaning or scope of the judgment, the Court shall construe it upon the request of any party.

ARTICLE 61

1. An application for revision of a judgment [can] *may* be made only when it is based upon the discovery of some fact of such a nature as to be a decisive factor, which fact was, when the judgment was given, unknown to the Court and also to the party claiming revision, always provided that such ignorance was not due to negligence.

2. The proceedings for revision [will] *shall* be opened by a judgment of the Court expressly recording the existence of the new fact, recognizing that it has such a character as to lay the case open to revision, and declaring the application admissible on this ground.

3. The Court may require previous compliance with the terms of the judgment before it admits proceedings in revision.

4. The application for revision must be made at latest within six months of the discovery of the new fact.

5. No application for revision may be made after the lapse of ten years from the date of the [sentence] *judgment.*

ARTICLE 62

1. Should a [State] *state* consider that it has an interest of a legal nature which may be affected by the decision in the case, it may submit a request to the Court to be permitted to intervene [as a third party].

2. It [will] *shall* be for the Court to decide upon this request.

ARTICLE 63

1. Whenever the construction of a convention to which [States] *states* other than those concerned in the case are parties is in question, the Registrar shall notify all such [States] states forthwith.

2. Every [State] *state* so notified has the right to intervene in the proceedings [:]; but if it uses this right, the construction given by the judgment will be equally binding upon it.

ARTICLE 64

Unless otherwise decided by the Court, each party shall bear its own costs.

Chapter IV: Advisory Opinions

ARTICLE 65

1. The Court may give an advisory opinion on any legal question at the request of whatever body may be authorized by or in accordance with the Charter of the United Nations to make such a request.

2. Questions upon which the advisory opinion of the Court is asked shall be laid before the Court by means of a written request[, signed either by the President of the Assembly or the President of the Council of the League of Nations, or by the Secretary-General of the League under instructions from the Assembly or the Council.] [   ]

[The request shall contain] *containing* an exact statement of the question upon which an opinion is required, and [shall be] accompanied by all documents likely to throw light upon the question.

ARTICLE 66

1. The Registrar shall forthwith give notice of the request for an advisory opinion to [the Members of the League of Nations, through the Secretary-General of the League, and to any States] *all states* entitled to appear before the Court.

2. The Registrar shall also, by means of a special and direct communication, notify any [Member of the League or State] *state* [admitted] *entitled* to appear before the Court or international organization considered by the Court, [(] or, should it not be sitting, by the President[)], as likely to be able to furnish information on the question, that the Court will be prepared to receive, within a [time-limit] *time limit* to be fixed by the President, written statements, or to hear, at a public sitting to be held for the purpose, oral statements relating to the question.

3. Should any [Member or] *such* [State] *state* [referred to in the first paragraph] *entitled to appear before the Court* have failed to receive the *special* communication [specified above] *referred to in paragraph 2 of this Article*, such [Member or State] *state* may express a desire to submit a written statement[,] or to be heard; and the Court will decide.

[2] *4.* [Members,] States[,] and organizations having presented written or oral statements or both shall be [admitted] *permitted* to comment on the statements made by other [Members, States,] *states* or organizations in the form, to the extent, and within the [time-limits] *time limits* which the Court, or, should it not be sitting, the President, shall decide in each particular case. Accordingly, the Registrar shall in due time communicate any such written statements to [Members, States,] *states* and organizations naving submitted similar statements.

ARTICLE 67

The Court shall deliver its advisory opinions in open [Court] *court,* notice having been given to the Secretary-General [of the League of Nations] and to the representatives of Members of the [League] *United Nations,* of *other* [States] *states* and of international organizations immediately concerned.

ARTICLE 68

In the exercise of its advisory functions[,] the Court shall further be guided by the provisions of the *present* Statute which apply in contentious cases to the extent to which it recognizes them to be applicable.

Chapter V: Amendment

ARTICLE 69

Amendments to the present Statute shall be effected by the same procedure as is provided by the Charter of the United Nations for amendments to that Charter, subject however to any provisions which the General Assembly upon recommendation of the Security Council may adopt concerning the participation of states which are parties to the present Statute but are not Members of the United Nations.

ARTICLE 70

The Court shall have power to propose such amendments to the present Statute as it may deem necessary, through written communications to the Secretary-General, for consideration in conformity with the provisions of Article 69.

TABLE OF CASES

BIBLIOGRAPHY OF MATERIAL CITED

Government and Other Official Publications

TREATY COLLECTIONS

Agreements Concluded at the Hague Conference, January, 1930 (London, 1930).

Aranda, A., República de Perú, Collectión de los tratados, convenciones, capitulaciones, armisticios. Vol. V (Lima, Peru, 1895).

Descamps, Baron, et L. Renault, Recueil international des traités du XXe siècle (Paris, 1901–1907).

League of Nations, Treaty Series.

Malloy, W. M., Treaties, Conventions, International Acts, Protocols, and Agreements between the United States of America and Other Powers (Washington, D.C., 1910).

Martens, G. Fr. De, Nouveau recueil général de traités (3d ser., Leipzig, 1931).

Tratados, convenciones, protocoles y demás actos internacionales vigentes celebrados por la República Argentina (Buenos Aires).

Treaties, Conventions, International Acts, Protocols and Agreements between the United States and Other Powers, 1910–1923 (Washington, D.C., 1923). Supplement to Malloy.

COURT DECISIONS

Published periodically

Cases Decided in the Court of Claims of the United States (Washington, D.C.).

Decisions of the Comptroller of the Treasury (Washington, D.C.).

Official Opinions of the Attorneys General of the United States (Washington, D.C.).

Reports of Cases at Law and in Chancery Argued and Determined in the Supreme Court of Illinois (Bloomington, Ill.).

Reports of Cases Decided in the Supreme Court of the State of Indiana (Indianapolis, Ind.).

Reports of Cases Argued and Determined in the Supreme Court of the State of Vermont (Burlington, Vt.).

Reports of Cases Determined in the Supreme Court of Wisconsin (Chicago and Menasha).

The Northwestern Reporter (St. Paul).

United States Reports (New York).

OTHER PUBLICATIONS

Acts of the Conference for the Codification of International Law (1930), Bases of Discussion (1929) Nos. C. 351. M. 145. 1930. V., C. 75. M. 69. 1929. V.

British and Foreign State Papers (London).

Colombia, Boletín del Ministerio de Relaciones Exteriores (Bogotá, 1910).

League of Nations, Official Journal.

United States, Congress, Congressional Record (Washington, D.C.).

United States, Congress, House of Representatives, Hearing before the Sub-Committee of House Committee on Appropriations, First Deficiency Appropriation for 72d Cong., 2d Sess.

United States, Department of State, Bulletin (Washington, D.C.).

United States, Department of State, Papers Relating to the Foreign Relations of the United States (Washington, D.C.).

United States, Department of State, Papers Relating to the Treaty of Washington (Washington, D.C., 1872).

United States Statutes at Large (Washington, D.C.).

Venezuela, Exposición que dirige al Congreso Nacional, Ministro de Relaciones Exteriores (Caracas, Venezuela).

Venezuela, Libro Amarillo, Ministro de Relaciones Exteriores (Caracas, Venezuela).

References Bearing on International Arbitration
Does not include citations of pleadings

Acrement, A., La Procédure dans les arbitrages internationaux (Paris, 1905).

Alvarez, A., Des occupations des territoires contestés à propos de la question de limites entre le Chili et la République Argentine (1903) 10 Revue Générale de Droit International Public 651.

American and British Claims Arbitration, Report of Fred K. Nielsen (Washington, D.C., 1926).

Anderson, C. P., The Costa Rica–Panama Boundary Dispute (1921) 15 American Journal of International Law 236.

Anderson, L., El laudo Loubet; contribución al estudio de limites entre Costa Rica y Panamá (San José, Costa Rica, 1911).

Argentina, Ministerio de Relaciones Exteriores y Culto de la República Argentina, Arbitraje Argentino en la cuestión de límites entre las repúblicas del Perú y de Bolivia; libro azul (Buenos Aires, 1909).

Audry, L., La Revision de la sentence arbitrale (Paris, 1914).

Auer, P. de, The Competency of Mixed Arbitral Tribunals (1928) 13 Transactions of the Grotius Society xvii.

Balasko, A., Causes de nullité de la sentence arbitrale en droit international public (Paris, 1938).

Balch, T. W., "Arbitration" as a Term of International Law (1915) 15 Columbia Law Review 590 and 662.

Basdevant, Jèze, and N. Politis, Les Principes juridiques sur la compétence des juridictions internationales (1927) 44 Revue du Droit Public et de la Science Politique 45.

Bishop, C. M., International Arbitral Procedure (Baltimore, 1930).

Blanco, C., La Validez de las sentencias arbitrales y el Tribunal Permanente de Justicia Internacional (1932) 21 Revista de Derecho Internacional 50.

Bolivia, Ministerio de Relaciones Exteriores de la República de Bolivia, El arbitraje entre las repúblicas de Bolivia y el Perú y su última negociación sobre fronteras; documentos diplomáticos (La Paz, Bolivia, 1909).

Borchard, E. M., The Mavromattis Concessions Cases (1925) 19 American Journal of International Law 728.

—— Strength and Weakness of the New International Court (1922) 4 Illinois Law Quarterly 67.

Borel, E., Les Voies de recours contre les sentences arbitrales (1935) 52 Academie de Droit International, Recueil des cours 5.

Brierly, J. L., The Hague Conventions and the Nullity of Arbitral Awards (1928) 9 The British Yearbook of International Law 114.

Bureau, P., Le Conflit italo-colombien (Affaire Cerutti) (Paris, 1899).

Bustamente, A. S. de, Panama–Costa Rica Boundary Controversy; Opinion Given by Dr. Antonio S. de Bustamente (Panama, 1921).

Caballero de Bedoya, R. V., État actuel de la question de la Cour Permanente de Justice Internationale considerée comme instance de recours (1932) 10 Revue de Droit International 142.

Caldwell, R. H., A Study of the Code of Arbitral Procedure Adopted by the Hague Peace Conferences of 1899 and 1907 (Carnegie thesis, 1921).

Carlston, K. S., Conflits de compétence entre organismes internationaux, 67–72 Journal du Droit International (Clunet) 730.

—— Importance of Procedural Rules in International Arbitration (1945) 1 International Arbitration Journal 58.

—— Procedural Problems in International Arbitration (1945) 39 American Journal of International Law 426.

Carroll, M. B., Postwar International Organization and the Work of the Section of International and Comparative Law of the American Bar Association (1945) 39 American Journal of International Law 20.

Castberg, F., La Compétence des tribunaux internationaux (1925, 3d ser.) 6 Revue de Droit International et de Législation Comparée 310.

—— L'Excès de pouvoir dans la justice internationale (1931) 35 Academie de Droit International, Recueil des Cours 357.

Central American Court of Justice, Anales de la Corte de Justicia Centro-americana (San José, Costa Rica, 1911–1917).

Chamizal Arbitration Award, The (editorial, 1911) 5 American Journal of International Law 709.

"Chamizal, El," Dispute between the United States and Mexico (editorial, 1910) 4 American Journal of International Law 925.

Claims Commission, Great Britain and Mexico. Decisions and Opinions of Commissioners, 1929–1930 (London, 1931).

Clarke, R. F., A Permanent Tribunal of International Arbitration; Its Necessity and Value (1907) 1 American Journal of International Law 342.

Corsi, A., Un Nouveau Traité d'arbitrage permanent (1899) 6 Revue Générale de Droit International Public 9.

Costa Rica, Secretaria de Relaciones Exteriores, Documentos relativos al conflito de jurisdicción territorial con la República de Panamá y sus antecedentes (San José, Costa Rica, 1921).

Darby, W. E., International Tribunals (3d ed., London, 1899).

Darras, A., De certains dangers de l'arbitrage international; affaire Cerruti entre la Colombie et l'Italie (1899) 6 Revue Générale de Droit International Public 533.

Dennis, W. C., Compromise—the Great Defect of Arbitration (1911) 11 Columbia Law Review 493.

—— The Necessity for an International Code of Arbitral Procedure (1913) 7 American Journal International Law 285.

—— The Orinoco Steamship Case before the Hague Tribunal (1911) 5 American Journal of International Law 35.

Dreyfus, F., L'Arbitrage international (Paris, 1892).

Dumas, J., Sanctions of International Arbitration (1911) 5 American Journal of International Law 935.

—— Les Sanctions de l'arbitrage international (Paris, 1905).

Erich, R., Le Projet de conferer à la Cour Permanente de Justice Internationale des fonctions d'une instance de recours (1931, 3d ser.) 12 Revue de Droit International et de Législation Comparée 268.

Feller, A. H., The Mexican Claims Commissions, 1923–1934 (New York, 1935).

—— The German-Mexican Claims Commission (1933) 27 American Journal of International Law 62.

Fiore, P., La Sentence arbitrale du président de la République Argentine dans le conflit de limites entre la Bolivie et le Pérou (1910) 17 Revue Générale de Droit International Public 225.

Fontecha, A. A. R. F., El Arbitraje entre Honduras y Nicaragua, rectificación documentada (Tegucigalpa, Honduras, 1908).

Garner, J. W., Appeal in Cases of Alleged Invalid Arbitral Awards (1932) 26 American Journal of International Law 126.

Garnier-Coignet, J., Procédure judiciare et procédure arbitrale (1930) 6 Revue de Droit International 123.

Goldschmidt, L., Observations supplémentaires relatives aux réglement pour tribunaux internationaux (1875) 7 Revue de Droit International et de Législation Comparée 423.

—— Projet de réglement pour tribunaux arbitraux internationaux (1874) 6 Revue de Droit International et de Législation Comparée 421.

Guermanoff, D., L'Excès de pouvoir de l'arbitre (Paris, 1929).

Habicht, M., The Power of the International Judge to Give a Decision "Ex Aequo et Bono" (London, 1935).

Hagerup, F., Affaire Cerruti—sentence arbitrale du 6 Juillet 1911 (1912) 19 Revue Générale de Droit International Public 268.

Hart, H. L., Experiment in Legal Procedure (1931) 72 Law Journal 392.

Hertz, W. G., Essai sur le problème de la nullité (1939, 3d ser.) 20 Revue de Droit International et de Législation Comparée 450.

Hill, N. L., The Influence of Disputants over Procedure in International Courts (1934) 21 Virginia Law Review 205.

—— The Interpretation of the Decisions of International Courts (1934) 22 Georgetown Law Journal 535.

Hoijer, O., La Solution pacifique des litiges internationaux (Paris, 1925).

Honduras, Límites entre Honduras y Nicaragua, mediación del gobierno de Estados Unidos; alegatos, pruebas y dictamenes presentados por Honduras (New York, 1921).

Hudson, M. O., International Tribunals Past and Future (Washington, D.C., 1944).

—— The Central American Court of Justice (1932) 26 American Journal of International Law 759.

Informe presentado á la nación por el Ministerio de Relaciones Exteriores del Ecuador, June 30, 1921 (1921) 1 The Republic of Ecuador (New York) 9.

Institut de Droit International, Projet de réglement pour la procédure arbitrale internationale (1877) Annuaire de l'Institut de Droit International 126.

Jacoby, S. B., The Permanent Court of International Justice as a Court of Appeals (1936) 22 Virginia Law Review 404.

Jenks, C. W., Equity as a Part of the Law Applied by the Permanent Court of International Justice (1937) 53 Law Quarterly Review 519.

Jessup, P. C., The Palmas Island Arbitration (1928) 22 American Journal of International Law 735.

Kamarowsky, L. A., Le Tribunal international (Paris, 1887).

Kellor, F., and M. Domke, Arbitration in International Controversy ([New York] n.d., issued by Commission to Study the Organization of Peace and American Arbitration Association).

Kellor, F., A Science of Arbitration (1946) 1 (New Series) The Arbitration Journal 19.

Lammasch, H., Die Lehre von der Schiedsgerichtbarkeit in Ihrem Ganzen Umfange (Stuttgart, 1914).

—— Die Rechtskraft internationaler Schiedssprüche (Kristiania, 1913).

Lansing, R., The Need of Revision of Procedure before International Courts of Arbitration (1912) 6 Proceedings American Society International Law 158.

Lapradelle, A. de, L'Arbitrage international en 1897 (Chronique Internationale) (1898) 10 Revue de Droit Public et de la Science Politique, Part 2, 525.

—— L'Excès de pouvoir de l'arbitre (1928) 2 Revue de Droit International 5.

Lapradelle, A. de, and N. Politis, Recueil des arbitrages internationaux (Paris, 1905).

Lauterpacht, H., The Legal Remedy in Case of Excess of Jurisdiction (1928) 9 The British Yearbook of International Law 117.

Le Roy, H. S., American and British Claims Arbitration Tribunal (1926) 12 American Bar Association Journal 156.

Limburg, M., L'Autorité de chose jugée des juridictions internationales (1929) 30 Academie de Droit International, Recueil des Cours 523.

Lisboa, H. C. R., Revision des sentences arbitrales (1902, 2d ser.) 4 Revue de Droit International et de Législation Comparée 62.

MacDonald, J., and C. R. Barnett, The American-Mexican Claims Arbitration (1932) 18 American Bar Association Journal 183.

McKernan, L. W., Special Mexican Claims (1938) 32 American Journal of International Law 457.

McNair, A. D., Constitutional Limitations upon the Treaty-Making Power, in R. Arnold, Treaty-Making Procedure (London, 1933) 1.

Malauzat, A., La Cour de justice arbitrale (Paris, 1914).

Mediación del Secretario de Estado de los Estados Unidos en la Controversia de Límites entre la República de Nicaragua y la República de Honduras (Washington, D.C., 1920).

Mérignhac, A., De l'autorité de la chose jugée en matière de sentence arbitrale (1898) 5 Revue Générale de Droit International Public 606.

Mérignhac, A., Traité théorique et pratique de l'arbitrage international (Paris, 1895).

Moore, J. B., History and Digest of the International Arbitrations to Which the United States Has Been a Party (Washington, D.C., 1898).

—— International Adjudications (New York, 1931).

—— International Arbitration, 4 Collected Papers of John Bassett Moore (New Haven, 1944) 200.

—— Memorandum on Uti Possidetis; Costa Rica–Panama Arbitration (Rosslyn, Va., 1913).

—— Specific Agencies for the Proper Conduct of International Relations, 5 Collected Papers of John Bassett Moore (New Haven, 1944) 300.

—— Opinion of J. B. Moore as Counsellor for Honduras, Honduras-Nicaragua Boundary Mediation before the Secretary of State of the United States, 1920–1921, in 5 Collected Papers of John Bassett Moore (New Haven, 1944) 129.

Morelli, G., La Théorie générale du procès international (1937) 61 Academie de Droit International, Recueil des Cours 257.

Morgan, M., The Work of the Mixed Claims Commission, United States and Germany (1926) 4 Texas Law Review 399.

Murdock, V. O., International Judicial Organization (1944) 69 Annual Report of the American Bar Association 373.

Nicaraguan Mixed Claims Commission, Report of Nicaraguan Mixed Claims Commission transmitted with Report of Its President to the Secretary of State of the United States (N.P., 1915).

Niedermayer, H., Das Völkerrechtliche Nicht-Urteil, Normen und Methode seiner Festellung, 26 Frankfurter Abhandlungen zum modernen Völkerrecht (Leipzig, 1931).

Nielsen, F. K., Progress in Settlement of International Disputes by Judicial Methods (1930) 16 American Bar Association Journal 229.

Nippold, O., Die Fortbildung des Vehrfahrens in Völkerrechtlichen Streitigkeiten (Leipzig, 1907).

North Atlantic Coast Fisheries Arbitration, Proceedings (Washington, D.C., 1912).

Nys, E., La Revision de la Sentence arbitrale (1910, 2d ser.) 12 Revue de Droit International et de Législation Comparée 595.

Orfeld, L. B., Equity as a Concept of International Law (1929) 18 Kentucky Law Journal 31 and 116.

Palmas Island Arbitration, Report of Fred K. Nielsen (N.P., 1928).

Panamá, Secretaria de Relaciones Exteriores, Controversia de Límites entre Panamá y Costa Rica (Panama, 1914).

Permanent Court of Arbitration, Proceedings of the Hague Peace Conferences, Conference of 1899 (Carnegie translation, New York, 1920).

Permanent Court of Arbitration, Proceedings of the Hague Peace Conferences, Conference of 1907 (Carnegie translation, New York, 1920).

—— Conférence Internationale de la Paix, La Haye, 18 Mai–29 Juillet, 1899. Ministère des Affaires Etrangères (The Hague, 1899).

—— Reports to the Hague Conferences of 1899 and 1907, by J. B. Scott (Oxford, 1917).

—— The Hague Conventions and Declarations of 1899 and 1907, by J. B. Scott (New York, 2d ed., 1915).

—— The Hague Court Reports, by J. B. Scott (New York, 1916).

—— The Hague Court Reports, by J. B. Scott (New York, 2d ser., 1932).

Permanent Court of International Justice, Series A, Collection of Judgments (Leyden, Holland).

—— Series A./B., Judgments, Orders and Advisory Opinions (Leyden, Holland).

—— Series B., Collection of Advisory Opinions (Leyden, Holland).

—— Series C., Pleadings, Oral Statements and Documents (Leyden, Holland).

—— Statute and Rules of Court (Leyden, Holland, 1936).

—— Series D., Collection of Texts Governing the Jurisdiction of the Court (Leyden, Holland).

Pierantoni, A., La Nullité d'un arbitrage international (1898) 30 Revue de Droit International et de Législation Comparée 445.

Politis, N., La Justice international (Paris, 1924).

Raestad, A., Le Recours à la Cour Permanente de Justice Internationale contre les sentences des tribunaux d'arbitrage internationaux pour cause d'incompétence ou excès de pouvoir (1932, 3d ser.) 13 Revue de Droit International et de Législation Comparée 302.

Ralston, J. H., The Law and Procedure of International Tribunals (Stanford, 1926).

—— Supplement to 1926 Revised Edition of the Law and Procedure of International Tribunals (Stanford, 1936).

Recueil des decisions des tribunaux arbitraux mixtes (Paris, 1922–1930).

Reinsch, P. S., The Concept of Legality in International Arbitration (1911) 5 American Journal of International Law 604.

Renault, L., Le Différend entre la Bolivie et le Pérou et l'arbitrage international (1909) 16 Revue Générale de Droit International Public 368.

—— Une Nouvelle Mission donée aux arbitres dans les litiges internationaux (1894) 1 Revue Générale de Droit International Public 44.

Revon, M., L'Arbitrage international, son passé—son présent—son avenir (Paris, 1892).

Rolin-Jaequemyns, G., Quelques mots sur la phase nouvelle du différend

Anglo-Américain (1872) 4 Revue de Droit International et de Législation Comparée 127.

Root, E., The Importance of Judicial Settlement (1910) Proceedings of American Society for the Judicial Settlement of International Disputes 11.

Rouard de Card, E., Droit international; l'arbitrage international dans le passé, le présent et l'avenir (Paris, 1877).

Rundstein, S., Le Caractère juridique des différends internationaux (1934, 3d ser.) 15 Revue de Droit International et de Législation Comparée 377.

—— La Cour Permanente de Justice Internationale comme instance de recours (1933) 43 Academie du Droit International, Recueil des Cours 5.

Sandifer, D. V., Evidence before International Tribunals (Chicago, 1939).

Scelle, G., Une Instance en revision devant la Cour de la Haye, l'affaire de la Orinoco Steamship Company (1911) 18 Revue Générale de Droit International Public 164.

Schätzel, W., Rechtskraft und Anfechtung von Entscheidungen internationaler Gerichte, 6 Frankfurter Abhandlungen zum Kriegsverhütungsrecht (Leipzig, 1928).

Some Opinions, Articles and Reports Bearing upon the Treaty of Trianon and the Claims of the Hungarian Nationals with Regard to Their Lands in Transylvania (London, 1929).

Stoykovitch, S., De l'autorité de la sentence arbitrale en droit international public (Paris, 1924).

Strupp, K., The Competence of the Mixed Arbitral Courts of the Treaty of Versailles (1923) 17 American Journal of International Law 661.

—— Le Droit du juge international de statuer selon l'équité (1930) 33 Academie de Droit International, Recueil des Cours 357.

Teyssaire, J., and P. Solere, Les Tribunaux arbitraux mixtes (Paris, 1931).

Tripartite Claims Commission, United States, Austria and Hungary, Report of Robert W. Bonynge (Washington, D.C., 1930).

Turlington, E., Comments on the Rules of the Special Mexican Claims Commission (1936) 3 Journal of the District of Columbia Bar Ass'n 22.

United States, Department of State. Arbitration Series No. 3 (Washington, D.C., 1932), No. 5 (Washington, D.C., 1934), and No. 6 (Washington, D.C., 1934).

United States, Department of State, Foreign Relations of the United States, Papers relating to, 1902, Appendix, part 2. Pious Fund of the Californias, Report of Jackson H. Ralston (Washington, D.C.).

United States–Chilean Claims Commission, Report of George H. Shields, Agent of the United States (Washington, D.C., 1894).

United States–Germany Mixed Claims Commission, Administrative Decisions and Opinions of a General Nature, 1926–1932 (Washington, D.C.).

United States–Germany Mixed Claims Commission, Opinions and Decisions in the Sabotage Claims Handed Down June 15, 1939, and October 30, 1939 (Washington, D.C.).

—— First Report of Robert C. Morris (Washington, D.C., 1922).

United States–Mexican Claims Commission under Convention of September 8, 1923, Opinions of Commissioners (Washington, D.C.).

Venezuelan Arbitrations of 1903, Ralston's Report (Washington, D.C., 1904).

Venezuelan Arbitration before the Hague Tribunal, 1903, Report of William L. Penfield, American Agent (Washington, D.C., 1905).

Verdross, A., L'Excès de pouvoir du juge arbitrale dans le droit international public (1928, 3d ser.) 9 Revue de Droit International et de Législation Comparée 225.

Verzijl, J., La Validité et la nullité des actes juridiques internationaux (1935) 15 Revue de Droit International 284.

Weiss, A., L'Arbitrage de 1909 entre le Bolivie et le Pérou (1910) 17 Revue Générale de Droit International Public 105.

Williams, J. F., The Tribunal for the Interpretation of the Dawes Plan (1928) 22 American Journal of International Law 797.

Witenberg, J. C., L'Organisation judiciaire, la procédure et la sentence internationales (Paris, 1937).

Yotis, C., La Question ultra petita à propos d'un arbitrage entre la Grèce et la Bulgarie (1926) 52 Journal du Droit International (Clunet) 879.

Other Publications

American Law Institute, Restatement of the Law of Judgments (St. Paul, 1942).

Arnold, R., Treaty-Making Procedure (London, 1933).

Bidau, E. L., Derecho internacional público (Buenos Aires, 4th ed. 1924).

Bluntschli, J. K., Le Droit international codifié (Lardy translation, Paris, 1895); also edition of 1886.

Boitard, J. E., Leçons de procédure civile (13th ed., Paris, 1879).

Bonde, A., Traité élémentaire de droit international public (Paris, 1926).

Bonfils, H., Manuel de droit international public (Paris, 1898).

Bry, G., Précis élémentaire de droit international public (Paris, 1910).

Bulmerincq, A., Das Völkerrecht (Freiburg, 1884).

Butler, C. H., The Treaty Making Power of the United States (New York, 1902).

Calvo, C., Le Droit international théorique et pratique (Paris, 5th ed. 1896).

Carnazza-Amari, G., Traité de droit international public (Paris, 1880–1882).

Clark, C. E., Code Pleading (St. Paul, 1928).

Code de procédure civile (Dalloz, Paris, 1936).

Council on Foreign Relations, Survey of American Foreign Relations (New Haven, 1929).

Creasy, E. S., First Platform of International Law (London, 1876).

Cruchaga Tocornal, M., Nociones de derecho internacional (Madrid, 3d ed. 1923).

Dalloz, Nouveau Code de procédure civile (Paris, 1922).

Deák, F., The Hungarian-Rumanian Land Dispute (New York, 1928).

Dumbauld, E., Interim Measures of Protection in International Controversies (The Hague, 1932).

Fauchille, P., Traité de droit international public (Paris, 1921–1926).

Ferguson, J., Manual of International Law (The Hague, 1884).

Fiore, P., Nouveau Droit international public (Antoine translation, Paris, 1885).

Fitzmaurice, G. G., Do Treaties Need Ratification? (1934) 15 British Yearbook of International Law 113.

Flores, P., History of the Boundary Dispute between Ecuador and Peru (New York, 1921).

Foster, John W., Diplomatic Memoirs (Boston and New York, 1909).

Funck-Brentano, Th., et Sorel, A., Précis du droit de gens (3d ed., Paris, 1900).

Genet, R., Traité de diplomatie et de droit diplomatique (Paris, 1931–1932).

Grotius, H., De Jure belli ac pacis (Kelsey translation, Washington, D.C., 1925).

Hall, W. E., A Treatise on International Law (8th ed., Oxford, 1924).

Heffter, A. W., Das Europäischer Völkerrecht der Gegenwart auf den bisherigen Grundlagen (8th ed., Geffcken, Berlin, 1888).

Hohfeld, W. H., Fundamental Legal Conceptions (New Haven, 1923).

Hudson, M. O., International Legislation (Washington, D.C., 1931–1941).

Hyde, C. C., International Law Chiefly as Interpreted and Applied by the United States (2 ed., Boston, 1945).

Kellershohn, M., Des Effets de l'annulation pour excès de pouvoir (Bordeaux, 1915).

Kent, J., Commentaries on American Law (13th ed., Boston, 1884).

Le Fur, L., Précis de droit international public (Paris, 1937).

Louter, J. de, Le Droit international public positif (Oxford, 1920).

Moore, J. B., A Digest of International Law (Washington, D.C., 1906).

Moore, J. W., and J. Friedman, Moore's Federal Practice (Albany, 1938).

Moses, F., International Legal Practice (1935) 4 Fordham Law Review 244.

Mouskhéli, M., L'Équité en droit international moderne (1933) 40 Revue Générale de Droit International Public 347.

Munro, D. G., The Five Republics of Central America (New York, 1918).

Nielsen, F. K., International Law as Applied to Reclamations (Washington, D.C., 1933).

Olivart, R., Tratado de derecho internacional público (Madrid, 1903).

Oppenheim, L., International Law (4th ed., London, 1928).

Our Treaties of Peace with the Central Powers (1927) 40 Harvard Law Review 752.

Phillimore, R. J., Commentaries upon International Law (London, 1857).

Pike, J. A., and H. G. Fischer, Federal Rules Service (Chicago, 1939).

Planas Suárez, S., Tratado de derecho internacional público (Madrid, 1916).

Politis, N., Le Problème des limitations de la souveraineté et la théorie de l'abus des droits dans les rapports internationaux (1925) 6 Academie de Droit International, Recueil des Cours 5.

Pradier-Fodéré, P. L. E., Traité de droit international public (Paris, 1885).

Pufendorf, S., Le Droit de la nature et de gens (Amsterdam, 1734).

Rivier, A., Principes du droit des gens (Paris, 1896).

Rolin-Jaequemyns, G., Chronique du droit international, 1871–1874 (1875) 7 Revue de Droit International et de Législation Comparée 70.

Santamaría de Paredes, Don Vicente, A Study of the Question of Boundaries between the Republics of Peru and Ecuador (Van Dyke translation, Washington, 1910).

Satow, E., A Guide to Diplomatic Practice (3d ed., London, 1932).

Schwarzenberger, G., International Law; Volume 1—International Law as Applied by International Courts and Tribunals (London, 1945).

Sunderland, E. S., Joinder of Actions (1920) 18 Michigan Law Review 571.

—— The Machinery of Procedural Reform (1924) 22 Michigan Law Review 293.

Taylor, H., A Treatise on International Law (Chicago, 1901).

Twiss, T., The Law of Nations (2d ed., Oxford, 1875).

Ulloa, A., Derecho internacional público (Lima, Peru, 1929).

Vattel, E., Le Droit de gens (ed. 1758, Fenwick translation, Washington, D.C., 1916).

Zivilprozessordnung (Liebmann, Berlin, 1930).

INDEX